Read What Others Are Saying
About This Amphibious Operations Series...

▐ Enough gripping drama, heroism, and heartbreak in McGee's almost encyclopedic *Solomons Campaigns* to supply Hollywood with material for a century.
— *Marine Corps League Magazine*

▐ If your children or grandchildren have ever asked, "What did you do in the war?" point them to McGee's books. Throughout you will find yourself saying, "Yup, that was us," and I guarantee you'll have renewed respect for the guy you see in the mirror every morning.
— *Howard Clarkson, USS LCI National Assn.*

▐ McGee is no novice when it comes to writing. . .nor is he an armchair historian. He has lived through much of what he writes about.
— **Sea Classics Magazine**

▐ *Amphibians Are Coming!* is a long-awaited dream since it deals with my kind of war. You've brought great pride and joy to thousands who were there and to future generations who will learn how America fought in World War II.
— *John A. McNeill Sr., USNR, Officer-in-Charge, LCT-159*

▐ Little has been written about service in the U.S. Naval Armed Guard in which nearly 145,000 men served. . .McGee remedies this deficiency in *Bluejacket Odyssey*. . .the book has value for historians.
— *Naval History Magazine*

▐ *Solomons Campaigns* will form a definitive account of naval, sea, and land operations in the South Pacific where America's response to Pearl Harbor began. . .a thoroughgoing historical record and analysis that historians and scholars will find invaluable.
— *Library Journal*

▐ McGee's *Amphibians Are Coming!* describe miracles: Bringing LSTs and other landing vessels into high production in a short time; bringing together untrained officers and men to perform tasks which should have taken months of training; making all this work under unbelievable combat conditions.
— *Mel Barger, Author of* Large Slow Target

▐ The result is a masterpiece. . . .The indexes and appendices are the book's crown jewels. Future authors will benefit from McGee's efforts in *Solomons Campaigns*.
— *Leatherneck, Magazine of the Marines*

▐ *Solomons Campaigns* will become the definitive work on the campaigns.
— *John Cummer, President, USS LCI National Association*

■ Your books brought tears to my eyes. A "must read" for all sea services veterans and their descendants.

—Charles C. Espy, Lt (jg), USNR, SS Thomas Nelson, Armed Guard C.O.

■ You are writing facts. How do I know? I was in Task Unit 32.4.4 and lost my ship on 23 June 1943, just as you write.

—L. Ray Weathers, Boatswain Mate 2/c, USN, USS Deimos *(AK-78)*

■ McGee has not only done exhaustive research into the documentation of how the amphibious forces were built, but has added the words of the men who took the theory of the amphibious doctrine and the new machines to sea. His dedicated work will surely help keep the day-to-day naval record of the "Greatest Generation" from being lost.

—John Lorelli, Author of To Foreign Shores, U.S. Amphibious Operations in World War II

■ As a Marine who landed on Guadalcanal on 7 August 1942, *Solomons Campaigns* is the most comprehensive book that I've read on the war in the Solomons. It brought back memories of those very dark days. Semper Fi.

—William J. Carroll, President, Guadalcanal Campaign Veterans

■ To say Bill McGee is a serious naval historian is an understatement. As they say in the Navy, well done!

—W. C. Hilderbrand, Capt, CEC, USN (Ret), CEC/Seabee Historical Foundation

■ *Solomons Campaigns* is perfectly balanced between riveting history, personal narratives, and pleasing layout packed with photos, maps, and illustrations. As the son of a Flotilla Five veteran of the Pacific, McGee's books are a fine tribute to all who served in that theater.

—Ron Swanson, Editor, The Flotilla, LCT Flotillas of WWII

■ *Amphibians Are Coming!* is a "must read" for all Armed Guard and merchant mariners and their families.

—C.A. Lloyd, Chairman, USN Armed Guard Veterans of WWII

■ Having experienced a full measure of life at sea during WWII, I find your military histories detailed, vivid, accurate. They capture the essence of that war.

—Anthony P. Tesori, USNR, Gunnery Officer, LST-340

■ The tragic voyage of Task Unit 32.4.4 still haunts me after all these years. Your eyewitness accounts of the June 1943 action are spellbinding. I couldn't put the book down.

—Roy Lucy, Radioman 3/c, USNR, USS Aludra *(AK-72)*

■ As a *Skylark* veteran, your military histories mean a lot to us, more than you'll ever know.

—Len Honeycutt, Radarman 1/c, USN, USS Skylark *(AM-63)*

Sabine *(AO-25), with three hoses deployed, refuels* Enterprise *(CV-6) during the approach phase of the Tokyo Raid. (National Archives)*

Neosho *refuels* Yorktown *(CV-5) just prior to the Battle of the Coral Sea. Note the difficulty the crew was having while trying to work in the heavy seas smashing over the well deck (one seaman in the center has even fallen down). Problems such as these led to the universal adoption of the elevated cargo spar decks for winches and other handling gear. (National Archives)*

AMPHIBIOUS OPERATIONS IN THE SOUTH PACIFIC IN WORLD WAR II

VOLUME III

PACIFIC EXPRESS

Logistics:
The Heart of the Battle for Guadalcanal
August 1942–February 1943

RAdm Richmond Kelly Turner, USN (left), and MajGen Alexander A. Vandegrift, USMC, review logistics plans on the flag bridge of USS McCawley *(AP-10) during Guadalcanal operations, July–August 1942. (Courtesy Naval Institute Press)*

"During the first four months of Operation WATCHTOWER,
eighty percent of my time was given to logistics. . .
we were living from one logistic crisis to another."
*—Rear Admiral Richmond Kelly Turner,
Commander Amphibious Task Force 62*

It was RAdm Turner's belief that in no part of naval combat operations did logistics require a larger part of a commander's attention than in our early amphibious operations. Guadalcanal logistics centered on troops, planes, food, ammunition, aviation gas, and—during the first two weeks—getting the airfield into condition to operate aircraft.

Amphibious Operations in the South Pacific in World War II

Volume III

PACIFIC EXPRESS

The Critical Role of Military Logistics in World War II

Edited by William L. McGee

with Sandra McGee

 **PUBLICATIONS**

Tiburon, California

2009

Pacific Express: The Critical Role of Military Logistics in World War II/Edited by William L. McGee with Sandra McGee

    Includes appendix, abbreviations, notes, glossary, bibliography, and index
    ISBN 978-0-9701678-8-0 (Volume III)
    ISBN 978-0-9701678-9-7 (3-Volume Set)

LIBRARY OF CONGRESS Control Number: 2009920374

I. Pacific Express: The Critical Role of Military Logistics in World War II – title.
1. Solomons Campaigns – Guadalcanal, New Georgia, Bougainville – History – 1942–1943.
2. U.S. Shipbuilding – History – 1939–1945 – Liberty ships and Victory ships – U.S. Maritime Commission, War Shipping Administration, Rear Admiral Emory Scott Land.
3. Advance Base Construction and Mobile Service Squadrons in WWII – History – 1941–1943.
4. Naval Transportation Service – History – 1939–1945.
5. U.S. Navy Construction Battalions (Seabees)/U.S. Marine Corps Engineers/USMC/ Pioneer Battalions/U.S. Army Engineers – History – 1942–1945.
6. U.S. Merchant Marine and U.S. Naval Armed Guard – History – WWII 1939–1945.
7. U.S. Army Transportation Corps/Army Transport Service – History – WWII – 1939–1945.
8. U.S. Coast Guard-manned vessels in the Pacific Theater of Operations in WWII – History – 1941–1945.
9. War Shipping Administration – Summary WWII cargo transported – amount, where and when.
10. Lessons Learned in the Solomons – History – 1942–1943.
11. U.S. Merchant ship casualties in the Pacific Theater of Operations in WWII – History – 7 December 1941–10 August 1945.

Printed in the United States of America on acid-free paper.

First printing

Published by BMC Publications
(A BMC Communications Company)
Tiburon, CA 94920
www.BMCpublications.com

Front cover photo credits, clockwise from top center: First Division Marines storm ashore on Guadalcanal, D-Day, 7 August 1942 (National Archives); Cargo unloaded from a pontoon barge onto an Amtrack (USNCB); Bulldozer known as "Old Faithful" to the 26th NCB on Tulagi, 1943 (Naval Historical Center); USAAF B-24 bomber takes off from island airfield as Seabees spread coral while widening the runway (National Archives); Seabees lowering a completed bridge on its bearings (USNCB); LST-340 on fire, 16 June 1943 (Ralph K. Brown).

Dedication

To the millions of unsung, home-front warriors who built
the ships, tanks and planes during World War II.

To the unheralded U.S. Navy Seabees, U.S. Army and
U.S. Marine Corps Engineers who built and manned
the many Advance Bases in the Pacific.

To the skilled U.S. Navy crews who manned the Fleet's mobile
Service Squadrons throughout the vast reaches of the Pacific.

To the civilian sailors and U.S. Navy gun crews who manned
the U.S. Merchant Marine cargo ships, transports, and tankers,
and delivered the goods to our amphibious forces.

And to the many U.S. Coast Guardsmen who filled the
critical role of manning hundreds of U.S. Army and Navy
long-haul vessels as well as thousands of amphibious landing
ships and craft in the Pacific Theater of Operations.

Books by William L. McGee

Amphibious Operations in the South Pacific in World War II

Vol. I

The Amphibians Are Coming! Emergence of the 'Gator Navy and its Revolutionary Landing Craft

Vol. II

The Solomons Campaigns, 1942–1943: From Guadalcanal to Bougainville, Pacific War Turning Point

Vol. III

Pacific Express: The Critical Role of Military Logistics in World War II
Editor with Sandra McGee

Bluejacket Odyssey, 1942–1946: Guadalcanal to Bikini, Naval Armed Guard in the Pacific

---

The Divorce Seekers: A Photo Memoir of a Nevada Dude Wrangler

with Sandra McGee

Meet the Editors

*William L. McGee
and Sandra McGee*
(Photo Joanne A. Calitri)

William L. "Bill" McGee was born in 1925 on a ranch in Montana. Ships have always figured prominently in his life. In 1942, he worked as a welder building Liberty ships and LSTs at the Kaiser Shipyard in Vancouver, Washington. Later that same year, he enlisted in the U.S. Navy and volunteered for the Naval Armed Guard, a special branch of the Navy that defended merchant ships, their cargo, and crews from enemy air and submarine attacks. From 1943 to 1945, he served in the Pacific Theater in three Liberty ships and one Victory ship.

Following his discharge in 1946, McGee returned to cowboying and worked as the head dude wrangler on an exclusive Nevada divorce ranch 20 miles south of Reno that catered to wealthy divorce seekers who came for a six week divorce. In 1950, he left cowboying and made a successful transition into the business world. He founded a San Francisco import-export company and was a shipper on several former WWII merchantmen. An interest in the entertainment industry led to a 32-year career in radio and TV broadcasting. McGee is the author of numerous books on broadcast advertising and is the recipient of many broadcasting awards. After a brief "retirement" in 1985, McGee turned his interest to research and history writing.

Sandra McGee was born and raised in Southern California, and studied ballet and piano. In her thirties, she believed her passion for these arts might also be served on the business side of the curtain. She helped co-found a professional ballet company in Santa Barbara, California and became a publicist for performing arts groups. Her interest in history and attention to detail teams nicely with her writer-husband, and together they have worked on numerous books and screenplays.

Contents

The story of the greatest shipbuilding program in America's history.

Source: Frederic C. Lane, *Ships for Victory—A History of Shipbuilding under the U.S. Maritime Commission in World War II* (1951).

The story of the vital logistics services supporting the U.S. Armed Forces operating in the Pacific. Logistics challenges are examined—proof positive that naval warfare is not all blazing combat.

Sources: Rear Admiral Worrall Reed Carter, USN (Ret), *Beans, Bullets and Black Oil—The Story of Fleet Logistics Afloat in the Pacific During World War II* (1953); Vice Admiral George Carroll Dyer, USN (Ret), *The Amphibians Came To Conquer—The Story of Admiral Richmond Kelly Turner* (1971); Samuel Eliot Morison, *Breaking the Bismarcks Barrier, 22 July 1942–1 May 1944* (1950).

Source: Bureau of Supplies and Accounts, Department of the Navy, "History of the Transportation Division, Bureau of Supplies and Accounts" (1944).

Sources: Department of the Navy, *Building the Navy's Bases in
World War II—History of the Bureau of Yards and Docks and the
Civil Engineer Corps, 1940–1946,* Vols. 1 and 2 (1947); Lieutenant
(jg) William Bradford Huie, CEC, USNR, *Can Do! The Story of
the Seabees* (1944); Lieutenant Mark H. Jordan, CEC, USN, "Saga
of the Sixth"; Captain Larry G. DeVries, CEC, USNR, "Seabees
on Guadalcanal," *WWII Naval Journal* (July/August 1994); Claude
S. Gulbranson, USNR, "History of the First Special U.S. Naval
Construction Battalion, 1942–1946" (1994); Publications of the
Marine Corps Historical Center (1944).

Sources: John Gorley Bunker, *Liberty Ships – The Ugly Ducklings of World War II* (1972); Vice Admiral Emory S. Land, USN, *Winning The War With Ships* (1958); William L. McGee, *Bluejacket Odyssey, 1942–1946—Guadalcanal to Bikini, Naval Armed Guard in the Pacific* (2000); Bruce L. Felknor, ed., *The U.S. Merchant Marine at War, 1775–1945* (1998).

Sources: Chester Wardlow, *The Technical Services—The Transportation Corps: Responsibilities, Organization, and Operations* (1951); David H. Grover, *U.S. Army Ships and Watercraft of World War II* (1987).

Sources: Publications of the U.S. Coast Guard Historian's Office: Robert M. Browning Jr., "The Coast Guard and the Pacific War" (1995); Robert Erwin Johnson, "Coast Guard-Manned Naval Vessels in World War II" (1993); Robert L. Scheina, "The Coast Guard at War" (1987). Winn B. Frank, "Farewell to the Troopship," *Naval History* (January/February 1997).

Source: Vice Admiral Emory S. Land, USN, War Shipping Administration, "The United States Merchant Marine at War: Report of the War Shipping Administrator to the President " (15 January 1946).

Source: William L. McGee, *The Solomons Campaigns, 1942–1943—From Guadalcanal to Bougainville, Pacific War Turning Point* (2002).

Maps

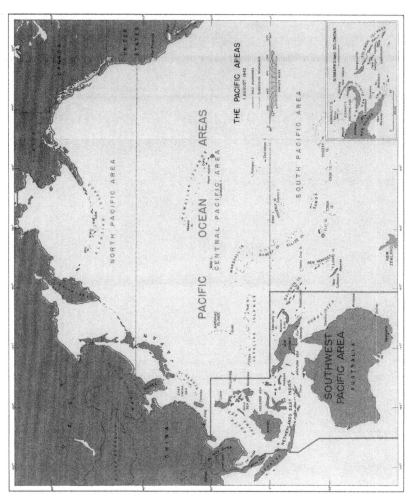

Map 1: The Pacific Areas, 1 August 1942

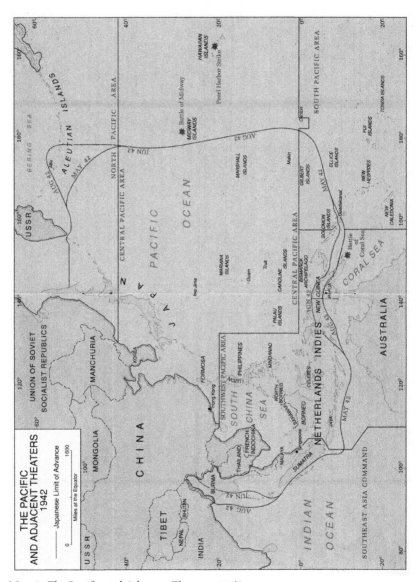

Map 2: The Pacific and Adjacent Theaters, 1942

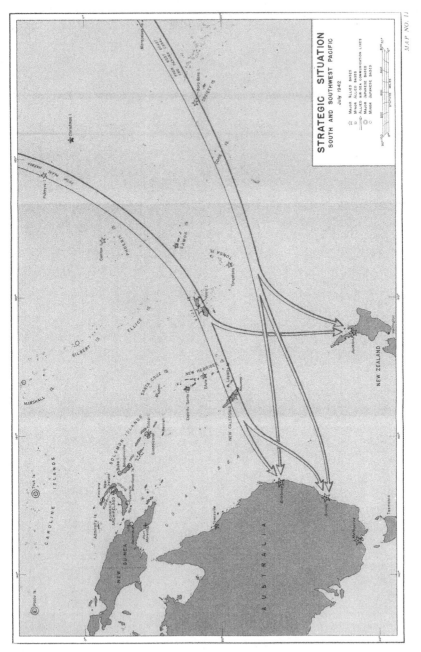

Map 3: Strategic Situation, South and Southwest Pacific, July 1942

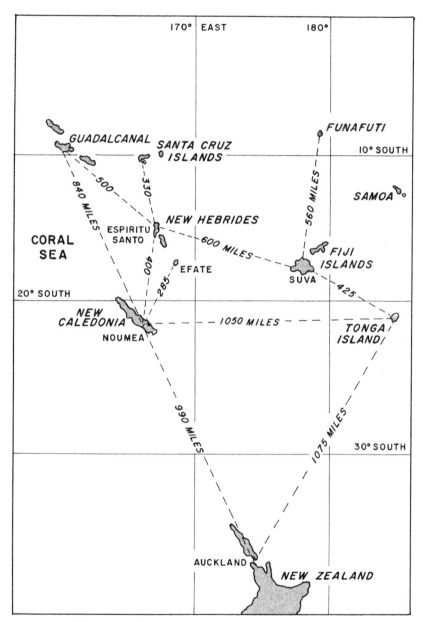

Map 4: Guadalcanal supply lines

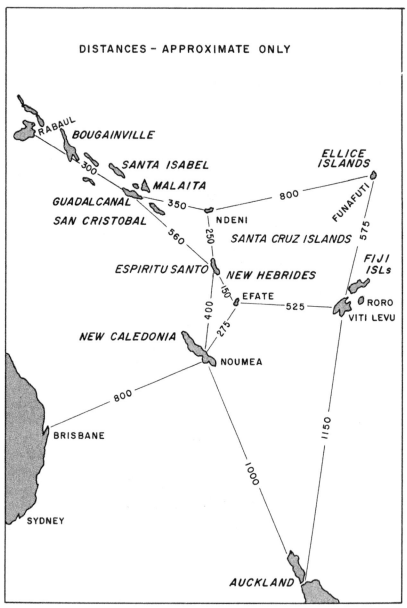

Map 5: South Pacific distances

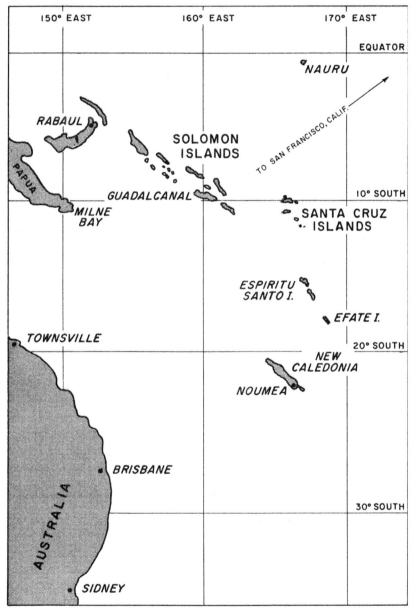

*Map 6: Solomon Islands: Espiritu Santo, New Hebrides;
and Noumea, New Caledonia*

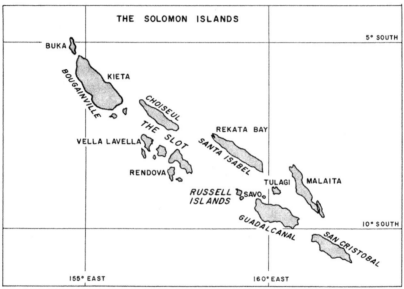

Map 7: The Solomon Islands

Foreword

Dennis R. Blocker II (right) with his grandfather, Clifford Lemke, S1/c, LCI (G)-449, c. 1991.
(Courtesy Blocker Family)

"In World War II, 16.1 million men and women served in the U.S. Armed Forces. For every *one* who served in combat, *ten* served in a support role." This is a staggering fact which is not only claimed but proven in this, the final book in William L. McGee's trilogy, *Amphibious Operations in the South Pacific in World War II.* Such a work is long overdue as the men and women of WWII are passing at a rate of more than 1,000 per day and taking their stories with them. This is why *Pacific Express* is so vitally important to the recorded history of WWII.

Few medals adorn the chests of civilian merchant mariners who crossed the vast Pacific Ocean on a merchant ship. Likewise the "Armed Guard" felt rather unarmed as they defended these ships. Who will tell the stories of the Marine engineers and navy Seabees who built the bases and paved airfields while under sniper fire? Who will tell of the navy amphibious forces that delivered the guns and ammunition, bombs, grenades and rockets, aviation gas and black oil, tanks, trucks, uniforms, medical supplies, construction equipment, food, water, and a million other items that kept the Americans and her Allies fighting? Is it any wonder that the men and women who made this happen are called the "Greatest Generation"?

For me, WWII is all black and white. The troops are all high-glossed and the aircraft fly with bits of lint and dust stuck to them. This is how I know WWII, not because I was born during the Depression (I was born in

1974), but because I am the grandson of three WWII veterans. My great-grandfather, a private in the Army's 30th Infantry Division, died from a German artillery barrage in Holland in October 1944. My two grandfathers both served in the navy's Amphibious Forces. Grandpa Blocker served on an LST in the Atlantic and was torpedoed. Grandpa Lemke served on LCI (G)-449, the subject of a book I am writing titled, *Sitting Ducks.*

There is a picture I have of my arm around Grandpa Lemke's shoulder. I am beaming with happiness and he is looking up at me beaming with pride. I will always treasure that picture because now I know what he went through, and that somehow he managed to come home, raise a family, and provide for them, even though he had seen many of his friends die. Amazing.

Also amazing is the story of the men who delivered the goods to the farthest reaches of the Pacific. In reading this wonderful book, *Pacific Express,* we, the future generations, will gain a true understanding of the Second World War and will know how it was won. And one day we will sit *our* grandchildren on our laps and ask, "Did I ever tell you how World War II was really won?"

—*Dennis R. Blocker II*
National LCI Association Historian, Pacific War

Preface

I am often asked, "What compelled you to write this book?" After all, there already exists many fine books on the important subject of logistics in warfare, albeit many out-of-print or hard to find. However, after nearly two decades of reading, researching, and writing three other books about the Pacific theater in World War II, I felt compelled to complete this third volume in my trilogy, *Amphibious Operations in the South Pacific in World War II*, for two reasons.

First, to honor all the men and women—military and civilian—who served in logistical support roles for our front line combat personnel in World War II. I felt these non-combatant service personnel were (and are) often overshadowed by those who served in combat. However, statistics show that there were ten supportive personnel for every one combatant in the U.S. Armed Forces in World War II.*

Second, since the mid-1990s, with the able assistance of Samuel Loring Morison (grandson of famed World War II naval historian, Admiral Samuel Eliot Morison), I had been gathering books and archival documents on the subject of logistics in warfare. I noted, of all the fine books already written on the subject, each one was primarily focused on a particular component of what I now term the "Pacific express."

Since the majority of these books or documents were authored in the mid-twentieth century, I could now compare their contents with new and declassified information. (Remember, during the war, most information was classified or "top secret.") I now had answers to many of my questions.

---

* Warfare and Armed Conflicts, A Statistical Reference (Washington, D.C.: National Archives and Record Administrator) 584.

So rather than write a new book on the subject, I decided to change course and tie all these fine, earlier works together under one cover as a *collection* of works by other writers, all experts on their respective subjects—such as Admirals Worrall Reed Carter, Emory Scott Land, and Richmond Kelly Turner—as well as published authors like Frederic C. Lane, John Gorley Bunker, Bruce L. Felknor, and David H. Grover. Now, as editor, I condensed or excerpted text from these experts and structured this book much like a reading and reference work to save busy readers and researchers time. Therefore, each chapter stands alone with its sources identified at the beginning, and any applicable notes, figures, tables, charts and photographs at the end.

I am very grateful to all my sources for allowing me to condense, excerpt or quote from their fine works. Particular attention has been paid to acknowledge all these sources in detail, both in the chapters and the Bibliography. Many of these works, having been published following World War II, are now out-of-print. However, copies may still be found from online booksellers like Amazon.com. Other works, such as Frederic Lane's *Ships for Victory*, have been reprinted.

Due to space limitations, it is not within the scope of this book to single out and honor the contributors of all logistics support personnel who served as part of the "Pacific express." However, if this book somehow stimulates history buffs and descendants of World War II veterans to continue their search for knowledge through the fine sources used here, this editor's purpose will have been fully achieved.

Editorial Method

Each chapter follows a similar format. The chapter opens with an "Editor's note" describing the chapter's focus and a few words about the excerpted material and its author(s). The guest authors' texts are left unaltered, even when modern usage may dictate something different, e.g., a different spelling or capitalization of a word. Only minor changes in punctuation have been made. Extremely long paragraphs may have been divided into shorter ones for easier comprehension by the reader. Excerpts may include notes that appeared in the original sources; however, the note numbers will be different in this book. In some instances, the note numbers from the original source are indicated by a second superscript Arabic numeral. Notes added by the editor are at the bottom of a page and are indicated by asterisks or other symbols. When parts of a work have been omitted, the omissions are indicated within the text by three ellipsis dots. If an omitted section of an excerpt may be important to the reader, a brief summary is provided by an Editor's note. For consistency of style, in treating units of measurement (gun bores, speed rates, tonnage), military ranks, and dates, a military writing guide was followed. The editors hope this explanation will help the reader get the most out of this book.

The Story Behind the Story

I've always loved going to sea. In 1993, I launched the writing of *Bluejacket Odyssey, 1942–1946,* while on a six week freighter trip to South America, and the results were very productive. So in 1999, I booked passage on another freighter for a 90-day, round-the-world trip.

My objective was to lay out all the material I had gathered for this third volume in my trilogy, *Amphibious Operations in the South Pacific in World War II,* and to develop a working Table of Contents. The tentative title was to be *Pacific Express—America's World War II Military Supply System.* I had a concept in mind for this volume: a collection of the best writings on the subject of logistics in warfare by other historians. I would then excerpt or condense and, where applicable, update if new information was available. I already had permission from several publishers, such as the Naval Institute Press, to draw on material they had published. (I'm a believer in not reinventing the wheel.)

The MV *Cho Yang Atlas,* of German ownership and registry, was new, having been delivered in 1998. The ship was large; 965 feet, 63,645 dead-weight tons, and designed to cruise at 24 knots. In spite of her size, the

Atlas crew numbered just 27; German officers with a South Pacific (Gilbert Islands) crew.

Four nice cabins accommodated up to eight passengers. My cabin was a two-room suite, outside facing, carpeted, and air-conditioned. My "living room" had a sofa, mini-refrigerator and bar, and electronics that included a TV and VCR. Passengers shared the dining room and lounge with the ship's officers.

The main ports-of-call on the 90-day itinerary were Long Beach (embark), Calif.; Oakland, Calif.; Kaohsiung, Taiwan; Hong Kong; Singapore; Suez Canal (transit); Le Havre, France; Rotterdam, Netherlands; Hamburg, Germany; Suez Canal (transit); Columbo, Sri Lanka; Port Kelang, Malaysia; Hong Kong (second call); Pusan, South Korea; Osaka, Japan; Tokyo, Japan; and Long Beach (disembark), Calif.

The many days at sea were exactly what I wanted—peace and quiet to work at my desk; occasional breaks in a chair on deck; social contact at meals with the officers and other passengers. For exercise, I did two or three laps, stem to stern, around the main deck once or twice a day, regardless of the weather.

I stayed in touch with my beautiful wife, Sandra, by fax. She had been invited to join me, but elected to stay home. (When I returned, she surprised me with the completion of remodeling work we had been putting off and a new car.)

This freighter trip proved to be as productive as the first one. I not only developed a working Table of Contents for *Pacific Express*, I completed the first draft writing and condensation of 75 percent of the material. From various ports-of-call, I mailed pages to my excellent manuscript typist, Jan Adelson, and she had the manuscript keyed before I returned home. Later, when the manuscript was nearly completed, Spencer Boise (who had read several previous manuscripts) gave *Pacific Express* an initial read and provided constructive comments about its format and content. (A freighter trip may not be for everyone, but it's perfect for a writer or reader. For those who are tempted, I can recommend Freighter World Cruises, Inc., www.freighterworld.com.)

For various reasons, the nearly-completed manuscript sat on the shelf for eight years. In 2008, Sandra came to my rescue and offered to help me finish it. With her background in writing and publicity, and attention to detail in editing, it was a good match. There aren't enough words to thank her, but I keep trying.

Welcome aboard. I hope you enjoy your cruise on the *Pacific Express.*

—William L. McGee

Introduction

In the words of Admiral Worrall Reed Carter, one of the U.S. Navy's foremost experts on logistics support in the Pacific theater during World War II:

> "From 7 December 1941, when the Japanese attacked Pearl Harbor, until they admitted defeat in August 1945, our fleet continuously grew. During those stirring and difficult times, the accounts of ship actions, air strikes, and amphibious operations make up the thrilling combat history of the Pacific theater. Linked inseparably with combat is naval logistic support, the support which makes available to the fleet such essentials as ammunition, fuel, food, repair services—in short, all the necessities, at the proper time and place and in adequate amounts. This support, from advanced bases and from floating mobile service squadrons and groups, maintained the fleet and enabled it to take offensive action farther from home supply points than was ever before thought possible."
>
> —*Adm W. R. Carter, USN (Ret), Commander*
> *Naval Bases South Pacific, 1942; Commander famed*
> *"floating" Service Squadron Ten, 1944–45.*

Now consider this statistic: A total of 16.1 million men and women served in the U.S. Armed Forces in World War II:

- Average length of active duty: 33 months

- Average time served overseas: 16 months
- Percent serving abroad: 73%
- Percent who never served abroad: 27%
- *Ratio of support troops to combat troops: ten-to-one**

This support-to-combat ratio of ten-to-one makes sense if you consider all the manpower it took to build, operate and maintain the many advance bases around the world. In the case of seagoing personnel, the Merchant Marine and Army Transportation Corps manned thousands of ships with crews made up of civilian and military personnel. The U.S. Navy had hundreds of auxiliaries—such as cargo, transport, hospital, stores, repair, tankers and ammunition ships—all classified as non-combatants even though many of them experienced enemy attacks from time to time. And these are just two examples that illustrate the need for manpower support.

For source material for this three-volume series, *Amphibious Operations in the South Pacific in World War II,* Samuel Loring Morison (grandson of famed World War II naval historian, Admiral Samuel Eliot Morison) researched and gathered archival documents and recommended books on the following subjects:

- The new landing ships and crafts and their crews.
- Amphibious operations from Guadalcanal to Bougainville.
- Seabee construction and stevedore battalions.
- Marine Corps engineers and pioneer units.
- Emergency shipbuilding under the Maritime Commission.
- Logistical challenges in the Pacific.
- Naval service squadrons.
- Manning the long-, medium- and short-haul vessels with U.S. Navy, Coast Guard, Merchant Marine, and Army crews to keep the "Pacific express" pipeline filled.

---

* Source: Department of Defense and the U.S. Census Bureau, and U.S. Army Military History Institute; Warfare and Armed Conflicts, A Statistical Reference (Washington, D.C.: National Archives and Record Administrator) 584.

The first two points became the subjects of *The Amphibians Are Coming!* and *The Solomons Campaigns, 1942–1943*, Volumes I and II respectively in the series. The last six points—and then some—are the subjects covered in this Volume III.

Due to space limitations, it is not within the scope of this book to profile every military or civilian service or agency that was a component of the "Pacific express." In fact, it is with due apologies that we, the editors, had to agree to cut three logistics services at the last minute. The Army Engineers were slated for a much larger role in the book. The Army's Service of Supply (later Army Service Force) and the Navy's Bureau of Supplies and Accounts—both procurers of supplies for shipment overseas—receive brief mentions, but not the full chapters we had visualized for them.

However, it is believed that the major components of the "Pacific express" that are covered in the following pages will reinforce this statistic: For every individual who served in blazing combat during World War II, ten—men and women—served in a support role.

—Sandra McGee

Part I

SHIPS FOR VICTORY

*The story of the greatest shipbuilding
program in America's history.*

"The War Shipping Administration and Maritime Commission came into
the military picture only when their affairs involved logistics. However, this
was becoming more and more the case and, therefore, I evolved one of my pet
phrases: Logistics equals Transportation. Transportation equals Logistics."

*—Vice Admiral Emory S. Land, USN, Head of Maritime
Commission and War Shipping Administration during
World War II, and author of* Winning the War with Ships

Chapter 1
Ships for Victory

Editor's note: This chapter is a condensed and edited summary of
shipbuilding under the Maritime Commission between 1941 and
1945. It is also a story about logistics and the political power and
intrigue between Washington movers and shakers during this
period. The reader who lived through the 1930s and '40s will
recognize most of the leading players. The younger reader will
learn how our thirty-fourth president, Franklin Delano Roosevelt,
mustered the nation to prepare for war.

Imagine this scenario: The U.S. Navy desperately needed
new combatants and auxiliaries, and the Maritime Commission
was ordered to build thousands of cargo ships, transports and
tankers in order to provide worldwide logistical support for the
U.S. armed forces. At the same time, America had lend-lease
commitments to the United Kingdom and Russia. There was no
quick and easy solution to this challenge because of the limited
number of operating shipyards.

Text excerpted with the permission of The Johns Hopkins University Press from
Frederic C. Lane, *Ships for Victory—A History of Shipbuilding under the U.S.
Maritime Commission in World War II* (1951, 2001). Photographic plates at the
end of the chapter are from the collection of the Maritime Commission and its
successor agency the Maritime Administration.

Sometimes the Joint Chiefs of the Armed Forces had to settle the differences between opposing agencies; other times the issues had to be settled by the Commander-in-Chief. But this behind-the-scenes battle for shipyard ways, steel plate, and propulsion equipment was waged throughout the war. In the end, the United States came out the winner.

Following the end of World War II, President Roosevelt directed every federal agency to prepare ". . .a final report that will sum up both what was accomplished and how the job was done." In 1946, Frederic C. Lane, a history professor at the Johns Hopkins University, was invited by the U.S. Maritime Commission to take on this task in its behalf. The result was *Ships for Victory—A History of Shipbuilding under the U.S. Maritime Commission in World War II*. At 881 pages, Lane's book is by far the most definitive work on shipbuilding in World War II and tells the story of the greatest shipbuilding program in American history.

On a personal note, ships have figured prominently in this editor's life. In 1942, I was a welder at the Kaiser Shipyard in Vancouver, Washington, while waiting to join the Navy. Then, while serving in the Naval Armed Guard, 1942–45, I shipped out on three Liberty ships and one Victory ship. Later, during the 1950s, working in the world trade business, I was a shipper on several former WWII merchantmen.

The editors are grateful to The Johns Hopkins University Press for permission to excerpt from Lane's *Ships for Victory*. For the interested reader, this fine work was reprinted in 2001 in softcover with a new preface by Arthur Donovan.

The Shipbuilding Industry

Closer integration of the [shipbuilding] industry with government agencies in a nationally planned program began before Pearl Harbor and was intensified after the declaration of war. Full wartime integration was carried out through two sets of controls. Like the rest of American industry, shipbuilding was subject to the rules and regulations issued by special agencies such as the War Production Board and the War Manpower Commission created to act only during the war. More direct and firm, however, were the controls resulting from the fact that the government became the industry's only customer, a customer ready to buy all that the industry could produce, and more. Government orders fixed the production goals of the shipyards, and government contracts formulated rules stipulating how corporations should operate.

These procurement activities of the government were administered for shipbuilding by two agencies, the Navy Department and the United States Maritime Commission. The Navy and the Maritime commission each directed and coordinated a section of the shipbuilding industry. Consequently the history of American shipbuilding in World War II falls into two parts.

For the shipbuilders under the Maritime Commission, the first main task was to build merchant ships faster than they were being sunk. In 1941 and 1942, shipping losses exceeded new construction. The Axis powers were not only winning the war on land, they were winning the war at sea, and if they continued to sink more tonnage than was built they would succeed in cutting their enemies' lines of supply. The perilous and feverish race between sinkings and construction was not definitely won until 1943.

After the triumph over the submarine menace, the need for cargo ships continued to be intense, for again, as in World War I, a "bridge of ships" was essential to the American Army. The shipyards under the Maritime Commission provided the bridge, delivering in 1939–1945 roughly 50 million deadweight tons of large cargo carriers and tankers.[1] In 1943 alone, they built 18 million tons, more than the total merchant fleet under the flag of the United States in 1939.[2] See Figure 1.

TOTAL TONNAGES OF PRINCIPAL TYPES
Of Vessels Delivered In Maritime Commission Program, 1939-1945

MILITARY MINOR TANKER VICTORY CARGO LIBERTY CARGO STANDARD CARGO

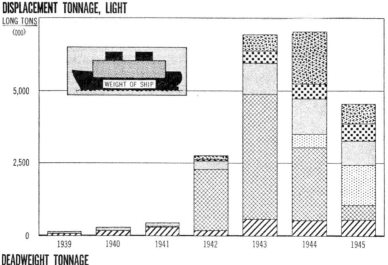

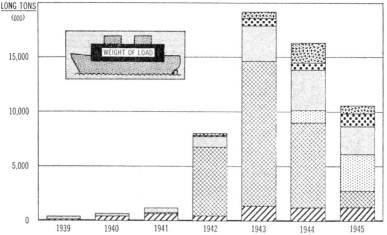

FIGURE 1. Source: Fischer, *Statistical Summary*, Tables B-3 and B-4. Vessels built in the United States for foreign governments and all vessels over 2,000 gross tons constructed in the United States for private concerns, as well as deliveries to the U. S. Maritime Commission, are included because all this construction was programmed by the Maritime Commission.

Merchant ships were not the only kind built under the Maritime Commission. Since more transports and naval auxiliaries were needed than could be built in yards under contract to the Navy, they were built in Maritime Commission yards. In the fall of 1944, most of the Maritime Commission shipyards on the West coast were building vessels classified by the Commission as "military" types. Some of these vessels classified as "military" were designed purely for military use—for example, the tank-carrying ships for effecting landings on enemy beaches (the LST's) or the aircraft carrier escorts, commonly known as "baby flattops" (Table 1). But most of the vessels built by the Maritime Commission and classified by it as "military" were transports, attack cargo ships, or oilers. Their designs were basically those of merchant vessels modified to meet military needs. Although these ships could be converted into merchant vessels and were counted as merchant vessels by the American Bureau of Shipping (Figure 2), they were built for delivery to the Army or Navy and were considered military types by the Commission. In terms of cost, military types constituted 23 per cent of the Commission's shipbuilding for 1939–1945.

In analyzing the importance of these different types, it is necessary to distinguish between deadweight tonnage and displacement tonnage. Deadweight tonnage is the weight of the cargo that a ship can carry without overloading. Displacement tonnage, light, is the weight of the ship itself, before it has been loaded. The addition of the deadweight tonnage to the displacement tonnage, light, gives the total displacement, namely the weight of water displaced by the fully loaded ship. For the study of industrial activity, displacement tonnage, light, is the best indication of a ship's size. . . .

The totals for the whole Maritime Commission program are impressive no matter how they are measured. Under Maritime Commission contracts, 5,601 vessels were delivered, and additional deliveries of merchant vessels in 1939–45 for private companies and foreign governments bring the grand total up to 5,777 vessels. Their construction consumed a total of about 25 million tons of carbon steel and engaged the labor of 640,300 workers at the peak of employment.[3] . . .

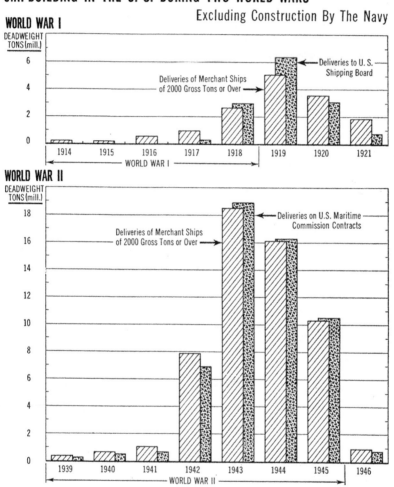

SHIPBUILDING IN THE U. S. DURING TWO WORLD WARS

WORLD WAR I   Excluding Construction By The Navy

FIGURE 2. Sources: U. S. Shipping Board, *Sixth Annual Report,* June 30, 1922, pp. 266-67; Fischer, *Statistical Summary,* Table B-3; Vessel Cargo Data Branch of MC (for deliveries to MC in 1946); and American Bureau of Shipping, *Bulletin,* January 1949 (for deliveries of merchant ships).

TABLE 1

VESSELS DELIVERED IN U. S. MARITIME COMMISSION PROGRAM
1939-1945

| | Number | Tonnage in thousands of tons* | | |
		Displacement (Light)	Deadweight	Gross
Grand Total................	5,777	22,218	56,292	39,920
By Type of Contract				
Maritime Commission........	5,601	21,478	54,102	38,490
Private....................	111	539	1,581	997
Foreign...................	65	201	608	433
By Type of Ship				
Standard Cargo†...........	541	2,496	5,349	3,834
Emergency Cargo (Liberty)....	2,708	9,412	29,182	19,447
Victory Cargo.............	414	1,851	4,492	3,151
Tankers...................	705	3,707	11,365	7,061
Minor Types..............	727	1,562	2,601	1,980
Military Types.............	682	3,188	3,303	4,452

* Displacement tonnage (the weight of the ship) and deadweight tons (the weight of the cargo) are both measures of weight based on the long ton of 2,240 pounds. Gross tonnage, in contrast, is a measure of the volume of the closed-in space on the ship. It is the cubic carrying capacity measured in cubic feet (100 cubic feet to the ton). An average freighter carrying 10,000 deadweight tons has a displacement, light, of about 4,000 tons, and cubic capacity of about 6,000 gross tons. Passenger liners have large gross tonnage compared to their displacement or deadweight.
† Includes passenger-and-cargo types.
Source: Fischer, *Statistical Summary*, Tables B-3 and B-4. Figures rounded off so that columns may not add.

Both 1943 and 1944 were record-breaking years in which 1,849 and 1,786 vessels were delivered, with a total displacement tonnage of 6.9 and 7.0 million tons, respectively. (Figure 1)

Comparison with the shipbuilding being done at the same time for the Navy is difficult because ordnance and armament are large items in the total cost for the Navy, and the greater complexity of warships makes a comparison in terms of displacement tons inadequate. The final products are hardly more comparable than a barracks and a fortress. The direct cost of ships delivered in 1941–1945 was about $18 billion for the Navy, exclusive of ordnance, about $13 billion for the Maritime Commission.

A striking contrast between the Navy expenditures and those of the Maritime Commission is in the way they were distributed by shipbuilding areas (Figure 3). Actually the money spent flowed through the shipyards,

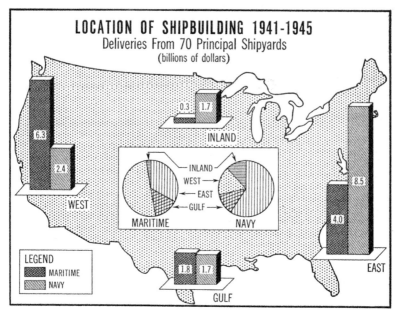

FIGURE 3. Source: Fischer, *Statistical Summary*, Table H-7.

which were the assembly points, back all over the country to the steel mills and to manufacturers who made engines, boilers, cables, and innumerable other components. But the records compiled enable us to follow the money only as far as the shipyards. . . .

The Maritime Commission Before the War

The U.S. Maritime Commission was created by the Merchant Marine Act of 1936 in order to modernize the American merchant marine. It was expected to achieve this aim by a judicious distribution of subsidies among applicant shipbuilding and ship-operating companies. These subsidies to American private enterprise were intended to make up for the differential between their costs and the costs of their European competitors. As these differentials in costs were of two kinds, so were the subsidies. Companies operating passenger ships or freighters could apply for a subsidy to compensate for their higher costs and enable them to operate in competition with foreign ships sailing the same routes. The Commission was empowered to grant such subsidies if it found that the route served was essential and if the operating company had an acceptable plan for replacing its old ships with modern ones.

The cost of the new ships would be higher if they were built in American yards than if built in foreign yards, and this differential was the basis for the second kind of subsidy which the Commission was empowered to grant, a constructions subsidy. If an operating company was ready to make a contract with a shipbuilding company for a ship the design of which was approved by the Commission and the Navy, the Commission was empowered to pay the builder a subsidy equal to the difference between his costs and foreign costs of building.[4] The conception of those who drafted the Merchant Marine Act of 1936 was that the Maritime Commission would be a quasi-judicial body, for it would pass on applications for differential subsidies.

It had judicial functions too in its power to review the agreements on rates made by the various shipping pools and in this respect could be compared to the Interstate Commerce Commission.[5] It was also instructed to operate schools for merchant seamen and officers, and was here enjoined to take the initiative. And it was expected to accomplish its main function— the replacement of over-age ships by new ones of approved designs—by acting on the applications for constructions and operating subsidies submitted by interested companies. . . .

Joseph P. Kennedy was made the first Chairman [of the Maritime Commission]. . . .When Mr. Kennedy resigned in February 1938, Rear Admiral (later Vice Admiral) Emory Scott Land, USN (Retired), already a member of the Commission, became its Chairman. Under his leadership the Commission and its staff set to work to get modern freighters built for the American merchant marine without waiting for applications from the industry for construction subsidies. The Commission, not the private companies, took the initiative; and consequently it functioned more like an operative agency, less like a judicial agency, than had been contemplated in the Merchant Marine Act of 1936.

The Commission drew plans for modern fast cargo ships, invited bids from shipyards, played newcomers against old-timers to beat down prices, and then awarded contracts—all without any assurance of being able to sell the ships to operators. This procedure was authorized as a last resort by Title VII of the Act of 1936, which required that such construction directly by the Commission be subject to the express approval of the President.[6] In general, Commissions are thought of as instruments of Congress in contrast to Departments which are instruments of the President, but the reliance of the Maritime Commission on Title VII made it in large measure an agency of the Executive.

The active or operating role assumed by the Commission was one factor which tended to cause more power to concentrate in the Chairman. Another reason for the dominating position which Admiral Land held as the Commission's chairman from 1938 to 1946 was the close personal relationship between him and President Roosevelt. Their friendship had begun in the Navy Department some twenty-five years earlier when Roosevelt was Assistant Secretary from 1913 to 1920. During six of those years, "Jerry" Land was a Lieutenant or Lieutenant Commander in the Bureau of Construction and Repair. Their friendship continued in the twenties when both were associated with the Daniel Guggenheim Fund for the Promotion of Aeronautics, and was renewed when President Roosevelt, in March 1933, nominated Rear Admiral Land to be Chief Constructor of the Navy and Chief of the Bureau of Construction and Repair.[7] Since Admiral Land was a naval constructor, not a line officer, this post placed him at the top of his profession. He was detached from it and, at his own request, placed on the retired list in April 1937, when he was then only fifty-eight years old and as agile and tireless as ever. His "retirement" caused some to wonder, but its meaning became clear when President Roosevelt appointed him that same month to the Maritime Commission and then, sending Mr. Kennedy to London as Ambassador, made Admiral Land the Chairman of the Commission.

Admiral Land's personality contained many qualities likely to appeal to Franklin Roosevelt and qualities important in explaining the performance of the Commission under his chairmanship. He set a very high value on personal loyalty—loyalty to one's superior, to friends, and to subordinates who were loyal in turn. He worked, moved, and thought with startling rapidity. In his office, he went through a host of papers, dictating or revising memoranda and leaving his characteristic "L" on innumerable reports. Even across a desk, however, his cold, bold eyes and quick sallies conjured away the wrapping of bureaucracy and recalled instead the dangerous swordplay of Viking ancestors. A flair for salty phrases led him occasionally to make impolitic pungent remarks in after-dinner speeches, but shone to his advantage before Congressional committees where his footwork was just as agile as it had been on the football field in 1900 when he went through the Army line on a trick play to score the Navy's winning touchdown.[8] He was not inclined to belittle in the least his own importance, but he knew how to disarm critics by down-to-earth disclaimers of infallibility.

Even across a desk, his cold, bold eyes and quick sallies conjured away the wrapping of bureaucracy...

"I got my start in life by working from sunrise to sunset, with my hands, for $10.00 a month and keep," asserted Admiral Land frequently, insisting he was no "brass hat."[9] From schooling in Cannon City, Colorado, he went to Wyoming as a cowpuncher and student at the university, and from Wyoming was appointed to the Naval Academy. When he graduated in 1902, he was tops in athletics and sixth in his studies. After a post-graduate course in naval architecture at Massachusetts Institute of Technology, service with Admiral Sims in London in 1918, many years in the Construction Corps of the Navy, a brief period of work in aeronautics (he took up flying when fifty and qualified for a pilot's license), and the four years as chief of the bureau in charge of the Navy shipbuilding, he was a proud member of the "shipbuilding fraternity," and accepted as its highest honor, election in 1940 to the presidency of the Society of Naval Architects and Marine Engineers. In Admiral Land, the Maritime Commission had a chairman who was highly esteemed and thoroughly at home in the Navy and in all the shipbuilding industry. . . .

When Admiral Land became Chairman in 1938, he gave primary attention to the external relations of the Commission—its contact with the White House, with Congress, with other agencies—and to its program and public relations as a whole; but as early as May 1937, he had made arrangements to have Commander Howard L. Vickery brought over from the Navy's Bureau of Construction and Repair to act as his assistant.[10] On September 26, 1940, Howard Vickery, then Commander, later Vice Admiral, became a Commissioner, having been appointed on Admiral Land's recommendation; so there continued to be one Commissioner in charge of construction. . . .[11]

From the point of view of the production of ships, the heart of the Commission was the Technical Division. It had a special status because it was directly supervised first by Commander Vickery as special assistant to Admiral Land, and later by Admiral Vickery as Commissioner. He was placed by Commission action in charge of all matters related to construction. . . .[12]

The balance sought in the membership of the Commission was a balance of abilities. Admiral Land, when first appointed, was outstanding as a naval constructor, and as Chairman proved highly gifted in handling public relations and political contacts. Admiral Vickery was a production man. Captain Macauley was skilled in maritime labor relations. Mr. Woodward was a lawyer. When these four composed the Commission, a man of business experience was sought to round out the combination. If its members could so work together as to pool their capacities, such a commission might administer an agency better than one man. But the Commission form was to be subjected to a severe strain by the war.

The Long-Range Program

The undisputed leadership which Admiral Land held in the Commission in 1941 was due in part to his success in carrying through a program for new construction. This prewar construction was very small compared to the production of the war years, but the building of 1938–1940 was extremely important in preparing for the work done in 1941–1945. It laid the foundations in shipyards, in designs, and in forming a trained staff for the Commission.

Merchant shipbuilding had come to a very low ebb in the United States when the boom after World War I collapsed, and it made only a slight revival under the Merchant Marine Act of 1928. Most of the fleet, having been built in 1918–1922, would in 1942 be twenty years old, which was generally considered obsolescent. Out of a total of 1,422 ocean-going vessels (2,000 gross tons and over) registered in 1942 under the American flag, 91.8 per cent would be twenty years old, as would all the 225 government-owned ships, most of them in moth balls from World War I. Most of the dry-cargo vessels were of 10- to 11-knot speed. Although twenty-nine large combination passenger-and-cargo vessels had been built under the subsidy provisions of the Merchant Marine Act of 1928, the United States had no liners to rival the British "Queens," and 60 per cent of the combination passenger-freight vessels were near obsolescence.[13]

The first ship contracted for through the Maritime Commission was a symbol, the *America*, the largest liner ever built in the United States. It was not nearly so big as the huge luxury liners of the French and British, the *Normandie* and the *Queen Mary*, which were the record makers of the North Atlantic traffic, but in some features such as fireproofing it excelled even these famous ships, and it was a notable advance in American passenger vessel construction. The contract was awarded September 30, 1937, and the *America* was intended for operation by the United States Lines to give the American merchant marine a representation of which it could be proud in the most publicized of all trade routes.[14]

More needed than the highly publicized liners were dry-cargo carriers. Speedy tankers, too, were wanted as auxiliaries for the Navy. Subsidies to increase the speed of tankers of the *Cimarron* class to 18 knots were among the first subsidies to be paid by the Commission, for this extra speed was reckoned a "defense feature."[15] But American oil companies had kept up their tanker fleets; the glaring deficiency in the American merchant marine was in dry-cargo vessels. The main problem of the Commission was to build speedy, efficient freighters.

Although everyone favored the building of new freighters, practical agreement on what to build was another matter. The Navy, the Commissioners, and the prospective operators found difficulty in agreeing. The Navy was given an important voice in the matter by the Merchant Marine Act of 1936. The possible use of the vessels by the Navy in time of war was a main reason why the national government was interested in new construction. All contract plans and specifications for the proposed vessels were to be submitted by the Commission to the Navy Department for approval, so that the Navy could urge any changes it deemed necessary to make possible the speedy and economical conversion of ships into naval auxiliaries. On this basis the Commission assumed the cost of all national defense features.[16] The Navy's conception of the kind of ships desired was naturally one-sided, but it was an important side and had to be considered.[17] At the other extreme was the point of view of the ship-operating companies. Whereas the Navy wished as speedy ships as possible for tactical reasons, the shipping companies wished economy in operation even at the sacrifice of some speed. Even within the Commission there was sharp divergence of views as to the way in which the Commission should proceed and the type of ships that should be built.

> **The possible use of the vessels by the Navy in time of war was a main reason why the national government was interested in new construction.**

How these divergences of view were reconciled or overridden is another story. Important for the shipbuilding of World War II is the fact that they had been overcome by positive action in which the Commission took the initiative under Admiral Land's leadership. Merchant shipbuilding was booming as war drew nearer, and the revival of the industry was along the lines laid down by the Maritime Commission in its "long-range program." It was called a long-range program because it was the answer to the Congressional injunction that the Commission make a definite plan for replacing obsolete vessels in sufficient volume to serve essential trade routes. It called for the building of 50 ships a year for ten years.[18] Although that does not seem a large program when in retrospect we compare it to the production during the war years, it seemed highly ambitious in 1938 when the first contracts in the long-range program were awarded.

After World War II began in Europe, the demand for shipping increased, as it usually has in time of war. With a more favorable market for the ships and with their potential use as naval auxiliaries growing more urgent, the long-range program of the Maritime Commission was accelerated. On August 27, 1940, the Commission voted to speed up that program so that 200 ships would be contracted for prior to July 1941. Contract authorization was raised $50 million by the Second Deficiency Appropriation Act of 1940. Before the end of October 1940, 47 ships had been delivered and contracts had been awarded for 130 more. The long-range program was proceeding well ahead of schedule. . . .[19]

The group of men who were the guiding spirits determining the design of the ships for the long-range program came together even before the formation of the Maritime Commission. Acting on a suggestion from the Navy, the Shipping Board Bureau of the Department of Commerce in 1934 engaged George G. Sharp, consulting naval architect, together with J. E. Schmeltzer and William G. Esmond of his staff, to work on the design of standard types of merchant vessels acceptable to the Navy.[20] The Navy's representatives on the joint board which met with these architects included the then Commander Howard L. Vickery, and occasionally James L. Bates.[21] When shipbuilding began to pick up, Mr. Sharp returned to the affairs of his firm of naval architects,[22] but Messrs. Schmeltzer and Esmond continued with the Shipping Board Bureau until they were transferred with the rest of its staff to the Maritime Commission. The organization of the new Technical Division was completed in 1939 by making James L. Bates the Director, Mr. Esmond the head of the Hull Section, and Mr. Schmeltzer of the Engineering Section. In July 1940, after the standard cargo vessels had proved brilliantly successful, Mr. Schmeltzer was made Associate Director of the Division in recognition of his primary responsibility for designs of propulsion equipment.[23]

As the long-range program materialized in more and more ships to be designed and inspected, additional units were formed within the Technical Division. A Preliminary Design Branch investigated the possibilities of various types of ships, developed initial plans, tested models, and worked up tentative drawings and calculations. Both for the hull and for the engines, separate sections were formed to turn these preliminary plans into exact specifications, and other sections checked the detailed working plans which were prepared by the constructor's naval architect. A Materials Section investigated materials and equipment of many kinds. There was an Interior and Styling group also, and a Clerical Section. To find what ship-yards were capable of building the vessels being planned, an Investigation Section was formed. Later it was absorbed by the Construction Section which sent inspectors into the yards to report on the way the work was progressing and see that it was being done according to specifications. A Trial Board reporting directly to the Commission was formed to pass on acceptance of vessels.

In 1940, after the ships of the long-range program had been in use long enough, a Performance Section within Technical was charged with drawing lessons from their operation, especially from any breakdowns.[24] Thus various units in the technical staff of the Commission were planning, supervising, and replanning the long-range program as it grew in volume.

Recruiting the technical staff was a serious problem. . . .The Commission was constantly losing good men to the new shipyards which were being formed to construct ships for the long-range program. . . . [However,] in recruiting its own staff, as well as in its relations to the shipbuilding companies, the Technical Division became an educational institution giving important training in naval architecture and marine engineering.

Alongside the development of the technical staff which planned and inspected new construction, grew an auditing staff in the Finance Division. The Merchant Marine Act of 1936 limited the profits of the builders to 10 per cent of the contract price; consequently the Commission's representatives checked over a company's statement of cost to see whether some of the price stated in the contract could be recaptured by the Commission as excess profit. For this purpose resident auditors were sent to all yards working on the Commission contracts. . . .

Standard Types of Cargo Vessels

The ships designed before the war for the long-range program continued during the war to be the Commission's ideal of what they would like to build. They were commonly called "standard types" to distinguish them from the other main groups of types—emergency, military, and minor. Even under the pressure of war, the Commission succeeded in building so many of the standard types that its "long-range" program of completing 500 of these vessels in ten years had been exceeded by 1946. The standard dry-cargo carriers were called C-types. They were of three sorts, C1, C2, and C3, the letter indicating that they were cargo ships and the number showing the relative size. Their main characteristics are shown in Table 2.

Compared to the freighters built before 1939, all of the C-types were remarkable for their speed. The *Challenge*, one of the first of the C2's, completed her maiden voyage from Boston to Cork, 2,742 nautical miles, in 6 days, 18 hours, and 38 minutes—an average speed of 16.82 knots, although the design speed of the C2 was only 15.5 knots.[25] Because of their better lines and improved propulsion machinery, these 15.5-knot ships had about the fuel consumption per nautical mile of the earlier 11-knot ship. At its sea trials in June 1939, the *Challenge* "chalked up a new world's

TABLE 2

CHARACTERISTICS OF SOME PRINCIPAL TYPES BUILT BY
MARITIME COMMISSION*

	Liberty	C1	C2	C3	Victory
Length, overall.......	441' 6"	417' 9"	459' 6"	492'	455' 3"
Beam, moulded.......	56' 11"	60'	63'	69' 6"	62'
Draft, loaded.........	27' 8"	27' 6"	25' 9"	28' 6"	28' 6"
Deadweight tonnage...	10,419	9,075	8,794	12,500	10,734
Bale capacity.........	500,245	452,420	536,828	732,140	453,210
Speed, knots.........	11	14	15.5	16.5	16.5

* For costs and displacement tonnage of these types see Table 20.
Source: Booklets prepared by the MC Division of Vessel Disposal and Government Aids and "Liberty Ship Stowage and Capacity Booklet," prepared for the Commission by the Bruce Engineering Co., New York.

record for fuel economy with a fuel consumption of 0.552 pounds per shaft horsepower per hour for all purposes." Its high speed cross compound turbines developed 6,000 shaft horsepower and drove the propeller shaft at 92 revolutions per minute through double reduction gears.[26] While their speed made these ships attractive to the Navy as potential auxiliaries, their combination of speed and economy enabled them to meet the needs of competitive commercial operators.

Most of the C-types were powered with turbines, and the basic reason why they could combine speed and economy was the progress made in building double reduction gearing which reduced the very rapid revolutions necessary for an efficient turbine to the relatively slow revolutions necessary in the efficient propeller. But Diesel engines, which did not require double reduction gearing, were installed on many C2's.[27] Few Diesels had been installed in American merchant vessels before the Maritime Commission launched its program, and Admiral Land considered recognition of the feasibility of the Diesel to be one of the main contributions of the Maritime Commission to the technical development of the shipbuilding industry.[28]

The other major contribution to which he pointed with pride in 1939 was the high pressure, high temperature steam turbine power plant being installed on C3's. Indeed, the C3 was an extremely fast ship for a cargo carrier. The design speed was 16.5 knots, but one of the first group built, the *Sea Fox*, on her official trials in March 1940, attained a speed of 19.5 knots and showed a fuel consumption rate of 0.563. These ships had a shaft hp. of 8500. A modified form of the basic C3 design providing for 95 to 192 passengers was also built. One was the round-the-world passenger liner *President Jackson* delivered in 1940.[29]

Much less ambitious were the C1's. Having a speed of only 14 knots, they were not up to the general standard required for Navy Auxiliaries, but were believed suitable for some particular trade routes. Five were delivered in 1940, twenty-nine in 1941, powered partly by turbines and partly with Diesel engines. But the chief source of pride to the technical staff of the Commission when the war began was the excellent performance of the C2's and C3's.[30]

Also a source of pride but a dream which existed only on drawing boards was the trans-Pacific passenger liner with the design designation P4-P. To compete with rumored Japanese liners, it was to have a speed of 24 knots. It would be 760 feet long with a beam of 98 feet and be propelled by two turbines, each of 29,000 shp. operating on reheat regenerative cycles. Since its speed and size made the P4-P potentially an airplane carrier, that possibility was kept in mind in its design. For example, smoke stacks were placed on one side so as to leave room for a flight deck. Other P (passenger ship) designs of various sizes (P1, P2, and P3) were included in Admiral Land's long-range program. Although none of these was built before the war, the technical staff of the Commission had worked on the basic problems which arose when the construction of such ships for transports was decided on during the war.[31]

Also a source of pride but a dream which existed only on drawing boards was the trans-Pacific passenger liner. . .

For tankers, similarly, design designations (T1, T2, and T3) were used to indicate various sizes, but before 1941 the only tankers built with Maritime Commission aid were those of the high speed *Cimarron* class, the T3-S2-A1, which were built with designs furnished by the Standard Oil Company of New Jersey[32] and for which the Maritime Commission paid only the cost of defense features.

All dry-cargo and passenger ships built under Maritime Commission contracts embodied a large number of improvements in addition to their more efficient propulsion machinery. . . .New aids to navigation, improved fireproof design, and better life-saving equipment also served to make the C-ships among the safest vessels afloat.

Since the Maritime Commission was charged with rebuilding morale among American seamen as well as replacing obsolete and inefficient vessels, a notable feature of all its vessels was better accommodations for officers and crew. The crew were given cabins in the house amidships instead of being bunked altogether in the traditional forecastle. Proper mess rooms were provided, as were hot and cold running water, and many more ventilator fans. . . .

From the point of view of commercial operation, an essential feature of the C-types was their equipment for handling cargo. On most, this consisted of 14 or 15 five-ton booms and one thirty-ton boom. All were worked by electric winches. They were rigged to 10 king posts which formed so prominent a part of the profile characteristics of the C-types.[33]

The methods used in constructing the C-types anticipated some features of the wartime program. Welding was just coming into extensive general use on large merchant vessels. In the Commission's design, riveting was replaced by welding to such an extent as to save a substantial amount in the weight of the hull and so secure greater deadweight carrying capacity. . . .[34]

More definitely connected with Commission policy was the trend towards standardization and the effort to apply methods used in mass production. Traditionally, operators determined the design of each ship according to their particular ideas of the special needs of the ports and routes in which they intended to operate the ship. The C-types, in contrast, were designed initially by the Maritime Commission after consultation with many operating companies and with trade associations whose suggestions were compromised and combined as far as possible so as to produce a standard ship adapted to a variety of needs. Modifications were then made to meet special needs of individual operators, but many components and items of equipment were the same. . . .

Another form of saving through standardization was by awarding contracts, not for one ship at a time, but for groups of four to six identical ships. This simplified the preparation of working plans, the ordering of materials, and the control of construction in a yard.[35] The type awarded to a yard was adapted to its equipment and most of the smaller, new yards were standardized on one type.[36] Although American shipbuilding in 1940 was far from the technique of multiple production developed during the war, it was already moving in that direction in building the Maritime Commission's standard cargo vessels.

The Shipyards of the Country in 1940

The value in 1941 of this long-range program lay not only in the ships it had produced but at least equally in the shipyards which as a result were then operating. The slump in shipbuilding after the First World War had threatened to cripple the industry. This was the more serious because naval architecture was an intricate science. Dominating the clatter and seeming random dispersion of a shipyard, guiding the work of its huge cranes, heavy presses, and other special equipment were the calculations of highly trained engineers and experienced managers. Their practical and theoretical knowledge had to be kept employed if the industry was to survive and have in it the possibility of sudden growth to meet a new emergency.

In the lean years from 1922 to 1938, only the very strong shipbuilding companies were able to keep going. The strongest survivors may be called the Big Five: Newport News, Federal, New York, Sun, and Bethlehem. Because of their equipment, the high reputation of the engineers, the location of their yards, and their corporate or banking affiliations, they were the best placed for securing the scanty orders for tankers, ore carriers, and Navy vessels which offered some nourishment during the barren period.

The Newport News Shipbuilding and Dry Dock Company was the oldest and perhaps the most experienced in the country. It had been founded by the railroad magnate, C. P. Huntington, in 1890 and since that time had built ships of all kinds, including battleships. In 1940 it was outfitting the *America*. The Federal Shipbuilding and Dry Dock Co. of Kearney, New Jersey, was a subsidiary of U.S. Steel. The New York Shipbuilding Co. at Camden, New Jersey, founded in 1899, had built battleships, cruisers, and passenger liners. During World War II, it built entirely for the Navy; from 1936 to 1946 it had no Maritime Commission contracts. The Sun Shipbuilding and Dry Dock Company, Chester, Pennsylvania, was a subsidiary of Sun Oil Company and constructed many tankers for that concern and other oil companies.[37]

Bethlehem's position was unique in that it held a leading position in the three fields of steel manufacture, shipbuilding, and ship repair. . . .Altogether Bethlehem was building ships in four yards in 1940: at Fore River, Massachusetts; Staten Island, New York; Sparrows Point near Baltimore, Maryland; and at San Francisco, California.[38]

In addition to the Big Five, two other shipbuilders, both of primary importance to the Navy, were active even during the depth of the shipbuilders' depression: the Electric Boat Company at New London, Connecticut, which built submarines, and the Bath Iron Works, at Bath, Maine, which built destroyers.[39] The Bath Company was drawn into the Maritime Commission program in 1940 when it contracted to build four C2 freighters. . . .

When war began in Europe and shipping boomed, new companies entered the field of shipbuilding, and in 1940 Admiral Land boasted that seven practically new yards had been developed by the Maritime Commission.[40] Three of these were on the Gulf and four on the West coast, whereas the Big Five were all concentrated in the Northeast, except for the Bethlehem San Francisco yard building for Maritime. The new yards were small, but they were seeds from which came establishments of importance during the war and they were scattered, as was desirable from the point of view of national defense and the labor supply. At the end of 1940, they were:[41]

(1)   Tampa Shipbuilding and Engineering Co., at Tampa, Florida, which was building Diesel-powered C2's on three ways.

(2)   The Ingalls Shipbuilding Corp. at Pascagoula, Mississippi, which was building C3's on four ways in a yard which was celebrated as the first constructed in the United States "exclusively for the building of welded ships." It was an offshoot of the Ingalls Iron Works of Birmingham, Alabama.[42]

(3)   Pennsylvania Shipyards, Inc. at Beaumont, Texas, had laid the keel for a C1. Its two ways were designed to have room for four such ships, since ships were launched sideways. Another special feature of its launchings was the use of bananas to grease the ways.

(4)   Consolidated Steel Corp. Ltd., at Long Beach, California, was building two C1's in the one long way in their recently acquired Craig yard. Here also side launchings were used.[43]

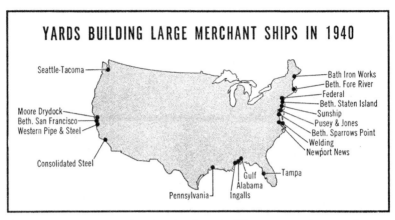

FIGURE 4. Class I yards, that is, those building ocean-going vessels over 400 feet in length. Source: Fischer, *Statistical Summary*, Table E-1, and Reynolds' Way Charts.

(5)   Western Pipe and Steel Co. was also working on two C1's in a new yard in San Francisco using side launchings.

(6)   Moore Dry Dock Co. of Oakland, California, primarily a repair company with three ways, was engaged in outfitting three C3's.

(7)   Seattle-Tacoma Shipbuilding Corp., in the new yard it was building at Tacoma, Washington, had two C1's on the ways and three in outfitting as the year 1940 ended.[44]

In addition: (8) The Pusey and Jones Corp. at Wilmington, Delaware, was building a C1; (9) Gulf Shipbuilding Corp. at Chickasaw, Alabama, was starting two C2's, of which it laid the keels in 1941; and (10) Alabama Dry Dock and Shipbuilding Co. at Mobile was at work on a private tanker, as was (11) Welding Shipyards, Inc. of Norfolk, Virginia. Altogether the yards working on large merchant ships at the end of 1940 totaled 19.[45] To the eleven already mentioned should be added: (12) Newport News Shipbuilding and Dry Dock Co., building C3's and private cargo ships on six of its ways; (13) Federal Shipbuilding and Dry Dock Co., about half full of Navy work but building merchant vessels under private contracts on five of its ways; (14) the eight ways of Sun Ship—as the Chester Yard was commonly called—which were filled half with private tankers, half with C-types. In the Bethlehem yards, C-types or tankers were being built on seven ways at Sparrows Point (15), four ways at Fore River (16), two ways at Staten Island (17), and two ways at the San Francisco yard (18). Finally, (19) the Bath Iron Works had C2's under construction on two ways.

Since in some yards, particularly those which launched sideways, there was more than one building berth on a single way, the total number of building berths occupied with ocean-going merchant shipbuilding on January 1, 1941, was 53.[46]

None of these shipyards, neither the yards of the Big Five nor of the smaller new companies, had any idle ways in the fall of 1940. What was not filled by the Commission's long-range program or by the small amount of unsubsidized private building was filled by the Navy's program.

The expansion of the Navy's program not only required the full use of existing shipyards but called for the building of new yards.

After years in which new construction was very slight, a substantial amount of Navy building was approved in 1934. Then came, in 1938, the Twenty-Percent Expansion Act and on top of it, in June 1940, the Eleven-Percent Expansion Act. This construction seemed like a lot until France fell and Germany controlled all the coasts from the Arctic to Portugal. Immediately, in July 1940, a Seventy-Percent Expansion Act increased the authorized tonnage of the Navy from 1,724,480 tons to 3,049,480 tons, a two-ocean Navy. Consequently all yards were fully occupied before the Maritime Commission started its emergency program, and mostly with Navy contracts.[47]

The expansion of the Navy's program in July not only required the full use of existing shipyards but called for the building of new yards. Some abandoned yards, such as the Cramp Shipbuilding Company of Philadelphia, where the cranes had rusted away, were provided by the

Navy with money to re-equip the yards and resume construction. Small yards such as the Gulf Shipbuilding Corporation, were given contracts for destroyers and the facilities with which to build them. Some of the Navy building, especially of auxiliaries, was placed in Gulf or West coast yards, but most of it was on the northeast seaboards where the yards were best equipped and their labor most experienced.[48]

The building of warships began to crowd out merchant ships in some yards. Especially heavy were the demands of the Navy on the Big Five. Newport News took so many Navy contracts in 1941 that it became absorbed, as New York Shipbuilding had been all along, in work on battleships, carriers, and cruisers. Federal took contracts for 5 cruisers and 37 destroyers, leaving only a little room for merchant building.[49]

Three of Bethlehem's four yards were assigned to do Navy work entirely—Fore River, which was the largest, Staten Island, and the San Francisco yard. The latter, which had been revived by the Maritime Commission as a modest 3-way yard, added more ways and appropriate machine, plate, pipe, and sheet-metal shops to take on Navy work, as did also Fore River, Staten Island, and the repair yard at San Pedro.

All these yards were destined for Navy work as soon as ships under contract for the Maritime Commission and on the ways were finished.[50] Only Sparrows Point remained free for merchant shipbuilding. Sun Ship, which had done no building of naval types, was induced to take contracts for auxiliaries, seaplane tenders and destroyer tenders.[51] Even the smaller shipbuilding companies which had been brought to life by the Maritime Commission, such as Tampa and Ingalls, were drawn into the Navy's plans.

The Consolidated Steel Corporation, which was building for the Maritime Commission at Los Angeles, agreed to build at Orange, Texas, a plant for the construction of destroyers.[52] Moore Dry Dock and Seattle-Tacoma added new facilities for the same purpose.[53]

These contracts did not directly interfere with the work on ships previously ordered by the Commission for its long-range program, but they were a drain on the skilled managers and engineers of even those shipbuilding companies which the Maritime Commission thought of as peculiarly its own.

Compared with the capacity or equipment of the American ship-building industry, the Navy's program was enormous. The estimated cost of vessels under contract was $5 billion.[54] On June 1, 1940, only 6 private yards were working on Navy orders. By February of the next year, there were 68. The bulk of these contracts were let in September of 1940 as soon as Congress appropriated the money.[55] From that time on, not only were the ways filled, but also the shops which manufactured gears, turbines, and all the other machinery essential to a ship.

Making new ship ways was relatively easy and the steel output was still large enough to handle the demand. The greatest difficulty was in obtaining machinery because of the scarcity of machine tools. In terms of shipbuilding, that meant a scarcity of cranes, gear hobbers, gears and turbines. To meet that situation, the Navy was given priority by the Vinson Act of June 28, 1940. By issuing a certificate of priority, the Secretary of the Navy could reserve for Navy building any scarce component, and he did reserve accordingly those items of machinery most difficult to obtain for the building of fast merchant ships.[56]

Compared with the Navy's building, the Maritime Commission's long-range program was but a drop in the bucket. The 177 ships which had been contracted for prior to October 15, 1940 were estimated to cost $438,200,000.[57]

Between October 1940 and July 1, 1941, the Commission planned to award contracts for 23 more vessels estimated to cost $101,100,000.[58] Trifles compared to the Navy's $5,000,000,000! But small as was the merchant shipbuilding program, it was being seriously interfered with by the Navy's priorities, especially on turbines and gears.

Congestion was already intense in the American shipbuilding industry when, in October of 1940, a British Merchant Shipping Mission assembled in New York to plan an emergency program.

Emergency Shipbuilding Before the Declaration of War

The Inception of the Emergency Program

In the winter of 1940–1941, Britain was straining every moral and material resource to resist the kind of lightning war by which Hitler had overwhelmed France during the previous summer. The Nazis controlled all the coast of Europe from Lapland to the Pyrenees. German aircraft and submarines, operating from much better bases than they had had in World War I, seemed likely to strangle Britain by destroying its shipping.

PROGRAMS FORMULATED IN 1940 AND 1941
For Tonnage To Be Delivered In 1942

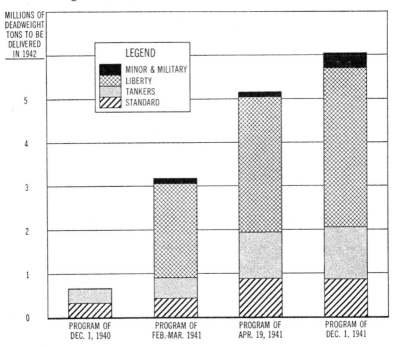

FIGURE 5. Private and British shipbuilding in the United States are included as well as ships contracted for by the U. S. Maritime Commission. Source: Fischer, *Statistical Summary*, Table A-2.

The ships of the United States were forbidden to enter the combat area by the Neutrality Act which had been passed in November 1939, but President Roosevelt was pushing various methods of aiding Britain while at the same time strengthening the defenses of the United States in the western hemisphere. The exchange of fifty destroyers to the British in return for the lease of naval bases in Newfoundland and other British territory in America was arranged in September 1940. Other forms of aid to Britain were to follow before long. Although the United States was making preparation for war (Congress passed the Selective Service Act in September 1940), it was not yet at war. Preparations were referred to as "the defense effort."

Under these conditions three emergency shipbuilding programs were laid on top of the accelerated long-range program during 1941. They form three waves of expansion:

- The first wave consisted of 60 ships contracted for by the British and 200 which were announced on January 3, 1941, for the United States.
- The second wave came in April after Congress passed the act providing for transferring merchant ships and other forms of aid to Britain under the formula of "lend-lease."
- The third rolled in gradually during the rest of the year, until on December 7, 1941, the Japanese attack opened the flood gates for two even bigger waves.

In each wave of expansion before the declaration of war, the officials of the Maritime Commission were called on to make decisions that later had important effects on the way the subsequent wartime programs were carried out. The atmosphere in which decisions were made and also the other agencies with which they were worked out kept changing. The very first wave was clearly a part of aid to Britain at a time when no general formula for giving aid, such as lend lease, had yet been worked out or received legislative approval.

Coordination of the national economy for the nation's defense was still a long way off; the war organization of the economy existed only in embryo, under the National Defense Advisory Commission (NDAC). Under the chairmanship of William S. Knudsen, the NDAC was drawing leading industrialists to Washington and giving the "New Deal" administration a general view of how to mobilize industrial resources. Shipbuilding plans were routed through the NDAC to be fitted into the general effort. Admiral Land was in charge of the shipbuilding section of the NDAC as well as Chairman of the Maritime Commission, and acted in both capacities in preparing plans for the President or in advising the British.[59]

Although there was general concern over Britain's ability to resist the Nazis, opinion in Washington was divided during the winter of 1940–1941. . . .Emotions ran high in discussions of how much, how generously, or how selfishly the United States should aid Britain, but there was no doubt some aid would be given, and the British Merchant Shipping Mission which had assembled in the United States in October 1940 was assured that they could do some building in American yards.

The British were prepared to back an extensive program involving the construction of new yards. They recognized that new yards could hardly be expected to produce any ships before 1942, and they discovered at once that they could not have fast ships, for there were not enough of the needed turbines and gears, not even enough to supply the Navy and the Maritime Commission's long-range program. But they obtained permission to build 11-knot 10,000 ton freighters.[60] The British mission worked in consultation with Admirals Land and Vickery who on November 12 approved its general plan.[61]

Official approval of the locations selected for new yards by the British was recorded by the Commission on December 11, at a time when emergency construction by the United States was being planned also. Workmen were just clearing the sites where the British ships were to be built when President Roosevelt announced at a press conference on January 3, 1941 that the United States would build 200 similar ships.[62]. . .

The idea that the United States should build 11-knot freighters such as the British would have to build was not relished by Admiral Land. What was later to be called the Liberty Fleet was in 1940 conceived of as an evil, perhaps a necessary evil, but an evil to be avoided if possible. The energies of the Maritime Commission were focused on the standard types. The decision that there must be additional construction to meet the emergency was made at the White House, and as a consequence the Commission accepted as a necessity late in December of 1940 the diversion of its energies from the goal which had been set up in peaceful times. . . .

In spite of Admiral Land's efforts, standard types had no place in the first wave of expansion. Indeed, according to the principles Land himself had advanced, there was no room for them at the moment in a program attempting something like a mass production of ships. "The proper procedure for the production of ships in quantities," he wrote November 8, "is to settle on the type of ship, which in quantity production for quick delivery, (considering the excessive load on the auxiliary building and turbine building capacity of this country), is a simple type of cargo ship with reciprocating engines, boiler pressure of 200 to 220 lbs., with all steam auxiliaries. The quantity of ships desired and the times at which deliveries are required should be established."[63] After Christmas, he was busy applying these principles to an American building program, but a program developed because of Britain's immediate peril. . . .[64] [Space limitations prevent detailing the Maritime Commission's wave-upon-wave of expansion throughout the war, thus some highlights are provided. The next challenge for the Maritime Commission was the selection of sites and the problem of size. Shipyards ranging in size from 4 to 14 ways were considered possibilities and the problem of location was a question of political dynamite. –Ed.]

Selecting the Sites and Managers

First to be definitely agreed to were those sites which Todd Shipyards included in its plans. South Portland, Maine, and Richmond, on San Francisco Bay in California, were approved as sites for British building on

December 11, 1940; and three other widely scattered yards, at Los Angeles, at Houston, and at Portland, Oregon, were approved for the American program on January 10, 1941.[65] Although precise locations were selected by members of the Todd group, all these yards were in places which had been included in Admiral Land's first list, that of November 8. Three being on the West coast, one on the Gulf and one at the other extreme in Maine, they were all located where new supplies of labor could be found without competing directly with the already busy shipbuilding centers of the Northeast. . . .

At the opening of 1941, nine yards with a total of 65 ways were approved to build in two years the desired total of 260 ships at the following locations:[66]

No. Ways

South Portland, Me.—
Todd-Bath Iron Shipbuilding Corp. for the British 7
Baltimore, Md.—Bethlehem-Fairfield Yard 13
Wilmington, N.C.—North Carolina Shipbuilding Co. 6
Mobile, Ala.—Alabama Dry Dock and Shipbuilding Co 4
New Orleans, La.—Delta Shipbuilding Co. 6
Houston, Texas—Houston Shipbuilding Corp. 6
Los Angeles (Terminal Island), Cal.—California Shipbuilding Cp. 8
Richmond, Cal.—Todd-California Shipbuilding Corp. for British 7
Portland, Oregon—Oregon Shipbuilding Corp. 8

First and last, the main concern in launching the emergency shipbuilding program was to enlist the leaders of the shipbuilding industry. The Big Five, who had most of the "shipbuilding brains" on their payrolls, were not eager to join in or were prevented from doing so by the Navy's claim that its work should have priority. . . . [They all] had so many Navy contracts there was little hope of getting any more merchant building into that yard. . . .[However], on January 10, New York Shipbuilding announced that they would build emergency ships at a new plant at Wilmington, North Carolina.[67]. . .

In the second half of January 1941, terms were finally arranged for a Bethlehem subsidiary to operate a new emergency yard named, because of the suburb in which it was located, Bethlehem-Fairfield.[68]. . .

Accordingly the Maritime Commission then turned to a leading ship-building company of the Great Lakes, the American Ship Building Co. Since the Liberty ships could not be built on the Lakes (being too long to pass the locks) the shipbuilding talent of the Lakes region was drawn upon by arranging with American Ship Building for the operation of the yard at New Orleans. A new company called the Delta Shipbuilding Co. was formed for that purpose.[69]

Thus two of the nine new emergency yards were operated by old-line companies, Bethlehem and Newport News. One was in the hands of a company transplanted from the Great Lakes, and one, at Mobile, was in the hands of managers of a repair company. All the other five, the five first approved, were under the combine headed by Todd Shipyards Corp., a new team. With the old-line yards busy with naval building and unable to supply experienced management for many new yards, the Commission had to turn to a relatively inexperienced group.

Under the Todd name had been gathered together a wide variety of men whose managerial talents had been displayed in various fields. Todd Shipyards itself had one of the very largest ship repair organizations with yards on all coasts and strong financial backing. It had built ships during World War I and led in the formation of the new Seattle-Tacoma shipyards. The ability of its president, John D. Reilly, as a man of bold decisions was spotlighted by newspapers and by *Fortune*, "the Magazine of Business," under the title: "Biggest Splash in Emergency Construction will be made by Todd." A second figure in the combination, also ranking high in the shipbuilding fraternity, was "Pete" (William S.) Newell, head of the Bath Iron Works. . . .

Henry J. Kaiser's only previous connection with shipbuilding was joint ownership with Todd in the Seattle-Tacoma Shipbuilding Corp. . . .[Kaiser] built up a reputation on the West coast contracting for all kinds of construction, and then brought together other construction firms to join in the achievements which won him fame as "Fabulous Kaiser."[70] His group built the Hoover and Grand Coulee dams, and the Bay Bridge from San Francisco across to Oakland, his headquarters. He was an organizer and a salesman, full of ideas and readiness to tackle the "impossible." Working for him were "six of the smartest young men in the country," men barely over 30, who, it was said, "keep the promises that Henry makes.[71]

In shipbuilding the kingpins among Henry Kaiser's young men were Edgar Kaiser, his son, and Clay Bedford. The former became head of the emergency shipyard at Portland, Oregon; the latter became general manager at Richmond, California, where the yard known originally as Todd-Cal, later as Richmond No. 1, was located, and where other yards were later built for the Maritime Commission. The third emergency yard on the West coast, that of the California Shipbuilding Co., at Los Angeles, (commonly known as Calship), was managed by associates of Kaiser in the Six Companies, at first by the McCone-Bechtel organization, later by J. A. McCone. On the East coast, William S. Newell was in charge of the emergency yards at South Portland, Maine. The fifth yard of the Todd group, that at Houston, Texas, was most directly under Todd management. Ownership in all seven yards (counting the two building for the British) was divided between Todd Shipyards Corp. and the Kaiser group, with Bath Iron Works Corp. owning a part also in the Maine yards.[72]. . .

In the perspectives of early 1941, an emergency program of 260 merchant ships, on top of the Navy's huge program and on top of the accelerated long-range program, seemed very large indeed. . . .

The Second Wave of Expansion

The second wave of expansion was directly linked to Congressional approval of the lend-lease program. It contained provision for more Liberty ships, for more C-type freighters, and also for government-built tankers.

After lend-lease was provided for by the Defense Aid Supplemental Appropriation Act, approved March 27, 1941, Admiral Land was called

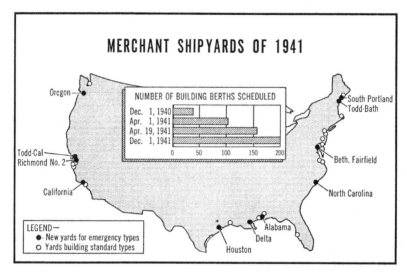

FIGURE 6. Class I yards. Names of the yards building standard types, many of which were much expanded in 1941, are given on Figure 4.

to advise how the funds should be allocated for about 200 more ships. He successfully urged on President Roosevelt that at least half the 200 be C-types.[73] Construction of tankers was decided on in addition, and between the President's initial approval in general and the final authorization of contracts by the Commission, the number of ships was increased.

The program was referred to the Office of Production Management (OPM) which was created in January 1941 to continue the work of the NDAC in directing the "defense effort." On April 17, the OPM approved a total of 306 new ships, and they were incorporated in the Commission's program of April 19, 1941, namely: 112 Emergency ships, 24 C1's, 46 C2's, 52 C3's, and 72 tankers. . . .

More shipways were needed to build the added standard and emergency cargo ships, and they were provided by adding to yards in existence, or at least yards of existing companies. . . .

At the same time, the emergency yards which were just starting were told to increase the number of their ways. . . .

The Third Wave

The first two waves of expansion were clear-cut moves; each was pro-grammed and announced as a whole. For each there was one decisive Congressional action and Presidential authorization. The third wave was a composite and dragged out from spring until late 1941. It was composed of four elements at least: (1) small vessels designed for transfer to the British, (2) ore carriers, (3) sea-going tugs and concrete barges, and (4) major types such as had been the exclusive concern of the two previous waves of expansion. Each of these elements in the program was a response to a different and distinct aspect of the general shortage of shipping.

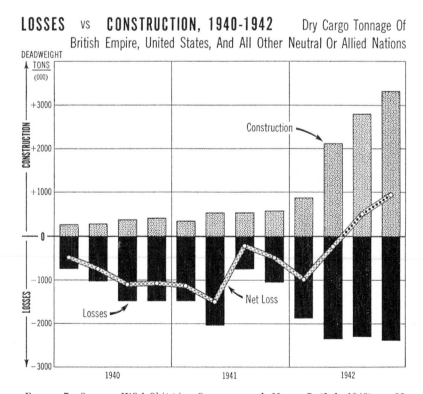

LOSSES vs **CONSTRUCTION, 1940-1942**   Dry Cargo Tonnage Of British Empire, United States, And All Other Neutral Or Allied Nations

FIGURE 7. Source: *WSA Shipping Summary,* vol. II, no. 7 (July 1945), p. 22.

The program of April 19, 1941 had hardly been formulated before Sir Arthur Salter of the British Mission pointed out to Admirals Land and Vickery in detail that more was needed. Assuming the current rate of sinkings and the adequacy of the April program, when combined with British building, to make up for losses once that program was fully underway, Sir Arthur stressed the very urgent need for tonnage during the first half of 1942. . . .

The shipping situation in 1941 was directly responsible also for expanding in June and July the program for Libertys and C-types. . . .

Before the declaration of war the Maritime Commission had programmed, in addition to the British building and a little private building, almost 5 million tons for 1942 and a productive capacity of over 7 million tons for 1943. Quite a contrast to the 341,219 tons which were the total deliveries of 1939.

Popularizing the Program

Not only was the emergency shipbuilding well underway before Pearl Harbor, but basic steps had been taken to present the program to the general public as a national enterprise in which they could join with pride. President Roosevelt himself led off by explaining in his fireside chats and news conferences the need for ships to defend America by aiding Britain.[74]. . .

Out of the nature of the shipbuilding industry arose two special forms of publicity: naming of ships and the launching ceremony. These were both matters of symbolic value, touched with emotion and inherently important therefore in public relations.

Naming the product is half the battle in any advertising campaign. The ship which was to win popular interest under the generic name "Liberty ship" started off under the severe handicap of being known as the "ugly duckling" because the President in his January announcement of the emergency building program referred to it as a "dreadful looking object" and *Time* magazine reported it under the heading "Ugly Ducklings."[75]. . .

The new name, modified finally into "Liberty ships," was fixed in the public eye and ear by the widely publicized festivities celebrating the launching of the first of the type at the Bethlehem-Fairfield yard on September 27, 1941. It was proclaimed Liberty Fleet Day, and on Admiral Land's urging the President personally took part. The ceremony was eminently successful in catching public attention; and by the time the talk was over and newspaper articles had been written all over the country, "Liberty fleet" had become "Liberty ships."[76]. . .

The nature of shipbuilding created a stirring ceremony well fixed by tradition, the launching. . . .In the new yards, launchings were ceremonies for the workmen as well as for the management, and for the public. . . .When the yard at Portland, Oregon, was ready to launch its first ship, *The Star of Oregon,* it served Coca-Cola and other similar refreshments to the workers in a general open-house celebration. . . .Other new yards planned similar extensive and popular celebrations of their first launchings.

In later launchings, workmen's wives were chosen to sponsor many ships. After production was in full swing and ships were being built so fast that one was launched every other day, launching ceremonies were abbreviated, but more persons than ever before had a personal interest in launchings.[77]

Like the rest of the Commission's activity, the effort to put patriotic drives back of the shipbuilding program was intensified after Pearl Harbor; but before that attack solidified the nation and deepened its danger, many of the main lines of policy had been determined. Basic decisions had been made in public relations and in the selection of shipyards and their managements. Equally important were the decisions already made in regard to ship design and the forms of contracts.

Design and Initial Procurement for the Liberty Ship

The Basic Design Decision and the Working Plans

Standardization of the type ship to be built was the first essential for the success of the emergency program. Speed and economy within a particular yard depended on having that one yard build one design. . . .In the United States, where new yards were being built, standardization was attempted on a nationwide basis. Nationwide standardization gave two major advantages: specifications and drawings to guide ship construction once prepared, could be rapidly reproduced for use in additional yards; and the procurement of components could be organized in a steady, flexible flow from a number of vendors supplying interchangeable articles to a number of shipyards. . . .

While the [Maritime] Commission was negotiating contracts with the shipbuilders, basic decisions were still being made about design plans and procurement. These decisions were implemented with celerity through a private enterprise under William Francis Gibbs, the head of Gibbs & Cox, Inc., [one of the nation's foremost architects]. . . .

The history of the design which was to hold a dominant place in shipbuilding during the first part of World War II is very different from that of the designs of other Maritime Commission ships.

When the Maritime Commission launched its emergency program, Gibbs & Cox was already engaged to take care of procurement and prepare working plans for the British ships built in this country[78]. . . .[Consequently] Gibbs was prepared to play a similar big role in the American program. . . .

The history of the design which was to hold a dominant place in shipbuilding during the first part of World War II is very different from that of the designs of other Maritime Commission ships. Hitherto design of ships built under the Maritime Commission had been developed in the Commission's Technical Division, which was accustomed to working on the designs long before any contracts were made with builders.[79] When the emergency program was decided on, there was no time to do more than choose among existing designs and then to make some modifications to meet special needs. . . .

On the day after the President's broadcast concerning the emergency program, January 4, 1941, James L. Bates, the Commission's Director of the

Technical Division held a conference with Messrs. Esmond, A. MacPhedran, E. P. Rowell, and I. Wanless, members of the Division who were directly concerned with matters of design.[80] He explained that the question of design of the emergency ship would be threshed out on January 8 when William F. Gibbs would arrive for a conference. The main characteristics were to be like those of the 60 ships the British were building: length about 440 feet, speed 11 knots, and weight-carrying capacity about 10,000 tons. Like the British they would have reciprocating engines, the only kind obtainable. Two changes from the British specifications had been decided on during the evening of January 3 after the President's announcement. In consultation with Mr. Bates, and with Mr. Schmeltzer, the Associate Director of the Division, Admiral Vickery decided that construction would be facilitated by the adoption of water-tube instead of Scotch boilers and oil firing instead of coal.[81]

Any alternate to the designs being used by the British Merchant Shipping Mission would have to be ready for presentation on January 8. The crux of the matter, as Mr. Bates saw it, was whether Gibbs & Cox, who were already busy revising the British plans for use in American shipyards, would be willing to undertake in addition the preparation of another entirely different set of plans.

Working plans had to be obtained quickly and in large numbers for distribution to several yards, and Gibbs & Cox was the only organization capable, at that moment, of handling this particular mass production of blue prints. . . .

No decision on alternate designs was reached at the meeting on January 8 with Gibbs and several representatives of the shipbuilding companies. Nor was one reached on January 13. A decision had to be made soon and the responsibility fell primarily on Admirals Land and Vickery.

Admiral Land decided in favor of the British design.[82] The fabricating required for this design could be managed in mass production with only a slight increase in man-hours over that required for the Commission design. The latter was untried, as compared with the former. Moreover, work could begin much sooner if the British design were used, since Gibbs & Cox were already preparing drawings for American shipyard use.[83]

Adoption of the British design meant that Gibbs & Cox would perform the functions of marine architect for all the emergency yards. To cooperate with Gibbs and with the companies building the emergency ships, the Maritime Commission created a whole new division, the Division of Emergency Ship Construction, which was carved out of the existing Technical Division, with the idea that, as Admiral Vickery explained, ". . .when the job is done—we will wash the whole division right out."[84] It was created to operate on an emergency basis and get results fast, even at the sacrifice of some of the painstaking procedures which were part of the usual practice of the Technical Division.

Except for the approval of shipyard plans, which will be discussed later, the most pressing task of the new division was to approve the working plans which were being prepared by Gibbs & Cox. . . .To speed up the work, [William G. Esmond and John E. P. Grant (hull plan and engineering plan sections) were transferred] to New York in February and established an office at 21 West Street, in the same building with Gibbs & Cox. They made it a practice to consult with the agent's draftsmen while plans were being drawn, interpreting specifications according to the Commission's needs. This became known informally as "bedside" approval. It had the obvious advantage of doing away with the necessity of sending plans back and forth and meant that very little time needed to be spent on examination of the finished plans.[85]

The extent of the work that had to be done by Gibbs & Cox in preparing working plans was not realized at first. . . .In spite of their large staff and wide experience, Gibbs & Cox found they had bitten off almost more than they could chew. This was reflected in delays and misunderstandings. Their wheels did not always mesh with those of the Commission which employed them. . . . [However] it should not be forgotten that the whole program did proceed at a rapid pace, and a mass of design work was accomplished in a short time. On the whole, Messrs. Grant and Esmond got along very well with the Gibbs & Cox staff. If there was some confusion, there was also ability and drive, which in the end resulted in achievement.[86]

Modifications in Design

Many changes distinguished the American "Liberty Ship" from its British prototype. The larger changes, such as the single central deckhouse, were decided on in the Commission and embodied in the specifications, but many others originated in the drawing of the working plans....

It will be noted that many changes made the ship more comfortable for the crew than was the case with the British "Ocean" type. At the same time, many items were omitted which had become standard on American vessels. These omissions were decided upon with the idea that this was an emergency ship and that cost should be made as low as possible without sacrificing seaworthiness or serviceability. . . .

In addition, there were about thirty-five deviations from the Commission's own standards for fire-proofing and crew comfort. . . .

Before actual construction had progressed very far, a few additional changes were made. Mr. Harry Hunter and Mr. Robson, of the British Supply Council, met with Messers. Grant and Esmond, of the Commission, and C. A. Ward, of Gibbs & Cox, to consider changes which marine experience indicated were desirable. The most important was the substitution of ¼" steel in conjunction with plastic armor, instead of ¾" steel, as protection for the chart and wheelhouse and radio room. . . .Other suggestions made at this time, which were adopted, included the addition of ventilators for the machinery space and the substitution of mechanically operated davits for manually operated ones. . . .

Also, the original plans called for five-ton booms only, but the need to load tanks and other heavy equipment necessitated the installation of fifteen-, then thirty-, and finally fifty-ton booms.[87] . . .

The minor changes just enumerated did not affect the vessel's appearance. It was the single midship house in place of the fore and aft houses, the different cargo-handling equipment, and the solid weather-deck bulwark instead of chain rails that made the Liberty ship look different from the "Ocean" class vessel. . . .

This does not take into account the deck space which became an important consideration. Except for the midship housing and fore and aft gun turrets, there were no important deck obstructions for the whole of the Liberty's 441'6" overall length. . . .

Purchasing Through a Central Agent

The purchase of components and materials for the Liberty ships was closely connected with the preparation of working plans because the same naval architects had an important role in both operations. To secure the advantages of large-scale purchasing and flexibility in deliveries, the Commission undertook to furnish the builders of Libertys with steel, engines, and nearly all other materials and components instead of leaving each shipyard individually to buy its own material as was done by the yards in the long-range program.

As early as December 1940, Admiral Land advised the President that there should be a central control through which material would be "purchased and apportioned to the contracting yards as the working schedules require.". . .But he showed no desire to build up a bureaucracy to perform these functions, although that became necessary later. Instead, Adm. Land proposed that purchasing and allocating be done for the government by a private firm under contract to act as agent.88 It was the quickest way to get started. Accordingly the system of centralized procurement and government-furnished materials was introduced at the outset of the program, but through a private company acting as agent for the government.

If procurement was to be centralized under a private firm, Gibbs & Cox was the obvious choice. In spite of the slight differences between the American Liberty, the British Ocean type, and the Canadian Forts, the standardization was sufficient so that very many components would fit interchangeably into any of these ships. From the point of view of broad industrial planning, British and American emergency shipbuilding was all one operation.

Politically and legally the British building and that of the Maritime Commission were of course quite distinct, and the Commission was careful not to assume responsibility for the terms of the arrangements made between the British Mission and private American corporations. But as a problem in scheduling, the two programs were one. . . .

As naval architects for the companies building for the British, Gibbs & Cox had already arranged to handle procurement for the Todd-Bath and Todd-California yards. It was usual for a shipbuilder to have his naval architect draw up the precise specifications of the materials and parts he would need and invite bids from vendors. The actual purchasing was usually left to the shipyard—it decided which bids to accept—but for the 60 British ships, Gibbs & Cox were to do the buying also and to arrange deliveries so that everything would reach each shipyard at the right time. Having placed the orders, they would tell the vendors exactly when and where to deliver; in short, they would schedule the flow of materials.[89]

By January 29, 1941, the Commission had in effect made up its mind that Gibbs & Cox would do the ordering also for the 200 American Libertys.[90] In April, 112 more ships were added so that in the summer Gibbs & Cox was buying and setting tentative delivery dates on the basic materials for 372 ships, more than ten times the total national output two years before. . . .

On March 31, 1941 Mr. Gibbs presided at a meeting in New York with representatives of the shipyards. Besides members of his own organization and of the Commission, there were present representatives of the Bethlehem, Newport News and American Ship Building companies. The purpose of the meeting was to discuss ways of purchasing and expediting materials and to decide in as much detail as possible just what would be done by the Maritime Commission, by Gibbs & Cox, and by the individual shipyard. It was agreed that the Commission would do the expediting. . . .

Problems typical of the whole organization for mass production arose in connection with the engine. The basic design used on all the 372 ships for which Gibbs & Cox was ordering was British and the plans had to be redrawn to adapt them to American industrial practice.[91]. . . As a result, 80 British working plans had to be expanded into about 550 plans. . . .

Interchangeability was an important factor in the building of boilers. In this case the design used on the British ships was not being followed on the

American, which used a water-tube boiler designed by Babcock & Wilcox Co. It was placed athwartship with the firing aisle fore-and-aft, instead of transversely as in the case of the British coal-fired Scotch boilers. . . .Boilers for the first 200 emergency ships were supplied by Babcock & Wilcox, Combustion Engineering, and Foster-Wheeler, at the rate of nine, six, and three per week, respectively. These companies were selected by Gibbs & Cox and the Maritime Commission because they had extensive works and were experienced manufacturers of boilers and boiler parts. When the program was enlarged to 312 ships, four more boiler manufacturing companies were given contracts.[92] . . .

The Break with Gibbs & Cox

Throughout the first half of 1941, Gibbs & Cox and the staff of the Maritime Commission worked very closely together, almost as one organization, in the preparation of plans and the placing of orders. Then they parted company and Gibbs & Cox dropped out of the emergency shipbuilding program, which they had done more to organize than had any other one firm. In July and August they were finishing the last of the plans. At the same time the Commission was reorganizing its staff to take over procurement.[93] Gibbs & Cox had placed the orders for the 60 British and 312 Liberty ships which were authorized in the first two waves of expansion in the Maritime Commission's program. For the additional ships of the third wave, ships to be paid for by the appropriation bill which passed Congress in August 1941, the Commission was preparing itself to do the buying. . . .

The following December Admiral Land summed up for an Appropriation Committee the story of the stiff bargaining, "We felt that we paid plenty for it and they felt that we did not pay enough, so we just split business with them and said, 'Good-bye boys,' and kissed each other on both cheeks, and we are running our own show now."[94] Gibbs & Cox kept very busy with work for the Navy, which was turning out destroyers with great rapidity and paying the usual fee on each.[95]

The role of Gibbs & Cox in the emergency program was characteristic of the transitional period when the nation was not at war, when it was politic to refer not to preparations for war but to the "defense effort," and when preparations were governed by the intent of interfering as little as possible with the peacetime system of business.

After mobilization of the nation was vigorously taken in hand by government bureaus, Gibbs & Cox remained important in the preparation of designs and working plans. During the transition period, Gibbs & Cox also provided the instrument for quickly centralizing procurement, a centralization which was a necessary consequence of the decision to have the Commission supply materials and components for the Libertys.

Expansion and Reorganization After Pearl Harbor

The Fourth Wave of Expansion

The Japanese attack and the declaration of war by Germany changed both the shipbuilding program and the conditions affecting its success. Sinking of merchant vessels took a pronounced turn for the worse because German submarines attacked the coastwise shipping lanes that run from the mouth of the St. Lawrence to the Gulf of Mexico and the Caribbean. Overall they found unarmed and unescorted freighters and tankers an easy prey in that area during the first half of 1942. The huge loss in merchant vessels—6.4 million deadweight tons in the first half of 1942—made fast construction in the Maritime Commission yards ever more urgent. But building for the Navy was also desperately needed immediately after Pearl Harbor. At the same time Army commanders, looking ahead to the time when the men they were training would be brought into combat, demanded transports as well as cargo carriers. Under such pressure the Maritime Commission's program underwent two more waves of expansion, the fourth and the fifth. . . .

The declaration of war was also a signal for closer common action at the highest political levels, and, before Christmas, the Prime Minister of Britain crossed the ocean to confer at the White House concerning the objectives and materials of war. During January 1942, the shipbuilding goal was set as the delivery of 8 million tons in 1942, an increase of roughly a third. For 1943, 10 million tons were planned. Admiral Vickery, who was called on to say whether it could be done, replied that it would be no problem to get 10 million in 1943 if production in 1942 could be stepped up to 8 million.[96]. . .

For the program as a whole, the speed-up in rate of production was estimated as about 25 per cent, giving roughly five ships per way per year instead of four. Accordingly it was necessary to add a few new yards for major types to meet the boost in objectives of nearly a third which was ordered by the President in January 1942.[97]

Two new yards were built by a company headed by Henry Kaiser, who now organized new shipbuilding companies of his own in which Todd Shipyards had no shares. Kaiser and his associates also acquired full ownership at this time of the West coast yards they were managing and sold to Todd Shipyards their interest in the Todd-managed yards elsewhere. The new Kaiser company received contracts to build and operate for the Commission a basin shipyard known as Richmond No. 3, with five basins, located near the yards already being operated by Kaiser in Richmond under

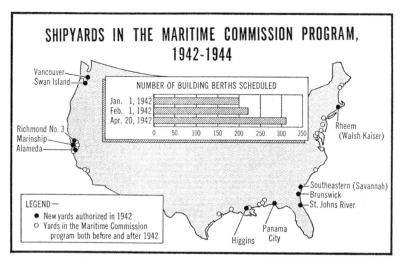

FIGURE 8. Class I yards. Names of yards built before 1942 are on Figures 4 and 6.

the immediate direction of Clay Bedford, and to build and operate likewise a new yard at Vancouver, Washington, near the yard of the Oregon Shipbuilding Co. directed by Edgar Kaiser.[98]. . .

The Fifth and Final Wave

After the fourth wave of expansion, Admiral Land reiterated his warning: "The shipbuilding cup is full to overflowing."[99] The Maritime Commission was under all kinds of pressure to build more shipyards and try new types of ships, but like the Navy it felt that it had its hands full. At a conference in the office of Admiral S. M. Robinson, Chief of the Bureau of Ships, on January 15, 1942 with a representative of the Office of Production Management "it was definitely determined that any additional shipbuilding beyond that discussed at this conference was in excess of the capacity of the shipbuilding industry in the United States." They agreed not to build any more unless so ordered by the President of the United States. [100]. . .

They were so ordered. Pressure from the Army demanded more and more ships. Sinkings were running over a half a million tons a month[101] and, on the other hand, the Army was training men with the intent of making 1,800,000 ready for overseas service by the end of December 1942, and 3,500,000 ready by the end of 1943. Less than half that number could be maintained as a fighting force overseas, so General George Marshall wrote to the President on February 18, 1942, unless steps were taken "to increase the tempo of the shipbuilding program to a much higher figure. . . .The war effort of the United States, less what can be done by the Navy, will be measured by what can be transported overseas in troops and materiel."

The next day, February 19, 1942, Admiral Land had a conference in President Roosevelt's bedroom. The impossible must be done, the objective must be lifted again, from a total of 18 million tons in 1942–43 to 24 million tons. The President asked that plans be made to build 9 million tons in 1942 and 15 million tons in 1943. "I realize," wrote President Roosevelt in the memorandum in which he confirmed this decision, "that this is a terrible directive on my part but I feel certain that in this very great emergency we can attain it."[102]. . .

The actual rate of production in February and early March 1942 was only about 2½ ships per way per year. In order to try for the new objective it was decided to build more shipways. It was done by adding to existing yards and by creating wholly new yards at new locations. . . .

For additions to existing yards, the Maritime Commission turned to the West coast. Again, as in the previous month, Admiral Vickery looked for aid to the Kaiser management because of its outstanding record at that date. The companies under old-line management had not yet shown what they could do. . . .But out on the West coast, Oregon Ship was getting a ship ready to launch 71 days after keel laying, and Richmond, yard No. 1, which worked for the British but was under the same management as nearby Richmond No. 2 and No. 3, was finishing the second round off the ways in about 80 or 90 days for each ship.[103]. . .

It was decided to increase to 12 ways the Vancouver yard which had been begun just the previous month, and to build a new 10-way yard on Swan Island. . . .[It was also decided] that Richmond No. 2 should be expanded from 9 to 12 ways. . . .A little later 3 more ways were added in a sort of annex originally called No. 3A, later No. 4; and thus the Kaiser yards on San Francisco Bay, with a total of 27 ways, almost equaled in the number of their shipways the yards of Sun on the Delaware. Although the Richmond yards were not contiguous nor under a single corporation, they were quite close together and were all under the same general manager, Clay Bedford.[104]

An entirely new yard also was established on the West coast by enlisting part of the management previously associated with Calship. . . . [S. D. Bechtel of the "Six Companies" group] was able to enlist men from the allied construction companies and from Calship, and to fabricate the steel for his first ships in the facilities of that company, 400 miles away [south] of his new yard at Sausalito, Marin County, across the Golden Gate bridge from San Francisco. Admiral Vickery approved verbally the site as one he knew well enough already and on the same day that Mr. Bechtel presented his plans told him to go ahead: "I am betting on your fellows; I expect you to produce."[105] The new yard, later called Marinship, did in fact deliver five ships in 1942.[106]. . .

Marinship was a 6-way yard, one of five new 6-way yards which were begun to meet the President's new directive of February 19, 1942. . . .

Even after all contracts for new yards had been awarded, in April of 1942, the Commission's building schedule did not come up to the President's directive of 9 million tons for 1942. The expansion in shipways was about 40 per cent,[107] but very little indeed could be expected off the new ways within the remaining months of 1942. The schedule of April 20, 1942 provided for a total of 7,715,800 tons in 1942. The hope of reaching that goal and if possible doing better depended mainly on speeding the work in existing yards, but in April the rate of production in most of the yards was disappointing. . . .

This fifth wave of expansion in facilities was so large as to make it extremely unlikely that the number of shipways would be the limiting factor in the program. The bottleneck was more likely to be steel or engines. . . .

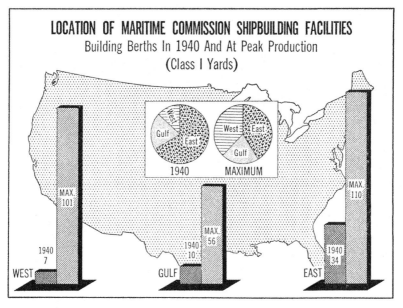

FIGURE 9. Number of building berths utilized for Maritime Commission shipbuilding on January 1, 1941 and maximum number. Source: Fischer, *Statistical Summary*, Table E-1.

The Commission Under the War Powers

[During the war] Admiral Vickery became the man directly responsible for running the shipbuilding program, while other Commissioners had other specialties. This increased specialization within the Commission was partly a result of Presidential action and partly a matter of mutual agreement among the Commissioners. The increase came particularly in those fields in which Presidential intervention was real or potential. . . .

The Chairman of the Commission [Admiral Land] did not become entirely absorbed in any one specialty, for he remained the chief channel of contact with Congress and the President in regard to all the Commission's activities. But he was pulled away from shipbuilding by his appointment as Administrator of the War Shipping Administration on February 7, 1942.

In creating the War Shipping Administration, the President used his authority under the First War Powers Act to take away from the Maritime Commission some of its former powers. Actually the same people kept on performing many of the same functions as before, since Admiral Land was at once made Administrator, and kept the WSA and the MC closely linked together. . . .

[These new responsibilities] required much of Admiral Land's attention. Consequently he had less time to handle the host of problems which were created by the acceleration of the shipbuilding program. They were left to Commissioner Vickery, whose rank in the Navy rose as his task increased in importance. A Commander when the emergency program started in 1941, Howard L. Vickery was named on February 4, 1942 to the rank of Rear Admiral.[108]

In organizing the WSA, Administrator Land made Commissioner Vickery the Deputy Administrator for Ship Construction within the WSA[109] This served the purpose of tying the two organizations closer together. . . .

By the summer of 1942 the turmoil of reorganization was subsiding. The separation of the WSA and decentralization of construction supervision by the Maritime Commission staff had been carried through. The staff to supervise the new forms of shipbuilding contracts had been organized in such a way as to centralize procurement and decentralize the supervision of construction. This plan was adhered to throughout the war. All the emergency yards had been started and the corporations to manage them had all been selected. Shipbuilding programs had been expanded by the fourth and fifth waves to such a point that there were no big bursts of expansion thereafter.

The Victory Ship

The Desire for Faster Cargo Carriers

In 1943, while the yards were setting their all-time record in the production of Liberty ships, the schedulers and designers in the Maritime Commission were making preparations for the production of various new types, of which the most important was the Victory ship, a faster type of cargo carrier. It was to be constructed in the emergency yards. . . .The plans were not put into effect immediately because they were opposed by the War Production Board [WPB]. Its opposition led to a violent controversy between the Maritime Commission and the WPB, a controversy finally settled by the Joint Chiefs of Staff. At the end of 1943, the Commission's program had become more diversified and more closely meshed with specific military needs.

The extent to which standardization, the dominant thought at the inception of the emergency program, had been compromised even before the end of 1942, is shown by the Commission's program No. 11 formulated on December 17, 1942. It scheduled for delivery in 1943: 230 standard-type of dry-cargo carriers (C1, C2, C3), 209 tankers, 16 ore carriers, 69 frigates, 50 escort aircraft carriers, 54 landing ships, a number of types of Army and Navy transports, and 1,262 Liberty ships, in addition to minor and very special types such as the concrete and wooden ships. . . .Deliveries of the new Victory type would not come until 1944 or possibly late 1943. By that time the Liberty ship would no longer bulk large in the Commission's program and standardization would to that extent be sacrificed.

One reason for this change was the steel shortage. The fastest yards were going to be forced to slow down anyhow in order not to run out of steel. Consequently, the Commission planned to put the steel allotted it to more efficient use by building faster ships.[110] When lack of steel limited the program for 1943 to 16 million tons, the Commission's program called for building as much as possible of that tonnage during the first half of the year, for the carrying capacity was needed as soon as possible.[111] During the later months of the year, when production would have to slow down anyhow in order not to use up more steel than had been promised for the year and in order not to exceed the Presidential directive, yards could afford the time to change over to a new type. The planning for this change began as early as August 1942. At that time standardization had already fulfilled its main purpose by enabling facilities and labor force to expand to such an extent that shipyards could use all the steel available and more.[112]

Another reason for the change, a reason that might have caused diversification in the program even if there had been no steel shortage, was the cumulative effect of demands for faster ships. Many demands for specific faster types were made by the Navy, not only for definitely military types such as the escort aircraft carriers, but also for C2 or C3 cargo ships to be converted into tenders or some other kind of auxiliaries.[113] For use as cargo carriers also, faster ships were being demanded, both for wartime use and for postwar competition. The 11-knot Liberty ships never would have been built at all if propulsion machinery could have been secured for faster vessels. As Admiral Vickery said, "It was a case of those ships or none at all. We are hopeful that expansion of turbine and gear production facilities may relieve the situation somewhat and we will be able to build more of the better ships."[114]

Newspaper opinion reflected and added to the criticism of the slowness of the Liberty ship. It became somewhat strident as submarine and bombing attacks became more menacing. . . . Shipping interests were also unhappy about the construction of slow vessels in large numbers. J. Lewis Luckenback, President of the American Bureau of Shipping, voiced this feeling in his semi-annual report given on July 29, 1941 in the presence of Admirals Land and Vickery. . . .

When toward the end of August 1942, Sir Amos Ayre, Director of Merchant Shipbuilding in the United Kingdom, came to America and made a tour of the shipyards,[115] Admirals Land and Vickery learned about the fast standard cargo vessels then under construction in England.[116] The British decision to build faster ships was preceded by a careful consideration of such factors as deadweight, labor and material requirements, available berths, routes, number of voyages and so forth.[117] They found that vessels of from 12 to 15 knots were frequently put into 10-knot convoys, which meant that their extra speed was wasted. Therefore, the British concentrated on a 15-knot vessel of about 10,000–12,000 tons deadweight with single screw and Diesel engine. Later on, two such engines with twin screw were used on larger vessels, giving a speed of 17 knots. The production of geared-turbine sets was increased through simplification and standardization.[118]

Shortly after Sir Amos Ayre's visit, Admiral Vickery had the Technical Division start work on the design of a new vessel of 15 knots. The approach to this new design was from the Liberty ship rather than from the C-type ship because the simplicity and standardization of the former type would facilitate production in quantity. From the start, it was decided to have the new vessel roughly equal the 10,000 ton deadweight of the Liberty ship.[119]. . .

The Hull Design of the Victory Ship

While the main problem, propulsion machinery, was still unsolved, the Preliminary Design Section of the Technical Division worked out a basic design for the new vessel, allowing for slight modifications in case reciprocating engines, Diesels, or turbines were to be used. From the start it was clear that no such box-like design as that of the Liberty would serve for a ship designed to make 15 knots. Assuming a reciprocating engine of 5600 horse-power and about 100 revolutions per minute, the basic dimensions of a design called the AP1 were worked out in September 1942, as follows:

LWL	445'
Beam	63'
Depth	38'
Designed draft	28'
Designed speed (80 percent of designed power)	15 knots
Designed power	5800 ihp.
Number of holds	5
Type of accommodation	Same as EC2-S-C1

After the plans had been worked on for a month, Mr. Bates, Director of the Technical Division, showed them to John E. Burkhardt and James B. Hunter at the Quincy shipyard of Bethlehem Steel. The Bethlehem people agreed to assist in the preparation of the new design and, if their work-load permitted, to prepare working plans. They also agreed to make a plating model while the Commission prepared the lines, secured Model Basin results, and made calculations of weight and stability. . . .

At a conference with his staff on November 21, Mr. Bates reviewed the characteristics agreed upon and repeated the guiding principles laid down by Admiral Vickery. Deadweight must equal that of the Liberty ship and the speed must be 15 knots. As regards improvements, "they are not only not desired, but are not to be accepted, unless it can be shown that they are essential to acceptable performance, and at the same time that they can be incorporated without prejudice to prompt procurement."

One important change was made in the vessel's dimensions. Its beam was changed from 63' to 62'[120]. . .when it was discovered that several of the yards, particularly Bethlehem-Fairfield, had ways that were too narrow for construction of a ship with a 63' beam.[121] This difference of one foot may appear to have been inconsequential, but the change affected the other dimensions and also involved the question of stability.

It was not easy to accept the ban on improvements. The War Shipping Administration asked that the new design provide for greater loading on deck than was permissible on the Liberty ships. This required the use of steel shapes other than those which the steel companies were accustomed to supply. The objections of the steel companies were finally overcome by Admiral Vickery, however, after discussions with the officials of WPB. Provision was made thereby for larger permissible deckloads.

As discussion of details progressed, the need for improvements became more insistent. It was a natural desire of the designers and planners to have the new vessel move away from the Liberty towards the C2; they thought it desirable to add such items as searchlights and gyrocompasses, for example, if they were available. In January 1943, Admiral Vickery approved the general policy of improving on the EC2 design whenever conditions of manufacture and design were such that no delay in procurement would result. Longer booms and improved winches were decided upon on this basis. Other features were dictated by military considerations—for example, lifeboat davits capable of handling landing craft.

While the form of the hull was being worked out, the characteristics of the propulsion machinery were still in doubt. The hull lines had been planned on the assumption that the ship would have an engine of 6000 shp. and a speed of 15 knots. It became apparent, however, that turbines of 8500 shp. might be available for some ships of the new type. Consequently, Admiral Vickery asked that basic plans for the machinery space provide that the bolting arrangements be the same no matter which engine was used, and that the hull lines be such that the ship could also operate economically at the higher speeds appropriate to the more powerful propulsion machinery. Designing the lines of the hull so as to provide for this range in power of the engine required some sacrifice in optimum performance. As finally developed, the Victory Ship used slightly more power at 15-knot speed than did the C2; but, in spite of its greater deadweight tonnage, it used less power than the C2 at speeds of 16 knots or more.[122]

For working plans for the new type, the Commission turned first to the Shipbuilding Division of the Bethlehem Steel Co. Late in December 1942, the Commission's staff was told it was expected that 1,600 of the new type would be built with plan approval and procurement in Washington, and with working plans being prepared by Bethlehem.

In January it was announced that Bethlehem was too busy with its work on the troopships being built at Alameda, and that George G. Sharp's office would prepare the working plans for the new type. At a meeting in that office on January 20, 1943, with representatives of several yards, Mr. Bates explained the reasons for the new design and expressed the desire of the Commission to secure basic agreement on working plans to be developed by Sharp, it being understood that the individual yards could modify the plans to suit their particular methods of construction. . . .

The yard's representatives, in the interest of uniformity, expressed a general desire to have all changes, after construction had begun, come direct from Washington. They also suggested that an effort be made to correlate the requirements of the Bureau of Marine Inspection and Navigation, and the Navy.

By the end of March 1943, the characteristics and specifications for the new emergency vessel were settled.[123] Since the new vessel grew out of the Liberty ship, the basic idea being a vessel of the same deadweight but with 15-knot speed, it is interesting to compare it and the Liberty (Table II). They were both full scantling ships with the machinery space between holds No. 3 and No. 4, and a total of five holds. Cargo handling gear was also similar, consisting, on the new ships, of fourteen 5-ton booms, one 30-ton, and one 50-ton boom. Unlike the Liberty ship, it had an extra deck in holds No. 1, No. 2, and No. 3 for the stowage of package goods, and used electricity rather than steam for anchor windlass, for steering, and for some pumps.

In appearance the ships were similar, with the single large house amidships. However, on the new ship, in order to simplify construction, a straight line sheer was adopted forward and aft and a forecastle added to prevent the sheer from being excessive forward and to make the vessel more seaworthy. Another change, in the interest of decreasing construction man-hours, was the spacing of frames at 36" instead of 30". While this reduced the number of frames, it required the use of heavier ones and resulted in a slight increase in steel weight. . . .

The crew was fixed at 51 as against about 44 on the Liberty and in both types of ships they were berthed in the midship house. Twenty-nine gunners were berthed in the poop deck house. . . .

Armament consisted of a 5" gun aft and a 3" gun forward. The latter was on an emplacement capable of supporting another 5" gun if the guns should be available. There were also eight 20mm guns—four amidships, two on the forecastle, and two on the poop deck. . . .

The increased dimensions and speed of the new vessel called for different lines. The bow was semi-V-shaped, the stern was the "cruiser" type, and there was a 15 per cent parallel middle-body. As in the case of the Liberty, construction was facilitated by taking special care to avoid furnaced plates.[124]

The Search for Engines

The propulsion machinery most satisfactory for a hull of this type would be turbines, provided the supply was adequate. The foresight which the Commission had shown in June 1941 in building new plants for the manufacture of turbines was showing results in the second half of 1942. As early as May 22, 1942, General Electric had begun delivery of C3 turbines from a site which had been only a barren swamp a year before. But most of the turbines from the new plants were earmarked for standard-type freighters or tankers.

Yards which had been first planned for Liberty ships were changed over to faster types as rapidly as turbines were available.[125] To meet military and shipping needs, Alabama Ship, Marinship and Swan Island became tanker yards.[126] Then, when more turbines and gears from the new plants became available, North Carolina Ship was changed over from Libertys to C2's in accordance with the original plan that turbines from the new factories would be used to build more of the standard types.[127] Some turbines of the C3 type might be available for use in the new type but not nearly enough to equip the 500 to 800 ships a year which were being planned.

Accordingly, there was no prospect of having enough turbines for all the ships of the new design; and when on September 9, 1942, Mr. Schmeltzer told the Engineering Section that they must find a way of raising the 2500 hp. of the Liberty ship to 5600 hp. for the new standard vessel, he said it would be necessary to stick to the reciprocating engine. Drawings must be prepared and a pilot engine built and tested; they would then be ready to go into quantity production. The matter was most urgent.

Obtaining a satisfactory reciprocating engine of 5600 hp. was not going to be easy. . . .

Collision with the Controller of Shipbuilding

December 1942.   WPB's Production Vice Chairman, C. E. Wilson, brought into WPB to take charge of turbines and ship production the celebrated naval architect, William Francis Gibbs, who on December 19, 1942 became Controller of Shipbuilding. . . .

Admirals Land and Vickery voiced their opposition to the appointment on the grounds that the firm of Gibbs & Cox, with which Mr. Gibbs was not severing his connection, was too deeply involved in Navy work for him to act impartially.[128] . . .

The indefiniteness of Mr. Gibbs' authority was disturbing. His responsibilities and powers were established by an exchange of letters between WPB and the Navy Department,[129] and within WPB he assumed authority over its Shipbuilding Division of which the functions were to "coordinate and facilitate the efforts of the Army, Navy, Maritime Commission, Coast Guard, Lend-Lease Administration, and other war agencies in the construction of ships on schedule and in the production of materials and parts. . . ."[130] . . .

Meanwhile, arrangements were being made with the Navy to carry out tests of the first Lentz engine. It was expected the tests would be completed in March 1943. While planning for the use of Lentz engines in most ships of the new type (the EC2-S-AP1), the designers also completed plans for the use of other engines. The designation EC2-S-AP2 was given to a design providing for a 6000 shaft hp. C2 turbine; the EC-S-AP3 was the same vessel when provided with a 8500 shaft hp. C2 turbine; the EC2-S-AP4 was a design using Diesel propulsion. The final separation of the new ship from the Liberty ship in the minds of its creators was signalized by changing its design designation from EC2 to VC2 on April 28, 1943, and by general adoption of the name "Victory Ship."

By that time, contracts had already been awarded for construction of the new type: on April 20, 1943, to Oregon Ship and Calship for deliveries of AP3s, with the C3 turbines, to begin in April 1944; and on April 22–May 6, to Bethlehem-Fairfield, Richmond No. 1 and No. 2, Delta, Houston, and Southeastern, for AP1s, with the Lentz engines.

Meanwhile, Admiral Land began to hear of conferences at which the Maritime Commission was not represented. He saw evidence that, as he wrote to Harry Hopkins, "there may be some ganging up on the Maritime Commission and involved therein, either directly or indirectly, is the fine Italian hand of our friend Gibbs."

January 1943.   The Maritime Commission's plans were now on a collision course with the plans for standardizing and scheduling which were being formulated in WPB.

The preparation of working plans for the Victory was going forward in the office of George Sharp, a firm of naval architects which had been most closely connected with the Commission's designs of standard types—but not with the Liberty ship, for which, it will be recalled, the working plans were provided by Gibbs & Cox.

This was the situation when William Francis Gibbs and the WPB began to interfere. The feud went on for the better part of a year between the U.S. Maritime Commission and the War Production Board—or should we say Land and Vickery vs. Nelson and Gibbs. . . .

Spring 1943.   Representatives of the turbine manufacturing industry got together to work out details for quantity production of a standard turbine and reported that the prospects were good. This was the basis for an agreement on one of the points at issue.

At a conference of Messrs. Wilson and Gibbs, and Admirals Land and Vickery, on April 30, 1943, the Commissioners consented to drop the Lentz engines if enough turbines could be produced, and WPB agreed to drop its opposition to the Lentz engine if they could not.[131] Thereafter the Lentz engine was no longer an important issue. . . .

The path towards a solution was found in the plans for standardization and the various alternatives of increased production worked out by a group of consultants drawn from the companies manufacturing turbines. They developed plans for standardization in building a simplified type of 6000 hp. turbine (6600 shaft hp maximum) and presented them at a meeting on May 8 and 9. . . .The general characteristics of the "Victory" turbine were agreed to at this meeting, and starting with these characteristics each manufacturer was to proceed with his own design. . . .

All turbines should fit the same ship's foundation without structural change and all steam, drain, and lubricating connections should be identical. . . .Enough progress had been made to indicate that a standard turbine could be produced in quantity and reasonably soon.[132]. . .

On the basis of the plans of the turbine manufacturers, the Maritime Commission agreed definitely on May 12, 1943 to drop the Lentz engine, and the WPB on its side authorized approval of facilities and components for Victory ships.

Just how many yards were to be changed over to Victorys or at just what rate continued in dispute, however.[133] For Oregon Ship, WPB's approval of necessary facilities was held up until July 1943.[134]

The new schedule for ship production which the Maritime Commission prepared May 14, 1943 on the basis of using turbines instead of the Lentz engine provided only 260 Victory ships to be delivered in 1944, instead of the 524 in the April program. . . .In conferences with the turbine manufacturers, it expressed hope of getting back to its April goal of 524 Victory ships in 1944 and of getting as much as 90 units per month in 1945. Its July program called for delivery of 340 Victory ships in 1944. (Figure 37)

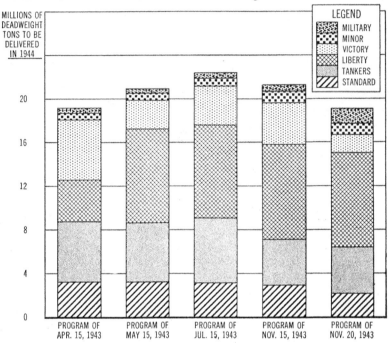

PROGRAMS FORMULATED IN 1943 For Tonnage To Be Delivered In 1944

FIGURE 37. Source: Fischer, *Statistical Summary*, Table A-4.

Resolving the Conflict with WPB

In the final analysis, the Joint Chiefs settled the heated controversy over building a faster type of merchant vessel in August 1943.

How much the intensity of this conflict was due to the nature of the issues and how much to personalities is one of those questions which documents cannot answer conclusively.

William Francis Gibbs retained throughout his service as Controller of Shipbuilding his connection with the firm of Gibbs & Cox, which had its own organization of naval architects and marine engineers.

The Technical Division of the Maritime Commission, in contrast, took pride in the program developed by the long, full-time effort of Admiral

Vickery and the staff he had developed and organized. They were intent on building the best ships they could. Mr. Gibbs' efforts to change the program seemed to Admiral Vickery and his staff unwarranted and unnecessary interference. On September 11, 1943, Mr. Gibbs resigned as Controller of Shipbuilding.[135]

One result of the controversy was that fewer Victory ships were built than had been programmed at the beginning of the year. Plans to build Victorys in the emergency yards in the South were abandoned. The Liberty yards of the West coast began their launching of Victory Ships, not in the closing months of 1943, as originally planned, but during the first half of 1944.

Turbines of the C3 type were delivered before the Victory yards were ready to receive them and, in November 1943, the Commission had to arrange for storage at Toele, Utah, of turbines on their way from New England to the West coast.[136]

The first Victory ship to be built was delivered by Oregon Ship on the last day of February, 1944; and only 15 were delivered before May 1944: 11 from Oregon Ship and 4 from Calship.

Later, Victory ships were also built at Bethlehem-Fairfield, Richmond No. 1 and No. 2, and Vancouver. All the Victorys built at the latter yard were the modified form of the Victory design which began in May 1944 to fill the shipways of the West coast Victory yards: namely, the VC2-S-AP5, the attack transports.

Military and Minor Types

Landing Ships and Escort Vessels

Military Types occupied 103 of the 251 building berths in the Maritime Commission's Class I yards in August 1944 and formed 24 per cent of the total production of that year measured in displacement tons.[137] . . .

When the possibilities of multiple production became manifest in the summer of 1942, it was decided that the Maritime Commission yards could find room to build landing craft and escort vessels and also produce enough merchant ships to meet the goal of 24 million tons by the end of 1943. Fifty aircraft carrier escorts and 60 LST's were built in yards which in February had been planned for Liberty ships.

In many instances military types were built in yards originally planned for merchant ships, either because vessels begun as C-types in the long-range yards were finished as military types, or because yards which finished their contracts for merchant ships received new contracts for military types to be delivered in 1944. In short, the main reason why military types were built, not in yards under the Navy, but in yards under the Maritime Commission, was that there was more capacity available in the Maritime yards. . . .

So many different military types were built under Maritime Commission contracts that they cannot all be covered here. However, a few details about the landing ships, the "baby flattops," and various types of transports will show the difficulties involved in this aspect of the Maritime Commission's shipbuilding and will emphasize its importance to the Armed Forces.

Landing Ship Tank (LST).   A large landing-craft program was decided on in April 1942 as part of the plan for taking the offensive in Europe in the summer of 1943.[138]. . .By May 1942, the Navy assigned contracts for the construction of 300 LST's to be completed by June 1943.[139]

The design of the LST had been discussed by representatives of the British Admiralty with the Navy as early as November 1941, and it had been decided in December that the Maritime Commission should work out the plans.[140] But after the Maritime Commission had developed the plans and entered into negotiation to make contracts with shipbuilders, strategic planners set production schedules calling for the utmost speed.

Admirals Land and Vickery decided they could not assume responsibility for meeting these production schedules unless they had control of the procurement of the machinery, namely, Diesel engines. Allocation of these engines was controlled by the Navy which needed them for other craft also and was unwilling to give up control. Consequently, the Navy Bureau of Ships was placed in charge, and the drawings and specifications for the LST developed in the Preliminary Design Section of the Maritime Commission were turned over to the Navy.[141]. . .

The Navy awarded contracts to the yards with which the Maritime Commission had been in negotiation for the building of LST's, and, in order to reach the required total of 300 by June 1943, the Navy also called on the Maritime Commission to build 90 LST's in yards already under contract to it for other types.

Admirals Land and Vickery were reluctant to use for the construction of LST's any yards that were building Liberty ships, for it would badly upset the production schedules. They agreed to do so, however, because the only alternative, in view of the decision at the highest level of command, seemed to be that the Navy would give contracts to these yards. In that case the Maritime Commission might never get the yards back for the Liberty program.[142]

Bethlehem-Fairfield was given a contract for 45 vessels (reduced in October at the Navy's request to 30)[143] and consequently disrupted its work on Liberty ships. . . . Delivery of the 30 vessels was completed in February 1943, nineteen days behind the contract schedule, but ahead of the completion of the Maritime Commission's other contracts for LST's.[144]

Construction of the other 45 LST's was assigned on May 28, 1942 to the Kaiser Co., Inc. to be built in new yards from which no ships had yet been delivered.[145] The prospect of having to interrupt the multiple production of Liberty ships had brought spirited protests from Henry and Edgar Kaiser.[146] Their protests had some success, for the LST's were kept out of the existing yards at Richmond. Instead a new yard was built, Richmond No. 4. It built 15 LST's; the other 30 built by Kaiser were constructed at the Vancouver yard near Portland, which broke off its work on Liberty ships after launching only two and clearing away two which were only half built. . . .

The LST's were part of "one of the most outstanding high-speed efforts of the whole war effort," in which the Navy encountered very severe problems in trying to build on exceedingly short notice.[147] It disrupted much of their building program, especially work on destroyer escorts.[148] Its effect on the Maritime Commission program was estimated by Admiral Land to have meant the loss of 75 Liberty ships.[149]

Escort Aircraft Carriers (CVE's).   While planning and preparing in 1942 to take the offensive on the other side of the Atlantic, the Anglo-American alliance was suffering very heavy shipping losses in American waters, even within sight of the coast, and in the Pacific was barely able to stop the Japanese in the Coral Sea and at Midway. These problems intensified the need for escort vessels of various kinds, and again the Navy turned to the yards of the Maritime Commission.

Aircraft-carrying escort vessels constructed by converting merchant types had been under consideration by the Navy for some time. A Moore-McCormack C3 was converted to an escort aircraft carrier at Newport News in March–June 1941. Other conversions followed, and in May 1942, work on this type [dubbed "Baby Flattops"] concentrated at the Seattle-Tacoma yard, which had been working on C3's under Maritime Commission contracts but which took Navy contracts and came accordingly under the supervision of the Bureau of Ships thereafter.

A total of 8 of the C3-S-A2 escort aircraft carriers, intended for delivery to the British, were completed in various yards under the Maritime Commission in 1942–43.

The main escort aircraft carrier program of the Commission consisted of the 50 built by Kaiser. Contract plans and specifications for this design (S4-S2-BB3) were developed by the Maritime Commission's Technical Division using its P1 design as a basis for the hull form and were finished with the cooperation of the Navy, which aided especially in designing the flight deck.

George G. Sharp, acting as design agent for the Kaiser company, developed the working drawings, and the hull lines were drawn under the supervision of James L. Bates. Construction was in accordance with accepted standard marine commercial practice for both hull and machinery, with the Navy specifications for C3 conversions applied where appropriate. Because the output of turbines, gears, and Diesels was all pre-empted for other designs already in production, the design provided for reciprocating steam engines of the five-cylinder Skinner uniflow type capable of developing 5,400 horsepower on each of two shafts. They would give a speed, it was hoped, of 20 knots.

The length overall was 490 feet, the light displacement 6,890 tons. The flight deck was longer than on the converted C3's, and the fact that the S4-S2-BB3 was designed from the beginning for its specific function gave it a number of other advantages, such as its two screws and separate machinery spaces. On the other hand, it lacked certain features which would have been incorporated as a result of war experience but for the fact that its design was "frozen" in order to speed deliveries by the methods of multiple production for which Henry Kaiser was famous.[150]

The decision to have these escort aircraft carriers built by Kaiser was stated by President Roosevelt to the Navy and the Maritime Commission at the conference at the White House on June 8, 1942. Kaiser's plan was to build them in the 12-way Vancouver yard as soon as that yard had finished its 30 LST's. Why then did not the Navy let the contract and take over the supervision of this yard as it had taken over the supervision of the C3 aircraft carrier escorts being built at Seattle-Tacoma? The Navy wanted the ships but did not want Kaiser. Accordingly Admiral Land and Colonel McIntyre presented the case at the White House; Henry Kaiser also saw the President; and the construction of the 50 escort aircraft carriers of new design in the Kaiser Vancouver yard was agreed to on the basis that the construction of these, as of all other Kaiser-built ships, would be supervised by the Maritime Commission's staff, and the Maritime Commission should develop the design.[151]

When the contract was awarded, Henry Kaiser underestimated the time required in preparation before multiple production could begin for a ship of this type. Because of Kaiser's optimism[152], the Commission's schedule of July 25, 1942 envisaged the delivery of 4 in February 1943 and completion of 50 by the end of the year. The first delivery was July 8, 1943. After the first round was off the ways, construction picked up speed and, in the fourth, round 6 were delivered in one month, June 1944, and the contract completed July 8, 1944.[153] In view of the size and the amount of complex equipment involved in a vessel of this type, it was a notable achievement in multiple production.

Transports

Whereas the LST's and CVE's were built for military use, most transports were potential passenger ships, or combination passenger and cargo ships. In some cases that affected the design, and may have been one reason why so many different kinds of transports were built. Also the Army and Navy had various and changing ideas about what kinds of transports they wanted. The resulting difficulties are fully illustrated in the history of the C4's.

The C4 design originated in the plans developed by naval architect, George Sharp, in 1941 for a cargo ship for the American Hawaiian Lines and in the plans for its conversion into a troopship prepared at the same time so that it would be possible to proceed with the building of either type without delay. In his design, changes for conversion into a troopship were kept at a minimum because of the thought that these vessels would be turned over to the American Hawaiian Steamship Co. for use as cargo ships after the emergency.[154] In the latter part of October 1941, the Maritime Commission took over Sharp's design and subsequently developed from it a number of designs both for cargo carriers and troop ships.

Two shipyards were constructed to build C4's. The first to be authorized was the five-basin Richmond No. 3 yard of Kaiser Co., Inc. . . .The second yard destined to build C4's was an extension of the Sun Shipbuilding and Dry Dock Co. at Chester, Pennsylvania which was called Sun No. 4. . . .It was to be an 8-way yard constructed on land already owned by Sun lying directly north of the North Yard. . . .

After the delays in constructing and equipping the two yards— Richmond No. 3 and Sun No. 4—came delays because of changes in the designs and specifications of the ships.

The contracts awarded Sun in August 1942 called for the C4-S-B1 design, a cargo ship which was primarily a tank carrier. Much time was spent developing a design to make possible the self-loading and discharge of tanks through interior and exterior ramps, but only one ship was finished on this design.[155] In September 1943, the Joint Chiefs decided that the 49 other C4's at Sun should be converted to Army troopships in order to fill the requirements for transportation of troops overseas in accordance with the decisions of the Quebec Conference.[156] Even 7 unfinished first-round ships were to be changed to the transport design (C4-S-B2).[157] Actually, 6 of Sun's C4's were turned over incomplete to the Navy to be converted into hospital ships and 8 were finished as troop ships.[158] In 1944 or 1945 there was another change, and the last 5 C4's built by Sun were again cargo ships (design C4-S-B5).[159]

At Richmond there was never any doubt that the C4's would be transports.

At Richmond there was never any doubt that the C4's would be transports. But within the same basic transport design a great many modifications were possible. Both at Richmond and at Sun, construction was impeded by a larger number of modifications of this kind. Some arose from problems of armament and stability, desire to increase the troop-carrying capacity, and efforts to increase resistance to battle damage.[160] Only one aspect of these many changes can be considered here in any detail—that connected with the uncertainty over what branch of the government should operate the ships.

There was a struggle going on among the Navy, and Army, and the Maritime Commission's "Siamese twin," the War Shipping Administration, for control of shipping. This contest over who would operate the ships affected various features of their design and especially the provision for accommodations for crews, since the Navy's requirements in this respect were quite different from the Army's or the civilian standards followed by the War Shipping Administration.

When plans for the C4 transports were first drawn, the Maritime Commission proceeded on the assumption that they would be operated for the Army by the WSA, or by the Army with civilian crews, and that therefore the Navy need not be consulted about their design.[161] The Navy, on the other hand, kept in mind the possibility that the C4's might some day be turned over to them to be manned by naval personnel and for that reason strove to bring the ships as close to Navy standards as possible. Other questions besides that of accommodation for the crew were involved in the suggestions made by the Navy in the summer of 1942, but Admiral Vickery's instructions to the Commission's Technical staff were that since "the arrangements lay entirely between the Maritime Commission and the Army, the desires of the Navy Department should be ignored and the matter allowed to simmer."[162]

The "simmering" threatened several times to come to a boil. and a new arrangement was made in February 1943 which provided that crew spaces on C4 vessels "should be altered to their maximum capacity" so that if the Navy should be called on to man the vessels at the last moment "the vessels could be blown up to meet naval personnel requirements."[163]. . .

Another change. In March, the Army reluctantly agreed to have Army transports manned by naval personnel. Official notice came to Admiral Land in April in a letter setting forth the recent decision to assign the C4 ships to the Navy under bareboat charter, and stating that the Bureau of Ships would review the plans of the ships to see what changes would be necessary.[164]

Throughout the remainder of the spring and summer, the Navy suggested modifications and changes.[165] In the latter part of October, Carl Flesher, Director of the West Coast Regional Office, telegraphed Admiral Vickery: "If you can find some way to stop the Navy Department from requesting so many changes, it will assist us greatly in new construction and conversion work in San Francisco area."[166]

Unfortunately this conversion to naval transports was not the last change these vessels were to undergo. The following summer, the Commission was informed by the Naval Transport Service that the Navy was not in a position to man the C4 transports and could not therefore accept delivery of the vessels.[167] This left the Commission with the problem of converting the vessels for merchant crews to meet Coast Guard standards for merchant ships.[168]. . .

Changes in the design of the vessels did not account for all the difficulties encountered in the construction of the C4's. Not only were the contractors delayed in completing the facilities, as had been explained, but they were slowed down by deficiencies in their labor force and supervisory personnel. . . .

This was the result, Vickery concluded, of "a dilution of management, necessary dependence upon inexperienced personnel, and a lack of sufficient personnel." Consequently contracts were revised or canceled with the balance of the C4's built elsewhere. . . .

The final record on construction of C4's was as follows:[169]

Troop transports built at Richmond No. 3 35
Troop transports built at Vancouver. 10
Troop transports built at Sun (including incomplete
    hospital ships) 14
Tank carrier built at Sun. 1
Cargo ships built at Sun 5
Total. 65

No other transports (perhaps no other ships) had as confused a record of changes in design and contracts as did the C4's.

Navy Attack Transports (APA's).   Thirty-two Navy APA's built by the Commission with design S4-SE2-BD1 were a purely military type. They were smaller with shallow draft, provided with divided machinery compartments, and were arranged to carry large amounts of combat equipment so that they were rated by the Navy as APAs, attack transports.

They were built by the Wilmington yard of Consolidated Steel Corp., which finished its deliveries in April 1945, three months ahead of contract schedule. This achievement of Consolidated stood out the more by contrast with the difficulties of Walsh-Kaiser, which was building for the Navy attack cargo ships of the same dimensions (S4-SE2-BE1)

The first keels for these two variations of the S4 type were laid at about the same time, but Walsh-Kaiser, hampered by having frigates and Libertys in the yard, did not finish its BE1's until August 1945.[170]

Victory Transports.   More numerous than any other type of transport were those built on the Victory ship design. Working plans, specifications, and procurement for the Victorys were pushed rapidly as soon as the controversy with WPB was settled in August 1943.[171]

In October of 1943 Admiral Vickery, while on a visit to London, stirred up controversy by some remarks about the commercial possibilities of the Victory in postwar competition,[172] but their suitability for wartime needs came to the forefront of attention again in November 1943 when the Joint Chiefs informed the Maritime Commission that 130 attack transports, as well as a number of other military types, should be added to its program.

This required a reduction in the program for merchant shipbuilding so that the yards could be used for these military types, and the Commission's program of November 20, 1943 revised accordingly the schedule for 1944 and 1945.[173] Some of the new military needs were met by converting C-types, but the demand for 130 attack transports was met mainly by a modified form of Victory ship, VC2-S-AP5 design.

The Victory transport was enough like the Victory ships already planned so that there was no violent disruption of the continuity of production and procurement when yards which were constructing Victory freighters, or preparing to, built Victory transports instead.

Richmond No. 2 changed over directly from Liberty ships to Victory transports in May and June of 1944. Calship and Oregon which had laid keels for Victory freighters in November 1943, launched two to four rounds of this design and then changed over to the Victory transports.

Another West coast yard organized for multiple production, Kaiser-Vancouver, was assigned Victory transports in place of the tankers it had expected to build when it completed the aircraft carrier escorts, and it, too, was laying keels of AP5s in April and May of 1944.

Altogether the Commission built 117 transports of this one design, VC2-S-AP5.[174] In constructing these transports the Commission was able to use fully the methods of multiple production, although in procurement and in labor force it encountered difficulties.

Other Military Types

Many other military types could be mentioned—Navy tenders, five designs of Navy oilers, gasoline coastal tankers, other cargo attack ships, hospital transports, other troop transports, and attack transports.[175] Frequently the military types were conversions of ships begun as C-types. In instances in which change of type took place after work was far advanced, or the specifications were changed substantially while work was in progress, the tearing out of what had just been built seriously damaged the morale of workers. . . .

It was impossible to explain to the workmen the military reasons back of the changes. Even in retrospect, only a technical military historian could pass any judgment on them. They upset both scheduling and morale and were one reason why building for the military increased the administrative and industrial problems out of all proportion to the total tonnage produced.

(Source: Lane, *Ships for Victory*, 1–100, 138–172, 574–636.) ∎

Endnotes for Chapter 1

Abbreviations Used in Notes

MC   Maritime Commission

gf   General files

WSA   War Shipping Administration

PR   Press Release

Bland Committee—House, Committee on the Merchant Marine and Fisheries

Truman Committee—Senate, Special Committee Investigating the National Defense Program

[1] Rounded off totals for "Major Types" from Table B-3 in Gerald J. Fischer, *Statistical Summary of Shipbuilding under the U.S. Maritime Commission during World War II* [Historical Reports of War Administration, U.S. Maritime Commission, No. 2] (Government Printing Office, 1949).

[2] Ibid. The merchant fleet of the United States in 1939 totaled 12 million tons; that of the world, 81 million.—U.S. Maritime Commission, *Report to Congress* for the Fiscal Year ended June 30, 1948 (Government Printing Office, 1949), p. 64.

[3] Fischer, *Statistical Summary,* Tables B-3, B-4, and G-2, and estimate by Fischer for steel consumption on basis of sources he cites in ibid., Section F notes.

[4] Merchant Marine Act, 1936, 49 Stat. 1985, Titles I, V and VI.

[5] Statements by ex-Commissioner Thomas M. Woodward to Frederic C. Lane, June 25, 1946, Notes in MC, Historian's Collection, Research file 105.

[6] U.S. Maritime Commission, *Report to Congress* for the period ended October 25, 1939. (Government Printing Office, 1940), pp. 4–5.

[7] Memorandum by Land to Frederic C. Lane, June 23, 1948, in MC, Historian's Collection, Research file 118.1.1.

[8] This biographical sketch is based mainly on the "Biography" prepared Sept. 30, 1944, by the MC, Division of Public Information, and on Donald E. Keyhoe, "You Can't Sink This Admiral," *American Magazine,* Mar. 1940, pp. 21, 68, whose version of the Army-Navy game of 1900 is even more dramatic than that in *The Sun,* Baltimore, Monday morning, Dec. 3, 1900, which I have followed.

[9] E.g., Senate, *Maritime Commission Nominations, Hearing,* before a Sub-committee of the Committee on Commerce, 75th Cong., 1st sess., Apr. 10, 1937.

[10] Kennedy to Claude A. Swanson, Secretary of the Navy, May 3, 1937, in Land reading file.

[11] Land to Schuyler Otis Bland, Aug. 29, 1940; Land to Senator Josiah W. Bailey, Aug. 29, 1940, in MC, Historian's Collection, Land file.

[12] MC Admin. Order No. 41, Dec. 28, 1937. He was made Rear Admiral Jan 22, 1942 (confirmed by Senate, Apr. 9, 1942) and Vice Admiral, Oct. 24, 1944 (confirmed by Senate, Nov. 27, 1944).

[13] *Economic Survey of the American Merchant Marine* (Government Printing Office, 1937), pp. 36–39. *The Use and Disposition of Ships and Shipyards at the End of World War II, A Report prepared for the United States Navy Department and the United States Maritime Commission by the Graduate School of Business Administration, Harvard University, June, 1945,* printed for the use of the Committee on the Merchant Marine and Fisheries, Document No. 48 (Government Printing Office, 1945, cited hereafter as *Harvard Report*), p. 174.

[14] Robert Earle Anderson, *The Merchant Marine and World Frontiers* (New York, 1945), p. 71; MC Minutes, Sept. 30, 1937, pp. 1772–74. A general view of the long-range program is Emory S. Land, "Building an American Merchant Marine," the *Annals* of the American Academy of Political and Social Science, CCXI (Sept., 1940), 41–48.

[15] MC Minutes, Dec. 21, 1937, p. 2498; *Marine Engineering and Shipping Review,* Mar., 1939, p. 103.

[16] Merchant Marine Act, 1936, 49 Stat. 1985, Secs. 101, 501 and 502.

[17] Kennedy to Swanson, June 10, 1937, in MC general files (cited hereafter as gf) 107-5; Land Memorandum for files, Aug. 9, 1937, in MC, Historian's Collection, Land file.

[18] Land to the Commission, Dec. 20, 1938, in Land file, and Gerald J. Fischer, "The Programming of Ship Construction by the U.S. Maritime Commission 1938–1945" (typescript, Nov. 27, 1946 p. 8, in MC Historian's Collection, Research file 202.1.

[19] U.S. Maritime Commission, *Report to Congress* for the Period Ended October 25, 1940, pp. 6–8, gives the misleading impression that it was expected that their construction would be completed July 1941. But see Land to Harold D. Smith, Oct. 23, 1940 in MC gf 506-1, and Fischer, *Statistical Summary,* Table A-2.

[20] J.W. Barnett, Acting Chief of Division of Loans and Sales, U.S. Shipping Board Bureau, to Acting Director, Aug. 7, 1934. The plan for engaging a naval architect for the work is described in the letter of Mar. 16, 1934, same to same. Both in MC gf 505-1.

[21] Memorandum on meetings of the "Committee on Standard Merchant Vessels" in MC gf 505-1. The notes on the meeting of Aug. 27, 1934 contain the earliest use I [F. Lane] have seen of the well-known designations T2, C2, and P2.

[22] J. M. Johnson, Acting Secretary of Commerce, to Claude A. Swanson, Secretary of the Navy, July 3, 1936, in MC gf 505-1. See *Harvard Report*, pp. 174–80, on the gradual revival of both Navy and merchant shipbuilding.

[23] J. M. Chambers (approved by Vickery) to J. L. Spilman, Classification Division, C. S. C., Mar. 30, 1940, in MC, Personnel Division files.

[24] Administrative Orders and Quarterly Reports of the Technical Division analyzed in Blanche D. Coll, "Administration of Functions Assigned to the Technical Division, 1937–1947" (typescript, Mar. 10, 1947) in MC, Historian's Collection, Research file 106.

[25] *Marine Engineering and Shipping Review,* Oct. 1939, p. 469.

[26] Ibid. July 1939, p. 305; and H. Gerrish Smith, "Events of 1939 Prove Wisdom of U.S. Shipbuilding Policy," in ibid., Jan. 1940, p. 50. See also J. E. Schmeltzer, "Engineering Features of the Maritime Commission's Program," in *Transactions* of the Society of Naval Architects and Marine Engineers, XLVIII (1940), 332–70.

[27] Most of the "C" Diesel ships had single reduction gearing between the two or four Diesel engines and the line (propeller) shaft. The ships with low speed Sun Doxford engines, like the C2-SUs, had no reduction gearing.

[28] *Maritime Engineering and Shipping Review,* Aug. 1939, pp. 355–56.

[29] Ibid., Nov. 1940, pp. 92, 108.

[30] E. S. Land, "Some Policies of the U.S. Maritime Commission," in *Transactions* of the Society of Naval Architects and Marine Engineers, XLVIII (1940), 258–76.

[31] Ibid., and J. E. Schmeltzer, "The Commission's P4-P Design," in *Marine Engineering and Shipping Review,* Feb. 1941, p. 75.

[32] Statements by E. S. Dillon, Feb. 28, 1949.

[33] General descriptions in the article by Admiral Land, "Some Policies," above cited and in Robert Earle Anderson, *The Merchant Marine and World Frontiers.* Detailed descriptions of specific ships in many articles in the *Marine Engineering and Shipping Review* in 1939 and 1940.

[34] H. Gerrish Smith, in *Marine Engineering and Shipping Review,* Jan. 1940, p. 50.

[35] Land, "Some Policies," pp. 266–67, and H. Gerrish Smith in *Marine Engineering and Shipping Review,* Jan. 1940, p. 49.

[36] Fischer, *Statistical Summary,* Table C.

[37] *Harvard Report,* pp. 167–74.

[38] Testimony of A. B. Homer, Vice President, Bethlehem Steel Company, in Senate, *Investigation of the National Defense Program, Hearings* before a Special Committee Investigating the National Defense Program, 77th Cong., 1st sess., pt. 6, July 15, 1941, pp. 1550–53. Hereafter cited as Truman Committee, *Hearings.*

[39] *Harvard Report,* pp. 172–73.

[40] House, *Independent Offices Appropriation Bill for 1942, Hearing* before the House Subcommittee of the Committee on Appropriations, 77th Cong., 1st sessl, pt. 1, Dec. 19, 1940, p. 442.

[41] A basic source for this survey of the state of shipyards in 1940–41 is the set of "Way Charts" prepared by Joseph T. Reynolds under the direction of Gerald J. Fischer and F. C. Lane in the office of the Historian, U. S. Maritime Commission, 1946–47. They are based on the records kept by the U. S. Maritime Commission Production Division and by the Navy, Bureau of Ships, supplemented by letters from shipyards. Cited hereafter as Reynolds' Way Charts.

[42] *Marine Engineering and Shipping Review*, Jan. 1940, p. 35; and Nov. 1943, p. 166; Dec. 1943, p. 180; Jan. 1944, p. 196; *Fortune*, July 1943, p. 218.

[43] *Consolidated Steel Corp., Annual Report for 1944.*

[44] *Marine Engineering and Shipping Review*, Mar. 1941, p. 54.

[45] That is, building ocean-going vessels over 400 feet in length.

[46] Fischer, *Statistical Summary*, Table E-1, but the figure for building berths there given, 51, does not include the two ways at Bath Iron Works because those ways were shorter than the standard used in that table to determine building berths.

[47] *Harvard Report*, pp. 176–77.

[48] House, *Navy Department Appropriation Bill for 1942, Hearings* before the Subcommittee of the Committee on Appropriations, 77th Cong., 1st sess., Feb. 1941, pp. 668–72, 690–91, 722–28.

[49] Ibid., p. 666.

[50] Testimony of A. B. Homer before the Truman Committee, *Hearings*, pt. 6, p. 1558; House, *Navy Department Appropriation Bill for 1942, Hearings*, p. 668.

[51] Ibid., pp. 671–72, 723, 726.

[52] Ibid., p. 723; *Consolidated Steel Corp. Annual Report for 1944.*

[53] House, *Navy Department Appropriations Bill for 1942, Hearings*, p. 723.

[54] Ibid., p. 668.

[55] Ibid., p. 238–39. The figure 68 includes builders of small craft.

[56] Charles H. Coleman, *Shipbuilding Activities of the National Defense Advisory Commission and Office of Production Management, July 1940 to December 1941.*

[57] MC, *Report to Congress* for period ended Oct. 25, 1940, p. 7.

[58] Land to Harold D. Smith, Oct. 23, 1940 in MC gf 506-1.

[59] Coleman, *Shipbuilding Activities of NDAC and OPM*, pp. 1–2; *The United States at War*, pp. 23–52.

[60] The British plans were politically approved on Oct. 30, 1941 by Secretary of the Treasury Morgenthau who was then the clearing house for aid to Britain. *Journal of Commerce*, Nov. 1, 1940.

[61] C. T. Ballantyne, British Purchasing Commission, to Philip Young of the President's Liaison Committee, Nov. 13, 1940, and Knudsen to Young, Nov. 18, 1940, in MC, Historian's Collection, Vickery file "1940—Shipyards and

Construction Data," which is a collection of the series of memoranda of Nov. and Dec. 1940.

62 *Journal of Commerce*, Dec. 27, 1940; Samuel I. Rosenman, ed., *The Public Papers and Addresses of Franklin D. Roosevelt*, Vol. IX, *War—and Aid to Democracies* (New York, 1941).

63 Land to Knudsen, Nov. 8, 1940, in gf 506-1.

64 An American emergency program for building 200 ships is assumed by Admiral Land's Memorandum for the President, Dec., 1940, in gf 507-1.

65 MC Minutes, pp. 15753–15753-A, Jan. 10, 1941.

66 Press Release 804, Jan 8, 1941, (in MC gf 105-2) said that the sites for building the 200 ships had been selected. For dates of Commission action, Jan. 10–17, see Fischer, *Statistical Summary*, Table E-5.

67 *Journal of Commerce*, Jan. 10, 1941, p. 22. The contract was not approved until Jan. 17.

68 Land to the President, Dec. 26, 1940, Land reading file; Minutes, pp. 15834–15834-A (Jan. 17, 1941).

69 MC Minutes, pp. 15834–15834-A, Jan 17, 1941; E. B. Williams, "The Delta Shipyard," *Marine Engineering and Shipping Review*, Apr. 1943; Outline of the Plan for Construction and Operation of a Shipyard, and the Building of Ships in It, at New Orleans, and for the U.S. Maritime Commission, in MC gf 507-3-5. The urging which induced the American Ship Building Company to join reluctantly is set forth by W. M. Gerhauser in House, *Investigation of Shipyard Profits, Hearings* before the Committee on the Merchant Marine and Fisheries, 79th Cong., 2d sess., 1946, pp. 518–20, 267–268.

70 In addition to Henry J. Kaiser Co. and The Kaiser Company, the other construction firms were W. A. Bechtel Company, Bechtel-McCone-Parsons, General Construction Co., Morrison-Knudsen Co., MacDonald & Kahn, Inc., and Pacific Bridge Co.

71 *Fortune*, Oct. 1943, p. 147 ff.; see also *Fortune*, July 1941, pp. 124 ff.; Frank J. Taylor, "Builder No. 1," *Saturday Evening Post,* June 7, 1941.

72 Corporate arrangements and management are fully discussed in House, *Investigation of Shipyard Profits, Hearings.*

73 Land to the President, Mar. 27, 1941 and Apr. 2, 1941, both in MC gf 506-1. Also Land to General J. H. Burns, Mar. 28, 1941 in Land reading file.

74 Press Release 881, MC gf 105-2, Apr. 9, 1941.

75 Press Conference of Jan. 3, 1941 in *The Public Papers and Addresses of Franklin D. Roosevelt* (New York, 1941), IX, 647; *Time*, Jan. 13, 1941, p. 14.

76 PR 1033, Sept. 24, 1941 and PR 1032, Sept. 25, 1941, in MC gf 105-2. Commissioner Macauley referred to them as "Liberty Ships" in an address on Sept. 4, 1941. In gf 105-5.

[77] MC Minutes, p. 18916 (Sept. 12, 1941); p. 20100 (Dec. 12, 1941); p. 20158 (Dec. 16, 1941).

[78] The "Office Memoranda" of the Technical Division, Maritime Commission, define the usual relations of the Maritime Commission, the shipyard and the Marine Architect. Precedents are also discussed in the long "Memorandum" by R. E. Anderson, May 22, 1942, in gf 507-1-4, Feb. 7, 1941. An itemized list of the services of Gibbs & Cox is filed under Apr. 5, 1941 in Emergency Construction Div. file QM8-A3-2.

[79] Office Order No. 43, Series of 1939, Sept. 21, 1939, in Technical Div. files; Admin Order No. 37, Suppl. No. 1, Dec. 13, 1938; Office Order No. 18, Series of 1938, May 24, 1938, in Technical Div. files; Quarterly Reports, Technical Division, July 1, 1939–Dec. 31, 1940.

[80] Memorandum, "Design C2-S-C1," Jan. 6, 1941, in Wanless File, EC2-S-C1, Correspondence.

[81] This account of discussion of details of the new design is based on David B. Tyler, "Construction and Operation of Liberty Ships from the Technical Point of View," Oct. 23, 1946, in Historian's Collection, Research file 111-1a.

[82] Note made by Admiral Land on a draft of this chapter.

[83] Wanless, "History of Emergency Ship Design"; J. E. Schmeltzer to Chairman, May 15, 1941, in gf 507-1-4; notes by David B. Tyler on interview with Mr. Bates; MC Minutes, pp. 18447–49, Commissioner Dempsey's prepared statement in the Truman Committee, *Hearings,* pt. 5, June 3, 1941, p. 1466, said: By adopting the design and following the plans which Gibbs & Cox "had prepared" for the 60 ships "under construction for the British. . .it was possible to effect a material saving in the main essential, time," and to take advantage of what Gibbs & Cox had already done in procurement.

[84] House, *Emergency Cargo Ship Construction, Hearings* before the Subcommittee of the Committee on Appropriations, 77th Cong., 1st sess., on H. J. Res. 77, Jan. 18, 1941, p. 16.

[85] W. G. Esmond, Chief of Hull Section, Emergency Ship Construction Division to Director, Emergency Ship Construction Division, Apr. 21, 1941, in Production Div. files QM8-A3-0-1.

[86] Interviews with Messrs. Grant and Esmond, June and July 1947 in MC, Historian's Collection.

[87] Historical Notes by W. G. Esmond, in W. E. Spofford, "History," pp. 92–98.

[88] Land to the President, Dec. 26, 1940, in MC gf 507-1.

[89] W. F. Gibbs describes his arrangements with the British in his testimony, House, *Navy Department Appropriation Bill for 1945, Hearings,* 78th Cong., 2d sess., p. 3870, and in a letter to Admiral Land, May 7, 1941, in MC gf 507-1-4, par. 11.

[90] At that date began a flood of letters telling engine manufacturers and others that the contracts for components would be let through Gibbs & Cox. MC gf 507-1 and 507-1-1.

[91] They were designed by the North Eastern Marine Engineering Co., Ltd., a Division of Richardson, Westgarth & Co., Wallsend-on-Tyne.

[92] Minutes of Meeting, Feb. 21, 1941; J. E. Schmeltzer to Gibbs & Cox, Att. W. F. Gibbs, May 29, 1941 in Emergency Ship Construction Division file, QM8 S51.

[93] Vickery to Commission, July 25, 1941, with Admin. Order No. 37, Suppl. 42.

[94] House, *Independent Offices Appropriation Bill for 1943, Hearings* before the Subcommittee of the Committee on Appropriations, 77th Cong., 2d sess., on the Independent Offices Appropriation Bill for 1943, Dec. 9, 1941, p. 277.

[95] House, *Navy Department Appropriation Bill for 1945, Hearings*, 1944, p. 4028. Mr. Gibbs' testimony before that Committee, pp. 3986–4027, is a vigorous defense of his fees.

[96] House, *Production in Shipbuilding Plants, Executive Hearings*, pt. 3, June 28, 1943, pp. 915–16.

[97] Statement of Land in House, *Fifth Supplemental National Defense Appropriation Bill for 1942, Hearing*, Feb. 12, 1942, p. 100.

[98] MC Minutes, pp. 20502–04 (Jan. 13, 1942); p. 20491 (Jan. 10, 1942).

[99] House, *Fifth Supplemental National Defense Appropriation Bill for 1942, Hearings*, 77th Cong., 2d sess., Feb. 12, 1942, p. 95.

[100] Land reading file, Jan. 17, 1942. Memo to Admiral Robinson and W. H. Harrison.

[101] Data on sinking from *WSA Shipping Summary*, Vol. II, No. 1, p. 18 (Jan. 1945).

[102] MC, Program Collection, Feb. 21, 1942. The President to Admiral Land, with memorandum from Marshall to the President attached. At another conference at the White House, attended by representatives of the Army, the WPB and the MC but with no representative of the Navy present, the President reiterated on Feb. 23 the need for increasing the amount of merchant marine tonnage. Land reading file, Feb. 23, 1942.

[103] Vickery's bar charts, in MC, Historian's Collection.

[104] House, *Higgins Contracts, Hearings*, pp. 252–53; Fischer, *Statistical Summary*, Table E-5.

[105] Testimony by S. D. Bechtel in House, *Production in Shipbuilding Plants, Hearings*, June 22, 1943, pp. 691–708. MC Minutes, pp. 21362–64 (March 12, 1943). The telegrams and replies are in gf 507-1 under the dates cited.

[106] The initial contract for the yard and Liberty ships was awarded to W. A. Bechtel Co., a partnership. Late in 1942 the joint venture was changed to Marinship Corp. House, *Investigation of Shipyard Profits, Hearings*, 1946, pp. 249–51.

[107] Additions totalled 99 but the loss of Seattle-Tacoma made the net gain only 91. The total planned was thus raised from 221 building berths to 312, counting Higgins as 44.

[108] Information from MC personnel files.

[109] WSA Administrative Orders Nos. 1 and 2.

[110] Land (written by Searls) to Nelson, Aug. 25, 1942 in MC Historian's Collection, Douglas file, "Construction."

[111] Statements by G. J. Fischer. July program minus military and minor types.

[112] See Admiral Vickery's retrospective statements in House, *Independent Offices Appropriation Bill for 1945, Hearings,* pp. 705–06 (Dec. 9, 1943).

[113] The Land file in MC, Historian's Collection contains many requests.

[114] MC Press Release No. 991, Aug. 14, 1941.

[115] Vickery to Clay Bedford, Aug. 28, 1942, MC, Historian's Collection, Weber reading file.

[116] Land to Lane, May 11, 1949.

[117] Sir Amos L. Ayre, "Merchant Shipbuilding During the War," in Institution of Naval Architects, *Transactions,* vol. 87 (1945), p. 3.

[118] *Ibid.,* pp. 13–14.

[119] Bates to J. Lewis Luckenback, Sept. 18, 1942, in MC, Technical Division files, A.B.S., pt. 3.

[120] Notes on conference on new EC2 design, Nov. 21, 1942, in MC, Technical Division, Preliminary Design Section, Correspondence file, VC2-S-AP1, 1942–43.

[121] Wanless to Vickery, Sept. 23, 1942, in Preliminary Design Section Correspondence file, EC2-S-C1.

[122] Wanless to Lane, Oct. 29, 1950, and Nov. 16, 1950 in MC, Historian's Collection.

[123] Tyler, "Victory Ship Design," pp. 19–25.

[124] Tyler, "Victory Ship Design," pp. 25–27.

[125] Vickery's memorandum on the Victory Ship, and Tyler, "Victory Ship Design," pp. 6, 9–10. Vickery's memo on Victory Ship: In long hand on the back of letter paper bearing his home address, Admiral Vickery wrote out a summary of his planning for the Victory ship and how it had been interfered with. This document which is without title is in the Historian's Collection, Vickery file, "Victory Ship Program."

[126] *Ibid.,* and Reynolds' Way Charts; for Swan Island, MC Minutes, pp. 22180–82 (June 11, 1942).

[127] MC Minutes, p. 23789 (Dec. 17, 1942).

[128] Land to Files, Jan. 26, 1943 in MC Historian's Collection, Land file.

[129] Chaikin and Coleman, *Shipbuilding Policies,* p. 90, note 169.

[130] *Ibid.,* p. 29.

[131] Memorandum of Conference held in the office of Charles E. Wilson, Apr. 30, 1943, in Land file; Vickery's memo on Victory Ship, cited above.

[132] Tyler, "Victory Ship Design," pp. 49–54. A long record of this meeting is in the Vickery file in the MC, Historian's Collection.

[133] Chaikin and Coleman, *Shipbuilding Policies*, p.172; C. E. Wilson to Ralph Cordiner, May 13, 1943; J. A. Krug to Staff, May 14, 1943 in WPB file 324.10412.

[134] Vickery's memo on Victory ship; Tyler, "Victory ship Design," p. 74. Wilson to Land, July 3, 1943 (above cited) defends this refusal to approve facilities for changing yards from Liberty to Victory ships. Transcripts of telephone conversations between Vickery and Wilson, July 27, and Vickery and Murphy, July 28, in MC, Historian's Collection, Vickery file.

[135] *New York Times,* Sept. 12, 1943; Chaikin and Coleman, *Shipbuilding Policies,* p. 91.

[136] MC Minutes, pp. 26749–50, Nov. 9, 1943. Quarterly report of the Survey and Schedule Branch of the Production Division, Oct. 26, 1943.

[137] Fischer, *Statistical Summary,* Tables E-8 and B-5.

[138] Dwight D. Eisenhower, *Crusade in Europe,* pp. 38–39; George E. Mowry, *Landing Craft and the War Production Board, April 1942 to May 1944,* [Historical Reports of War Administration, War Production Board Special Study no. 11] (Washington: Civilian Production Administration, 1944, reissued 1946) pp. 6 ff.

[139] Letters in MC Technical Division files, S1, Nov. 21, 1941 and Dec. 11, 1941, cited in Helen E. Knuth, "The Building of LST's by the Maritime Commission," pp. 2–3, 7. Miss Knuth's research is the basis of most of this account of building the LST's.

[140] Ibid.

[141] Ivan J. Wanless to F. C. Lane, Nov. 16, 1950.

[142] Statement by William A. Weber, recorded May 7, 1946.

[143] N. L. Rawlings to Land, Sept. 23, 1942, in MC gf 506-15-3; MC Minutes, p. 23092 (Oct. 1, 1942).

[144] Knuth, "The Building of LST's," pp. 17–19.

[145] Land to Kaiser Inc., May 28, 1942, in MC gf 506-15-2.

[146] Edgar Kaiser to Vickery and Henry Kaiser to Vickery, both May 16, 1942 in MC gf 506-15-2.

[147] For detailed information on the design, construction and manning of the new landing craft, see William L. McGee, *The Amphibians Are Coming! Emergence of the 'Gator Navy and its Revolutionary Landing Craft,* Vol. 1. –Ed.

[148] Mowry, *Landing Craft,* pp. 5–6, 23–24.

[149] Land to W.F. Gibbs, WPB, Jan. 21, 1943 in MC gf 107-155.

[150] Reports in MC, Historian's Collection, Research file 111; confirmed by interview with James L. Bates, June 21, 1949.

[151] Ibid., and statements of Admiral Land, Mar. 22, 1949; MC Minutes, p. 27251 (Jan. 4, 1944), getting this contract is part of the Kaiser legend. See *Fortune,* Oct. 1943, p. 255.

[152] Statement by J. L. Bates, June 21, 1949.

[153] Program Collection, pt. II, and Reynolds' Way Charts.

[154] Memorandum from Ivan Wanless, Chief of Preliminary Design Section to Chief of the Final Design Section, Oct., 28, 1941, in MC gf 506-14-1. Cited in Helen Knuth, "The C-4 Shipbuilding Program," a typescript prepared under my [Frederic C. Lane's] direction. Miss Knuth's research is the basis of this section.

[155] Knuth, " The C4 Shipbuilding Program," pp. 20–21.

[156] Leahy to Land, Sept. 17, 1943, in MC gf 506-14-3.

[157] Reynolds' Way Charts; attachment to Robert Haig to Vickery June 17, 1944 and McInnis to Haig, Sept. 3, 1943, in gf 506-14-3.

[158] Minutes, p. 28745 (June 13, 1944) for completion of 8 as troop ships; Minutes, pp. 28943–44 (July 4, 1944) for delivery of 6 incomplete to the Navy. In Fischer's *Statistical Summary,* Table C, the C4-S-B2s turned over to the Navy for completion are listed as cargo ships because they were not delivered to the Commission as military types.

[159] Reynolds' Way Charts.

[160] Knuth, "C-4 Shipbuilding Program," pp. 19–23, based on the many letters on the subject in MC gf 506-14-2, 506-14-1, 506-14-3. Richmond built C4-S-A1s.

[161] Report of Conference held with Bates, McPhedran, Wanless, Haynes, Smith, Vickery, Flesher and Shulters, Nov. 19, 1941, in MC gf 506-14-1; House, *Production in Shipbuilding Plants, Executive Hearings,* pt. 3, June 23, 1943, p. 899.

[162] Bates, Memo. for Files, June 27, 1942, in MC gf 506-7-1.

[163] Bates, Memo for Files, Aug. 4, 1942, in MC gf 506-14-1 and Huntington Morse to Land and Vickery, Feb. 27, 1943 in MC gf 507-14-2.

[164] Knuth, "C4 Shipbuilding Program" pp. 25–26; Horne to Land, Apr. 30, 1943, in MC gf 506-14-2.

[165] Wanless Memo for Files, May 7, 1943, in MC gf 506-14-1; Report of Conference in office of George Sharp, May 26, 1943, in MC gf 506-14-1; Land, Memo for Admiral King, CNO, Sept. 15, 1943, in MC gf 506-14-2; Admiral James Pine to Land, Oct. 26, 1943, in MC gf 506-14-1.

[166] Flesher to Vickery, Oct. 28, 1943, in MC gf 506-14-1. For award of contract for conversion to Navy design see Minutes, p. 28636 (June 1, 1944).

[167] Bates to Vickery, July 6, 1944, in MC gf 506-14-1.

[168] Ibid., also Green, Asst. Supt. Vancouver Yard to C.H. Johnson, Tech. Asst. to Vickery, July 11, 1944; Vickery to Kaiser Co., Richmond, Aug. 12, 1944 in MC gf 506-14-2.

[169] Two of the transports included in the 35 built at Richmond No. 3 completed their outfitting at Vancouver. Knuth, "C4 Shipbuilding Program," pp. 15–17, and Reynolds' Way Charts.

[170] MC, "Permanent Report of Completed Ship Construction Contracts," House; *Walsh-Kaiser Co., Inc., Hearings,* p. 262; Reynolds' Way Charts.

[171] C. H. Johnson to Technical and Procurement Divisions, Sept. 3, 1943 and Vickery to various suppliers, Sept. 3, 1943 in MC gf 506-22-1, and Tayler, "Victory Ship Design," p. 81.

[172] Tyler, "Victory Ship Design," pp. 82–87.

[173] Joint Chiefs of Staff to Land, Nov. 9, 1943, and schedule of Nov. 20, 1943, in MC Program Collection.

[174] Kaiser-Vancouver began work on its C4's only after finishing 31 AP5's—Reynolds' Way Charts. Vancouver, between the completion of its own AP5's and its building of C4's, outfitted 5 of the AP5's built at Calship, and Moore Dry Dock outfitted 4 of the AP5's built at Calship in order to finish them within the time limit set by the Joint Chiefs.—MC Minutes, pp. 31793–95 (Apr. 26, 1945).

[175] Fischer, *Statistical Summary,* Table A-1 of Form 106.

PLATE I.

Above, Side launching of a C1 at Consolidated Steel's Long Beach yard. *Lower left*, A C2-F, one of the fast freighters built by the Maritime Commission during the Chairmanship of E. S. Land, Vice Admiral, USN (Ret.) *(lower right)*.

Henry J. Kaiser *(left)* and W. S. (Pete) Newell *(right)* planned new shipyards to build freighters like the *Ocean Courage (above)* for the British and to build for the Maritime Commission a modified form of the same design, the Liberty ship *(below)*. Vessels of the British Ocean class were often called Libertys.

PLATE XXI.

Above, Victory ships crowd the outfitting docks at Calship while being completed as attack transports. *Center,* the Victory cargo ship (VC2-S-AP2). *Below,* a Victory transport (VC2-S-AP5) under way.

PLATE XXIV.

Above, the coastal cargo ship (C1-M-AV1) of which 218 were delivered in 1944–1945 for the needs of the Navy in the Southwest Pacific. *Left,* concrete ships being launched from basins at Tampa, Florida. *Below,* the powerful sea-going tug (V4-M-A1) of which 54 were constructed for the Maritime Commission. They formed part of the tug armada that towed concrete caissons across the English channel to form the artificial harbors off the Normandy beaches.

PLATE XXVI.

Upper left, bulkhead and forward section of tanker on ways. *Upper right*, lifting a forepeak section. *Lower left*, completing main deck of a Victory ship. *Lower right*, cutting scrap steel for use in welding schools.

Part II

LOGISTICS CHALLENGES IN THE PACIFIC

The story of the vital logistics services supporting the U.S. Armed Forces operating in the Pacific. Logistics challenges are examined—proof positive that naval warfare is not all blazing combat.

"A sound logistic plan is the foundation upon which a war operation should be based."

—*Admiral Raymond A. Spruance, USN (Ret)*

Chapter 2
Advance Bases and Floating Service Squadrons

Editor's note: This is the story of the vital logistics services supplied to U.S. Naval and Army forces in the Pacific Theater from 1941 to 1945. Unlike a technical study, this story will not attempt to furnish complete statistical figures. Rather, it will focus on logistics in order that those interested in naval history may realize that naval warfare is not all blazing combat.

Webster's defines logistics as "the branch of military science having to do with procuring, maintaining, and transporting materiel, personnel and facilities." While fighting is at times the deciding factor in warfare, it is possible only when the logistics needs of the fighters have been anticipated and met. German armies perished in the bitter Russian winter from lack of supplies, as had Napoleon's army before them. History is full of such tragedies, and every operations planner should realize his utter dependence upon logistics.

Excerpted from Rear Admiral Worrall Reed Carter, USN (Ret), *Beans, Bullets, and Black Oil—The Story of Fleet Logistics Afloat in the Pacific During World War II* (1953); Vice Admiral George Carroll Dyer, USN (Ret), *The Amphibians Came To Conquer—The Story of Admiral Richmond Kelly Turner* (1971); and Samuel Eliot Morison, *History of United States Naval Operations in World War II*, Vol. 6, *Breaking the Bismarcks Barrier, 22 July 1942–1 May 1944* (1950). The illustrations were selected by the editor from numerous archives.

During World War II, the United States was faced not only with the vastly increased demands created by forces of unprecedented magnitude, but the distances over which all supplies and services had to move before they could be effective, and by the need to charter, buy, and build enough ships to deliver them to where they were badly needed. Moreover, the technical advances made by modern science involved many items with multiple components—some of them mechanically intricate and of every imaginable sort. If a shortage developed, men might die uselessly. There was potential tragedy in every move made.

Therefore, dry as it may seem at first sight, what follows is nevertheless the highly significant record of what was done to support our combat units for their bloody work and of the means by which battered ships and men were repaired.

Rear Admiral Worrall Reed Carter, USN (Ret), was well qualified to write on the subject of naval logistics in the Pacific during World War II. As Commander Naval Bases South Pacific in the fall of 1942, Carter helped build up the shore facilities which supported the Solomons operations. From February 1944 to July 1945, he headed the famed "floating" Service Squadron Ten in support of the operations in the far reaches of the Pacific. The following excerpt is from Carter's *Beans, Bullets and Black Oil—The Story of Fleet Logistics Afloat in the Pacific During World War II.*

Service Force Beginnings

From 7 December 1941, when the Japanese attacked Pearl Harbor, to when they admitted defeat in August 1945, our fleet continuously grew. During those stirring and difficult times, the accounts of ship actions, air strikes, and amphibious operations make up the thrilling combat history of the Pacific Theater. Linked inseparably with combat is naval logistic support, the support which makes available to the fleet such essentials as ammunition, fuel, food, repair services—in short, all the necessities at the proper time and place and in adequate amounts. This support, from advanced bases and from floating mobile service squadrons and groups, maintained the fleet and enabled it to take offensive action farther from home supply points than was ever before thought possible. . . .

The advantages of logistics afloat and near the fleet operating area had long been recognized by many naval commanders and no doubt by others who gave the matter analytical thought. But there was skepticism, too. For example, it took a long time to satisfy everyone of the practicality of fueling under way at sea. Also, there were those who were skeptical of the capabilities of tenders and repair ships. Such vessels were looked upon as able to accomplish a certain degree of minor repair and upkeep, but for support of any consequence a navy yard or shipyard was for years thought necessary. . . .

After World War I, the Base Force was formed as part of the U.S. Fleet. This was, in fact, the beginning of the Service Force and its duty was service to the fleet, although it continued to be called the Base Force until the U.S. entered World War II. In concept and principle, it was sound, and its organization for the work then deemed practical was good. As a result, valuable and efficient services were rendered to the fleet, and some ideas of greater future accomplishments took root.

The fuel-oil tankers, fresh and frozen food ships, repair ships, fleet tugs, and target repair ships were administered and operated by the Commander Base Force. Ammunition ships were administered and usually operated by Naval Operations (OpNav). The navy yard schedule for overhaul was arranged but the allotment of funds for the work was controlled by the type commanders.

The destroyer tenders and submarine tenders were not administered or operated by the Base Force, and only occasional servicing jobs, either of emergency nature or beyond the capacity of the tenders, were performed directly on destroyers and submarines by the Base Force ships. The term "directly" is used because the Base Force often supplied the tenders with fuel, food, and ammunition, with which they in turn serviced the destroyers and submarines.

The Base Force also made arrangements for water and garbage disposal, and usually ran the shore patrol. The distribution of the enlisted personnel was, in varying degrees (depending upon the ideas of the Commander in Chief), handled by the Base Force. . . .

The fleet air arm was a separate organization with its own tenders furnishing its own services, although while assigned for photographic, target, and some observation work, the planes received temporary servicing from the Base Force. The aircraft tenders, like those of the destroyers and submarines, received some services from the Base Force which in turn were passed on to the planes. When the *Langley, Lexington,* and *Saratoga* joined the fleet, the Base Force took on the principal part of the responsibility for their fuel, food, and gun ammunition and made arrangements for regularly scheduled overhauls. All special equipment and planes, and many alterations due to experimental changes and improvements, were handled directly through the bureaus without reference to the Base Force.

Fueling underway at sea was instituted as part of the annual exercises. Fuel connections were designed and installed, and "at sea" rigs were supplied in order to carry out this part of the schedule. Fueling underway at sea was then looked upon somewhat as an emergency stunt which might have to be resorted to in wartime, and therefore probably required occasional practice. Few ever thought it would become so routine a matter that it would be accomplished with ease in all kinds of weather except gales. . . .

Unfortunately, just as we were ready to move to further accomplishment, the depression years arrived, funds were severely restricted, and the Base Force came to a slowdown without opportunity for improvement and advancement in operating technique.

This period was immediately followed by the Roosevelt years of emergency. The sudden expansion of all categories of naval personnel left little opportunity for anything but the fundamentals. In consequence, no great advance in Base Force technique or organizational coordination of fleet logistics were made until the war was in its second year.

The Navy Department knew that expansion of the fleet called for a proper balance in its auxiliaries, but because of the lack of detailed knowledge, there was no sound formula for finding that balance. So it was estimate and guess, with the authorizations always a little on the light side because of the need for combat units whose construction alone would tax the capacity for the building plants.

As a result, in 1940, the operating force consisted of 344 fighting ships and, to service them afloat, 120 auxiliaries of various types.

While in the 15 years from 1925 to 1940, destroyers, cruisers, and carriers had more than doubled in numbers, the auxiliaries had not. The most notable increase had been in seaplane tenders and oilers, but there were too few of the latter to permit their being kept with the operating units long enough to improve their at-sea oiling technique. Instead, they had to be kept busy ferrying oil.

During the first year of President Roosevelt's declared limited national emergency in 1940, there were authorized 10 battleships, 2 carriers, 8 light cruisers, 41 destroyers, 28 submarines, a mine layer, 3 subchasers, and 32 motor torpedo boats; a total of 125 combat fleet units. Because of the lack of logistic knowledge and foresight, the auxiliaries ordered to service this formidable new fleet numbered only 12: 1 destroyer tender, 1 repair ship, 2 submarine tenders, and 2 large and 6 small seaplane tenders. The war plans, it is true, included the procurement and conversion of merchant ships for auxiliary and patrol purposes, but nothing came of this provision. Because of the shortage of merchant shipping, little could be done without causing injury elsewhere.

Also during 1940, the Oakland, Calif., Supply Depot was acquired and the existing port storage depots at several points, notably San Diego, Calif.; Bayonne, N.J.; and Pearl Harbor, T.H.; were expanded.* Still no one seemed to give much consideration to the delivery and distribution of supplies to ships not at those bases to receive them.

---

* "T.H." was the abbreviation for Territory of Hawaii. Hawaii later became a state in 1959. —Ed.

The Base Force war plans for an overseas movement visualized two somewhat vague schemes:

- The fleet would fight at once upon arrival in distant or advanced waters and gain a quick victory (or be completely defeated), and the base would be hardly more than a fueling rendezvous before the battle. Afterward (if victorious) with the enemy defeated, there would be plenty of time to provide everything.
- The advanced location would be seized, the few available repair and supply vessels would be based there, and the remaining necessary facilities would be constructed ashore.

The trouble with this thinking lay in the fact that if the enemy refused early action there was no assurance that the base could be held with the fleet not present. On the other hand, the fleet, if present, could not be serviced without adequate floating facilities while necessary construction was being accomplished ashore. How little we really knew in 1940 as compared with 1945 shows in a comparison of the service forces active at both times.

In 1940, the Base Force Train included a total of 51 craft of all types, among them 1 floating dry-dock of destroyer capacity. By 1945, the total was 315 vessels, every one of them needed. The 14 oilers which were all the Navy owned in 1940 had leaped to 62, in addition to merchant tankers which brought huge cargoes of oil, aviation gasoline, and Diesel fuel to bases where the Navy tankers took them on board for distribution to the fleet.

No less than 21 repair ships of various sizes had supplanted the 2 the Navy had five years before. The battleships had 3 floating dry-docks, the cruisers 2, and the destroyers 9, while small craft had 16. Hospital ships had risen from 1 to 6, and in addition there were 3 transport evacuations vessels. Ammunition ships numbered 14, plus 28 cargo carriers and 8 LSTs (Landing Ship, Tank).

The number of combatant ships had increased materially, and it is natural to ask if the auxiliaries should not have increased comparably. The answer is, of course, yes. But the increase of combatant ships had been visualized, and the building programs were undertaken before the war began. It flourished with increased momentum during the early part of the war, long before the minimum auxiliary requirements could be correctly estimated and the rush of procurement started.

The original planners had done their best, but it was not until the urgency for auxiliaries developed as a vital element of the war that we fully realized what was needed and met the demand. Merchant ships were converted whenever possible, and this, with concentrated efforts to provide dry-docks and other special construction, produced every required type in numbers that would have been considered preposterous only a short time before.

When the Japanese attacked Pearl Harbor, Rear Admiral W. L. Calhoun commanded the Base Force there and had his flag in the USS *Argonne*. Overnight his duties increased enormously. Thousands of survivors of the attack had nothing but the clothes they wore, which in many cases consisted of underwear only. These naval personnel had to be clothed, fed, quartered, re-recorded, and put on new payrolls with the utmost expedition in order to make them available for assignments anywhere. There were hundreds of requests for repairs, ammunition, and supplies of all kinds.

Calhoun expanded his staff to three times its original size, and despite the excitement, confusion, diversity of opinion, uncertainty, and shortages of everything, he brilliantly mustered order from what could easily have been chaos. Calhoun, soon promoted to vice admiral, continued as Commander of the Service Force until 1945, and the remarkable cooperation, hustle, and assistance rendered by his command are unforgettable. This was especially true in the advanced areas. Any duty to which the term "service" could be applied was instantly undertaken on demand. This contributed enormously to the fleet efficiency, and, in consequence, to the progress of the campaign.

No single command contributed so much in winning the war with Japan as did the Service Force of the Pacific Fleet. It served all commands, none of which could have survived alone. Neither could all of them combined have won without the help of the Service Force. It is deserving of much higher public praise than it ever received, and, most of all, its activities should be a matter of deepest concern and study by all who aspire to high fleet commands.

At the time of the Pearl Harbor attack, the Base Force had a few more vessels than in 1940, but otherwise was substantially unchanged. . . .In San Francisco, it [the Base Force] was represented by the Base Force Subordinate Command (Rear Admiral C. W. Crosse), which had been established in June of 1941 to give quicker and more direct service on the West Coast and to aid in more efficient procurement and shipment for the mid-Pacific.

The early Service Force was organized around four squadrons: Two, Four, Six and Eight:

- Squadron Two included hospital ships, fleet motion-picture exchange, repair ships, salvage ships, and tugs.
- Squadron Four had the transports and the responsibility for training. This was the tiny nucleus of what eventually became the great Amphibious Force, or Forces.
- Squadron Six took care of all target-practice firing and of the towing of targets, both surface and aerial. Six also controlled the Fleet Camera Party, Target Repair Base, Anti-Aircraft School, Fleet Machine Gun School, and Small Craft Disbursing.
- Squadron Eight had the responsibility for the supply and distribution to the fleet of all its fuels, food and ammunition.

Growth and changes came. In March of 1942, the name was changed to Service Force Pacific Fleet. Headquarters had already moved ashore from the USS *Argonne* to Pearl Harbor Navy Yard, and later moved again to the new administration building of the Commander in Chief Pacific, in the Makalapa area outside the navy yard. In July of 1944, the Service Force moved into its own building, a huge three-story, 600-foot structure adjacent to the CinCPac headquarters. The organizational and administrative changes were dictated by the increasing requirements of the war.

Squadron Four was decommissioned and its transports given to the Amphibious Force. By the summer of 1942, the rapidly changing conditions of the war caused a further reorganization and Service Force was realigned into four major divisions: Service Squadrons Two, Six, and Eight, and Fleet Maintenance Office. Except for some additional duties, the functions of the three numbered squadrons remained unchanged. The Fleet Maintenance Office took over all hull, machinery, alteration, and improvement problems involving battleships, carriers, cruisers, and Service Force vessels.

The Service Force Pacific Subordinate Command at San Francisco continued its original functions and expanded as the tempo of the war mounted. It became the logistic agency for supplying all South Pacific bases.

By August of 1942, operations in the South Pacific were of such critical nature, with the campaign against the enemy in the Solomons and Guadalcanal about to begin, that the Service Squadron South Pacific Force was authorized to deal directly with Commander in Chief, Commander Service Force Pacific, and Commander Service Force Subordinate Command at San Francisco. . . .

Guadalcanal Logistics Review

Vice Admiral Robert L. Ghormley had been Commander South Pacific (ComSoPac) since May 1942. As such he was charged with the conduct of the Guadalcanal operation under the overall direction of Admiral Nimitz. In late July 1942, not counting attack transports which are considered combatant vessels, we had 15 logistic vessels in the South Pacific.* The repair ship *Rigel* was in Auckland, New Zealand. At Tongatabu were the destroyer tender *Whitney*, hospital ship *Solace*, stores ship *Antares*, the fresh and frozen food ships *Aldebaran* and *Talamanca*, the ammunition ship *Rainier*, and two district patrol craft, YP-284 and YP-290, both with provisions. Two more YPs, the 230 and 346, were at Efate, New Hebrides. The seaplane tender *Curtis* and the two small plane tenders *McFarland* and *Mackinac* (the former a converted destroyer) based at Noumea, New

---

* Technically the transports were still APs at the time of the landings. They were not converted and redesigned APAs until early 1943. —Ed.

Caledonia, while the limited repair ship *Argonne* sailed 10 July 1942 from Pearl for Auckland.*

Fuel Shortages

In late July 1943, the fleet oilers *Cimarron* and *Platte* were to be at Tongatabu to supply oil for the amphibious force ships staging, and the fleet oiler *Kaskaskia* was scheduled to leave Pearl on 20 July. At Noumea, there were to be 225,000 barrels of fuel oil brought by chartered tankers, and the same amount brought about 2 August. Over at Tongatabu, the old, slow Navy tanker *Kanawha,* with a capacity of 75,000 barrels, was station oiler.

On 19 July, the chartered tanker *Mobilube* arrived at Tongatabu, but after fuel had been pumped from her into Rear Admiral Noyes' *Wasp* group of Task Force 18, Rear Admiral Kinkaid's *Enterprise* group of Task Force 16, and two of the transports, the *President Adams* and *President Hayes.* The latter pumped the rest of her cargo into the *Kanawha* and left for San Pedro 27 July.

The vital importance of an adequate supply of fuel, and its timely and properly allocated delivery to the vessels of the South Pacific for the campaign about to begin, was clearly recognized by Ghormley, ComSoPac. The distances involved, the scarcity of tankers, and the consumption of oil by task forces operating at high speeds made the solution of this logistic problem difficult enough if the normal operating consumption was used for estimates. But what would constitute "normal" when the offensive was underway? Even more difficult to resolve was the margin of safety to cover unforeseen losses, excesses, or changes in operations. Furthermore, though Ghormley foresaw the situation and tried to anticipate it, his logistic planners were too few and had too little experience. That he had his fuel requirements constantly in mind is shown by his dispatches to Nimitz. Another thing that worried him was the lack of destroyers for adequate

---

* For a list of "Early Bird" service force vessels that arrived in the South Pacific in 1942, see the Ship List at the end of this chapter. —Ed.

escort and protection of his tankers even when he had the latter. This shortage of destroyers was felt by the task force commanders also and had considerable influence on all the operations.

In a dispatch of 9 July 1942, Admiral Nimitz said to Ghormley that he, Commander in Chief Pacific Fleet, would supply the logistic support for the campaign. Arrangements, he stated, had been made to have the oilers *Cimarron* and *Platte* accompany Task Force 11 leaving Pearl Harbor for the South Pacific, and that the *Kaskaskia* would leave soon after, about 20 July. The *Kanawa* would fuel Task Force 18 and then go to Noumea. The chartered tankers, already mentioned as bringing 450,000 barrels of fuel to that port, would be followed by others with about 225,000 barrels a month for the carrier task force. Nimitz also promised other requirements, such as aviation gasoline, Diesel fuel, and stores for the task force, would be supplied as Ghormley requested.

All this sounded like a comfortable amount of fuel oil and, based upon past experience, no doubt seemed liberal to the estimators. But past experience was not good enough. To begin with, the *Cimarron* and *Platte* had fueled Task Force 11 on its run down from Pearl. On 21 July, the *Platte* was ordered to pump her remaining oil into the *Cimarron,* proceed to Noumea, and refill there from the waiting chartered tankers. She took aboard 93,000 barrels of that oil and rejoined Task Force 11.

On 28 July, Admiral Ghormley ordered the ammunition ship *Rainer* and the tanker *Kanawha* to leave Tongatabu and proceed to the west side of Koro Island in the Fiji group. The ships were to arrive, escorted by Turner's amphibious Task Force 62, at the earliest practical time during daylight. The fleet tanker *Kaskaskia* was also ordered there to supply the needs of the Task Force which was to rendezvous there before proceeding to Guadalcanal. . . .

While this was occurring, Task Force 16, the Anzac Squadron, and part of the Amphibious Force joined Task Force 11 and took all the *Cimarron's* remaining fuel. As soon as the *Platte* rejoined, the former tanker was sent to Noumea to refill. She cleaned out the tankers there. The 225,000 barrels due at Noumea in the chartered tankers *E. J. Henry* and *Esso Little Rock* had already been diverted (one tanker to Efate, one to Suva), so Ghormley could hardly be blamed for feeling uncomfortable about the fuel-oil situation. [He desperately needed fuel] for his 3 carriers, 1 fast battleship, 11 heavy cruisers, 3 light cruisers, 40 destroyer-type ships, 19 large transports, 1 large and 3 small aircraft tenders, 8 service force vessels, and 499 airplanes of carrier- and land-based types. . . .

To remedy this acute shortage, on 1 August, Admiral Nimitz ordered the 2 large, fast tankers then available at San Pedro to proceed at the earliest possible moment to Noumea with black oil for diversion by Ghormley. This was in addition to the 200,000 barrels ordered delivered every 15 days. The *Gulfwax* was also ordered to sail from Pearl to replenish the storage supply at Samoa. The next day the tanker *Sabine* left San Pedro for the South Pacific, but would not reach the Fijis before two weeks had elapsed. . . .

With poor bases at Auckland, N.Z.; Fiji; Tongatabu, Tongo Islands; Noumea, New Caledonia; and Efate, New Hebrides, and the beginning of another one at Espiritu Santo, also in the New Hebrides, the Guadalcanal operation was begun. Not one of these bases was much more than a small airfield and a protected anchorage for ships while they took on fuel or supplies from service vessels.

Auckland was the "best" base because New Zealand could furnish food and some repair facilities; however, it was too far from the scene of operations. Tongatabu had no facilities other than a little storage convenience established by us, and it was also too far from the scene of operations. It was selected at a time when our caution was at its peak because it provided a submarine-protected anchorage behind reefs and was well beyond the range of Japanese land-based planes.

Of all of them, Noumea seemed the most suitable at this time. Its anchorage was large enough for all ships and was well-protected against submarine attack by islands and mine fields. Efate Island had two harbors, Vila and Havannah. The former was too small for more than one or two combatant ships, and the latter, while large enough at that time, had no protection against submarines. Suva in Fiji was, like Vila, too small, and the larger anchorage at Nandi was then unprotected.

So, with a far-from-desirable logistic situation and with the expectation of strong Japanese resistance, perhaps even full naval strength, the audacity of the Guadalcanal operation was evidenced in bold seizing of the initiative. The principal credit for this probably should go to Rear Admiral R. K. Turner, who was ever in the forefront in planning, directing, and carrying out an operation with skill, persistence, drive, and great courage. He thoroughly understood the difficulty of the support problem and worked unceasingly with all concerned in logistics, as he did with troop and combat-ship commands. He not only could, and did, think in the large, but he could also when necessary attend to small details such as procuring kegs of nails or bundles of steel landing mat. Reverses or confused action did not discourage him, but made him only the more persistent in having the action improved. Rear Admiral R. K. Turner's farseeing knowledge of the preparation in logistics in his campaigns throughout the war further served to mark him as the greatest of all amphibious commanders.

(Source: Carter, *Beans, Bullets, and Black Oil*, 1–10, 23–34.) ∎

❖ ❖ ❖

Editor: Rear Admiral Carter goes on to highlight the bloody six-month struggle for Guadalcanal. He also recounts the seven naval engagements between the American and Japanese fleets including America's severe defeat at Savo Island and its decisive victory in the three day Naval Battle of Guadalcanal.*

In the following excerpt from Vice Admiral George Carroll Dyer's chapter on logistics in *The Amphibians Came To Conquer—The Story of Admiral Richmond Kelly Turner,* Dyer

---

* For more on the six-month struggle for Guadalcanal, see William L. McGee, *The Solomons Campaigns, 1942–1943—Pacific War Turning Point*, Vol 2. —Ed.

summed up the four most apparent reasons for the slowness with which the Advance Bases Guadalcanal-Tulagi (code word: Cactus-Ringbolt) took shape in comparison to the speed and efficiency of many other Advanced Bases in the Pacific.

Logistics: August 1942–February 1943

1. There was no adequate Base Plan developed by higher echelons of command prior to the assault landing.

2. The Base Area was under Japanese gunfire or air attack a far greater number of times during the first four months of building than other bases. There was a definite lack of appreciation by the officer in over-all charge, Rear Admiral Turner, of the part that defensive tasks were playing in absorbing the time and energies of the Base Commander.

3. The lack of a clear mission at the Base Commander's level, with the immediate senior in command (Major General Vandegrift) being primarily concerned with work which would contribute promptly or directly to his offensive or defensive potentialities, and the next senior in the chain of command (Rear Admiral Turner) keeping a constant eye to future use of the Base.

4. A large amount of fuzziness in command lines with five seniors (ComSoPac, ComGenFirstMarDiv, ComAirSoPac, ComPhibForSoPac and ComSeronSoPac) all sending dispatches and letters direct to the Base Commander.

Editor: Dyer also described the Base Commander turnover during the early months of the Guadalcanal-Tulagi campaign:

At Guadalcanal, where the top commander of the two bases (Guadalcanal and Tulagi-Gavutu) had his headquarters, there were three changes of command at this level: Captain W. G. Greenman, USN; Captain Thomas M. Shock, USN; and Captain William M. Quigley, USN.

Captain Greenman lasted a month (7 November-12 December 1942) as he developed pneumonia and had to be shipped back to Pearl Harbor.

Captain Shock served from 12 December 1942 to 11 May 1943, then had to be invalided home. He had more than satisfied his Boss and the Army awarded him a Distinguished Service Medal. Although Guadalcanal took its toll on all ages, it was tougher on the older men. Greenman was 54 and Shock was 50.

Captain Quigley arrived 12 May 1943 and eventually received the promotion to Commodore which had been urged but never approved for his predecessors. Under his able command, the Advance Naval Bases of the Southern Solomons further developed and provided highly effective support, both operational and logistic, for the New Georgia Campaign.

At the Tulagi-Gavutu Base, there were four different commanding officers in less than five months: Lieutenant R. W. Pinger, D-V, USNR; Lieutenant Commander John C. Alderman, USN; Commander William G. Fewell, USN; and finally Commander Oliver O. Kessing, USN, soon to be promoted to Captain.

Commander James P. Compton, the first Commanding Officer of CUB One, also served for a short time as Commander Advanced Bases, Cactus-Ringbolt, before being named Chief Staff officer to Captain Greenman in November 1942.*

There was certainly no excuse for that kind of officer churn. The responsibility for seeing that the men at the front were well fed, clothed and armed should not have been passed around like some hot potato. This was finally recognized with the appointment of Captain Worrall R. Carter, USN, as Commander Naval Bases, South Pacific Force, in January 1943, after another plea from ComSoPac in November 1942 that "planning and development bases in this area are a major problem" but only after

---

* CUB is an advanced base unit consisting of all the personnel and material necessary for the establishment of a medium-sized advanced fuel and supply base. LION, the big brother of CUB, is a large advanced base unit consisting of all the personnel and material necessary for the establishment of a major all-purpose naval base. LION One on Espiritu Santo is visited later in this chapter. —Ed.

CominCH Admiral King had approved the creation of this additional echelon of command.

From a safe distance of 27 years, it may be pointed out that none of the operation orders dealing with WATCHTOWER [Guadalcanal] issued by naval command echelons prior to the landing, provided for scheduled or automatic resupply over the first 30 to 60 days of the operation. These orders contained no particular details regarding the follow-up movements for the *tremendous* logistic support which would be involved in building an Advanced Air Base, or the other essential facilities of a small Naval Operating Base at an overseas location.

CinCPac [Admiral Nimitz] issued his orders for building the Advanced Air Base by CUB One on 8 July 1942 but the Commanding Officer of CUB One did not receive a copy of it until after the [Guadalcanal] landings of 7 August 1942. This is logistics at its very worst, when the support forces are a month late in getting the word about the operations.

That the Line of the Navy, even those at the top echelon, learned fast about logistics is evidenced by this testimony of its senior officer in 1944: "This war had been variously termed a war of production and a war of machines. Whatever else it is, so far as the United States is concerned, it is a war of logistics. . . .The profound effect of logistics problems on our strategic decisions are not likely to have full significance to those who did not have to traverse the tremendous distances in the Pacific."*

(Source: Dyer, *The Amphibians Came To Conquer*, Vol. 1, 403–434.) ∎

⁘ ⁘ ⁘

---

* Quotation attributed to Admiral Ernest J. King to the SecNav, 23 April 1944.

Editor: Continuing from RAdm Carter's *Beans, Bullets, and Black Oil:*

More Logistics Build-Up in the South Pacific

By late fall of 1942, ammunition depots had been established at Noumea and Espiritu Santo, with a smaller one at Efate. All three handled aviation ammunition as well as larger materiel. There was more for the flyers at Guadalcanal.

Fuel-oil supply storage had been erected on Ducos Peninsula at Noumea with a capacity of 370,000 barrels of black and 30,000 barrels of Diesel fuel, together with a pier at which vessels could be unloaded and supplied. Our ships sailed on water but they moved on oil and the demand never ceased.

Over on Efate, at Vila, we had seven 1,000-barrel steel tanks for aviation gasoline, two 10,000-gallon Diesel tanks, and four buried 5,000-gallon aviation gasoline tanks, while at Havannah eight other buried tanks held 5,000 gallons each.

In the Tulagi area, we had ten 1,000-barrel tanks plus 12,000 barrels of aviation gasoline, a 60,000-barrel Diesel-oil storage, and a 280,000-barrel fuel-oil farm. Guadalcanal added storage for 1,300,000 gallons of aviation gasoline.

The storage, like the demands, mounted steadily. By July of 1943, we were erecting fifty 10,000-barrel fuel-oil tanks on Aore Island at Espiritu, as well as tanks holding 20,000 barrels of Diesel fuel, 17,000 barrels of motor gasoline, and twenty-three 1,000-barrel aviation-gasoline tanks. The fuel unit at Espiritu from November 1943 was one of the busiest of the many supply functions. Before that, fueling of the fleet had been by means of station tankers and incoming oilers.

The tank farms and fifty 10,000-barrel storage tanks were connected with a pipeline system and pumps capable of handling 350 gallons a minute. While the amount in storage was not large or the pumping rate high, in the light of previous close escapes from fuel shortages it was a comforting reserve equivalent of about five tanker-loads. In November 1944, the Noumea facilities were no longer necessary and dismantling was commenced.

The consumption of fuels and lubricants was tremendous. At Tulagi alone during the early part of 1943, the motor torpedo boats burned up 3,000 to 7,000 gallons a day and the airplanes about a thousand. By the end of that year, the PT boats burned about 5,000 gallons a day and the planes 5,000 to 10,000 gallons. Petroleum products carried afloat averaged 219,830 tons (approximately 1,300,000 barrels) a month for the first half of 1943, and were steadily increasing.

By October 1943, ComServRonSoPac sent a dispatch to Commander Subordinate Command San Francisco saying that his estimate of 17 black-oil tankers was not considered sufficient to fill the future requirements. It must be remembered that in this was included both fleet and shore supply, ServRonSoPac being responsible for both. This proved before six months had elapsed, not only that Ghormley's estimate of the previous August for the area had not been too large, but on the contrary, too small.

Lion One, Espiritu Santo

The mere technical definition of a LION as "a large advanced base unit consisting of all the personnel and materiel necessary for the establishment of a major all-purpose naval base" conveys little to anyone but those who have had experience with such an undertaking. In the South Pacific, LION One, under the able command of Captain J. M. Boak (later a commodore), by July of 1943 was rapidly making Espiritu Santo our principal base in the area. In detail, it consisted of facilities as varied as our needs. Its torpedo overhaul unit could handle five or six torpedoes a day. An aviation engine overhaul had a huge shop of many buildings, full of machinery and staffed with expert personnel capable of reconditioning 200 engines a month—no small activity in itself. The ship repair unit was completely housed by this time. Some heavy machinery had not yet been installed, but the general equipment and facilities were expected to be complete within a month and be capable of executing repairs as well as could be done by a regular repair ship.

The administration unit consisted of seven departments: operations, ordnance, captain of yard, supply, disbursing, receiving station, and executive. These covered in separate detail not only the activities ashore, but also boat pool and water transport system, the operation of the port director's service, inshore and harbor patrols, and so on.

The supply department had 36 buildings, each 40 by 100 feet, for general stores. The actual business done by its clothing and small stores section during May 1943 amounted to $175,000. On 28 June, needing more help, it received 244 seamen to supplement the 200 storekeepers and strikers already assigned.

Under the executive department came the six sections devoted to: clerical, fleet post office, welfare and recreation, Chaplain Corps, communications, and intelligence.

The LION, moreover, included activities for issuing pay checks, for camp maintenance, eight dispensaries completely equipped and staffed, and a 600-bed hospital. War involved not only tremendous effort and expenditure, but the systematic care of men.

Ammunition

The fast ammunition supply set up at Espiritu Santo was established by CUB One, the smaller brother of LION One. It was soon apparent that this was not sufficient and a much larger depot would be required. The first wave of munitions landed in December 1942, and from that time the stock continued to increase until September 1944, when it reached its peak. . . .

The depot overhauled and reconditioned a considerable amount of materiel, including more than 40,000 rounds of 5-inch/38-caliber, with the replacement of the projectile fuses. Until mid-1944, issues were made largely direct to the ships concerned. As the war moved westward, this grew steadily less and ammunition ships were loaded at the depot to go forward with the supply. At peak activity in March 1944, the depot serviced 120 vessels, large and small. . . .

In the torpedo overhaul shop at Espiritu, both fleet and aircraft torpedoes gave the 2 officers and 11 men more than they could do. . . .A mine depot at Espiritu Santo assembled and supplied the mines for any project. There was also at Noumea an ammunition depot with about 100 small magazines, 40 or 50 warehouses for ordnance materiels, all of them steel, and a large area of open storage, including mines and torpedoes.

Provisions and Stores

By the end of 1943, the Naval Supply Depot at Espiritu was operating on a 24-hour basis. Earlier in August, it had serviced its first large task force as a unit, though there had been individual vessels taken care of from time to time before that. Following the initial landings on Bougainville, three large cruisers were rushed down from there to Espiritu, a distance of more than 900 miles, for badly needed supplies. In short order they were loaded with 150 tons of provisions and general stores by means of barges securing alongside them in the stream.

At this time in late 1943, the supply storage unit, besides its sixty 40 by 100 feet warehouses, had extensive outdoor storage space approximating 400,000 square feet filled with supplies of all kinds. The fleet provision unit, with 24 large "reefers" (refrigerator boxes or rooms), and 5 warehouses had been receiving and issuing quantities of both fresh and dry provisions. Storage capacity was 2,500 tons of dry and 1,500 tons of fresh and frozen provisions.

The incoming stores section had the job of cargo segregation, and both this section and the outgoing stores unit were kept exceedingly busy. The supply depot had been constructed partly by plan, partly by trial and error. It had handled and issued large quantities of war materiels, worked its men overtime many a weary day, been cursed roundly any number of times, but had come through. At the depot, pier 4 extended some 200 yards into Segond Channel, and was capable of loading 2 large ships at once. Often it was impossible for the numerous vessels requiring supplies to secure alongside No. 4. In such cases ships' working parties were brought ashore, trucks were loaded with the necessary materiel and driven to another pier, unloaded into boats, and the supplies delivered by boats and barges alongside the waiting ships. . . .

Welfare and Fleet Recreation

Of importance among the many advantages officers and men alike of our forces enjoyed to a far greater degree than was possible for those of either the enemy or our allies, was our provision for relaxation and recreation, afloat as well as ashore. As far as was possible in the circumstances, our men were given under war conditions, the same types of recreational facilities they had enjoyed before the war at home. The effect upon general morale was admirable, the uplift healthful in every activity. The damning that was heard—and there was plenty of it, for sailors are notorious growlers—was mostly conversation, and did not result from the work or the overtime and mental strain.

Aore Island, for example, had a fleet recreation area which consisted, in addition to the swimming beach, soda fountain, and beer "parlor," of nine softball diamonds, one hardball diamond, three tennis courts, four volleyball courts, three basketball courts, one football and soccer field, three boxing rings, horseshoe courts, eight handball courts, and a theater district. Barbecue pits and picnic facilities rounded this out with something for nearly everyone.

Mafia Island also had a fairly large area for the Pallikulo Bay crowd, and many other recreation facilities were scattered about the Espiritu Santo base. . . .

At Havannah Harbor, Efate, there was a recreation area of less pretension, and it was while R. C. "Ike" Giffen's force was at anchor, some 8,000 cases of area beer were "lost" in shipment. It was suggested that they had been mistaken for landing-boat fuel as some of "Ike's" liberty boats handled poorly for a time. The laughter was as good a tonic as the missing beverage.

Maintenance and Repair

Naval battles mean hurt ships. The damage may be light relatively, or it may be serious. Whatever it is, the nearer the repair facilities the better.

Only in the most serious cases of major injuries beyond the ability of local facilities to repair, should a combatant vessel be sent back to a navy yard or shipyard. Such action takes the ship out of the active fleet for a considerable period, weakens our forces proportionately, may delay pending moves, and further exposes the cripple to attack en route while not in proper condition to fight off her enemy.

During early operations, our repair ships and advanced bases did everything they could, and the ship's forces themselves often accomplished wonders in patchwork and repair. These, however, were not sufficient, and floating dry-docks of various types and sizes were urgently needed. Ships had their bows blown off, their sterns blasted away, huge holes torn in their hulls by torpedoes whose explosions created a chaos that had to be seen at the time to be fully realized. Japanese shelling and bombing wrecked engine rooms, put turrets out of action, and touched off tremendous fires and magazine explosions that made the survival of the battered vessel almost a miracle. By getting the victim into a dock where she could be given full attention while still in the supporting area, priceless time and effort were saved repeatedly and the enemy could not know just how hard he had hit us at times.

By late fall of 1942, we had installed a ship-repair unit and a floating dry-dock, ARD-1, at Noumea. The floating docks of this type were 485 feet long and had a lifting capacity of 3,500 tons, which made them able to accommodate destroyers, submarines, and "landing ships, tank" (LSTs). . . .

The ship-repair unit was in operation by the summer of 1943 at Espiritu Santo, but it was never commensurate in size or capacity with some of the other activities there. Most of its effort was spent on necessary routine and emergency repairs to patrol craft, auxiliaries, landing craft, merchantmen, and vessels of the United Kingdom. It did, however, do some battle-damage repair work for our ships of all types, including fleet destroyers. Much of this was minor, thanks to later good fortune of war, and it was done well and willingly. . . .

In the Solomons at Florida Island—where as a starter we had only a motor torpedo boat base at Saspi, Tulagi, with the tender *Jamestown* concealed across the harbor against the mangrove jungle—in the spring of 1944 we had at Purvis Bay the AFD-13, destroyer tender *Whitney*, the repair ships *Medusa* (en route to southwest Pacific) and *Prometheus*, the battle-damage repair ship *Aristaeus*, and the repair barge YR-6. Valuable services were rendered. In addition to these floating services there were landing-craft repair units at Carter City on Florida Island near Purvis Bay and in the Russell Islands. Large boat-repair stations were at Turner City and at Gavutu Harbor on Florida. . . .

During the early part of the war practically all the work on small ships was done in New Zealand to take advantage of the docking facilities there. In January and March of 1943, the *Portland* and *New Orleans* went to Sydney, Australia, because major cases of battle damage could be handled only there. It became a fairly common practice also to send cruisers, destroyers, and similar ships there for dry-docking and rehabilitation.

During the early part of the war practically all the work on small ships was done in New Zealand to take advantage of the docking facilities there.

At Auckland, N.Z., repair facilities were such that 4 vessels of the attack-transport type could receive overhaul concurrently with smaller craft. The major part of the work was assigned to His Majesty's New Zealand Dockyard at Bevenport. When the jobs were greater than its capacity, they were farmed out to 112 independent firms, coordinated by the liaison officer in Auckland. In Wellington, a cargo ship could be completely overhauled while routine repairs and materiel work were being carried forward on 3 other similar vessels. Dunedin could give a cargo ship a complete overhaul but could not do simultaneous repair work.

All this repair work in New Zealand was under the direction of the Materiel Department of the Force Maintenance Office, and included repairs to materiel under the cognizance of armed guard officers on all War Shipping Administration vessels. Besides Auckland, several other bases in New Zealand supplied minor repair facilities. Auckland was the most important, however, and in 1943, in 11 months (February excluded), it repaired 282 vessels of all types. The monthly cost of repairs and alterations in this one port ran to about $100,000.

Havannah Harbor in Efate was a deep-water, torpedo-protected port nearer our activities than Noumea, and here for some months a number of combatant ships were based and serviced. On 15 January 1943, the repair ship *Rigel*, which had been doing great work at Espiritu Santo since 20 November 1942, arrived and rendered splendid tender and repair service under the able command of Captain Roy Dudley. She remained until relieved by the *Medusa*, 24 April 1943. Four days later the *Rigel* sailed to join the Seventh Fleet. . . .

The *Medusa* stayed in the New Hebrides until 27 March 1944 when she sailed to join the Seventh Fleet, with which she remained until war's end. . . .

General Activities

The duty of the service forces was not merely to keep abreast of the combatant fleet activities, but as far as possible to go ahead of them by being prepared in all respects before assistance was demanded. The difficulties of such an ambitious yet vital task were so great and depended upon so many elements beyond our control, that no account of the work can be wholly objective. The combat forces acted with greater confidence and dash as they became more aware that behind them waited more of the things they might need in either defeat or victory. The wounded were cared for immediately in the well-staffed and well-equipped hospital ships and base hospitals. The latter were established at Espiritu Santo, where a 600-bed hospital proper was reinforced by no less than 8 dispensaries; there were 2 base hospitals at Noumea—Fleet Hospitals Nos. 5 and 7, the former with about 1,000 beds, the second with about 2,000—backed up by a huge convalescent camp; one in Guadalcanal with 2,000 beds, one at Banika Island in the Russells with 1,300 beds, completed in March 1944; and still another at Efate.

The important supply of fresh or frozen foods was furnished by the fleet provision unit with 24 large reefers and warehouses at Espiritu Santo already mentioned, and 10 ships working out of Auckland to carry their vital freight wherever it was needed. Even this was not enough as our effort grew. In September 1943, the Commanding Officer of Service Squadron South Pacific estimated that he had exactly half enough ships to carry the provisions contracted for in New Zealand for 1944.

The activities there began in April 1942 under the direction of Commander H. D. Nuber of the Supply Corps, whose office was in Auckland. For some months that port was the main supply base and was able to fill the requisitions made on it.

By the time we landed on Guadalcanal, it was apparent that New Zealand was too far in the rear to be an operating base for directly supplying the forces afloat. From that time onward the principal supply to the fleet was made by United States provisions ships and the supply depots on advanced bases at Noumea and Espiritu. Beef, mutton, and other foods were, however, supplied to these sources from Auckland for some time thereafter. New Zealand also continued to supply large quantities of food to the shore forces.

More of everything was being called for day by day. In May 1943, it was reported that 17 more tugs, in addition to the 8 on hand, were needed; two more fuel-oil barges were demanded to supplement the 4 on hand; and 5 gasoline barges were required.

A month later the call for more went out again—9 Diesel-engine repair ships, 3 aviation stores (bulk) ships, 2 destroyer tenders, 6 LSTs as aviation stores issue ships, 4 landing-craft repair ships, 1 landing-craft tender, 10 tugs, 60 LCVPs (a 36-foot single-screw Diesel, built of plywood and very useful in handling stores up to about 5 tons or limited personnel)—per month for 6 months; plus 3 big salvage tugs (ARS's), and 2 motor-torpedo-boat tenders (AGP's). This was a time when the advantages of floating services were manifesting themselves strongly.

Many other facilities of smaller and less spectacular sorts were located at Noumea and Espiritu. Among them were the fleet post offices, with their eagerly perused letters from home, an anti-aircraft gunnery school, fire-fighting school with advisory instructors already mentioned, the motion-picture exchanges, gas plants, sections for the purchase of war bonds, and so on. All these went to make great bases which after a very short period of activity found themselves so far in the rear as to raise the question of whether the amount of shipping required to build them might not have supplied the necessary fleet support afloat, and been mobile and ready to go forward at short notice.

(Source: Carter, *Beans, Bullets, and Black Oil*, 49–62.) ∎

⁜ ⁜ ⁜

Editor: In spring 1943, prior to the New Georgia campaign, Guadalcanal was no longer known in code as "Cactus." The advance base on Guadalcanal was now referred to in dispatches as "Mainyard." In Rear Admiral Samuel Eliot Morison's *Breaking the Bismarcks Barrier, 22 July 1942–1 May 1944*, Morison described his tour of Mainyard with Commander Mainyard, Captain Thomas M. Shock.

"Mainyard"

A main yard it was with a thousand mainland factories and a hundred other bases funneling materiel into the supply dumps around Lunga Point.

To unfamiliar eyes all is a jumble; an office here, a workshop there, supply dumps everywhere. But the whole functions with the precision of the cruiser that "Tommy" Shock lately commanded.

Here is the radio station, underground at last but damp and hot. Watch those dispatches grow on the spindle as the operators translate the whine of the high-frequency into the clatter of typewriter keys. Over there is a switchboard, the telephone exchange.

Do you wish to call the airfield? Which one? There are several now besides Henderson. Suppose you want Public Works, as almost everybody in the Navy does. Which part of Public Works—the power plant, the road gangs, the Quonset hut builders, the telephone linemen?

We ride a jeep down lanes of coconut palms, past rows of green Quonsets. This is the armory, a small part of the Ordnance Department, which also runs an ammunition depot, demolition units, mine detail, torpedo "circus," and defense gun batteries.

Supply Officer is another hard-worked sailor man. Food, clothing, tools and stores of all kinds pass through his worried custody.

On the beach we find the Port Director installed in a hut which affords him a good view of the crowded Lunga roadstead. A cranky "spitkit" fleet, part of which runs regular ferry service to Tulagi, is under his jurisdiction. They are the least of his worries. Scores of small craft need repairs and attention. Merchant ships anchored in the roadstead want lighters and tugs. Transport skippers scream for pilots, charts, berthing and unloading instructions. Unwanted visitors want transportation to Tulagi, Purvis Bay, Aola, the Russells. "Can't send you today, Commander; come 'round tomorrow." No use arguing; he's "fightin' the war."

Captain of the Yard, an old Navy title that brings memories of mellowed stone buildings and green parade grounds, means something very different on this island. Here he is boss of "boys" from Malaita, each dressed in a lava-lava with a hibiscus flower in his startling coiffure, who work on roads, tote cased supplies and build a fine mess hall out of palm leaves (much cooler than imported architecture), all for a shilling a day.

Captain of the Yard is also chief of a fire department that proves to be necessary in spite of the prevailing damp; he runs a stockade enclosing the few Japanese prisoners; he supervises the homely services of mess cook, barber, laundryman and tailor, which are rendered under shrapnel-torn coconut palms.

The Medical Department, under a genial Harvard professor in uniform who is well named Colonel Friend, runs the hospital, pursues "bugs" in drinking water and mosquitoes in swamps and for morale purposes, trains a fine brass band. He wins the battle against malaria and has tropical ulcers—figuratively and literally—on the run. When our troops move up to Bougainville where the mosquitoes are even more numerous and deadly than in the 'Canal, the incidence of malaria will be reduced almost to zero.

With no more necessity to push Japanese off Guadalcanal, there have come the good and the bad of ordered life: motion pictures, daily tabloid full of jokes and gripes, Sunday services, officers' and enlisted men's clubs, a police force, courts martial and boards of investigation.

Captain Shock must also deal with many units beyond his jurisdiction although on the same island. Three hundred planes of the armed forces roost nightly on the Lunga plain; nearby are encamped hundreds of men to serve them with bombs, bullets, fuel and overhauls. Camped in cool, healthy area near Cape Esperance, the 43rd Army Infantry Division practices jungle tactics against the hour of the New Georgia landings. Not far away the 3rd Marine Division is limbering up for the next push.

Across Ironbottom Sound, Captain Oliver O. Kessing—better known as "Scrappy"—gives orders and dispenses hospitality at Government House, Tulagi. The sleepy old Chinatown, abandoned by its inhabitants early in 1942, has been completely razed and a city of huts erected; the cricket pitch of the former British residents has been turned into a baseball field; the golf links have been largely covered with buildings.

Up-harbor, where there used to be a native village called Sesape, a swarm of motor torpedo boats is moored and new barracks for their crews have been built across the harbor at "Calvertville."

On Florida Island, behind Gavutu and Tanambogo, which were captured only last August, Seabees are completing a seaplane base.

Port Purvis, next estuary to the east, is now a fleet anchorage where "Tip" Merrill's and "Pug" Ainsworth's task forces may rest by day. Hard by the Lord Bishop of Melanesia's palm-leaf cathedral, a new officers' club, "the Ironbottom Bay Club," is being built to provide interim refreshment for these night-riding sailors.

As the sun slips under the horizon by Savo Island, we pay social calls on some of the old-timers: Colonel "Harry the Horse" Liversedge, Lieutenant Colonel Griffith Corrigan of the Solomon Islands Native Defense Force. They dispense liquid hospitality from a battered gasoline tin. Sergeant Vouza, hero of the native constabulary, comes out of the shadows clad in GI shirt, loincloth, Silver Star and George Medal. He pays his respects to blond Sam Griffith and tells of hunting down stray Japs, a sport for which he feels proper sympathy is lacking among the newcomers. The talk looks back to Gavutu, the Tenaru and the Bloody Ridge, "the good old days" when we "fit" with General Vandegrift.

(Source: Morison, *Breaking the Bismarcks Barrier*, 100–103.) ■

⁌ ⁌ ⁌

Editor: In the Introduction to RAdm Carter's *Beans, Bullets, and Black Oil,* Admiral Raymond A. Spruance, USN (Ret), discussed planning for future operations in the Central Pacific:

When we started planning in the summer of 1943 for operations in the Central Pacific, it was obvious that the geography of the area which we hoped to capture had characteristics very different from those of the South Pacific. We did not know how fast we would be able to move ahead, but we did know that in the Gilberts, Marshalls, and Carolines, many of the islands had splendid protected anchorages in their lagoons. However, the land areas surrounding the lagoons were very small. These islands were only large enough, as a rule, to enable us to construct the always necessary air strips and to take care of the requirements of the atoll garrison forces. . . .The Marianas we knew had some good-sized islands in the group, but we also knew that not one of them had a protected anchorage large enough for fleet use.

This geography meant that the logistic support for our fleet during operations in the Central Pacific would have to be primarily afloat, in what developed into the mobile service squadron—first Service Squadron Four at Funafuti in the Ellice Islands and then Service Squadron Ten at Majuro in the Marshalls. The small beginnings of the idea in Service Squadron Four were absorbed into Service Squadron Ten soon after the latter came into being in February 1944 at Majuro.

The growth of Service Squadron Ten, its movement across the Pacific to successive bases at Eniwetok, then Ulithi and then Leyte, and its continuous and most efficient service to the fleet at these and numerous other bases where it stationed ships and representatives as our operations demanded, are achievements of which all Americans can be justly proud, but about which most of them have little or no knowledge.

(Source: Carter, *Beans, Bullets and Black Oil,* vii–ix.) ■

Editor: Continuing from Carter, *Beans, Bullets and Black Oil:*

Early in the fall of 1943, Admiral Nimitz ordered Commander Service Force to organize two mobile service squadrons. The idea was that as it advanced across the Pacific the fleet would base on one, capture its next objective, and there upon bring up the second. It would base on the second until still another forward area had been gained, whereupon the first service squadron would leapfrog over the second, and so on alternately. As will be seen later, this scheme was not used; but two service squadrons were nevertheless organized. . . .

Vice Admiral Calhoun designated his chief of staff, Captain H. M. Scull, as commander of the first service squadron to be formed, Squadron Four, to be based at Funafuti. It was commissioned 1 November 1943 and consisted of the destroyer tender *Cascade,* Captain Samuel Ogden, flagship, and 23 other vessels ranging from the repair ships *Phaon* and *Vestal* down through tugs and patrol craft to fuel-oil barges and 500-ton lighters. Captain Ogden was chief staff officer in addition to his duties in commanding his ship.

Rear Admiral Hoover had been ordered as Commander Aircraft Central Pacific to take station at Funafuti in the large seaplane tender *Curtiss,* which serviced the planes of Patrol Squadrons Fifty-three and Seventy-two. He was also senior officer present afloat, which actually made Scull's squadron a part of his command.

The organizational scheme accorded with Admiral Spruance's operation campaign order. This required that Commander Service Squadron Four establish and maintain a mobile supply base at Funafuti to supply the forces engaged; also that Four's assigned ships and others placed under its operational control should conform to the directives, plans, and needs of Commander Central Pacific Force (Spruance). Operational control of harbor facilities in Funafuti was delegated to Scull by Admiral Hoover.

The same command relationships were in force for the Marshalls campaign and the seizure of Kwajalein and Majuro; but in addition to Service Squadron Four mention was made in Spruance's operations order that Squadron Ten was being assembled, and that both Four and Ten were under the operational control of Commander Defense Force and Land Based Air, Admiral Hoover, who later became Commander Forward Area, Central Pacific.

In November 1943, the *Curtiss* and the *Cascade* reached Funafuti. The former remained until 31 December, when she went on to Tarawa, the *Cascade* staying until February 1944. During the November-February period, the *Cascade,* assisted by a rather limited assortment of yard craft, serviced 10 destroyers, 8 destroyer escorts, 6 landing ships (tank), 6 landing craft (tank), and various smaller types. The repair ship *Ajax*, Captain J. L. Brown, was present under temporary control of Service Squadron Four, and made repairs to LST, LCT, and PC types. The Diesel-driven repair ship *Luzon*, Commander E. R. Runquist, repaired landing craft, and the *Rainer,* Commander R. B. Miller, issued ammunition to the heavy cruisers *Chester* and *Pensacola*. On 22 November the *Vestal*, Commander W. T. Singer, after a year's service at Espiritu Santo where she did great work on war-damage repairs, came to Funafuti. Three days later she was alongside the small carrier *Independence* to make emergency repairs—the first war-damage repair undertaken by Squadron Four.

The *Independence*, torpedoed 20 November (D-day), her after engine room flooded, had a ruptured fire main, which left the after part of the ship without water pressure. After the transfer of aircraft and spare parts, and the removal of ammunition and gasoline from the cripple, the *Vestal* removed damaged protruding plating, dewatered and made tight the third deck, installed pipe jumpers to provide fire main pressure in the after part of the ship, and removed some blister plating. On 7 December the *Independence* sailed for Pearl, and thence to the United States for permanent repairs.

The *Vestal* remained at Funafuti doing various repair jobs, large and small, of every description. They kept the *Vestal* busy until she sailed for Majuro on 30 January 1944 to tackle the damage resulting from a collision of the battleships *Washington* and *Indiana* and to become a valuable unit of Service Squadron Ten until the end of the war.

Funafuti was not a good place because of the very rough water, which made boating and servicing difficult for ships and seaplanes. As soon as Tarawa was captured, most of the service except those for deep draft battleships and carriers were moved up to the Gilberts. It was soon clear that the enemy was not going to bring his navy out to contend for the Gilberts, and thereafter our heavy ships did not use Funafuti much but backed away to the better bases at Efate, Espiritu, Nandi, and Pearl.

As the war went on, the number of vessels assigned to the Service Force went steadily upward. With each new campaign our needs increased, and so did the number of ships. By September of 1943 the Service Force had 324 vessels listed, with 136 of them still to report. January of 1944 saw 510 ships listed, and in March no less than 990 vessels had been assigned, 290 of them still under construction or undergoing organization and training. Much of this increase was in patrol craft for Squadron Two and barges for Squadron Eight.

Barges and lighters of all types were being completed rapidly, but moving them from the United States to the areas of use was a problem. Having no means of propulsion, they had to be towed out to Pearl Harbor, and thence still farther westward, in the slowest of convoys. The departure of merchant ships and tugs hauling ungainly looking lighters and barges was not so inspiring a sight as that of a sleek man-of-war gliding swiftly under the Golden Gate Bridge and standing out to sea. Yet these barges, ugly as they were, proved invaluable in support of operations at advanced anchorages.

In February 1944, a new Squadron Ten went to Majuro in the Marshalls, soon absorbed first Squadron Four, and remained the mobile logistics forward area representative of the Service Force until the end of the war.

(Source: Carter, Beans, *Bullets, and Black Oil*, 87–93.) ■

Editor: Carter goes on to describe the invaluable contributions of the service force squadrons as the Fleet sweeps across the Pacific from the Marshalls to Okinawa in 1944 and 1945. However, due to space limitations, we will end our coverage of his history here.

Ship List
1942 Service Force "Early Birds" in the South Pacific

Includes the 23 vessels (APs, AKs, and AOs) in Task Forces 61 and 62 for the Guadalcanal-Tulagi Landings, 7–8 August 1942.

AD Destroyer Tenders
Whitney AD-4

AE Ammunition Ships
Rainier AE-5

AF Store Ships (Fresh/frozen foods)
Aldebaran AF-10
Talamanca AF-15

AG Miscellaneous Auxiliaries
Argonne AG-31 (Tender)

AH Hospital Ships
Solace AH-5

AK Cargo Ships**
Alchiba AK-21
Bellatrix AK-20
Betelgeuse AK-28
Fomalhaut AK-22

AKS General Stores Issue Ships
Antares AKS-3

AO Oilers
Cimarron AO-22
Kanawha AO-1
Platte AO-24
*Sabine AO-25

AP Transports***
American Legion AP-35 F
Barnett AP-11 F
Crescent City AP-40 F
Fuller AP-14 F
*George F. Elliot AP-105
Heywood AP-12 F
Hunter Liggett AP-27 F
*McCawley AP-10
Neville AP-16
President Adams AP-38
President Hayes AP-39
President Jackson AP-37
Alhena AK-26
Zeilin AP-9

AR Repair Ships
Rigel AR-11

AV Seaplane Tenders
Curtiss AV-4

AVD Seaplane Tenders (Destroyer)
McFarland AVD-14

AVP Small Seaplane Tenders
Mackinac AVP-13

YP District Patrol Vessels
YP-230, YP-284, YP-290 and YP-346

*   Lost during Solomons Operations.
**   All AK cargo ships reclassified AKA attack cargo ships in 1943.
*** All AP transports (except *George F. Elliot*) reclassified APA attack transports in 1943.

Source: Composition of Task Force, 2 June 1942. United States Fleet,
Headquarters of the Commander-in-Chief, Navy Department, Washington, D.C.

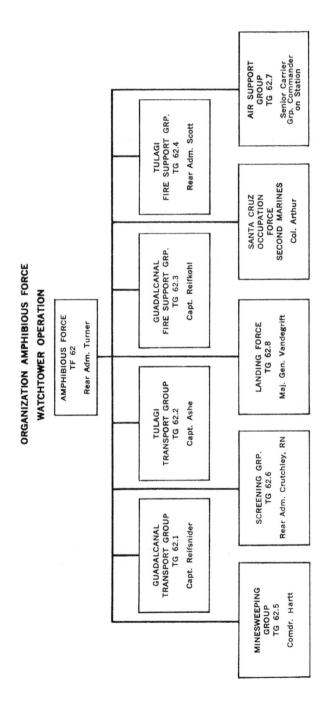

ORGANIZATION AMPHIBIOUS FORCE
WATCHTOWER OPERATION

AMPHIBIOUS FORCE
TF 62
Rear Adm. Turner

GUADALCANAL
TRANSPORT GROUP
TG 62.1
Capt. Reifsnider

TULAGI
TRANSPORT GROUP
TG 62.2
Capt. Ashe

GUADALCANAL
FIRE SUPPORT GRP.
TG 62.3
Capt. Reifkohl

TULAGI
FIRE SUPPORT GRP.
TG 62.4
Rear Adm. Scott

MINESWEEPING
GROUP
TG 62.5
Comdr. Hartt

SCREENING GRP.
TG 62.6
Rear Adm. Crutchley, RN

LANDING FORCE
TG 62.8
Maj. Gen. Vandegrift

SANTA CRUZ
OCCUPATION
FORCE
SECOND MARINES
Col. Arthur

AIR SUPPORT
GROUP
TG 62.7
Senior Carrier
Grp. Commander
on Station

(Source: Dyer, *The Amphibians Came To Conquer*)

Looking north down on station wharf at Pago Pago Harbor, Tutuila Island, Samoan Islands, circa 1942. (USNCB)

Fuel depot, coal docks and lower tank farm. Navy Yard, Pearl Harbor, Hawaii, 16 October 1941. (USNCB)

Control tower on Tafuna Airbase, Tutuila, Samoa, circa 1942–1944. (USNCB)

Guadalcanal landings. Amphibian tractors on the dock at Wellington, New Zealand, 20 July 1942, awaiting embarkation aboard ships of the Guadalcanal Invasion Force. (Naval Historical Center)

Pago Pago, Tutuila Island, Samoan Islands. View from ship alongside station wharf looking west. Note the cargo suspended in sling and trucks being loaded at forward end of ship. (USNCB)

USS *President Adams* (AP-38), 4 August 1942, probably taken at Noumea, New Caledonia, prior to the Guadalcanal operation. (Naval Historical Center)

PBY base showing ramps and fill ground, Epiritu Santo. (USNCB)

Guadalcanal-Tulagi landings. Attack on Solomon Islands. Guns and planes of the Pacific Fleet blast tiny Tanambogo Island, enemy stronghold in the Solomons, just prior to its capture by the Marines on 7 August 1942. In foreground, the famous causeway to Gavutu Island which the Marines crossed under heavy enemy machine gun fire. (National Archives)

Logistics nightmare. Guadalcanal landing site, 7 August 1942. (U.S. Marine Corps)

Sailors unloading gasoline drums from an LCT on the Morobe PT boat base waterfront, July–August 1943. (National Archives)

Marine Raiders maneuver cautiously through the coconut groves keeping an eye out for snipers in the treetops. They are also wary of the enemy elsewhere. (U.S. Marine Corps)

USS *Minneapolis* (CA-36), damaged in the battle of Lunga Point, Guadalcanal, at Tulagi Harbor for repairs. (USNCB)

Cimarron, first ship completed for the U.S. Maritime Commission, as she appeared during her trials in February 1939. (National Archives)

Cuyama (AO-3), shown here in the mid-decade, is beginning to show signs of old age. Fleet oilers were the "work horses" of the fleet. Charged with the task of keeping the fleet in black oil, they were constantly on the move. (Naval Historical Center)

Further evidence of the difficulties experienced by oiler crews as they attempted to conduct fueling operations in heavy seas. Here, *Kaskaskia* (AO-27) with "white water" on the well deck refuels *Enterprise* (CV-6) on 18 August 1942. (National Archives)

Chiwawa (AO-68), taken 20 June 1943. The first of the Bethlehem-built T3-S-A1s, she carried an extensive AA suite of four 3-inch 50s, two twin 40mms, twelve 20mms, and a single 5-inch 38 gun at the stern. (National Archives)

Fueling two ships at one time became the norm in the latter part of World War II. Here, *Kankakee* refuels light cruiser *Montpelier* (CL-57) in the Solomons on 13 January 1944 while a Fletcher-class destroyer approaches to starboard to receive fuel from that side of the oiler. Note the modifications that have been made to improve oiling at sea; particularly prominent are the large combination kingpost/ventilator shafts aft with their huge fueling booms. Other notable features include elevated cargo winches, a spar deck with its cargo of lube oil drums, and the addition of twin 40mm gun positions atop the after deck house. (National Archives)

By the end of World War II, refueling at sea was being conducted on a routine basis and had progressed to the point where two large warships could be serviced at the same time. This maneuver was not as easy as it may appear as there was always the risk that the oiler would be crushed by the two larger ships. Here, *Cahaba* (AO-82), shown 8 July 1945, refuels *Shangri-La* (CV-38) on her port side and *Iowa* (BB-61) on her starboard side. Note the calmness of the seas and the critically small distance between ships. (National Archives)

Chapter 3
The Naval Transportation
Service in World War II

On 26 January 1942, six weeks after the 7 December 1941 attack on Pearl Harbor, the Naval Transportation Service (NTS) was created as an independent division out of the Traffic Section of the U.S. Navy's Bureau of Supplies and Accounts (BUSANDA), Fuel and Transportation Division.

To operate, it required authority over various bureaus within the Navy itself to counteract some of the self-serving tendencies inherent in the naval organization. It also needed to know its relationship to the other agencies that already controlled navy shipping but belonged to other entities. For example, at the outbreak and during the prosecution of the war, the following agencies all controlled ships and shipping in some form, at some time:

- Naval Transportation Service
- Army Transport Service
- Strategic Shipping Board
- U.S. Maritime Commission's War Shipping Administration
- Bureau of Yards and Docks
- Fleet Support Services

The information for this chapter is from the Department of the Navy, Bureau of Supplies and Accounts, and is derived from the official documents, "History of the Transportation Division," dated 1 June 1944.

- Marine Corps
- Joint Military Transportation Command

According to the Joint Action Plan created before the war, the U.S. Navy was to handle all overseas shipments. The Army was to turn over the Army Transport Service and its assets, but this did not happen. Even so, one would expect the control of the Navy assets to have been clearly defined, but this, too, was not to be. The functions and responsibilities of the Naval Transportation Service were not clearly understood by other offices or bureaus in the Navy Department. Various agencies simply bypassed the NTS and satisfied their shipping requirements by any means necessary leading to inefficiencies, increased costs, and, more importantly, delays in getting vital materiel to the front.

NTS Mission and Organization

The mission of the NTS was not quite clear even to those in the organization. The source document from which this chapter is derived described it as a "kind of schizophrenia or split personality which has persisted from the beginning."

On the one hand, the NTS regarded itself as a shipping line that operated ships. Thus, it expected to man, operate and maintain those ships. The NTS expected to act as a fleet or task force, loading goods as ordered, and delivering where needed. This appears to have been the intention of the War Plan that provided for the Navy to "man and operate" the Army Transport Service and to "provide transportation" for the movement of forces overseas. Navy officers, although not thrilled with the operation of merchant vessels, felt this was a natural extension of their duties. Furthermore, the Navy was tasked with protection of the merchant fleet as well. In fact, the Navy was tasked with routing, escorting, and arming merchant vessels (hence the Naval Armed Guard), which then moved under Navy convoy escort. All in all, it was logical for the consolidated control of overseas shipping to be under Navy cognizance.

Intention and reality immediately clashed. The Navy lacked the personnel to man such ships. It did not have the organization to control them. (The NTS, formed after the attack on Pearl Harbor, had approximately two dozen employees.) And, perhaps most importantly, it had no liaison with the Army to effect such a change. In fact, in February 1942, when the War Shipping Administration was authorized to operate ships for the Army and Navy by Executive Order #9054, the Naval Transportation Service was excluded from any major participation in the operation of such a fleet.

So the operation of such a fleet fell to others. The NTS, even when vessels were assigned to it, almost immediately turned them over to other organizations. At the conclusion of the war, almost 4,000,000 deadweight tons of shipping were under Navy control, but the NTS operated only about a dozen ships.

On the other hand, this brings up the other side of the split personality, the NTS as a logistic agency acting in an administrative capacity for overseas transportation as part of a larger organization, the Bureau of Supplies and Accounts. In short, once the need for a shipment was determined, the NTS found the ships to deliver it. This "freight forwarding" function was the focus of the NTS for the entire war. In fact, that was its focus until 1949 when the Military Sea Transportation Service (MSTS) was formed from the core of the NTS. Even then, the Army and Navy argued about the setup.

As if traffic management and the movement of massive amounts of war fighting materiel were not challenge enough, other important tasks faced the NTS. They included the procurement of non-military type vessels for use as Naval auxiliaries; planning requirements for the Navy for overseas shipments; and administration of a system of port directors, both in country and at established bases overseas.

Instead of the original plan, penned between the Maritime Commission and the Navy in 1939, which called for the Navy to receive ships on a bareboat or time charter basis after they had been requisitioned by the commission, the Navy received allocations of ships, often for a single voyage. The Navy, that is, the NTS, acquired some 80 vessels, including provision ships, cargo carriers, transports, tankers, and hulls for conversion to auxiliary aircraft carriers. Most were turned over to the commission to be operated in a pool of ships targeted to transport goods as required by the military as a whole. Only when it was demonstrated, as in the case of fleet oilers and assault transports, that the ships should be manned by naval personnel, did the War Shipping Administration allow the ships to be transferred to direct Navy control.

The War Shipping Administration (WSA) policy called for increased efficiency of each vessel assigned to the Army or Navy for any given voyage. Upon delivery of shipments, the vessels reverted back to the WSA for loading and routing on the homeward voyage. The military, for security (and to maintain control), wanted long term control of the vessels.

The WSA, while maintaining its position, never fully settled the issue. Instead, high-level policy was left for the Joint Military Transportation Committee (JMTC) under the Joint Chiefs of Staff, which first met in March 1942. This committee provided overall guidance, but did so informally for nearly a year until it was granted a charter by the government acknowledging what it was already doing. The primary purpose of the JMTC was to coordinate the planning of the Army and Navy. This planning was supposedly settled in the Joint War Plan, which was immediately dropped at the beginning of the war leaving a void filled with bureaucratic in-fighting.

The result was that the NTS was to determine the Navy's particular requirements for shipping at which time the ships would be allocated. Thus, the planners had a huge responsibility and the difficult task of determining both the amount and timing of materiel required. Given the fluid nature of war in general, and war in the Pacific in particular, this was to be no easy task.

Transportation Planning

To conduct shipment planning and provide the requirements to the WSA, the NTS needed to know what initial movements were occurring and thus require materiel, what cargo would be shipped, and usage or experience factors with the various vessels in which the materiel would be shipped. It did not know any of these three items. To exacerbate the situation, the military felt the information flow should be from the logistics planners (in NTS) to the operational planners (military leaders) and that military leaders should not have to explain where, when, or why they were going to use the assets. This, however, was the exact information NTS had to provide to the WSA in order to get the necessary shipping allocated. As a result, the first estimate for shipping made by the NTS had very limited premises and stated, "No provision is made for requirements for shipping." The estimate of 53 additional vessels, in addition to the 60 the Navy already possessed for the six months following the estimate, proved grossly inadequate to the true need. And no improvement in the estimates was in sight or sought. The NTS had no way of knowing the factors by which the shipping requirement could be determined and wasn't pushing to get the information.

The Army was more specific and estimated a need for 590,000 additional troops overseas, some 110 cargo ships then under Army control, and an additional allotment of 18 ships per month for the remainder of the year.

This was enough to cause the NTS to scramble to update its estimate. It asked the Assistant Chief of Staff (Plans) for an estimate of the shipping required by the Navy for the remainder of 1942. The reply was that it was the function of the NTS to determine shipping requirements. Nevertheless, the Assistant Chief of Staff (Plans) proposed an estimating formula based on the last three months' shipping requirements, separating the requirements based on the Navy's area of operations for the Atlantic, Pacific, and Asiatic fleets, and adding a 50 percent factor for "possible" extended operations in the Pacific.

Since the NTS had no other way of estimating shipping, and was not to be out-done by the Army, it used the formula and updated the estimate to WSA from 53 ships to 106 vessels.

In fact, the need actually realized was for nearly twice the tonnage in the Navy's estimate. Had the pooling system initiated by the WSA not been in place, the Navy would have suffered greatly for such poor estimating and planning. Additionally, the pool system called for periodic review of requirements based on monthly allocations. This allowed NTS planners to get more accurate estimates and made the procurement of vessels easier. Even so, during submission of an estimate for 12 months leading into 1943, the NTS was so wide of its mark that three days after the estimate, a draft urgent request was sent to the WSA for an additional 50,000 tons for the first month of the estimate alone.

According to the NTS historian, the Navy was in constant danger of "embarrassment from its inability to forecast accurately" both with the WSA and the Joint Military Transportation Committee. In fact, embarrassment should have been the least of the worries of the NTS. There were fighting men on front lines who needed the supplies and materiels and they couldn't wait three months for the estimates to be accurate.

Attempts were made to improve the "back door method NTS had to use to acquire data," but mostly to no avail. If it were not for the efforts of some dedicated and persistent Port Directors working for the NTS, the year 1942 would have been even worse.

Port Administration

The best prepared part of the NTS system at the beginning of the war was the Port Director system. While still in peacetime, District Offices were set up in principal U.S. ports. Instructions were issued concerning mobilization of vessels for war, and procedures for convoy and routing were issued. The Navy carefully selected the port directors after a study of the problem. As a result, on 7 December 1941, there was a well staffed, instructed, and standardized system of continental port direction.

The War Plan called for the merchant fleet to be taken over by the Navy. This mobilization devolved to the Port Directors. They administered the movement of personnel and passengers to these ships as well as loading and unloading. They planned for the fueling and provisioning of the vessels, and, most importantly, they issued instructions directly to the captains or masters of the vessels and to convoy commodores for routing and communications procedures.

In spite of outstanding efforts in accordance with pre-war plans, the plans were modified when the war started. The WSA cut into the procurement and mobilization of the merchant vessels from the port directors. The NTS fleet was never as large as envisioned and thus the task of personnel management and husbanding by the port directors was reduced. The overall duties of the Port Director were reduced to harbor movements, berthing, routing, communications, and convoy formation.

The Port Director reported to the Commander-in-Chief as part of FX-37 for convoy concerns, and reported to the Chief of Naval Operations (CNO) and, more immediately to the NTS, for all other concerns.

As a result of this confused state of affairs, differences between port director responsibilities developed based on the personalities present and local political concerns. For example, on the West Coast, loading of vessels was the responsibility of the port directors; on the East Coast, loading was supervised by Navy supply officers.

The decentralized control of shipping and split chain of command for the port directors, as well as differences in the magnitude of the shipping between coasts, engendered sharply contrasting organizations and structures on the two coasts. San Francisco handled the largest portion of the supplies and war materiels for the war effort in the Pacific and thus developed a method of controlling the flow of goods quickly.

San Francisco: Point of Embarkation

When the war broke out, the Port Director in San Francisco had Piers 48, 49, 50A, and 50B in operation and was prepared to expand them. Further, he was ready to man them with stevedore labor. Thus, established stevedore labor was used to load vessels under the control of the Port Director.

The Naval Supply Depot in Oakland was still in pre-commissioning status, so the tasks were left to agencies already performing them rather than shifting to another model. This meant a Navy Supply Officer was responsible for loading the ships in Oakland. He, however, was not ready with an established stevedore labor pool. As a result, labor was recruited at the gates of the supply depot, something the San Francisco Port Director found disconcerting.

The Vice Chief of Naval Operations stepped in and established the Base Service Unit which was to work with the Naval Supply Depot in an advisory capacity, assisting them in the assembly, inspection, and preparation for shipment of materiel delivered to the depot. The Base Service Unit was designated to assist the Port Director in "loading."

Overseas Port Logistics

No consideration had yet been given to the logistic aspect at the other end of the supply chain—the various overseas island ports at which the supplies and materiel were discharged. There were no Port Directors from the NTS at overseas locations. The unloading of vessels was handled by in-theater military commanders as they saw fit.

The problems of overseas discharge of goods were noticed in April 1942 when Captain Davis, Port Director for San Francisco, sent an officer with stevedoring experience on a BOBCAT movement. (BOBCAT was code name for an Advanced Base standard materiel shipment.) The subsequent report noted shortages of equipment and weaknesses in the organizational structure. For example, the officer noted the low priority assigned to the task of discharging cargo (thus putting ships in danger of attack for longer periods and delaying the turnaround time of the vessels). He described the lack of supervision over working parties assigned to stevedoring (which were likely military personnel with little or no experience unloading vessels). He further noted lack of coordination with ashore organizations and between Army and Navy units in the same locale.

This lack of liaison in operational theaters extended from those theaters back to the NTS. This want of liaison between Washington and the operational areas was felt in the lack of shipping control and the lack of information flowing back to NTS for it to make accurate estimates of shipping needs. The shipping problem thus grew in breadth and complexity as the Pacific war escalated. The NTS appeared unable to cut across the tangled skeins of established practice and organization to establish itself as the dominant and controlling agency for transportation.

In late 1942, the difficulty and inefficiencies in the movement of supplies and war materiel came to a peak for several reasons including the widening operations in the Pacific, increased loss of vessels, and congested ports such as Noumea, New Caledonia, resulting in large numbers of merchant vessels waiting to discharge cargo in order to return for another load.

The WSA responded by trying to take further control over shipping. This effort, however, deprived the military services of control over the means of completing their assigned operations. The two factions continued to fight one another until they finally established a balance that kept goods flowing in spite of a shortage of shipping and no centralized control.

To further complicate the problem, a subcommittee report to the Joint Military Transportation Committee in February 1943, critical of the WSA, noted that "the shipping position of the United Kingdom is ever more critical than that of the United States." This provided impetus for a subsequent decision by President Roosevelt, after conferring with Prime Minister Churchill, to direct additional shipping to support the British. The WSA, attempting to comply, thus decreased the shipping available on the Pacific side.

The Navy finally recognized the crisis and the numerous competing parties involved, and began a search for the means to tighten the entire logistics structure.

Centralized Control

The first improvement made was to involve operational commanders in the estimates for shipping resources. The Navy authorized the disclosure of operational plans on a need-to-know basis to those attempting to coordinate shipping and logistic requirements. Further, the estimate would include personnel, supplies and materiel to establish Pacific bases, and also the maintenance requirements for such bases as well as the forces afloat.

This was the first time the Chief of Naval Operations had authorized the dissemination of operational plans for logistic purposes. This, too, was the first time theater commanders were required to submit maintenance requirements for bases and forces afloat.

As important as this improvement was, no provision was made for the continuation of this procedure. It was limited to the estimate created for December 1942 to June 1943.

A second improvement designated the Naval Transportation Service as the processing agency for the correlation and control of priorities for overseas shipments in the Pacific. Since this came from the Commander-in-Chief, i.e., the President and the Chief of Naval Operations, this was truly the birth of the NTS as the controlling agency for shipping logistics. Other bureaus were directed to supply the NTS with the requisite information to fulfill its functions, and since the order came from the very top of the Navy and government chain of command, the principle of centralized control residing in the NTS was finally established in fact.

A third improvement involved the establishment of port organizations by all theater commanders, as directed by the Vice Chief of Naval Operations (VCNO), to expedite the turnaround of cargo vessels and transports. The VCNO stipulated that the names of the port directors and their locations be transmitted to the NTS.

The very next day the directive was issued to the Bureau of Yards and Docks to organize special battalions of Seabees for stevedoring operations. The NTS immediately suggested that the battalions be coordinated directly under NTS authority and attached to the Port Directors organization wherever assigned.

Given the "status" of the NTS as indicated by the President and CNO, and the issues that had developed in Noumea where significant numbers of merchant vessels were delayed while waiting for the unloading of cargo—which hampered the war effort and increased the loss of merchant vessels as they lingered in port—the recommendations of the NTS were heeded. The NTS was in charge.

Army and Navy Coordination

At the end of 1943, the NTS was in control of overseas shipments. However, the Army was still submitting proposals for consolidation of logistics using Army methods. It was doing so at the urging of the WSA, which had requested closer coordination between the Army and Navy.

The needs of the two services were different and each had unique methodologies. The Army calculated maintenance requirements on a ton-per-man-per-month basis and was fairly accurate. The Navy based its planning on ships rather than men. Many ships were mobile; many were new. Thus, the location for support and the level of support—given that no usage data was available on the newer platforms—made the estimating problem significantly more demanding.

The Army thus wanted consolidation and the Navy wanted coordination. The Navy's position was that finally a centralized and newly functioning (if not yet efficient) organization controlled by the NTS existed. Changing it at this point would hamper the war effort. In March 1943, the two services reached agreement and published it in the "Basic Logistical Plan for Common Areas Involving Joint Army and Navy Operations."

Control of Theater logistics was ceded to locale military commanders under joint staffs. While this prevented the extension of NTS authority into operating areas, it did provide for a single point of contact for the NTS to coordinate shipping. Additionally, it decentralized the newly centralized system of shipping control. It did ensure that merchant ships in operational areas were efficiently utilized, space-wise, and were in direct support of operational requirements—that is, they were directly supporting the war fighter, the ultimate goal.

The remaining problem for the Naval Transportation Service was still the complete definition of its mission and the provision of a suitable organization to carry it out. The characteristics of the logistics problem were only just becoming clear in 1943.

(Source: Department of the Navy, Bureau of Supplies and Accounts, Report, "History of the Transportation Division," 1 June 1944.) ∎

Editor: In 1949, after the Second World War—and barely before the Korean War (1950–53)—the Naval Transportation Service (NTS), with the Army's agreement, became the Military Sea Transportation Service (MSTS) and took control of all overseas shipping needs. However tentatively, the joint era had begun. In 1970, the MSTS became the Military Sealift Command (MSC).

Chapter 4
Builders at the Front

"Every time I pass a bulldozer, I want to stop and kiss it."
—*Admiral W. F. Halsey, USN, Guam, 1945*

Principal sources for this chapter are the Department of the Navy, *Building the Navy's Bases in World War II—History of the Bureau of Yards and Docks and the Civil Engineer Corps, 1940–1946,* Vols. 1 and 2 (1947); and Lieutenant (jg) William Bradford Huie, CEC, USNR, *Can Do! The Story of the Seabees* (1944).

In addition to the above sources, special thanks are due the following who provided firsthand accounts of Seabee contributions, both of the construction and stevedore battalions: Lieutenant Mark H. Jordan, CEC, USN (Ret), and former Executive Officer of the famous Sixth Naval Construction Battalion, for furnishing a rare copy of the Battalion's history, "Saga of the Sixth: A History of the Sixth Naval Construction Battalion, 1942–1945"; Captain Larry G. DeVries, CEC, USNR, for sharing both his manuscript, "Builders at the Front," and *WWII Naval Journal* story, "Seabees on Guadalcanal"; Al Don, USN (Ret), former editor of the Seabee newsletter, "Can Do," for his critique of an early draft of this manuscript; Claude S. Gulbranson, USNR, and Secretary for the First "Special" Naval Construction Battalion, for furnishing a copy of the privately published, "History of the First Special U.S. Naval Construction Battalion, 1942–1946"; and the Marine Corps Historical Center for copies of "Engineering on Guadalcanal" (1944) and "Building Under Fire—Marine Corps Engineers" (1944).

Editor's note: This chapter profiles the engineering and construction skills of the U.S. Marine Corps and the U.S. Navy. The U.S. Marine Corps Engineers are profiled as their actions are chronicled on Guadalcanal during America's first offensive of World War II. This is followed by profiles of the two types of U.S. Naval Construction Battalions—or Seabees as they were called: the "NCB" for construction and the "Special" NCB for stevedoring. The chapter concludes with a summary of the many early Advance Base construction projects built in the South Pacific.

Special thanks are due the following authors who contributed firsthand accounts to this chapter: Lieutenant Mark H. Jordan, CEC, USN (Ret), and former Executive Officer of the famous Sixth Naval Construction Battalion; Captain Larry G. DeVries, CEC, USNR; and Claude S. Gulbranson, USNR, and secretary for the First "Special" Naval Construction Battalion.

U.S. Marine Corps
"First Ashore, First to Fight!"

Editor: The following monograph from the U.S. Marine Corps, "Engineering on Guadalcanal," describes the birth of the Marine Corps Engineers and their unsung special Pioneer unit of the First Marine Division. The monograph provides the background to understanding the difference between the young combat engineers trained primarily as infantrymen, and the seasoned Seabees—long on construction skills, but ready to fight when the need arises. It also provides yet another perspective on the Guadalcanal story.

Engineering on Guadalcanal

Since the founding of the Marine Corps on 10 November 1775, the "Soldiers of the Sea" have been primarily riflemen. But developments in military science forced the creation of special units trained for specialized tasks. Although small Marine Engineer units had been in existence for a number of years, the strength of the Corps was too small to warrant a separate Engineer Service. The early events of WWII, however, indicated the necessity of a larger proportion of engineer troops in combat divisions and so the Marine Corps Engineer Service was born. In the Guadalcanal campaign, components of this newly organized branch received their baptism of fire.

Among the special units comprising the 1st Marine Division were the 1st Pioneer Battalion and the 1st Engineering Battalion. Companies of these units were attached to infantry regiments and distributed throughout the troop transports comprising the Task Force. On the morning of 7 August 1942, the big guns of the escorting combat ships covered the landing of the infantry. In the boats carrying the leading infantry elements were small detachments of Pioneers and Engineers. As the infantrymen moved inland to establish the beachhead, the attached Engineers accompanied them while the Pioneers remained to organize the beach.

Pioneer officers immediately checked the actual terrain along the beach with the mental impressions they had obtained from studying aerial photographs. Markers were landed and set up to indicate the limits of the beach and the unloading points for various types of supplies and equipment.

Pioneer gun crews set up machine guns and prepared to keep hostile dive-bombers at a respectful distance. Very little time elapsed before boatload after boatload of essential materiels were being ferried from the transports and cargo ships lying off-shore. When these boats hit the beach the Pioneers took charge and manhandled stores across the soft sand and placed them in the beach dumps under cover of the coconut trees.

Small tractors driven by Pioneer operators were among the first pieces of motorized equipment ashore. These were needed to snake the large trucks and field guns out of the ramp boats and through the shallow water to the security of solid ground. The ultimate success of the landing operation depended on the rapid and efficient handling of many tons of combat stores in this initial phase of the operation. Pioneers struggled hour after hour under the blazing tropical sun carrying heavy loads through soft sand until they were moving on will power alone. When the Jap planes came over they dropped their loads and manned their guns. They won the admiration of the division by their performance.

In the first few hours after the landing, the Engineers accompanying the infantry threw an improvised bridge across the Ilu River which enabled the supporting heavy weapons and light supply vehicles to cross with no delay. Since the initial landing was made on a beach about four miles east of Lunga Point, and because the Japanese airfield was the key to the whole situation, the infantry units pushed rapidly ahead to secure it. This left the beach-head proper relatively undefended and the Engineer Battalion was called upon to organize a defensive position around it. True, it was a sketchy defense because of the length of the perimeter and the small number of troops to hold it, but it released badly needed infantry to do the more important job.

During the next few days the division moved to the area around the captured airfield, and the mountains of supplies and equipment landed by the Pioneers had to be hauled from the beaches to the supply dumps in the vicinity of Lunga Point. This movement was made by truck and the Engineers were required to erect temporary bridges across one river and to strengthen and rebuild existing bridges across others to enable them to pass the division loads.

The challenges were considerable:

(1)   In the initial landing, the Engineers lay vehicle paths of burlap covered with wire mesh over the sandy beaches.

(2)   The fierce tangle of the jungle was then cleared preparatory to building much needed roads and trails.

(3)   Deep jungle mud made even jeep travel difficult until better roadbeds were available.

(4)   Captured Japanese rollers were pressed into service as the Marine Engineers begin building the airfield.

(5)   As combat conditions permit, the Engineers improve the roads so heavy vehicles and additional traffic can proceed.

(6)   Quickly built pontoon bridges to allow troops and supplies to move forward over many streams.

(7)   Modern equipment soon has the fighter and bomber strips ready to handle the combat traffic soon to arrive.

Japanese attacks by air and sea were increasing in tempo. Our cargo ships and transports were forced to leave before they were completely unloaded. Consequently, only a small percentage of the engineer equipment was landed and, as a result, this unit had to rely on field expedients from the very start. Fortunately the Japs left a generous supply of heavy timber and no time was lost in utilizing it for construction purposes.

The primary job of the Engineer Battalion was to complete the airfield so that our own aircraft could use it. The Japs had done an excellent job on the landing strip, but they had started its construction from the ends and were working toward the center. When the engineers arrived there was a gap to be filled that required the movement of approximately 10,000 cubic yards of earth. A simple job if earth moving machinery had been available, but it wasn't. Engineers turned to with captured hand shovels, a few trucks—none of which were dumps—and a few small gasoline powered rollers. These latter pieces of equipment were found on the field somewhat the worse for wear. Splinters from the bombs and shells so liberally sprinkled over the area by our opening bombardment had completely ruined many of them. But the repair section of the Engineer Battalion salvaged parts from the more seriously damaged and repaired a few. The Jap machinery was pretty poor compared with high grade American made machines but it was better than nothing.

Earth was moved from the borrow pits by using Japanese dynamite to loosen it, shoveling it into trucks by hand, and then shoveling it out where needed. Working under the broiling tropical sun on short rations day after day was trying. But to this was added the hazards of working in the "V" ring of the bull's-eye from the Jap bombers point of view. They endeavored to slow up progress by dropping both high explosive and delayed action bombs along the landing strip. It was not possible to stop construction and the probability of casualties had to be accepted. Engineers dug the bombs out when necessary, exploded others in place, and then filled the craters.

About three weeks after the initial landing, work on the airfield had progressed in a satisfactory manner in spite of the Nipponese efforts to stop it. The landing strip was complete enough to take the planes several days ahead of schedule. Toward five o'clock one evening the air was filled with the hum of many motors. Men ran for the shelter of slit trenches. Then, as they gazed heavenward with curses on their lips, their eyes made out the big white stars on the wings of U.S. aircraft, and their curses turned to cheers. Fighter planes circled in perfect formation high overhead as the dive-bombers came sliding gracefully down toward the field. Around the edges of the strip tense-faced Engineers stood holding their breath, and as the wheels of the leading plane touched the ground lightly, an audible sound of relief was heard. As the plane slowed down and swung off the strip to a taxiway many watchers cheered and many throats were tight. After the last plane had landed safely, Engineer working details collected their tools and slowly walked away, but there was a spring to their step which seemed to say, "We did not fail."

Work continued on the airfield until a contingent of the 6th Naval Construction Battalion (Seabees) arrived September 1, 1942 to relieve the First Engineering Battalions. The engineers gladly relinquished the construction of the landing strip and its appurtenances to the Seabees and turned to their tactical engineering missions so necessary to the support of the infantry.

From the start of the operation, there were several other essential tasks that had to be performed concurrently with the airfield construction. The supply of pure water was an engineer function. The Water Supply Section of the Battalion set up and operated portable and mobile water purification units. These units filtered and chlorinated the river water which was then pumped into 3,000-gallon canvas storage tanks. Distribution was effected by means of two-wheel water trailers and the standard 5-gallon expeditionary cans. These units in operation supplied on an average of 40,000 gallons per day. The ability of the operators to make repairs under trying conditions with limited tools and improvised parts kept the units in almost constant operation in spite of occasional damage from bomb shell splinters.

Because supplies and ammunition had to move continually, the construction of roads and bridges was a major problem. When the infantry pushed their defensive lines deeper into Japanese territory, new supply roads—commonly called jeep tracks—had to be provided. The two angle-dozers with carryalls, power shovel, and half dozen dump trucks landed late in September for the Engineer Battalion were used extensively in this work. To see the sturdy American machinery cut its way through tropical jungles was a real pleasure. But the heavy demand for all types of work still necessitated lots of hand labor. When the supply of captured construction materiel was

Because supplies and ammunition had to move continually, the construction of roads and bridges was a major problem.

exhausted, natural materiels had to be used exclusively. Coconut logs were the handiest and were very plentiful; consequently they were used for every imaginable construction project.

Road blocks, anti-tank mine fields, land mines, anti-personnel mines, and some barbed wire entanglements were installed and maintained by the Engineer units. Demolition parties assisted the infantry by blasting holes for machine gun emplacements in the rocky ridges. The angle-dozers were occasionally used to clear fields of fire for infantry organizations dug in on jungle defense lines.

The usual procedure for Engineers is to "fight all day and work all night" but that was reversed in this campaign. During the first month and a half both the Engineer and Pioneer Battalions were camped in the jungle on the perimeter of the beachhead. Later they were moved to defensive sectors on the beach itself. The normal construction work and unloading activities were carried on in daylight, but when darkness fell these battalions were in their defensive positions. Many sleepless nights were spent with Japanese patrols in contact with their outposts. Because the Nips launched their big assaults at night these units participated in several heavy engagements. But the dawn always found them going back to their normal daytime routine.

When the 1st Marine Division left Guadalcanal, the Pioneer, Engineer, and Naval Construction Battalions were combined under a single head. Their missions still remained the same: namely, shore party work for the Pioneers, combat functions in direct support of the infantry for the Engineers, and heavy construction for the "Seabees." However, this general similarity of equipment and work warranted the unified command. And that is, in general, the present organization of the Marine Engineer Regiments.

After all is said and done, these Marine Pioneer Battalions are not so far removed from their pioneer forefathers who built their cabins and plowed their fields with their rifles within easy reach. Basically, these Marines are still riflemen, and as their trucks and tractors are building in the jungle, their rifles are kept within easy reach.

(Source: U.S. Marine Corps, "Engineering on Guadalcanal,"
Headquarters Bulletin, January 1944.) ∎

Building Under Fire, Marine Corps Engineers

Editor: Lieutenant Colonel James G. Frazer, USMC, served as the first Commanding Officer of the 1st Marine Corps Engineer Battalion on Guadalcanal from 7 August to 24 October 1942. In the following excerpt from *Building Under Fire—Marine Corps Engineers*, he related the challenges and focus of these fighting engineers who are "first on the beach."

The Marine Corps Engineers are a fighting part of a fighting team. Engineer organizations are heavily equipped with infantry weapons and the men are basically trained as infantrymen. Fighting to protect what they have built is not a catch phrase or a recruiting slogan. It is an expected and relished part of the job. In the Pacific Theater, Marine Divisions were used to spearhead certain offensive operations. The engineer units accomplish under fire the technical work so necessary to the successful completion of an attack. Attack planning is based upon the rapid completion of every task, utilizing local and natural materiels to the utmost. No attempt is made in the initial phases to perform heavy or permanent types of construction, which are left for follow-up units equipped for that type of work with heavy equipment.

An important engineer task commences as the bow of the first landing boat scrapes on the beach. When a landing is made on a hostile shore, the attacking troops must bring with them tremendous quantities of supplies and equipment. As this materiel is brought ashore from the transports and cargo ships, a shore party, also known as a Pioneer Unit of the Marine Engineer Regiment, takes over. It is their function to unload the small boats and move the supplies and equipment across the beaches into dispersed dumps. Shore party units are usually equipped with light tractors, bull-dozers and cranes for improving beach facilities and performing salvage operations. The shore party also is equipped with quantities of beach roadway matting. When this materiel is laid over the soft sand, it provides sufficient support for vehicles to move freely from the ramp-type landing boats to the firm ground.

Combat engineers were used as infantry for the first two days on Guadalcanal. They organized a defensive position to protect the supplies on the landing beach while the infantry pushed westward toward Lunga Point. When the Japanese base was captured, the engineers moved to the vicinity of the airfield, laid down their weapons, picked up their tools and started work. Japanese air and surface attack forced the Navy Task Force to withdraw before many of the ships were completely unloaded, leaving the engineers with no heavy earth-moving equipment and a very limited supply of hand tools. Reconnaissance parties located Jap supplies of construction timber, explosives and some machinery and utilized these and other expedients from the very start.

Marine Corps Engineers repaired some Jap trucks and these, along with the train and a few American trucks, hauled dirt to the air strip. Captured dynamite was used to loosen the earth, and captured hand shovels were used to load it.

When the original Combat Engineer Battalion was relieved of its work on the airfield [by the Sixth NCB] the personnel devoted their energy to other combat missions in all parts of the Division area. As the infantry pushed the Japanese back, road construction became a pressing problem. . . .Roads were pushed through while the engineers were harassed by sniper and mortar fire. In a few cases, cableways were erected across ravines, saving many hours of back-breaking work for carrying parties.

Bridges, on the other hand, presented an easier problem. Highly satis-factory floating foot bridges were improvised from scrap lumber and empty gasoline drums. These bridges were placed across streams within defensive positions to facilitate the rapid lateral movement of infantry troops. On one occasion a bridge of this type was constructed under artillery fire.

A small amount of standard military portable bridge equipment was available for vehicular bridges, and proved to be worth its weight in gold. It was used as a tactical bridge and was replaced by a permanent bridge as soon as conditions permitted, thus keeping the portable bridge available for emergency use.

(Source: Frazer, "Building Under Fire – Marine Corps Engineers," *Engineering News-Record*, February 1944.) ∎

Editor: The Marine Corps Pioneer units ensured the materiel was delivered to the beachheads enabling the Engineer battalions to commence the initial building of infrastructure. Then, while the battle continued to rage, the Navy's Seabees followed to build the extensive facilities that enabled the full effect of the Navy-Marine Corp team to be felt.

❖ ❖ ❖

U.S. Navy

Editor: When the Navy needed men who not only could build but also could take up arms and defend themselves and their installations, the U.S. Navy's Bureau of Yards and Docks organized the Naval Construction Battalions—popularly known as the Seabees (for the initials "C.B."). These battalions were made up of construction workers, officered by construction experts, and trained in combat method. Their motto, "Can do," was brilliantly proven in action.

The following excerpts profile the contributions of two different types of Seabee battalions—the Naval Construction Battalions for construction, and the "Special" Stevedore Naval Construction Battalions for stevedoring.

The Department of the Navy's comprehensive two-volume work, *Building the Navy's Bases in World War II—History of the Bureau of Yards and Docks and the Civil Engineer Corps, 1940–1946,* profiles the duties and responsibilities of the two specialties in the Naval Construction Battalions as well as the Civil Engineer Corps.

U.S. Navy Bureau of Yards and Docks (BuDocks)

The record of the Bureau of Yards and Docks, the Corps of Civil Engineers, and the Naval Construction Battalions in World War II is the story of a small component of the Navy which had a specific mission to support the Fleet, and which met that challenge by quick initial action, by meteoric expansion, and by the creation of new means and measures to achieve its objectives. Their role in the expansion of the naval shore establishment in the United States and the building of advance bases overseas enabled our armed forces to carry the war to the enemy's home waters, by sea and air, and to conquer him on his own soil.

The Bureau of Yards and Docks (hereafter "BuDocks") was a branch of the United States Navy and was established in 1842 to build and maintain navy yards, drydocks and other facilities relating to ship construction, maintenance and repair.

As the amount of wartime construction increased, it became evident that the Bureau's form of organization was no longer suitable for the greatly increased volume of work involved. As a result, on 1 December 1941, BuDocks was reorganized into five departments: Administration and Personnel; Progress Control and Statistics; Finance and Operating; Planning and Design; and Construction. As the war progressed, a sixth department, the Advance Base Department, was organized on 5 January 1944.

A senior officer of the Civil Engineer Corps was placed in charge as director of each department. Each department in turn was subdivided into divisions dealing with specific aspects of the work. The divisions, in turn, were subdivided into sections and sub-sections.

Before the Limited National Emergency was declared in 1939, there were fewer than 200 persons employed by BuDocks in Washington. By December 1941, the number had passed 1,000; by August 1944, almost 2,000 were employed.

When the Naval Construction Battalions (NCB) were authorized in January 1942, two departments of BuDocks worked closely with the NCB: Administration and Personnel, and Advance Base.

Administration and Personnel Department.   On 5 January 1942, the time of the authorization of the NCBs, four divisions were set up in the Administration and Personnel Department: Construction Battalion Recruiting Division, Construction Battalion Operation and Personnel Division, Construction Battalion Training and Inspection Division, and Construction Battalion Materiel Division.

The Construction Battalion Recruiting Division was established to expedite Seabee enlistments through meetings, publications, and other forms of publicity. This division also kept records of, and set standards for,

Seabee ratings. (This division ceased to operate in August 1944 when the recruiting program ended. From that time on, new Seabees were handled through the Bureau of Naval Personnel and the manning levels were replenished by inductees.)

The Construction Battalion Operation and Personnel Division was first organized in the Bureau; later it was transferred to the Bureau of Naval Personnel. The functions of this division were to establish complements for the battalions, handle movement and formation, maintain schedules of training and readiness dates, handle records of promotion recommendations, and maintain liaison on rating and promotion of enlisted personnel.

The Construction Battalion Training and Inspection Division established training policies and the inspection, supervision, and direction of Seabee training activities. This division was transferred to the Bureau of Naval Personnel in July 1944. Although the two divisions which were transferred to the Bureau of Naval Personnel became integral parts of that Bureau, they were manned by officers of the Civil Engineer Corps and they cooperated closely with BuDocks.

The Construction Battalion Materiel Division was charged with handling administrative and policy matters in connection with equipping, outfitting, and refitting construction battalions for duty overseas. Later the division was divided between the Advance Base Department and the Planning and Design Department.

Advance Base Department.   The Advance Base Department maintained liaison with the Chief of Naval Operations (CNO) and other Bureaus on Advance Base matters. This department made schematic studies of advance base layouts; developed new types of gear for advance base construction and operation; procured, tested, and shipped advance base gear; and had cognizance of the Advance Base Depots at Davisville, R.I.; Port Hueneme, Calif.; Gulfport, Miss.; and Tacoma, Wash.

U.S. Navy Civil Engineer Corps (CEC)

In 1867, the Navy created its Civil Engineer Corps (hereafter "CEC"), a staff corps of the United States Navy whose officers were professional engineers and architects, and acquisitions specialists. They were responsible for executing and managing the planning, design, acquisition, construction, operation, and maintenance of the Navy's shore facilities.

The expansion of the CEC's duties coincided with the expansion of United States bases and interests overseas, especially from approximately 1892 onward.

(Source: Dept. of the Navy, *Building the Navy's Bases in WWII*, Vol. 1, iii, vii, 61–71.) ∎

⁌ ⁌ ⁌

Editor: Lieutenant (jg) William Bradford Huie expands on the history of the CEC in *Can Do!:*

Prior to 1892, the United States had no bases outside the continental limits. On their few adventures outside continental waters, U.S. warships utilized friendly ports and the coaling stations maintained for merchantmen. The British fleet was master of the seas and, since Britain was generally friendly, the U.S. fleet concerned itself with North America. In line with our foreign policy as expressed in the Monroe Doctrine, the Navy was not an offensive weapon; it was the "first line of defense." In 1879, CEC officers surveyed a site at Pago Pago, Samoa. In 1892, the United States' first small but avowedly foreign base was opened there.

With the Spanish War, the U.S. extended its commitments from Puerto Rico to the Philippines. Unfortunately, the naval establishment did not expand proportionately, though Congress did authorize a few foreign developments. Work was started at Pearl Harbor in 1901; Puerto Rico in 1902; Olangapo in the Philippines in 1902; and at Guantanamo Bay, Cuba, in 1903. Dutch Harbor, Alaska, became a naval coaling station in 1902.

During World War I, there was some expansion of the shore Navy, but most of it was in the continental bases. It wasn't until 1938, after Munich and after Japanese intentions in the Pacific became obvious, that Congress took the shackles off the U.S. military.

The CEC, still working through private contractors with civilian labor, began to expand fuel, flight and housing facilities at overseas bases. Puerto Rico was still the most "Advanced Base" in the Atlantic. In the Pacific, there was Pearl Harbor, and that was primarily the extent of the U.S.'s naval presence. The tenuous line through Midway, Wake, and Guam to Cavite in the Philippines was too long, too thin, and too weak to be called a line of defense.

At the end of 1939, the Corps comprised 126 regular officers. By 1945, 10,186 were on duty.

> Editor: In January 1942, the challenges facing Rear Admiral Ben Moreell, CEC, USN, wartime Chief of BuDocks, were substantial. Continuing from Huie, *Can Do!:*

To iron out all organizational red tape, Admiral Moreell relied upon Captain John R. Perry, CEC, USN, a tall, red-headed Texan who specialized in damning torpedoes and driving full speed ahead. The first hitch developed over officers. To obtain officers, the CEC proposed simply to expand itself; to seek out construction engineers, commission them according to their civilian attainments, and put them in command of the Seabees. But command had always been the prerogative of line officers of the Navy. The CEC had never commanded; why should it now? Reluctantly, the Navy agreed to the innovation, and the CEC began commissioning civilian engineers for the Seabees in ranks up to Lieutenant Commander.

The second organization snarl was over "rates" [Ratings] for Seabees. Navy system called for every man to enter the Navy as an apprentice seaman with promotion to come only after he had proved himself in uniform. Normally this is an excellent plan, but the times were abnormal. Men wanted for the Seabees were skilled, experienced men; most of them had families; the draft wouldn't reach them for years. They would volunteer, but only if they had [financial] support for their wives and children.

Captain Perry asked the Bureau of Naval Personnel [successor to the Bureau of Navigation] for permission to enlist men for the Seabees in rates up to and including chief petty officer. This would mean a sliding scale of pay and allowances for Seabees from $50 to more than $200 a month. Naturally, the "regular" Navy men—men who had served in the Navy for sixteen years to become chief petty officers—would resent thousands of newly created Seabee rates. Captain Perry pointed out, however, that the Navy recognized civilian attainment in commissioning officers, and he contended that this same practice should prevail in enlisting men.

These two major concessions by the Navy—the granting of command to CEC officers and the approval for rates-on-enlistment for men—made the Seabee organization possible. The CEC expanded itself from the 126 officers of the 1930s to more than 8,000 officers [during the war], most of whom were assigned to the Seabees. The men were enlisted at an average rate of petty officer second-class—average pay and allowances $140 a month—making the Seabees one of the highest paid organizations in the service.

In short, the Navy made it possible for the cream of the construction industry to join the Navy "en masse." The civilian engineers became officers; the foremen became chief petty officers; the carpenters, machinists, earthmovers, etc., became rates in the ranks. The Navy did more than make an alliance with the construction industry; it simply absorbed a large portion of the industry with amazingly successful results.

In this process of absorption the Navy enjoyed the cooperation of both management and labor unions. The construction companies were asked to release all the engineers who could be spared, and most of them responded quickly.

The labor unions moved more cautiously. . . . [and wanted] a guarantee that Seabees would not be used on continental projects. . . .Admiral Moreell refused to give such a guarantee. He did, however, assure the unions that the Seabee organization was being built primarily for Advance Base work; that the CEC expected to continue building all continental facilities by private contract and civilian labor. . . .On this assurance he asked the unions for their cooperation in the recruiting drives, and most of the unions lent their aid. The Building Trades Council of the American Federation of Labor was particularly helpful. Approximately 80 percent of all men in the Seabees were union members.

(Source: Huie, *Can Do!* 61–64, 83–85.) ■

❖ ❖ ❖

Editor: Lieutenant Mark H. Jordan, CEC, USN (Ret), and former Executive Officer of the Sixth Naval Construction Battalion on Guadalcanal in 1942, recalled in a letter to the editor:

CEC officers were initially appointed from civil life and inputs from this source continue to this day, via either NROTC (Naval Reserve Officer Training Corps) or OCS (Officer Candidates School). The assignment of Naval Academy graduates to the Corps started about 1906. . . .The Naval Academy has never dominated the CEC. When I entered the Corps in 1940 (one of three Academy grads that year), the regular Corps, then about 120 strong, divided more or less equally between the Naval Academy and civilian sources.

The granting of command to CEC officers was indeed a major concession. In fact, the title first given to commanding officers of Seabee battalions was "officer in charge," a term which implied limited authority. Actually, under an order issued by the Secretary of the Navy in March 1942, officers in charge of Seabee units had all the authority of commanding officers. It was not until 1951 that the title became "commanding officer" in reality.

The men chosen were sent to a first-rate engineering school for a three-year course in civil engineering and upon graduation they became officers of the CEC. As such, they were not command officers (command was reserved strictly for officers of the line) but Engineering Duty Only officers in the line, concerned only with planning and contracting for whatever shore installations were authorized by Congress and ordered by the Secretary of the Navy.

(Source: Lt Mark H. Jordan, CEC, USN [Ret], letter to editor, 2 August 1996.) ■

Editor: Continuing from Huie, *Can Do!:*

Pre-WWII Civilian Contracts Awarded by BuDocks

Swiftly and methodically, the CEC began negotiating cost-plus-fixed-fee contracts with combinations of private contractors. The contractors began their big push to recruit workmen for the overseas jobs. Attracted by the high wages, thousands of men embarked for Newfoundland, Iceland and the British Isles; for the West Indies; for Sitka, Kodiak and Dutch Harbor; for Pearl Harbor and several nearby Hawaiian Islands; for Midway, Wake and Cavite; for Palmyra and Samoa.

Admiral Moreell and the Navy command watched the civilians embark with misgivings. Even in peacetime the use of civilians for advance base work has its handicaps. . . .And what if suddenly we were drawn into the war? The bombing plane has made this war different from all previous wars. Base construction is not only vulnerable to attack; it is the center of attack—the primary objective of the opposing forces.

On 6 December 1941, approximately 70,000 civilians were working on projects outside the United States. They were building the two Atlantic and three Pacific "roads".

On the north Pacific road: 895 were at Sitka; 2,396 were at Kodiak; 1,076 were at Dutch Harbor. Virtually all of these were Americans.

On the central Pacific road: 7,000 were in the environs of Pearl Harbor; 1,931 were at Midway; 1,149 were at Wake; 71 were at Guam; 3,412 were at Cavite; 207 were working on the Melinta Tunnel on Corregidor. Except at Cavite, most of these were Americans.

On the long road through the South Pacific—this road was scarcely begun—351 were at Palmyra; 462 were at Johnston; and 1,297 were at Samoa. All of these were Americans.

On 6 December, these people were doing war work for a nation at peace with the world. But on 7 December, their status had changed; they had become fair game for the bombs and shells of Germany, Italy and Japan.

Editor: Huie goes on to describe what happened to the civilian workers at Wake, Guam, Corregidor and Cavite after the 7 December 1941 attack. The final outcome: the Japanese shipped most of the survivors—now prisoners of war—to various prison camps from Shanghai to Santo Tomas, a name which connotes abuse and atrocity. The legal and human problems which arose as a result of their civilian status were very complex. In the end, President Roosevelt initiated action whereby the Government assumed financial responsibility for the men and their dependents.

Pearl Harbor Changes Game Plan

How did the civilian workers at bases which were not attacked by the enemy react to the news from Pearl Harbor? They reacted variously, as might be expected. Some of them gripped their tools harder, stuck to their jobs. At a few bases, many requested immediate transportation home. The general reaction confirmed what the CEC had long feared: the civilian-worker plan for advance bases was outmoded; it was not for this war.

In the darkest hours of our history we were condemned to mark time while a whole new organization for overseas construction was built. Thousands of civilians had to be evacuated from strategic areas, and they had to be replaced by skilled construction men who were armed, trained and equipped members of a military unit.

The Jap attack caught us short in many categories. Our shortage of first-class warships and planes has been widely discussed and is generally understood. What needs explanation is that the Japs caught us not only short of bases; they also caught us without an organization with which to build bases!

Our war in the Pacific and, to a lesser extent, our war in the Atlantic, had to mark time while we dismantled the private-contract-civilian-labor system for Advance-Base construction; while we enlisted construction men and built the Seabee organization; and while we substituted Seabees for civilians. When you understand what this meant in time, shipping and expense, you will understand why so many long, bitter months passed before an offensive blow could be struck in the Pacific.

Rear Admiral Moreell and the CEC would now have to substitute Seabees for civilians practically overnight. The men building the roads would have to be prepared to set aside their tools and pick up their rifles at the sound of a siren. Construction plans would have to be integrated with combat plans.

(Source: Huie, *Can Do!* 66–68, 79.) ∎

Naval Construction Battalions—Birth of the Seabees
"We Build, We Fight!"

Editor: The U.S. Navy's story of the Seabees is chronicled in the Department of the Navy's *Building the Navy's Bases in WWII*.

Battalions Authorized and Organized, 5 January 1942

After the 7 December 1941 attack on Pearl Harbor and the United States' entry into the war, the use of civilian labor in war zones became impractical. In fact, under international law, civilians were not permitted to resist enemy military attack; resistance could result in summary execution as a guerrilla.

On 5 January 1942, Rear Admiral Moreell was granted authority from the Bureau of Personnel to recruit men from the construction trades for assignment to a Naval Construction Regiment (NCR) composed of three Naval Construction Battalions (NCBs). This was the actual beginning of the renowned Seabees and Moreell personally furnished them with their official motto: *Construimus, Batuimus*—"We Build, We Fight."

Naval Construction Battalions were organized around the allowance of 33 officers and 1,081 enlisted personnel. They were organized in five companies including a headquarters company and four construction companies. The organizational allowance was designed to provide a self-sustaining unit with individual and organizational equipment, vehicles, supplies and materiel to perform construction work.

The original planning resulted in battalions being assigned as a functional component part of advanced bases known as CUBs, LIONs, and ACORNs, which were the code names for standard advanced naval bases.

Naval Construction Battalions were completely equipped, self-sustaining and able to construct airfields, roads, bridges and buildings at an advanced base and to install, operate and maintain its public utilities.

(Source: Dept. of the Navy, *Building the Navy's Bases in WWII*, Vol. 1, 133–150.) ∎

❖   ❖   ❖

Editor: Lt (jg) Huie continues with the Seabees story in *Can Do!:*

It is almost impossible to exaggerate the urgent need for Seabee battalions in December 1941. They had to be recruited, organized from scratch, then trained, equipped and transported to the job site. The war had to wait for them.

The Seabees were not really trained during the first months; they were just assembled, given their medical shots and equipped with whatever was at hand. There was no time for training. The First and Second Construction Battalions embarked from the West Coast for the South Pacific early in February 1942. The Third Battalion went to the Fijis; the Fourth to Dutch Harbor; the Fifth to Samoa. The Seabees had No. 1 priority on shipping— like volunteer firemen being rushed to the fire.

Twenty-five battalions had been shipped overseas before the CEC could stabilize on an eight-week assembly and training period. There were desperate shortages of ordnance, construction equipment and clothing, so the battalions had to be shipped out with "supplies and equipment to follow." On arrival at their jungle islands, the men had to barter, steal and improvise while they waited and hoped for all the stuff that was "to follow."

On 17 January 1942, ground was broken near Norfolk, Virginia, for Camp Allen, which was to take care of one regiment. This camp was put in commission on 13 March 1942 when 2,000 men arrived there for training.

National Youth Administration (NYA) camps were used until May 1942, when Camp Bradford was opened. The small NYA camps were scattered throughout the country. It was at these camps that many Seabees were assembled for their medical shots, outfitting and brief conditioning. Camp Bradford was ten miles from Camp Allen, but the two were operated as one training center.

It took months to lick the training problem. Camp Endicott, R.I., with a capacity of 11,000 men, was commissioned 11 August 1942; and Camp Peary, Va., with a capacity of 40,000 men, was opened in November 1942. These were followed by the commissioning of Camp Lee-Stephenson, Quoddy Village, Me.; the opening of the Recuperation Center at Camp

Parks, Cal.; and the development of the Advance Base Depots at Port Hueneme, Cal.; Davisville, R.I.; and Gulfport, Miss.

On 18 September 1942, about the time that the creation of the construction battalions slowed down to an orderly process, the Navy ordered the CEC to begin creating stevedore battalions of Seabees. A serious bottleneck had developed in the South Pacific. Ships could not be unloaded as fast as they arrived, and at one time 83 freighters were riding at anchor in the South Pacific waiting to be unloaded. Unloading difficulties were multiplied by the fact that we had no cargo docks north of Australia, and all cargo had to be handled first onto lighters, from the lighters to trucks, and thence to storage areas.

These stevedore battalions were designated as "Special" Seabee Naval Construction Battalions ("Special" NCBs), and the First "Special" was organized hastily and sent to Guadalcanal. Each "Special" NCB was organized around the nucleus of experienced stevedores, and the inexperienced men were given brief training on a dry-land model of a Liberty ship at Camp Peary.*

A later development was the Construction Battalion Maintenance Unit (CBMU). These units varied in size from 60 to 250 officers and men, and were designed to replace construction battalions after construction has been completed and the war had moved on, leaving only maintenance and operations tasks in its wake.

By 1943, with the pressure slacking off in both the Atlantic and the Pacific, the training period for Seabee battalions was gradually lengthened to three months. Battalions returning from overseas were given the military training which they had skipped in the dark days.

The Seabees began looking like a military organization as well as acting like one. On broad training grounds at the big camps, Marine Corps instructors taught the Seabees all the tricks of beach landings and jungle warfare. Tough bulldozer operators to whom fighting was an occupational sport were taught judo and bayonet tactics.

(Source: Huie, *Can Do!* 86–88.) ■

∴ ∴ ∴

---

* The First "Special" Naval Construction Battalion is profiled later in this chapter. —Ed.

Editor: In 1942, many Seabee battalions helped build the "service stations" to the South Pacific so that the "Pacific express" could deliver the tens of thousands of tons of supplies, equipment, ammunition, and fuel to the Solomons for the various units slated to participate in the move northward. The following excerpt from *Building the Navy's Bases in WWII* is a sampling— by no means exhaustive—of naval bases and facilities built by Seabees along the South Pacific road.

Seabees Build Advance Bases in the South Pacific

The first naval construction unit to deploy from the United States was designated the First Construction Detachment and landed on Bora Bora in the Societies Islands on 17 February 1942. Their mission was to construct a fueling station that would service the many ships and planes necessary to defend and keep open the sea lanes to Australia. This unit was nicknamed the "Bobcat" Detachment (code name for Bora Bora). Their efforts were later rewarded when the island's tank farms supplied the ships and planes that fought the historic Battle of the Coral Sea.

The Second NCB began work at both British and American Samoa only a few days after Lieutenant Sam Mathis' First NCB landed at Efate in the New Hebrides on 4 May 1942 to open up airstrips from which we could start bombing the Japanese on Guadalcanal.

In both the Fiji and Ellice island groups, vast construction projects were completed in 1942. A detachment of the Third NCB developed Nandi in the Fijis, while the 58th NCB and another detachment of the Third NCB developed Vunda Point.

Funafuti in the Ellice group was converted into a base in October 1942 by detachments of the First and Third NCBs; Nanomea was developed by the 16th NCB; Nukupetau by another detachment of the 16th NCB; Upolu by a detachment of the Second NCB.

Detachments of the 5th and 76th NCBs worked at Palmyra; detachments of the 5th and 10th NCBs worked at Johnston and Canton Islands.

(Source: Dept. of the Navy, *Building the Navy's Bases in WWII*, Vol. 2, 191–240.) ∎

Editor: Huie discusses the importance of these "roads and service stations":

Too often when we think of the Navy we think only of ships or dive-bombers or Marines; yet a modern fleet without great, far-flung bases—without piers, drydocks, airfields, vast storage and repair facilities—is like an automobile without filling stations.

The mobility of both the air and surface elements of a fleet is directly related to the number and location of the bases. Moreover, as the character of naval warfare becomes more complex, as the components become larger, more varied, and more numerous, so must the bases become larger and more complex.

The new American Navy dates from the September 1940 destroyer deal with Britain. By that deal we began to build the two "roads" to victory in the Atlantic: The Argentia-Iceland-Londonderry road through the North Atlantic; and the Miami-Trinidad-Natal-Ascension-Freetown road through the South Atlantic.

Simultaneously, we began building three "roads" across the Pacific: The Sitka-Kodiak-Dutch Harbor-Adak-Attu road; the Pearl Harbor-Midway-Wake-Guam-Cavite road; and the Bora Bora-Samoa-Fiji-Espiritu Santo-Noumea road to Australia, the Solomons and the Indies.

In the final analysis this war, like most of history's wars, boils down to a fight for roads. The roads [sea lanes] this time are the longest in history; indeed, they are as long as they can possibly be on a globe no larger than ours. Before America can bring her decisive industrial might to bear against her enemies, five roads must be completed: two to Germany, three to Tokyo. These roads must be broad, because of the weight and variety of the weapons and supplies which must flow over them. They must be safe from successful attack.

The problem Admiral Moreell and the Civil Engineer Corps faced was to accelerate construction of these five roads. Varying amounts of work had been done on each road; but all five roads had to be converted into super-highways in the shortest possible time. The Army and our British allies would help; but the job was a Navy job.

(Source: Huie, *Can Do!* 61–65.) ■

❖ ❖ ❖

Editor: Noumea, the important base on New Caledonia, was rapidly expanding thanks to the dedicated efforts of 13 battalions. According to the Bureau of Yards and Docks' excellent history of worldwide U.S. naval facilities in WWII, the following NCBs worked on one or more Noumea projects before the war ended: the 2nd "Special", 3rd, 6th, 11th, 19th, 20th, 24th, 33rd, 37th, 53rd, 73rd, 75th, 78th, and 88th.

Noumea, New Caledonia

Prior to the entry of the United States into the war, an Australian garrison was stationed on New Caledonia. In March 1942, by agreement with the French, U.S. Army Expeditionary Forces under Lieutenant General Alexander M. Patch occupied the island, and most of the Australian garrison was withdrawn.

Plans for building up Noumea as a main air and naval base were soon put into execution, and a detachment of the 3rd Naval Construction Battalion began construction of facilities on Ile Nou. However, no construction equipment or materiel was available until mid-August, so the early projects were accomplished with borrowed equipment.

The French power cable to the island had been accidentally cut in March, so the Seabees erected a power plant on Ile Nou. The Royal Australian Air Force had a modest seaplane base at Ile Nou which was taken over by the U.S. Navy to provide fueling and re-arming services for patrol planes and quarters for their personnel.

In August 1942, a Seabee detachment began assembly of pontoon barges, both with and without propulsion units. Most of them were turned over to the Army transportation pool for use in ship unloading.

On 1 December, the detachment assumed the operation of a 75-ton crane and its pontoon barge, which they had assembled. It was used to unload the three sections of LCTs, PT boats, landing barges, tank lighters, and P-38s—all carried as deck cargo on freighters.

Noumea had a large harbor, but servicing facilities were meager. Nickel Dock, 800-feet long with a 24-foot water depth, could take one large vessel. The wharf was equipped with three 7-ton cranes, but it had little storage area. Le Grand Quai, 1,400 feet long, with water depth of from 20 to 26 feet, had some 68,500 square feet of space in trans-shipment sheds, but had no crane.

Shortage of stevedore personnel impeded the unloading of ships during the summer months. All Navy personnel available were used for unloading, and the construction battalions, as they arrived, handled most of their own unloading.

Unloading at Noumea in the first half of December 1942 averaged 5,000 tons per day (about half the cargo of a fully-loaded Liberty ship), not sufficient to keep up with the rate at which cargo was arriving, so serious congestion of merchant shipping in the harbor resulted.

The 19th NCB, which reported at Noumea on 11 November 1942, started building an advance base construction depot, the first in the forward area. It comprised of eleven Quonset huts, one steel and two timber warehouses, an electric system, and an area for receiving, sorting, and shipping construction equipment and materiel.

For the 1st Marine base depot, the 19th NCB constructed two large piers, one 300-foot and one 200-feet long, and 20 frame warehouses having concrete decks. A vehicular bridge, 20 feet wide, was built at the depot to unload vehicles from barges.

During the first half of 1943, the construction at Noumea grew rapidly. On 1 January 1943, the 24th NCB, which had arrived in December, undertook the construction of a 600-by-72-foot timber pier at the northern end of the Nickel Dock.

A pontoon assembly depot (PAD) was established at Ile Nou and by March 1943, Seabees had completed the erection of buildings needed to house operations and had installed a narrow-gauge railway in the plant and storage area. The PAD was charged not only with the manufacture of the pontoons, but also with their assembly into barges, wharves, and other units as required.

Facilities at Ile Nou were increased to include an amphibious boat pool, a ship repair unit, a pontoon assembly depot, an aircraft engine overhaul base, a tank farm for aviation gasoline storage, a section base, and an anti-aircraft school.

In March 1943, the 2nd "Special" Seabees arrived to handle stevedoring.

At the repair base, facilities were provided for the repair and servicing of vessels as large as destroyers, and the base was also equipped to go into the stream and make repairs and alterations to vessels of the transport type.

Navy medical facilities at Noumea consisted of two 2,000-bed hospitals, MOB 5 and MOB 7. Several Seabee battalions cooperated in the construction of these facilities, using prefabricated metal huts, native structures, and frame buildings. A convalescent camp was added to MOB 7 later on.

At Noumea, a supply depot was also established to serve the South Pacific. It included 85 steel warehouses and a depot camp with all facilities. Steel magazines for an ammunition depot and warehouses for an aviation supply depot were also erected.

The land-plane facilities at Noumea were, in general, under the control of the U.S. Army. On the west shore of Magenta Bay, however, an auxiliary field with a single fighter runway was built for the Navy.

Because of the continued, and even increased, use of New Caledonia as a staging and rehabilitation area, and the island's position on the line of support to the forward areas in the Pacific, roll-up at Noumea would not get underway until late in 1944.

Espiritu Santo, New Hebrides Islands

When the Japanese moved into the Solomons and began construction of airfields on Guadalcanal, an Allied airbase in an advance area became vital. The choice of Espiritu Santo, 500 miles southeast of Guadalcanal in the New Hebrides, as a site for a major Army and Navy operating base, brought the U.S. bombers 400 miles closer to the Japanese positions and provided a staging area for the forthcoming Allied invasion of the Solomons. The base provided aircraft facilities capable of supporting heavy bombers, fighters, and two carrier groups; an accumulation of ammunition, provisions, stores, and equipment for offensive operations; and repair and salvage facilities for all types of vessels. It became a vital link between Henderson Field on Guadalcanal and the airfields at Noumea and Efate.

Espiritu Santo is the northernmost and largest of the New Hebrides Islands. It has an irregular outline, with numerous small islands near its shores. Heavily wooded and mountainous, particularly in the south and west where the highest peak rises to more than 6,000 feet, "Santo," as it is known locally, is about 75 miles long and 45 miles wide.

A small reconnaissance party of three men left Efate on 28 June 1942 to find an airfield site closer than Efate to Henderson Field. Espiritu Santo was chosen and, on July 8, a small group of Seabees of the Efate detachment arrived at Santo with a Marine anti-aircraft battery and a company of colored infantrymen to begin work on Turtle Bay airfield.

The Santo pioneers were given 20 days in which to construct the field. They worked day and night in the race against time using "make do" equipment.

A 6,000-foot runway was cleared and surfaced with coral in time to meet the deadline. On 28 July, the first fighter squadron came in and was followed the next day by a squadron of B-17s. The planes were fueled from drums and gave the Japanese in Guadalcanal its first big bombing on 30 July.

Army Air Force and Marine personnel poured into the island shortly thereafter, and after the Marines landed on Guadalcanal on 7 August, the new field at Santo gave vital support to that action.

The 6th and 7th NCBs arrived at Espiritu Santo in August 1942. The 6th NCB proceeded to Guadalcanal arriving in several elements between 1 September and 12 October 1942, where it fought in the battles for Henderson Field.

On 11 August 1942, when the 7th Battalion arrived, it immediately began construction of more extensive air facilities to support the Guadalcanal campaign. In 60 days, they completed a second fighter strip, 4,500 feet by 170 feet, with 7,500 feet of taxiways and 50 revetments. They then began work on two fields to support bomber operations. A runway, 5,000 feet by 150 feet, of steel mat on an 8-inch coral base, was constructed on the shores of Pallikulo Bay (Bomber Field No. 1). Working in cooperation with a company of the 810th Army Engineers, the 7th Battalion also cleared, graded and surfaced with coral a runway of the same dimensions at Pekoa (Bomber Field No. 2).

At the same time, both the 7th and the 15th were engaged in providing other necessary facilities for the base as a whole. The 7th erected 60 Quonset huts to be used as galleys, wards, operating rooms, dispensaries, and the like for CUB One Hospital, and 40 Quonset huts and warehouses for Base Hospital Three. Another hospital of 100 beds, including quarters, wards, mess hall, operating building, and other structures, was established by the 15th for Acorn 2 Hospital. In cooperation with the 35th Battalion, the 36th built 25 Quonset huts for quarters and wards, four steel warehouses, and extended the water system, lighting and roads at Base Hospital No. 3.

For a seaplane base, the 7th Battalion constructed a parking area, two prefabricated 85 by 100 feet nose hangars, warehouses, Quonset huts and two seaplane ramps in Segond Channel. These Seabees also established a PT-boat base, with extensive facilities.

The 36th, 40th, 44th and 57th NCBs later poured into Santo to expand it into a powerful base.

(Source: Dept. of the Navy, *Building the Navy's Bases in WWII*, Vol. 2, 221–232.) ∎

⁑ ⁑ ⁑

Editor: All of these pioneer Battalions were disappointed that they had not yet made contact with the enemy. In Lt Huie's words:

All of them continued to hope that their next assignment would be up where the bombs were falling. Every Seabee among them sorrowfully reported that they found nothing remotely resembling Dorothy Lamour; that drinking whiskey was painfully scarce; and that they preferred sawdust to another helping of Spam.

Virtually every one of these battalions had to unload its equipment onto pontoon barges, then drive the barges into strange beaches. Camps had to be cleared; weather had to be fought; disease had to be accepted with fortitude. Long waits for mail were the rule, not the exception. Yet morale continued wonderfully high among the men because (1) they were older construction men, accustomed to making homes for themselves under difficult, lonely conditions; and (2) they had volunteered to do a job on which they expected hardship.

Editor: The contest for the Solomons opened on 7 August 1942 when the 1st Marine Division (Reinforced) landed on the beaches of Guadalcanal and Tulagi as Operation WATCHTOWER, initiating a campaign that was to continue for six months. The principal objective of the first phase of the struggle, the battle for Guadalcanal, was to deny to the enemy, and to possess for ourselves, the airfield that the Japanese had been constructing on the island since early May 1942—soon to become known as Henderson Field. On 16 August 1942, the first element of CUB

One, an advance fuel and supply base, landed on Guadalcanal. This element, under Ensign George S. Polk, USN, consisted of five officers and 118 enlisted men, all navy petty officers of aviation support ratings.

Here is Commander Joseph P. Blundon's story, as told to fellow Seabee and author Lt (jg) William Bradford Huie, of how the Sixth NCB followed the Marines ashore, joined the fight for Henderson Field and, as a result, became the first Seabees to both "build and fight." Continuing from Huie, *Can Do!:*

Battle for Henderson Field

The Seabee story of Guadalcanal begins on the afternoon of 20 August 1942, when Commander Joseph P. "Paul" Blundon, CEC, USNR, Officer-in-Charge of the Sixth Naval Construction Battalion, arrived in a PBY off Lunga Point and promptly reported to General A. A. Vandegrift of the Marines. Commander Blundon recalled:

"I guess I was the first Seabee to go under fire. The Marines had been on Guadalcanal thirteen days, and they had a tiny beachhead around Henderson Field. While I was reporting to General Vandegrift, the Jap bombers came over and I hit my first foxhole. I just lay there and trembled with patriotism while the bombs fell around us.

"A few days later my Sixth NCB arrived, and we assumed full responsibility for the completion and maintenance of Henderson Field. The Japs had cleared an area 300 by 5,600 feet, but it was by no means finished. Two 1,800-foot sections at the ends of this area had been graded and while these sections were rough, our fighters could operate off of them. In the gap between the graded sections about 1,000 feet more had been partially graded, and the remaining 1,000 feet had not been graded at all.

"The Japs were shelling the field with howitzers, as well as bombing it night and day; and it was our job to keep the holes filled up while we finished the grading, laid the Marston mat, built hardstands and revetments, and helped solve the fuel and ammunition problems.*

"We had very little equipment. We had one carryall scraper—the big waddling machine that scoops up twelve cubic yards of earth—two bulldozers, six dump trucks, twenty-five flat-bottom Jap trucks, one motor patrol grader, one Jap tractor, and one Jap sheeps-foot roller. We also had 10,000 barrels of Jap cement, 18,000 feet of Jap soil pipe, plenty of Jap creosoted poles and a supply of Jap lumber. This Jap materiel and equipment saved our skins.

"The men in our Battalion had not been together more than ten days before we left the States. We had been given our medical shots, a little hasty military indoctrination, and then we had been formed into a Battalion and rushed to the South Pacific. We didn't kid ourselves. We weren't a trained military organization; we were just 1,100 partially armed civilians. We had one '03 rifle for each two men. That was all that could be spared us.

"But all of us were experienced construction men. We knew the value of team work. We knew how to take orders; and, more important, we knew how to execute orders. General Vandegrift assigned us a section of the beach to defend against Jap landings, and we figured we could defend that beach and still do the job at Henderson Field.

"We realized at the outset that the battle was going to turn on how fast we filled up holes and how fast we could

---

* A "hardstand" is a parking lot for one or more planes. The surface must be "hard" enough to support the plane's weight, which is concentrated in the few square inches of wheel surface touching the ground. Revetments are walls of earth piled up on three sides of the hand-stand to protect the plane from flying shrapnel.

develop that field. When the Jap bombers approached, our fighters took off; the bombers blasted the airstrips; and then if we couldn't fill up those holes before our planes ran out of fuel, the planes would have to attempt to land anyway, and they would crash. I saw seven of our fighters crack up in one bitter afternoon. From our point of view the battle of Guadalcanal was a race between the Jap artillery and their airplanes, and the Sixth Seabee Battalion.

"We played our cards fast. We pitched our camp at the edge of the field to save time. We dug our foxholes right up alongside the landing area. We found that a 500-pound bomb would tear up 1,600 square feet of Marston mat, so we placed packages of this quantity of mat along the strip, like extra rails along a railroad. We figured out how much sand and gravel was required to fill the average bomb or shell crater, and we loaded these measured amounts on trucks and placed the trucks under cover at strategic points. We had compressors and pneumatic tampers to pack the fill into the craters. We organized human assembly lines for passing up the pierced plank and laying it.*

"Then when the Jap bombers approached, every Seabee, including our cooks, manned his repair station. Our "crater crews" were lying in the foxholes right at the edge of the strip. The moment the bombers had passed over, these men rolled out of the holes and raced for the craters. While they were tearing away the twisted steel plank, our trucks roared out of hiding to dump their earth and gravel into the holes. The men with the compressors and pneumatic tampers leaped into the holes and began packing the dirt as it came in. Our human assembly lines began passing in the new steel plank

---

* The terms "pierced plank" and "Marston mat" are used interchangeably. The steel plank unit is approximately 16 inches wide by 10 feet long, with many holes "pierced" in it to reduce its weight. The planks have interlocking edges.

and laying it. Every man had to keep his eye peeled for Jap strafing planes, and when the Jap dived in, our men dived for the close-at-hand foxholes. The men who were working in the crater just used the crater as protection against the strafers.

"We found that 100 Seabees could repair the damage of a 500-pound bomb hit on an airstrip in forty minutes, including the replacing of the Marston mat. In other words, forty minutes after that bomb exploded, you couldn't tell that the airstrip had ever been hit. But we needed all of this speed and more. In twenty-four hours on October 13 and 14, [1942] fifty-three bombs and shells hit the Henderson airstrip!

"During one hour on the 14th, we filled thirteen bomb craters while our planes circled around overhead waiting to land. We got no food during that period because our cooks were all busy passing up the steel plank. There were not enough shovels to go around, so some of our men used their helmets to scoop up earth and carry it to the bomb craters. In the period from September 1 to November 18 [1942], we had 140 Jap raids in which the strip was hit at least once.

"Our worst moments were when the Jap bomb or shell failed to explode when it hit. It still tore up our mat, and it had to come out. When you see men choke down their fear and dive in after an unexploded bomb so that our planes can land safely, a lump comes in your throat and you know why America wins wars.

"Shell craters are more dangerous to work on than bomb craters. You have a feeling that no two bombs ever hit in the same place; but this isn't true of shells. A Jap five-inch gun lobs a shell over on your airstrip and blasts a helluva hole. What are you going to do? You know, just as that Jap artilleryman knows, that if he leaves his gun in the same position and fires another shell, the second shell will hit in almost the same spot as the first one. So a good old Jap trick was to give us just enough time to start repairing the hole and then fire the second shell. All you can do is depend on hearing that second shell coming and hope you can scramble far enough away before it explodes. But this is a gamble which is frowned upon by life insurance companies.

"Al Pratt (Lieutenant Alma P. Pratt, CEC, USNR) was in direct charge of the crater-filling crews. He was an earth-moving specialist; a stocky, serious-minded fellow who recovered quickly from any shock. One afternoon Jap artillery had chased him all over the strip. He had been knocked down twice by those "second shell" bursts, he was groggy and very dirty, yet he was still charging up and down the strip, bellowing for more speed.*

"In addition to our crater-filling efforts, we fought the Japs by working constantly to enlarge the operating surface of the field. Fighter planes can take off and land safely on a steel-matted area 75 by 2,500 feet. So, when we finished an area 150 by 2,500 feet, we had what amounted to two operating strips; since if we had craters on one side of this area we could rope off the damaged side and use the 75-foot-wide strip that was not damaged. Then, when we finally completed an area 150 by 5,600 feet, we had four fighter strips. With the larger area we still had only one safe bomber strip, but bombers carry so much more fuel than fighters that they can give you more time to make repairs.

"Several times in the early days before we got the field lighted we had to land planes after dark. In such emergencies Seabees would hold flashlights and form a human boundary around the landing strip. Death would literally hover over these men, since the planes, often partially out of control,

---

* Strangely, the Japanese used armor-piercing shells in shelling the Henderson strip. This worked to our advantage since, while the holes were 15 to 20 feet deep, they were relatively small in diameter and thus destroyed very little Marston mat.

would come in feeling their way, and if they caught a little air pocket even the brush of a wingtip would sever the head of any man holding a light.

"In spite of all our speed, however, I think we might have lost that fight had it not been for the emergency strip which we roughed out early in September. The Japs didn't discover we had this strip for a long time, and the stories I've seen about Guadalcanal don't even mention it. Yet we had it, and I think it saved the show for us.*

"This strip was about 2,000 feet from the Henderson strip and ran parallel to Henderson. At the start it was nothing more than a sage-grass field with grass eight to ten feet high. We went in there with machetes and cut the grass off to about eighteen inches high. Then we rolled the grass down, filled in the depressions, and we had a strip which was rough, but one which we used on plenty of occasions when we had more holes than we could fill on Henderson. Even B-17s could get down and get off on this grass in extreme emergency.

"In the final analysis, of course, it was the quality of the men of the Sixth Battalion which enabled us to win the airfield battle. All of them had volunteered for front-line work—and that's very important. Less than 10 percent of them proved unfit for duty under bombs. Compared to any outfit in the service, that's a low percentage. A few men just couldn't take it, but we weeded them out quickly. I think their number was miraculously low in view of the fact that we had had no realistic military training and very little training of any sort.

---

* This emergency strip was constructed under the direction of Chief Carpenter's Mate Walter Joslyn.

"The average age of the men was about thirty-five. Many of us were old enough to have been the fathers of the Marines who did the fighting. But I regard this as an advantage rather than a disadvantage. I think the older men stood up better under bombing than the younger men. The man of thirty-eight who has spent his life in active construction work is tough. He doesn't have the physical stamina of the boy of eighteen; he's not as reckless. But when the chips really go down and a job has got to be done, I'll take the experienced, level-headed man of thirty-eight.

"In our part of this war, it's experience and know-how that count. A man may be strong as a bull and ferocious as a tiger, but his hands must be skilled for the Seabees are the men who use America's machines to advantage. One skilled Seabee operating a twelve-cubic-yard carry-all can move as much dirt in eight hours as 150 Jap laborers. To repair the same bomb crater that we can repair in forty minutes takes the Japs three hours, and then they only fill the hole with dirt. They have no compressors or pneumatic tampers, and they have no steel mat.

"As a fighting man, either on the ground or in the air, the Jap is outmatched by the American. But the Jap is a capable, determined fighter, and he can give a good account of himself against the American. But when it comes to military construction, the Jap is hopelessly outclassed. While America had been building super-highways, skyscrapers and dams, the Japs have been building dog trails and fiber huts. As a fighting man, perhaps the Jap merits some respect from us; but as a construction man the Jap merits only the contempt which the Seabees have for him."

(Source: Huie, *Can Do!* 97, 39–45.) ■

Editor: Captain Larry G. DeVries, CEC, USNR, profiled the Sixth NCB and the events that led to the participation of the Seabees in the battle for Guadalcanal in his personal story, "Seabees on Guadalcanal."

Profile: Sixth Naval Construction Battalion

The 6th NCB, which was destined to be the first naval construction battalion to come under enemy fire, was activated at Camp Allen, Virginia, on 24 June 1942, and went from Gulfport, Mississippi, to Moffett Field, California, and on to San Francisco, California. It left for the South Pacific on 21 July on USS *President Polk* and USS *Wharton* with five other ships escorted by the light cruiser USS *Helena* (CL-50). The 6th NCB reached Espiritu Santo on 11 August via Pago Pago, Samoa.

On 20 August, Commander Joseph P. Blundon, CEC, USNR, who was Officer-in-Charge of the 6th NCB, arrived in a PBY, which landed off Lunga Point. He immediately called on General Vandegrift and his planning was directed toward work on Henderson Field. Commander Blundon requested two companies from his NCB at Espiritu Santo be sent forward with a number of extra men trained for special details such as water purification and machinery repair.

This first contingent landed on 1 September 1942 and consisted of 357 men and five officers under Lieutenant (jg) Thomas L. Stamp, CEC, USNR.*

Commander Blundon had departed by aircraft to Espiritu Santo on 27 August and returned on 29 August with Commander James P. Compton, USN, who was Commanding Officer of CUB-1, the first CUB-type base to be constructed.

---

* This landing took place just 24 days after the Marines' landing and about nine months after the attack on Pearl Harbor. —Ed.

Lack of transportation shipping, enemy action, and the need for other priority unit and supply shipments caused the 6th NCB to arrive in elements. The second element of 156 men from the 6th NCB departed Espiritu Santo on 29 August and arrived on Guadalcanal on 26 September. The third, fourth, and fifth elements arrived on 2, 9, and 12 October resulting in 1,002 men, including 17 officers on Guadalcanal-Tulagi by mid-October.

The construction work on Guadalcanal was centered around Henderson Field and the Naval Operating Base at Lunga and at Koli Point on Guadalcanal. On Tulagi [19 miles to the north of Guadalcanal across Sealark Channel] the construction effort was focused on Tulagi Harbor and the motor torpedo boat base supporting Motor Torpedo Boat Squadrons 2 and 3 as well as the seaplane base on Halavo peninsula on Florida Island.

At Lunga, the extension and improvement of Henderson Field absorbed the majority of the effort, especially for the first elements of the 6th NCB. . . .At times, the 6th NCB had 25–30 construction projects underway.

A detachment of the 6th NCB under Lieutenant Ben Marcus, CEC, USNR, was sent to Tulagi on 9 October. On Tulagi, the work included power generation and distribution lines, telephone and communication lines, water systems, fire systems, gun emplacements, sawmills, piers, gasoline and avgas storage tanks, a radio station and general construction for units assigned there. The harbor there was very important and at various times the heavy cruisers USS *Pensacola,* USS *New Orleans,* USS *Minneapolis,* the PT tender USS *Jamestown,* and the destroyer-seaplane tender USS *McFarland* were disabled and were worked on in the harbor. Construction work also took place on Gavutu, Tanambogo, and Halavo.

Units on Guadalcanal generally spent one year on the islands before they were sent to bases both in the South Pacific and in the United States for rest, replacements, and re-outfitting.

The 6th NCB was the first unit to depart Guadalcanal on 5 January 1943. The 6th NCB was the first naval construction battalion to suffer fatalities due to enemy action (Chief Machinist Mate Henry L. Thompson, killed in action 14 October 1942) and the first NCB unit to have members decorated for action under enemy fire. It was one of four NCBs to earn the Presidential Unit Citation during the war.

The Guadalcanal Campaign provided the proving ground for Naval Construction Battalions and their need in the campaigns to follow in the Pacific. At its peak over 258,000 Seabees and CEC officers were on duty in World War II. Eventually, 150 Naval Construction Battalions and 41 Construction Battalion "Specials" were established and served around the world on all continents. One hundred thirty-five Construction Battalion Maintenance Units were formed. One hundred eighteen Construction Detachments and five Pontoon Assembly Detachments were also formed. Other services, and the rest of the Navy itself, were lost on the distinction among the unit types. They all became known as Seabees.

(Source: DeVries, "Seabees on Guadalcanal,"
WWII Naval Journal, July/August 1994.) ∎

"Special" Stevedore Naval Construction Battalions
"Keep the hook moving!"

Editor: This section will focus on the First "Special" Stevedore Naval Construction Battalion—the first of many Seabee "Special" battalions whose primary function it was to stevedore—load and unload ships—but also, when necessity required, engage in construction and combat duties.

Claude S. Gulbranson, USNR, secretary for the First "Special" NCB, chronicles this history in the organization's privately published, "The History of the First Special U.S. Naval Construction Battalion, 1942–1946."

Battalions Authorized and Organized, 18 September 1942

In the fall of 1942, it became apparent that the Navy would be forced to organize special battalions of stevedores to handle the mountains of freight which had to be unloaded on open beaches in the Pacific Theater. The nature of the Pacific made stevedoring at the Advance Bases as hazardous and difficult as construction. An unloading ship was a prime target for the enemy.

All the normal difficulties of unloading were multiplied by the absence of piers on a forward island. There were no piers for two reasons: there had been no time to build them; and, until an island was secure from enemy attacks, it was foolish to build piers, since they would only be destroyed by enemy bombs. This meant that when a freighter arrived at a place like Guadalcanal, she had to anchor offshore and unload her cargo onto heaving barges; then the barges ran to the beach, where the cargo had to be handled onto trucks. This ship-to-shore process doubled the normal amount of stevedoring.

Ships sometimes swung around the "hook" for weeks before they could get unloaded, even in Noumea and Espiritu Santo. The absolute necessity of supplying cargo-handling equipment, cranes, tugs and the like, and, most importantly, experienced stevedore gangs for the march up the Solomons was a lesson learned the hard way during OPERATION WATCHTOWER.

Even granting that civilian ships' crews were willing to risk bombs and willing to work 'round the clock in drenching rains, additional stevedoring forces were necessary. Shipping space was short; the supply lines were long and tenuous, so it was imperative that ships be unloaded and turned around quickly at their destinations. At one time in 1942, eighty-three ships were lying at anchor in the South Pacific waiting to be unloaded.

The Navy needed stevedores and, as with the construction men, it seemed wise for the stevedores to be members of the armed forces, trained to fight as well as work, and subject to military discipline. Where a battle might turn on the handling of cargo under fire, it seemed unwise for all the armed contingents in an area to be dependent on the whims of a civilian crew.

Those circumstances, plus some impressive results turned in by Naval Construction Battalions when asked to unload ships during emergencies, convinced the Navy to organize "Seabee Special" Battalions for stevedoring. The Seabees would more than make up in enthusiasm, hard work, and long hours what they lacked in military experience.

On 18 September 1942, the authority for the organization of special-duty battalions, composed of personnel well qualified in cargo handling and ship loading, was granted. The Civil Engineer Corps (CEC) designated the stevedore battalions "Special" battalions and rushed plans for their creation.

Profile: First "Special" Naval Construction Battalion

As with the first construction battalions, the need was so urgent that there was little time to train the First "Special." To form the First "Special" Battalion, the CEC grabbed 95 men with stevedoring experience who had enlisted for service with the Construction Battalions, and added 900 others who knew something about rigging, and handling barges and small boats, and rushed the group to the Pacific where they were joined by the Second, Third and Fourth "Specials."

On 16 December 1942, the First "Special" became a commissioned activity with Lieutenant Commander William T. Powers as Officer-in-Charge. At that time, the unit was based at the U.S. Naval Construction Training Center, Camp Bradford, Virginia. It was then transferred to the training center at Camp Peary, Williamsburg, Virginia.

In January 1943, the First "Special" moved to the Advanced Base Depot, Port Hueneme, California, where it was organized into two echelons, then outfitted and trained as stevedore units.

Between 4 February and 5 March 1943, with both echelons thoroughly trained, they embarked on four merchant vessels (SS *Turner*, SS *Louis Joliet*, SS *Mormacren*, MV *Day Star*) with stopovers in Espiritu Santo. The Battalion was united as a single unit when the second echelon finally arrived at Guadalcanal on 2 May 1943, and would go on to personify Seabee ingenuity in the field of stevedoring.

First "Special" Arrives at Guadalcanal, 2 May 1943. When the First "Special" arrived at Guadalcanal on 2 May 1943, 120 men immediately went ashore to occupy the assigned campsite, while the remainder of the men stayed on board to discharge the battalion's initial equipment, including rolling stock, electrical, stevedoring, galley, water purification, camouflage, and mobile machinery; also, ship's service, medical supplies and equipment, auto maintenance, ad infinitum.

The First "Special" camp was located close to the Naval Operating Base (NOB), Lunga Point at Tenaru Beach. It was convenient in that marine transportation and beach unloading work presented no undue difficulties.

Climatic conditions on Guadalcanal created many difficult problems in regard to camp construction. The high humidity, frequent rains, and deep mire constantly menaced construction and improvements. During the first few weeks, many difficulties were encountered, since all available men were solely engaged in stevedoring work.

Of primary importance to the crew, a galley was immediately set up. As time went by, a well-planned frame structure was built with drainage facilities and a concrete deck. Foremost in importance among the problems faced was obtaining fresh provisions, and second, conveying the food to working gangs aboard ships in the roadstead.

The quarters of enlisted personnel went through a similar evolution of development. Originally, all tents were put on the ground. Later, as tonnage became available, wood decks were installed. However, the screening-in of all tents was a slow process since mosquito netting was a priority item.

During the first six weeks, stevedore work was limited to daylight hours, since the 'Canal was subjected to frequent enemy nocturnal air raids. Security reasons required that ships leave their anchorages in the strait at night. (This all changed for the better after the U.S. secured airfields on New Georgia.)

The First "Special" NCB was soon operating in an efficient manner. Orders for battalion operations were received by the officer-in-charge (OIC). They were, in turn, passed on to the executive officer for proper disposition.

The executive officer, acting directly under the OIC, was personally responsible for the proper administrative functioning of all operations. The remaining staff officers included officers of the Medical, Dental, Chaplain, and Supply Corps.

A staff of four officers was directly responsible to each company commander, who, in turn, was responsible to the executive officer for the administration of his company. Gangs of men, under the supervision of a chief petty officer, were responsible to the four junior staff officers.

Working hours during the first six months emphasized discharging priority cargo of the following types: a) materiel necessary for existence, b) equipment essential for expanding facilities, and c) equipment belonging to new units staging on the island.

Work assignments in the latter category took place at widely separate beaches; that is, Kukum, Tassafaronga, Kokum-buna, and Teterte. Subsequently, the field of operation was narrowed down to Kukum, Lunga, Tenaru, and Koli.

The First "Special" was responsible for the unloading of cargo and maintenance of barges. During the summer months of 1943, ships to be unloaded were so numerous that it necessitated the economical distribution of gangs over extended operations.

It took plenty of stamina and guts to work long, weary hours under the simmering heat of a tropical sun. Keeping the supplies rolling called for the monotonous routine of lifting and guiding while watching always for the enemy and maybe sleeping in a foxhole. Hours were not counted. Nature, too, was the enemy of these men. The winds stirred the sea violently, and the rains caused trucks to bog down. The insects bedeviled the men, and the threat of malaria hung over each man like a shadow. But there was a war to be won.

For the stevedores, the goal was to keep the hook moving (meaning the hook attached to a boom or crane that lifted the cargo nets and slings). Appropriately, their motto became "Keep the Hook Moving!"

This combination of conditions threatened to create inefficiency, fatigue and physical exhaustion. By the end of the first year's overseas duty, a total of 242 men had been transferred because of medical disabilities resulting mainly from malaria and/or occupational fatigue.

From the very first day of arrival at Guadalcanal, it could be seen that the critical item in the transfer of cargo from ship hold to lighter (barge-like craft) to truck to supply dump was the lighter. Any other difficulties could be remedied by putting more men to work or obtaining more trucks. However, to increase the capacity of barges to haul cargo, a whole new business had to be established to maintain the barges. The battalion assumed this task shortly after arrival.

For ferry service from ship to shore, the stevedores pressed into service anything that would float. There was a steady stream of LCMs, LCTs, and pontoon barges, including "Big Joe." "Big Joe" was the pride of the pontoon fleet, since it was able to take ashore 200 tons at a trip. The most successful barges were the ones made up of three rows of twelve pontoon cells. They had a normal capacity of seventy tons.

Maneuvering this motley assortment of floats and bringing them alongside a ship in a running sea was a tough job for the Seabee coxswains. The captain would roar, "Bring that barge alongside Number 3 Hatch!" and the coxswain would try to maneuver his barge in between the barges which were already taking cargo from Numbers Two and Four hatches. One captain, watching a young coxswain trying to maneuver his barge in a heavy sea, became exasperated and bellowed, "Take that damn thing out and anchor it and I'll come alongside!"

(Source: Gulbranson, "History of the First Special U.S. Naval Construction Battalion, 1942–1946.") ∎

Editor: John D. Case, from Tokeland, Washington, joined the Navy in October 1939. Now a Chief Boatswains Mate and First "Special" assistant beachmaster, Case had exactly the kind of civilian work experience for which the Seabee recruiters had been looking. He had worked on fishing boats in Alaska and had been a stevedore, rigger, and logger in the Pacific Northwest. By checking personnel records, the recruiters found him already in the Navy serving on a tugboat on the East Coast and arranged his transfer to the First "Special" NCB in December 1942 as a "charter member."

In an interview with the editor, John Case described the First "Special's" Headquarters Company and his many duties on Guadalcanal:

> "The Headquarters Company consisted of a Company Commander, Camp Maintenance Officer and a Security Officer. It was a very large ship's company with mechanics, carpenters, truck drivers, a large mess hall, and a rigging loft to make up gear for the stevedore gangs. Companies 'B' and 'C' consisted of ships handling personnel (stevedore gangs). They worked all cargo ships that came to the 'Canal. . . .
>
> "A Chief Bo'sun in charge of stevedore gangs had to study the manifest of a ship to determine the kinds of cargo in each hold and its destination, e.g., 'Canal dump site or transfer to another vessel. He would then assign five gangs to the ship, one for each hold. He might also serve as a Cargo Chief on one or more amphibious landing craft scheduled for an invasion. In this case, he would set up the manifest and supervise the battle loading of the vessel. In some instances, he might even be asked to stay with the ship for the invasion in order to supervise the discharging of cargo. . . .
>
> "Army engineers built the finger piers. The Army furnished us with extra personnel, when necessary, to work in our stevedore gangs or on barges, but always under our supervision. The Army came in later with

their DUKWs (2½ ton, 6 x 6 amphibious trucks) which speeded up the unloading process."

Editor: On numerous occasions, the First "Special" NCB was subjected to aerial attacks, many of which occurred while stevedoring units were working aboard ships. John Case recalls:

> "We were under orders to try to get the gangs ashore providing there was sufficient warning, otherwise they were instructed to stay aboard and help the ship's company. For example, they might help the deck force swing in, lower, and secure the booms and rigging to give the ship's gunners a clear shot at the attacking planes." *

Editor: Lt (jg) William Bradford Huie summed up the challenges of a Seabee stevedore's day in these three paragraphs from *Can Do!:*

Aboard ship the hatches are open, booms rigged, winches in neutral, the Seabee gangs are waiting. As the barge comes alongside, the cargo nets and slings move upward from the holds carrying tons of vital needs. Guns, grenades, serums, plasma, food, fuel, clothing, tobacco, bulldozers and tanks—they all moved upward high into the air, then over the side and down to the pitching barge, where the Seabees jump to lash them fast. Back goes the big hook for another load. "Keep that hook moving!" Once more the winches strain, the booms groan, the cables are taut as bow strings, and the endless procession increases in cadence as the crews warm up.

---

* John D. Case, interview by the editor, William L. McGee, 1995.

Deep in the holds of the ship, too far down to feel even the whisper of a breeze, the Seabees are stripped to their waists. Sweat pours in torrents, even filling their shoes, but they keep rushing. Always, the next lift must be ready when the hook comes back from its journey over the side. "Keep that hook moving! There's a war to be won! Our buddies on the beach need this stuff to throw at the Japs!"

The barges, with whitecaps licking at their gunnels, creep slowly ashore to be beached as far in as they can go. Then crawler cranes, moving like giant land crabs, creep up alongside, and once again there is that same steady rhythm of swinging hook as the precious cargo is transferred from barge to truck. The barges are needed back at the ship. "Keep that hook moving!" The trucks are a conveyor belt to the warehouse or, more likely, the open storage area.

(Source: Huie, *Can Do!* 175–176.) ∎

❖ ❖ ❖

Editor: Continuing from Gulbranson's history:

Operation of water craft along the shore of Guadalcanal was extremely hazardous because there was no protection from wind and ocean waves. The weather was such that the wind would come up every afternoon, resulting in heavy running seas. This made it difficult to hold boats, barges and other landing craft on the beach while they were being unloaded, resulting in many accidents. For example, seas splashing on the engine will kill it. Without power, the barge would then be washed broadside onto the beach, and wrecked, unless immediately pulled off.

For several months, unloading operations were carried out without any finger piers. Cranes on those piers would have been able to unload cargo directly into trucks for the run to the dump sites. This necessitated craft being beached in shallow water while being unloaded, and thus exposing their propulsion units to heavier pounding by waves.

In the early stages of barge operation, the First "Special's" men were unskilled as coxswains. Experience again proved to be the best teacher. Many times, barges were washed on to the beach because the coxswains, when backing off the beach, didn't go far enough astern before turning. And, many times, anchored barges were washed ashore because of broken lines or too-light anchors.

The 46th NCB did the heavy overhaul work on the barges and the First "Special" took care of running repair. The First "Special" was later given all maintenance work. An Army gasoline tank truck was salvaged from the Public Works Yard. Bulk gas could then be hauled and transferred into a pontoon tank on the deck of the maintenance barge. Prior to this time, the barges had been gassed by hand pumping from barrels.

A machine shop, where engines were completely overhauled, was set up on the beach. One side of a finger pier was reserved for repair use. Here, repairs to propeller shafts and rudders were effected. Since most of the barges had pontoons with holes in them, they were pumped out and the holes patched.

At one time, 50 barges were being run 24 hours a day. Later, when ship piers were built at Kukum, an average of 30 barges proved adequate.

The First "Special" had another very important job, the loading of military cargo from the huge stockpiles on Guadalcanal into LCTs, LSTs, LCIs and other amphibious craft for upcoming invasions. Their first challenge would be the New Georgia invasion.*

On numerous occasions, the First "Special" NCB was subjected to aerial attacks, many of which occurred while stevedoring units were working aboard ships. On 16 June 1943, one of the greatest air battles in the South Pacific was fought over the First "Special's" stevedores and the ships they were unloading. Two ships, the *Celeno* (AK-76) and LST-340, took direct

---

* The editor was reminded of this while reading the following in the Admiral Nimitz, CinCPOA, June 1943 Report to the Joint Chiefs, "During the month of June, the supplies and equipment for the New Georgia movement were collected at Russell Islands from the stockpiles in the Guadalcanal area. A total of 23,775 drums of fuel and lubricants, 13,085 tons of gear, and 28 loaded vehicles were thus moved." —Ed.

hits and were badly burned, then beached. Crew members were swimming everywhere while Japanese planes swooped low and strafed them in the water. The Seabee stevedores at Tenaru Beach came to the rescue in their small boats.*

Not all Seabee activities were work. Movies and an occasional camp show helped break the monotony, and the native families were friendly.

First "Special" by the Numbers.   During the first three months of its Guadalcanal duty, the First "Special" handled 112,407 tons of cargo from 33 ships off Guadalcanal. During this time, there were 26 air alerts and two very serious bombing raids.

During 16 months of operation on Guadalcanal, the following results were achieved:

> Tons of cargo unloaded 560,000
> Tons of cargo loaded 33,000
> Average tons of cargo per hatch hour. 13

The First "Special" was a proud and patriotic outfit. They worked long and hard days to "Keep the hook moving!" They were proud of being the first stevedore battalion working at the first Advance Base in direct support of our troops in the Pacific. (By the end of the war, there would be 39 Stevedore battalions.)

They won the thanks and admiration of the hundreds of freighter crews—Army, Coast Guard, Merchant Marine and Naval Armed Guard— for the prompt and efficient stevedore service they provided. And, it goes without saying, they were appreciated immensely by the troops on the front lines who needed that materiel and those supplies to survive and win.

(Source: Gulbranson, "History of the First Special U.S. Naval Construction Battalion, 1942–1946.") ∎

* * *

* This attack is detailed in Chapter 5. —Ed.

"Brass" Accolades for the Seabees

Editor: A few words from the "brass" on the importance of the Seabees' constructing and maintaining shore facilities around the world.

"Eighty percent of my time was given to logistics during the first four months of the WATCHTOWER operation because we were living from one logistic crisis to another."

—*Admiral Richmond Kelley Turner,*
Amphibious Task Force 62

"Had it not been for this chain of advance bases, the fleet could not have operated in the western reaches of the Pacific without the necessity for many more ships and planes than it actually had. A base to supply or repair a fleet 5,000 miles closer to the enemy multiplies the power which can be maintained constantly against him and greatly lessens the problems of supply and repair. The scope of the advance base program is indicated by the fact that the personnel assigned directly to it aggregated almost one-fifth of the entire personnel of the Navy."

—*Fleet Admiral Ernest J. King, Commander in Chief,*
United States Fleet, and Chief of Naval Operations

"The Marines were at Guadalcanal, thank God, but the Seabees were there, too.

The Marines did the fighting. . .the Seabees had nothing else to do but:

1. Build and operate Henderson Field,
2. chase Jap bombs and shells around the field and fill up the holes faster than the Japs could blast them,
3. build the docks and unload the ships,

4. cut a few million feet of lumber out of the swamps and convert it into docks, warehouses and barracks,

5. drain the swamps and kill the mosquitoes, and then

6. build a few hundred miles of roads."

—Lieutenant (jg) William Bradford Huie, CEC, USNR

"I do not know how we could have gotten along without the Seabees."

—General A. A. Vandegrift, USMC

". . .In the Solomon Islands campaign the Seabees demonstrated their ability to outbuild the Japs and to repair airfields and build new bases, regardless of conditions of weather. There can be no doubt that the Seabees constitute an invaluable component of our Navy."

—From the official report by Fleet Admiral Ernest J. King, Commander in Chief, United States Fleet, and Chief of Naval Operations

". . .the Seabees are the find of this war."

—Major General H. M. Smith, USMC

⋅⁝⋅ ⋅⁝⋅ ⋅⁝⋅

Editor: Continuing from the Department of the Navy's *Building the Navy's Bases in WWII:*

More Guadalcanal *and Tulagi* Construction

Guadalcanal Construction

Pagoda Hill Communications Tunnels.   During September 1942, Japanese bombing and shelling threatened vital radio and radar equipment, all of which was surface housed, so it became necessary to get the equipment under ground as soon as possible.

The 6th NCB undertook tunneling operations into Pagoda Hill, just a few feet from Henderson Field. Because of the urgency of the situation, three eight-hour shifts were put to work. Air spades, air drills, and hand shovels were used and Japanese cars, on Japanese rails, were used to remove the spoil. On 14 October, all equipment was moved from the Pagoda building on top of the hill into the tunnel just before a new Japanese shelling took place. In all, four such tunnels were built by the Seabees.

More Airfields.   To supplement Henderson Field, three secondary flight strips were built close by: Number One was a rolled-turf strip, 4,600 feet by 300 feet, constructed in three days, using Japanese equipment entirely; Number Two was a grading job accomplished with a single scraper and one bulldozer which pulled some Japanese trusses rigged into a drag; and Number Three was a rolled-turf strip used only for dispersal. The last two strips were on the front line at the time of construction. Marine patrols set up emplacements and stood guard while the construction work was underway.

The 14th NCB, which had landed at Koli Point in early November 1942, began work on an emergency fighter strip, later called Carney Field, in the Koli Point area on 5 December 1942.

Tank Farms for the Airfields.   Concurrent with construction of the airfields was the erection of tank farms. Late in October 1942, the 6th NCB started work on three 250-barrel tanks for aviation gas at Henderson Field. Up to that time, fuel drums had been discharged from cargo vessels onto landing barges, unloaded at the beach, and then transported by trucks to fuel dumps near the airfield. Such operations were labor intensive and, at times, it was impossible to furnish enough fuel to satisfy operating requirements. The three tanks were located so that the drums could be rolled from the trucks onto a rack then emptied into a trough discharging into the tank. Fuel for use on the field was drawn from the tanks into tank trucks.

In December 1942, additional storage volume was provided through the erection of one 1,000-barrel and two 10,000-barrel prefabricated steel tanks. The final step in the construction of the tank farm was the laying of a 6-inch welded pipeline connecting a distributing point on the beach to the various tanks.

The 26th NCB, which arrived on 26 December 1942, erected two additional 10,000-barrel aviation-gasoline tanks and nine 1,000-barrel tanks for Henderson Field and the supplementary fighter strips. At Kukum they built a tank farm providing storage for two million gallons of aviation gasoline, one million gallons of motor gasoline, and 42,000 gallons of diesel oil.

In March 1943, a detachment of 260 men from the 34th NCB, stationed at Tulagi, was ordered to Guadalcanal to take over the building of a 36,000-barrel tank farm at Koli Point begun by the 14th and 46th NCBs. The tank farm, with a total capacity of 1,300,000 gallons of aviation gasoline and 500,000 gallons of motor gasoline in thirty-five 1,000-barrel tanks and one 10,000-barrel tank, was completed by May 1943. The tanks were well dispersed and concealed in heavy jungle growth in seven groupings. A submerged line was installed to moorings off Koli Point to permit tankers to discharge their cargoes into the storage tanks.

Waterfront Facilities.   Until Guadalcanal was secured, waterfront facilities were virtually non-existent. Unloading from ships to beaches was accomplished by means of light landing-craft, tank lighters, and pontoon barges. Work parties of Marines and the 6th NCB generally did their own unloading, except during critical periods when the Marines had to man the front lines.

During the early months of the campaign, coconut-log ramps about 35 feet long and wide enough to accommodate a truck were constructed extending far enough offshore to float a landing craft at the outer end.

Later, three timber piers were built. The first was constructed by repairing an old enemy pier at Kukum, using creosoted telephone poles left by the Japanese. On the day that the pier was completed, enemy artillery got range on the area, forcing its temporary abandonment and the pier was left unused for several months. To substitute for it, two small piers were constructed at Lunga.

Harbor facilities were considerably extended during the latter half of 1943 after U.S. forces took control of the enemy airfields in the Central Solomons. The Seabees assembled pontoon barges to aid in unloading, and built finger piers at various locations around the island. Two T-shaped piers, having 40-foot water depth at their outboard ends, were constructed at Kukum. A pier to accommodate Liberty ships was also built at Point Cruz. One Army port battalion and four amphibious truck companies handled unloading operations.

Road Construction.   Initially, road construction on Guadalcanal was delayed by the pressing need to complete the airfields and by a shortage of equipment. When the 6th NCB was relieved of airfield construction about the middle of November 1942, its attention turned to road construction. No attempt was made to remove the layer of organic materiel which formed a sub-base for most of the roads, but a 12- to 18-inch clay blanket was placed over it, traffic-compacted, and surfaced with 6 inches of gravel. Later, the 14th and 26th NCBs added some 96 miles of road to the 24 miles built by the 6th NCB.

One of the more interesting tasks of the 26th NCB at Guadalcanal was the construction of the 1.2 mile "Guadalcanal-Bougainville-Tokyo Railway."

Repair and Storage Facilities.   Repair facilities on Guadalcanal were limited. Boat repair units at Lunga Point and Koli Point were equipped to handle repairs and to overhaul engines for small boats and landing craft only.

Quonset huts and 40-foot arch-rib warehouses were constructed by the Seabees for Navy and Army aviation supplies, for a naval supply depot, and for a medical supply depot.

In July 1943, a Navy construction-materiels depot was set up to supply all construction battalions with much-needed spare parts for repair of their equipment and with expendable materiels used in construction. By November 1943, an aviation repair and overhaul unit had been placed in operation to handle necessary repairs to structural sections of aircraft, manufacture sheet-metal parts, and repair stationary and moveable control surfaces.

Hospitals.   The principal naval medical facilities at Guadalcanal consisted of the 1,290-bed hospital for MOB 8, supplemented by a 300-bed hospital for Acorn 1. The work of the Seabees in hospital construction was severely hampered by lack of building materiels. To take care of the situation, temporary structures were improvised out of native materiel to accommodate the overflow of patients until permanent surgical facilities and other requirements could be completed.

Malaria Control.   The plan to use Guadalcanal for extensive staging operations was greatly handicapped by malaria, which rose to epidemic proportions during the rainy season. Accordingly, 14 officers and 650 men of the 63rd NCB, which had arrived on 11 June 1943, were assigned to malaria control. With assistance of native labor, Seabees removed logs, roots, and overhanging trees from the banks of streams and lagoons and submerged snags from the stream beds.

In small streams, this brought about an increase in the rate of flow so that breeding of the anopheles mosquito was checked. In the case of lagoons or the larger, slower-moving streams, clearing their banks permitted easier access for the oiling crews on their periodic missions.

In endeavoring to free lagoons on the flat coastal plains from anophelene larvae, it was necessary to surmount the obstacle of sandbars by devising a method to permit egress of infected lagoon water to the sea. Control methods included the clearing of the banks and the installation of culverts, fabricated from discarded oil drums, through the sandbars.

Complete swamp drainage on the 'Canal was found to be impossible; therefore, the swamps were ditched so that the water could collect in pools, where it could be oiled.

Native Labor and Materials.   Native labor was used principally in stevedoring operations, handling materiel at cargo and ration dumps, building native-type structures for warehouses and offices, clearing and oiling streams for malaria control, and, during the early stages of construction, as common labor on airfield construction.

Materiels found on Guadalcanal were widely used on construction projects. River gravel, mixed with sand-clay silt as a binder, provided support for airstrip steel-mat surfacing. Decayed coral was later used for runways, taxiways, and hardstands. Gravel and some coral were used for road construction. Good hardwood, mahogany, rosewood, and teakwood furnished piling and timbers for wharves and bridges. Many offices and warehouses were built of native poles, with side and roof materiels procured from the coconut tree.

The 61st NCB, from June 1943 to January 1944, set up and operated two sawmills which produced more than one million board feet of lumber, in addition to numerous piles for camp, bridge and pier construction. The 26th and 46th NCBs also operated sawmills.

The 63rd NCB built dock facilities at Tetere Beach. Using piling, caps, stringers, and decking obtained from the jungle, they erected a stage, 40 feet square, with a 12-foot driveway extending 60 feet to shore. A ramp on the seaward side facilitated unloading of heavy ordnance and equipment.

Battalion Credits.   A total of 17 Naval Construction Battalions, including 5 "Special" stevedore battalions, were assigned to Guadalcanal. All were subjected to intermittent air raids (until the fall of 1943), but the most severe punishment was taken by the 6th NCB during the first months of airfield construction. Other early battalions were under the constant strain that goes with frequent air raids, but they suffered no personnel losses.

By the end of 1942, the 14th, 18th, and 26th NCBs had reported to Guadalcanal, in addition to the original 6th NCB (which was transferred in January 1943).

During 1943, the 34th, 46th, 61st, 63rd, 53rd, and 27th NCBs arrived, as well as the 1st, 4th, and 9th "Special" NCBs.

Construction Battalion Maintenance Unit 501 (CBMU) took over part of the maintenance duties on Guadalcanal in March 1943. During the early months of 1944, CBMUs 532, 533, 518, and 520 assumed responsibility for maintenance and minor construction activities. By that time, all battalions, with the exception of the "Specials," had been withdrawn.

The 18th, 25th, and 58th NCBs staged through Guadalcanal with Marine divisions, and numerous other Seabee groups were at Guadalcanal for staging activities prior to forward movements.

The naval air base on Guadalcanal was disestablished on 12 June 1946.

Tulagi Construction

Concurrent with the building up of the large advance base on Guadalcanal, Tulagi, located across Iron Bottom Sound and part of the Florida Island group, was developed as a small naval base. It provided a well-protected harbor where large ships could anchor, and facilities were established for the reserve storage of fuel and diesel oil, and for the support of seaplanes, landing craft, and motor torpedo boats.

PT-Boat Base.   In October 1942, a detachment of 59 men of the 6th NCB was sent from Guadalcanal to Tulagi to build a PT-boat base at Sesapi. The strength of the detachment was later increased to 133 men.

First, an emergency outlet channel for Tulagi harbor was dredged and blasted to avoid having PT boats bottled up by enemy warships. Two PT-boat floating drydocks were assembled from pontoons; a 500-man camp was set up; and power and telephone systems to serve the island and harbor area were installed. The detachment also furnished a number of carpenter details to assist with the maintenance and repair of PT boats.

In addition, PT-boat facilities were constructed on the island of Macambo, with base housing at Calvertville on Florida Island. An existing concrete wharf at Macambo, in need of repair but still serviceable, was used, but it was necessary to build torpedo overhaul and storage facilities.

In July 1943, three PT Squadrons were using the Sesapi and Macambo bases. Two 1,000-barrel tanks for aviation gasoline were erected at Sesapi and eight 1,000-barrel tanks at Macambo, with loading line to the dock.

Halavo Seaplane Base.   Before leaving the Tulagi area in January 1943, the 6th NCB detachment began construction of a seaplane base at Halavo on Florida Island. The completion of this base became the major task of the 34th NCB when it arrived on Tulagi on 12 February 1943.

A tent camp was erected for 1,500 men and 300 officers. In planning for the seaplane facilities, due to the shortage of cement it was decided to use steel mat on the ramps and apron. A temporary mat ramp, 25 feet wide, had been completed when priorities for work at Halavo were reduced in May 1943 to allow concentration on work in the Russells and on Guadalcanal.

Priorities were then established as follows: 1) base roads, 2) a 12,000-barrel tank farm, 3) a small apron without mat.

Toward the end of June 1943, a squadron of 15 PBYs was added to the scouting squadron already operating from the base, and another temporary ramp of steel mat was laid for their use.

Construction of the tank farm was completed, including a filling line to the beach and a delivery line to the ramp. Thirty wooden buildings for administration and shops were constructed as fast as the output of the local sawmill permitted.

The Marston mat ramps were considered wholly satisfactory in service, and it was estimated that their substitution for concrete saved about two months' construction time.

Landing-Craft Repair Base. On 22 April 1943, instructions were received calling for the establishment of a base for landing craft in the Tulagi area. The base was to be self-sustaining and mobile, in the sense that disassembly and reshipment of its facilities to forward areas and resumption of normal operation could be accomplished with a minimum of delay. The base was to be capable of keeping 80 landing craft in repair.

The base called for was established by the 27th NCB at Carter City on Florida Island, between April and August 1943. Warehouses, tropical-hut housing for officers and men, and other camp facilities were provided. One 350-ton, 6 by 24 foot pontoon drydock for LCIs was assembled. On 22 August 1943, the operation of the repair base was taken over by Construction Battalion Detachment (CBD) 1008.

The 27th NCB also constructed facilities on Gavutu Harbor for the functioning of two amphibious boat repair and training centers, and the training of their crews prior to forward-area assignment.

The base at Turner City, on Florida Island, included camp facilities for 400 men and officers, a pier 10 by 130 feet, a 2 by 12 pontoon finger pier for small craft, and two steel arch-rib warehouses to be used as shops. At the base on Gavutu, steel arch-rib buildings were erected for shops and two

10,000-barrel aviation-gasoline tanks were built concealed in a hillside. An existing concrete wharf, 125 by 150 feet, providing 20-foot-draft berthing space, was repaired and equipped with a marine railway. These facilities were essentially completed by August 1943.

Hospital Facilities.   Illness was even more prevalent on Tulagi than on Guadalcanal. Medical facilities, as established, consisted of a 200-bed hospital at the Halavo seaplane base and the "Blue Beach" Hospital on Tulagi. The first 200-bed unit at Blue Beach, consisting of 35 Quonset huts originally part of CUB 2, was completed by the 27th NCB in May 1943.

Waterfront Facilities.   Waterfront facilities at Tulagi Harbor were improved and extended by the Seabees. The 6th NCB installed a five-ton stiff-leg derrick, built from Japanese structural steel and powered by a salvaged Japanese automobile engine on Government Wharf. The wharf, built of timber, was enlarged by the 27th NCB. The 27th also constructed Sturgess Wharf, with a 140-foot face and 40-foot water depth.

Tulagi Wrap-Up.   The Japanese did not bomb Tulagi until February 1943. However, from that time until the following June, the Seabees were subjected to occasional air raids. It should be noted that the gunners of the 27th NCB were given partial credit for downing three Japanese planes.

When CBMU 521 reported to Tulagi in December 1943, all the other Seabees had left with the exception of the 34th NCB. That battalion was relieved by CBMU 505 in March 1944.

Battalion Credits.   The 6th, 27th and 34th NCBs, plus the 9th "Special" NCB, were the major builders of the Tulagi naval base. Many landing ships, craft, and PT-boats considered it "home" after runs up the slot long after Tulagi and Guadalcanal had been secured.

Seabee Facts and Veterans Groups

- Many battalions took part in the transformation of the Southern Solomons from jungle to advance bases. Construction pioneers included the 6th NCB followed closely by the 14th, 18th, and 26th NCBs. The 27th, 34th, 46th, 61st, and 63rd NCBs all arrived in

1943. The First "Special" NCB was the pioneer stevedore outfit charged with relieving the unloading bottleneck at the 'Canal. They were followed by the 4th and 9th "Special" NCBs.

- As the Guadalcanal advance base developed, the Seabees were organized into the 18th Naval Construction Regiment. Later, when most construction work was completed and only maintenance was necessary, the full 1,100-man battalions were replaced by the smaller Construction Battalion Maintenance Units. Other battalions would use the 'Canal as a staging base later in the war.
- Approximately 325,000 men joined the Seabees during WWII; they already knew, or would soon learn, one or more of 60 skilled trades.
- Nearly 11,400 officers were commissioned in the Civil Engineer Corps during WWII; 7,960 of them served with the Seabees.
- The Seabees constructed more than 400 advance bases along five figurative "roads" (sealanes) to victory; all had their beginnings in the continental United States.
- In the North, Central, South and Southwest Pacific areas, the Seabees built 111 major airstrips, 441 piers, 2,558 ammunition magazines, 700 square blocks of warehouses, hospitals to serve 70,000 patients, tanks for the storage of 100,000,000 gallons of gasoline, and housing for 1,500,000 men.
- Seabees earned 33 Silver Stars and 5 Navy Crosses during World War II. However, they also paid a price: 272 enlisted men and 18 officers were killed in action. In addition to deaths sustained as a result of enemy action, more than 500 Seabees died in construction accidents. Pacific Seabees suffered more than 200 combat deaths during construction and fighting operations and earned more than 2,000 Purple Hearts.

(Source: Department of the Navy, *Building the Navy's Bases in World War II*, Vol. 2, 248–256.) ■

Seabee Veterans Groups

Editor: For information on specific Seabee Battalions, membership, reunions, or newsletters, Seabee veterans or their families may contact the following organizations: Navy Seabee Veterans of America, Inc., *www.nsva.org;* and CEC/Seabee Historical Foundation, *www.seabeehf.org.*

Amphibious Landings. First Division Marines storm ashore across Guadalcanal's beaches on D-Day, 7 August 1942, from the attack transport *Barnett* (AP-11) and attack cargo ship *Formalhaut* (AK-22). The invaders were surprised by the lack of enemy opposition. (National Archives)

Amphibious forces off Guadalcanal on D-Day, 7 August 1942. Four transports (AP) and a large number of small landing craft are present. (National Archives)

Unloading 500-pound bombs at Segi, New Georgia. Flotilla 5, LCT-65, July 1943. (National Archives)

Seabee and Engineer Construction. Bulldozer (minus blade) known as "Old Faithful" to the NCB 26 on Tulagi, 1943. Sign reads "Old Faithful, *Wake, *Midway, *Pearl Harbor, **Guadalcanal, Tokyo?" (Naval Historical Center)

Cargo being unloaded from a pontoon barge onto an Amtrack during WWII. (USNCB)

Prime mover and low bed trailer. (Courtesy Earnie Crippen, First Special NCB)

USAAF B-24 bomber takes off from the island's airfield as Navy Seabees work to spread coral while widening the runway. Other B-24s are parked in the distance. (National Archives)

Road construction. (USNCB)

New road to fighter strip No. 2. (First Special NCB)

Completed bridge being lowered on bearings. (USNCB)

Erection of warehouses. (First Special NCB)

Ramp construction. (USNCB)

Piledriver. (Courtesy Earnie Crippen, First Special NCB)

"Builders at the front" holding captured Japanese flag. (Courtesy Earnie Crippen, First Special NCB)

U.S. Navy radio station. (First Special NCB)

"Kill the Bastards! Down this road marched one of the Regiments of the United States Army. Knights Serving the Queen of Battles. Twenty of their wounded [   ] were bayonetted, shot and clubbed by the yellow bellies. Kill the Bastards!" (Courtesy Paul Clodfelder, First Special NCB)

Guadalcanal, Bougainville & Tokyo Express (G.B.& T. R.R.) hauls supplies from the beach to the supply depot on Guadalcanal, 1943. Construction by 26th NCB. (USNCB)

Seabee Stevedores. First Special NCB campsite on Guadalcanal, circa 1943–44. (Courtesy Claude S. Gulbranson, First Special NCB)

U.S. mail goes through with some help from Seabee stevedores. (Courtesy Claude S. Gulbranson, First Special NCB)

Seabee crane unloading a ship-to-shore vessel. (Courtesy Earnie Crippen, First Special NCB)

First Special NCB gear room, Guadalcanal, 1943–44. (Courtesy Claude S. Gulbranson, First Special NCB)

Seabee stevedore gangs "keep the hook moving" while unloading a Liberty cargo ship at a new Kukum Dock, Guadalcanal, September 1943. (National Archives)

Part III

MANNING THE SHIPS AND DELIVERING THE GOODS

"A total of 6,700 merchant mariners were killed or missing in action and presumed dead; 670 were made prisoners of war.

A total of 1,810 Naval Armed Guard officers and men were killed or missing in action and presumed dead; 14 were made prisoners of war."

—C. A. Lloyd, Chairman, USN Armed Guard Veterans of WWII

Chapter 5
U.S. Merchant Marine and
U.S. Navy Armed Guard

Editor's note: This chapter covers the manning of the merchant fleet—some 6,236 vessels strong—by two different crew types who served together in thousands of ships during World War II. The civilian members of the U.S. Merchant Marine operated the ships and the U.S. Navy Armed Guard protected the ships and their valuable cargo from enemy attacks. Together their mission was to "deliver the goods."

In the Foreword to William L. McGee's *Bluejacket Odyssey, 1942–1946—Guadalcanal to Bikini, Naval Armed Guard in the Pacific,* Charles A. Lloyd, chairman of the U.S. Navy Armed Guard Veterans of WWII, summarized the unique relationship between the U.S. Merchant Marine and the U.S. Navy Armed Guard.

Principal sources for this chapter are John Gorley Bunker, *Liberty Ships—The Ugly Ducklings of World War II* (1972); Vice Admiral Emory S. Land, USN, *Winning the War with Ships—Land, Sea and Air, Mostly Land* (1958); William L. McGee, *Bluejacket Odyssey, 1942–1946—Guadalcanal to Bikini, Naval Armed Guard in the Pacific* (2000); and Bruce L. Felknor, ed., *The U.S. Merchant Marine at War, 1775–1945* (1998).

The Allies nearly lost the war at sea in 1942 when our supply lines were stretched dangerously thin. In the end, the race between American ship construction and sinkings by the enemy was won by the Allied convoy system, naval superiority in combating the submarine menace, and an unprecedented shipbuilding program.

The U.S. Merchant Marine and Naval Armed Guard took part in every major campaign in World War II:

- There were only about 55,000 merchant seamen and officers sailing in December 1941. The War Shipping Administration established a recruitment/training program which turned out 262,474 graduates during the war. This program resulted in a peak sea-going force of 250,000 Merchant Mariners.
- Up to V-J Day, 733 American merchant vessels of over 1,000 gross tons were sunk during the war—victims of torpedoes, bombs, mines, and marine disasters largely caused by war conditions.*
- A total of 144,970 Armed Guard enlisted men and officers served on 6,236 merchant ships (American- and foreign-flag) between 7 December 1941 and 30 September 1945. Armed Guard personnel peaked on 1 November 1944 with a total of 112,108 men.
- A total of 6,700 merchant mariners were killed or missing in action and presumed dead; 670 were made prisoners of war.
- A total of 1,810 Armed Guard officers and men were killed or missing in action and presumed dead; 14 were made prisoners of war.

The merchant mariners who operated the ships were civilians, but they were also under government control and subject to disciplinary actions by the U.S. Coast Guard and, when overseas, by local U.S. military authorities. The Merchant Marine crews served alongside the Armed Guard and together we delivered the goods. In times of trouble, they passed

---

* The War Shipping Administration also controlled many foreign flag ships. Several hundred merchant mariners and Armed Guard personnel were lost serving on these ships. —Ed.

the ammunition and gave us a helping hand whenever needed. As Mike Molinari, an Armed Guardsman, said, "When a ship is sunk, there is no difference between the Armed Guard sailor and the merchant mariner. They fought and died together as brothers and shipmates. Nobody can take that away from them."

Merchant seamen were finally recognized as veterans by an act of the U.S. Congress in 1988, forty-seven years after America's entry into World War II, and after many thousands of those who had served had passed away. I stand proud to have supported their efforts to obtain veteran status.

The mission of each Armed Guard crew was to protect the ship and its valuable cargo and crew from enemy attacks and sabotage from the day we boarded each vessel until we were properly relieved upon completion of the voyage.

The USN Armed Guard Veterans and the American Merchant Marine Veterans accept each other as members in our respective veteran's organizations. This book is a fitting tribute to the U.S. Merchant Marine and the defenders of their ships, the U.S. Naval Armed Guard.

The Naval Armed Guard's motto was "We aim to deliver!" And we did—with the help of the merchant seamen, our escort vessels, and the grace of God.

—*Charles A. Lloyd, Chairman,*
USN Armed Guard Veterans of WWII

(Source: McGee, *Bluejacket Odyssey*, Foreword, xiii–xv.) ∎

U.S. Merchant Marine

Editor's note: Added to the Herculean task of building the war-time merchant fleet by Admiral Emory S. Land, Admiral Howard Vickery, and Captain Edward Macauley, was the problem of how the ships were to be manned. Historian John Gorley Bunker, a World War II merchant mariner, writes from experience having served on two Liberty ships, "plus a half-dozen other merchant types as fireman, oiler, deck engineer and purser." In the fol-lowing excerpt from Bunker's *Liberty Ships—The Ugly Ducklings of World War II*, he defines the problem of manning the ships; then describes the solution.

In 1940 the entire United States merchant marine, from ocean liners to towboats, included some 65,000 men (and a few women). By June of 1943 this seagoing force had increased to 85,000. A year later it numbered 175,000 and when the war ended in August, 1945, it had reached a high of 250,000.

Who were these men? Where did they come from? How did they acquire the training necessary to take the ships where they were going and bring them home again?

Wartime merchant seamen came from all parts of the United States and from some allied nations. Boys too young to enlist or be drafted joined the merchant marine. Men too old for the draft, or who for one reason or another were not accepted by the armed forces, found in the merchant marine an opportunity to take an active part in the war effort.

Some men went to sea for what in those days was good pay and some did so to escape military service, but these were not the overriding attractions for most wartime volunteers. A man could make good pay in shipyards and war plants without any of the risks of seafaring. And as for escaping the draft, many thousands of young men who were attracted to sea by wartime recruiting posters had little if any concept of what life in the merchant marine was like—or what pay or danger was involved.

Captain Hollie J. Tiedemann, superintendent of the St. Petersburg training station of the U.S. Maritime Service, believed that relatively few of the thousands of boys who passed through the government training schools were attracted by the promise of high wages. "Most of them," he said, "came with a desire to have a part in the war. Money was a secondary consideration. The many I had occasion to talk to had little idea when they arrived at the school just what the pay would be. They had heard that the merchant marine was a good place to see action in a short time and they were eager to get in it."

Early in the war, ships sailed with a nucleus of old-timers among the crew, but later there were so many new ships that there were not enough veterans to go around. Many new ships were fortunate if they had a dozen men in the unlicensed crew who had more than a voyage or two behind them.

An early Liberty would have a crew of seagoing men from the prewar merchant marine, plus a handful of newcomers. The boatswain might be a tanned and brawny Dane; some of the able seamen might be Norwegians or Swedes who had spent most of their lives in sail and steam. The firemen were probably veterans of the old coal-burners; and oilers might be old-timers who could squirt oil from a can into a thimble-sized oil cup with the engine doing 70 revolutions a minute and never spill a drop. Cooks might have been Filipinos, wiry little men who traveled together from ship to ship; spoke Tagalog, and gambled their earnings away at cards long before the ship had reached its first port.

Such typical prewar merchant sailors knew no home but a ship—they were conscientious, hard workers at sea and hard drinkers in port. They made good shipmates, for they did their jobs and expected others to do the same. They were the kind of men who went down with the *Catahoula,* the *Selma City,* the *Norlindo,* the *Afoundria,* the *Marore,* and a hundred other ships in the early days of the war. It is an eternal tribute to the quality of these men, rough, tough and unpolished as they were, that ships never lacked crews or missed a sailing date in the days when many of them had no guns or armed escorts to protect them.

Such quality was highly diluted later in the war. . . .

And, of course, there were the vociferous few seeking the fast buck; the kind for whom, as the saying went, there were only three kinds of time on board ship: sack time, coffee time, and overtime.

The ships kept sailing despite a critical shortage of key personnel, but it took almost superhuman efforts on the part of the War Shipping Administration (WSA) to juggle crews. Often a ship arriving from a foreign voyage would be tapped for an engineer, radio officer, boatswain, or perhaps even her master so that another ship that had completed loading its cargo could join a convoy on schedule. . . .

The amazing thing was that with such hodgepodge crews, the ships left port, for the most part maneuvered according to convoy plan, arrived at their assigned destination, and came home again.

Finding and training enough engineers, navigators and ship handlers was a far different matter from filling the required unlicensed billets aboard a ship. Handling a ship in convoy, especially in fog, dark of night, or evasive maneuvers, or taking it to a port halfway around the world was not something that could be left to novices.

Crewing the ships was a joint effort by the various maritime unions, government and steamship company hiring halls, and the government training schools, including the United Sates Merchant Marine Academy and the state maritime academies operated by Maine, Massachusetts, Pennsylvania, New York and California.

The War Shipping Administration conducted a nationwide recruiting drive in 1942 to find former seamen who had left the merchant marine for jobs on shore. More than 16,000 men with prior experience returned to sea by November of 1942, a time when the shipping industry was still experiencing heavy losses. . . .

A training division, the U.S. Maritime Service, was set up within the War Shipping Administration in July 1942 under Captain Edward Macauley. . . .

The Maritime Service operated seven training ships, but their activities were considerably curtailed by the dangers of wartime cruising. . . .

The largest of the training establishments for unlicensed seamen was the one at Sheepshead Bay, Brooklyn, New York. . . .Other schools were located at St. Petersburg, Florida, and at Avalon on Catalina Island off the Southern California coast.

Officer training schools were established at Fort Trumbul, Connecticut, and Alameda, California. There was an acute shortage of radio operators when the mass production of ships commenced and schools to train them were located at Gallup's Island in Boston harbor and at Hoffman Island, New York. . . .

The WSA schools for unlicensed men and officers, plus upgrading and refresher courses, turned out 270,000 graduates, including 10,000 officers from the U.S. Merchant Marine Academy and the state maritime academies. The short courses for upgrading unlicensed men to officer status produced 23,000 mates and engineers. Basic schools trained 155,000 men for shipboard jobs. More than 7,500 radio officers were trained as well as 5,300 pursers, who also served as pharmacist's mates.

During the summer of 1943 there were times when as many as 600 deck officers had no licenses . . .

During the summer of 1943 there were times when as many as 600 deck officers had no licenses, sailing on temporary emergency endorsements issued by the Coast Guard. There was always a greater shortage of engine-room personnel, and at the same time, as many as 1,000 engineers had no licenses. Hundreds of seamen who had sufficient sea-time requirements but lacked the official license were moved up into officer positions, and the ships went out, usually on schedule.

Every possible scheme was tried to find qualified people. Employers were asked to release men with prior sea experience, and veteran merchant seamen who had been drafted into the armed forces were released for service in the merchant marine. Hundreds of men were added to the merchant marine in this way. . . .

The age limit for enlistment in the Maritime Service was lowered to 16 years in May 1944 as a further expedient toward getting men. During the following week more than 7,000 adventure-minded youngsters volunteered at some 40 recruiting offices throughout the nation.

But it was not only the youngsters who showed up and wanted to go to sea. Men who were old enough to be their grandfathers, and who could have stayed at home and listened to war reports on the radio, chose to be back where the action was.

Percy P. Evans was 70 years of age when he signed on as engineer for the *Joseph R. Drake*. William Mallett had been chief engineer on the transport *America* in World War I; he returned to sea in World War II as chief engineer of the *John Davenport*. . . .

There could be a wide spread in ages among crews. When the *Oliver Wolcott*, left New Orleans "for ports of the world" in October of 1944, Chief Engineer Frank Aiken, and Chief Mate Hugh Young were both 67 years old. Radio Operator Herman Stone Jr. was 19, and Acting Second Mate John Shuttleworth was only 20. A dozen of the 44-man crew were under 20 and several were only 16. This was truly an all-American crew, from 15 different states.

Merchant Marine Crews

Editor: To put some numbers to the manning challenge, consider this: Based on a 1944 average of 41 Merchant Marine and 27 Armed Guard per ship, it would take 111,110 Merchant Mariners and 43,170 Armed Guardsmen to man 2,710 Liberty ships

The average Liberty ship carried a Merchant Marine crew of about 41 men. The combined crew averages for the Liberty ships were: Deck Dept., 17.3 men; Engine Dept., 13.0 men; Steward's Dept., 10.0 men; and total crew average including Master, 41.3 men.

A Victory ship crew averaged closer to 55 men. For the SS *Yugoslavia Victory,* it was Deck Dept., 21; Engine Dept., 19; Steward's Dept., 15; and total crew average including Master, 56.*

John Gorley Bunker described an average Liberty ship crew:

- Deck officers included the master, chief mate, second and third mates.
- Engine officers included the chief engineer and first, second and third assistants.
- The deck crew included a boatswain, six able seamen, three ordinary seamen, and a carpenter.
- Unlicensed engine room personnel included three firemen, three oilers, two wipers, and a deck engineer who took care of the deck winches, steam lines, radiators, and other equipment outside the engine spaces.
- The steward's department, always an important part of a Liberty ship's complement, included a chief steward, chief cook, second cook, night cook and baker, six messmen, and a galleyman.
- Each ship also carried a radio operator and a purser to take care of ship's business.

There were variations in manning, depending partly on contracts between the operating company and the unions manning the ship. Some vessels had no carpenter but did carry a deck maintenance man, a day-worker in the deck force. Many Libertys with Army cargo also carried a cargo security officer, a representative of the Army and not part of the crew. Libertys carrying troops had additional cooks and messmen. Many carried from two to four deck and engine midshipmen from the U.S. Merchant Marine Academy at Kings Point, New York. These cadets spent at least a year aboard ship as part of their four-year training program and served with distinction throughout the war. . . .

---

* During World War II, the editor served in the Pacific in three Libertys (SS *Nathaniel Currier,* SS *David Belasco,* SS *Thomas Nelson*) and one Victory ship (SS *Yugoslavia Victory*). Two voyage actions are covered later in this chapter. —Ed.

Pay scales in the prewar Merchant Marine were moderate at best. From 1940 on, the government approved special, additional compensation for crews on ships subject to enemy attack. This compensation was finally standardized, effective 24 February 1943, in the form of voyage, area, and attack bonuses.

A seaman was paid an additional 40 to 100 percent of his total wages, including overtime, during the time his ship was transiting certain areas considered subject to enemy action. . . .

Pay was further boosted by an "area bonus" of $5 per day for each day the vessel spent in any of three specified areas:

- Murmansk—the Atlantic and Arctic Oceans east of the Greenwich Meridian and west of 60 degrees east longitude, and north of 60 degrees north latitude.
- Mediterranean—east of a line from Cape Spartel to Cape Trafalgar, including the Adriatic and Aegean Seas.
- South Seas—the area bounded on the north by 20 degrees north latitude, on the east by 170 degrees east longitude, on the south by 20 degrees south latitude, and on the west by 120 degrees east longitude.

Finally, there was a bonus of $125 paid to each man if a vessel was under enemy attack at any port or anchorage.

It was no wonder that Armed Guard gunners, sharing the same dangers, felt that they were coming out on the short end and expressed their resentment against the better-paid merchant crew. . . .

The tremendous wartime expansion inevitably brought a larger share of laggards, misfits, and performers aboard ship. They served only to provide the number of "bodies" required by law before the ship could sail, contributed nothing to the success of the voyage, and often turned an otherwise happy ship into a trouble ship. . . .

"The principal cause of difficulties on board ship," said a WSA report of August 1945, were "clashes of personalities, intransigence, incompetence and negligence.". . .

Failure to join a ship on sailing day or being absent without leave were the major reasons for disciplinary action, providing close to 40 percent of the total number of cases. Negligence or incompetence on the job accounted for 27 percent of the disciplinary actions, with misconduct, including drunkenness and assault, contributing 14 percent. Censorship violations, pilferage, theft, and a variety of other offenses accounted for the rest.

(Source: Bunker, *Liberty Ships*, 19–24, 33–36.) ∎

❖ ❖ ❖

Editor: Vice Admiral Emory S. Land, USN, served as head of both the U.S. Maritime Commission and the War Shipping Administration during World War II. In Land's *Winning the War with Ships—Land, Sea and Air—Mostly Land,* the Vice Admiral bottom-lined his assessment of the merchant mariner:

Despite much criticism, these seamen did a noteworthy job. But to say that there was no trouble, or even that it was minor, would be to stretch the truth.

There is little or no romance in the merchant marine; no glamour, no sex appeal, no uniform for the sailor; and very little attention given to his welfare on the beach; in fact, little overall interest of any kind comparable to that for the military services. The only time the merchant marine is appreciated is in the time of a national emergency as an auxiliary to the armed services. In peacetime it is quickly forgotten.

Editor: Land explains the seriousness of the Merchant Marine labor problems:

Labor Relations

It should be remembered that a series of long strikes in the 1930s had brought the shipping industry to a standstill. When negotiations ended, merchant seamen had gained many of the rights they had long fought for. From this period, two very strong unions emerged: Joe Curran's National Maritime Union (NMU) and Harry Lundeberg's Sailors' Union of the Pacific (SUP).

When war came, it was obvious that great demands would be made on the Merchant Marine. Union leaders therefore vigilantly watched for any encroachment on the seamen's newly gained rights.

The maritime unions had won the right to control the hiring of all unlicensed personnel manning U.S. merchant ships. The prospect that the unions feared most was that war necessity might erode or demolish all the gains they had won for their members in years of bitter strikes and struggle.

When the American merchant marine was taken over by the WSA in April 1942 most seagoing personnel were members of maritime labor unions and were covered by collective bargaining agreements. Maritime unions agreed that the right to strike would not be exercised for the duration of the war, that the authority of the master of a ship in wartime operations would be strengthened, and that no changes would be made in collective bargaining agreements without WSA approval.

In the early months of the war, the unions and the WSA battled over various problems including:

(1)   The leasing or lending of U.S. flag merchantmen to Allied Governments and the use of their seamen to man them. President Roosevelt came up with a solution that gave the C.I.O. further cause to complain. On February 22, 1943, FDR wrote Admiral Land:

"...Norway undoubtedly has a dozen ready-to-move crews of experience. That is probably not as true in the case of other nations. This manning of ships to which we retain title by transferring them temporarily to a foreign crew which knows how to run the ship is a good thing because it relieves to some extent our own problem of placing an experienced crew on board."

On May 28, 1943, the President followed this line of thought further
in his letter to Prime Minister Winston Churchill:

> "Our merchant fleet has become larger and will con-
> tinue to grow at a rapid rate. To man its ever-increasing
> number of vessels will, we foresee, present difficulties of
> no mean proportion. On your side, the British Merchant
> fleet has been steadily dwindling. . .and you have in your
> pool as a consequence about 10,000 trained seamen and
> licensed personnel. Clearly it would be extravagant were
> this body of experienced men of the sea not to be used as
> promptly as possible. . . ."

(2)   The threat of the Navy taking over the Merchant Marine personnel because of reported incidents of drunkenness, insubordina-
tion and troublemaking by individuals whom the unions called
"performers." President Roosevelt put this rumor to bed when
he wrote Senator Radcliffe on May 2, 1942:

> "I have your letter of April 10th in which you refer
> to the current rumors that the officers and seamen of the
> Merchant Marine are shortly to be turned over to the
> Navy Department. I agree with you that at the present
> time such a move is not necessary, and would be unwise."

In spite of seemingly insurmountable differences at times, Joe Curran
and the National Maritime Union joined other unions in signing the
agreement with the War Shipping Administration that guaranteed their
bargaining rights but temporarily froze wages. The hiring halls were to
remain, and all government trainees would pass through them and be
given permits or trip cards.

A prewar division which allocated ships between the A.F.L. and C.I.O.
was maintained. A Maritime War Emergency Board with Captain Edward
Macauley as Chairman was given the power to decide on future changes

in pay and make decisions on hazardous duty pay which was ill-advisedly called a "war bonus."

Vice Admiral Emory S. Land reached the same conclusion many other high-level Washington people had when he wrote, "Criticism and attacks, even scurrilous ones, are the lot of any person who moves into the spotlight. In Washington, especially, the head that shows above the parapet gets shot at promptly."

(Source: Land, *Winning the War with Ships*, 192–207.) ■

∴ ∴ ∴

Editor: Continuing from Bunker's *Liberty Ships:*

General Operations

The next step after a ship was built, christened, and launched, was "delivery," which depended on how long fitting-out took. As an example, the *Richard Henry Dana. . .*was launched on 12 July 1942. Fitting-out was completed on 31 July, and then the ship was ready for delivery by the shipyard. It was turned over to the U.S. Maritime Commission and then to the general agent—in this case the American Mail Line—assigned by the War Shipping Administration to operate the ship for the government.

The brief, unceremonious delivery usually accounted for the first entry in a new ship's log, as it did for the *Dana* on 31 July 1942: "4:30 p.m. *Richard Henry Dana* officially delivered by the California Shipbuilding Corp. to the American Mail Line. Hull number 45, Calship. Hull number 294 Maritime Commission."

Loading began on 2 August. Guns were mounted three days later. Carpenters were completing the catwalks over the deckload on 10 August when Pilot Maland came aboard and the crew made preparations for getting underway. The ship began her maiden voyage, out of San Pedro, the next afternoon.

From the moment that the American Mail Line, as general agent, took delivery, it handled the myriad details of loading, provisioning, fueling, manning, and obtaining port clearance for the ship. Most general agents were well-known steamship owners and operators with long experience in the shipping business. But as wartime shipping increased tremendously, it strained the facilities of "old line" operators and new, lesser known firms were appointed as agents by the WSA.

It was a policy to appoint only firms with a background of deep-sea operations. Great pressure was put on the WSA and the Maritime Commission to grant general agency status to ill-equipped firms or to those set up as wartime ventures ready to assume an overnight corporate status for the prospect of a "quick buck." Many such applicants for general agency appointment were turned down for lack of sufficient experience, resources, and personnel, and because their appointment would serve only to pirate trained men from existing organizations. . . .

A steamship company acting as a general agent for the WSA experienced a meteoric increase in operations and personnel. Alaska Steamship Company, as an example, operated 17 ships before the war, only between Seattle, the Alaskan mainland and Aleutian ports. By the end of 1943, the company was agent for 82 WSA vessels engaged in worldwide operations.

Steamship company staffs had to be enlarged many times to handle the vast amount of detail connected with such far-flung operations. Operators had lost some of their best people, in many cases, to the Army and Navy and had to make up for it by working their staffs long hours, seven days a week. . . .Ships would never have been loaded and dispatched had it not been for the hard work put in by steamship company staffs.

General Agents Role

A general agent had to supply stores and fuel for the ship and arrange for tugs, pilot and customs clearance at the time of sailing. They arranged for berthing the ship and for cargo handling through a stevedoring firm.

They arranged for signing on a crew, prepared payrolls, and paid-off the crew when the voyage was ended.

A large part of the general agent's staff work involved compiling and submitting detailed voyage accounts to the WSA for every trip made by every vessel. Even the smallest expenditures during the trip had to be itemized and accounted for. All such expenditures were double-checked by WSA auditors who worked in the agent's own offices.

The general agent also had to arrange for representation in any foreign port where ships under its control might call, by appointing subagents, either American or foreign firms with experience in ship operation. Fees charged by subagents were added to bills submitted to the government by the agent.

The captain of a ship operating under agency agreement usually carried about $10,000 in cash for advances to the crew in foreign ports and for purchase of emergency supplies. Additional money could be obtained from subagents or from overseas offices of the WSA.

Maiden Voyage

After a ship was delivered, the next event was her departure on a maiden voyage, which might well be an around-the-world trip. For example, the *William B. Giles*, delivered on 29 August 1942, sailed from New Orleans in September, cleared the Canal Zone on 10 October, and headed for Cape Horn, via the Pacific. She reached Cape Town on 14 November and on 15 December was in Bombay to discharge cargo. More cargo was discharged in Colombo, Calcutta, and Madras. She loaded at Vizagapatam on 22 January 1943, crossed the Indian Ocean to Hobart, Tasmania, then sailed via Panama to Guantanamo Bay, Cuba and New York where she arrived on 17 April.

The *George Gipp* began her maiden voyage at Oakland, California, on 15 June 1943, sailed to Hobart, Tasmania, through the Suez Canal to Alexandria, Egypt, and completed her voyage arriving in Philadelphia on 17 October, having logged 21,739 miles. . . .

By the fall of 1944, ship operators working for the War Shipping Administration were supervising the use of more than 3,500 ships— 20,000,000 tons of shipping—and dispatching loaded ships from U.S. ports on an average of one every 30 minutes. And every pound of cargo cleared from American ports, as well as most of the imports brought back from overseas, had to be cleared by the ship operators.

Most of the WSA fleet was carrying Army cargo, with the next largest portion carrying Lend-Lease cargo. The rest of it was transporting essential raw materials and civilian commodities—everything from bauxite to salt and coffee—and some material for the Navy.

Besides the system of general agents and their subagents all over the world, ship operations were expedited by WSA offices, staffed by experienced shipping men, in major American and foreign ports serving the war zones. They were specialists in avoiding bottlenecks and scheduling docking and cargo-handling.

While the Merchant Marine officers and crews won most of the praise—and rightfully so—for moving wartime cargo around the world, their work would not have been possible without the unsung workers in the offices of the general agents. Their dedicated efforts enabled the ships to sail, as a WSA news release in 1944 pointed out:

> "Without the paper work and supervision of the ship operators, the great steel hulls of the merchant fleet might lie in harbors, rusting out their bottoms, or end in an unsolved tangle of misdirection and confusion. Thousands of workers for the ship operators keep long hours over typewriters, adding machines, manifests, declarations, insurance policies, war-complicated ship payrolls, and a thousand and one complex details to see that the planes, tanks, food and men reach the right place at the right time."

Arming the Ships

On 17 November 1941, Congress authorized the use of Navy guns and gunners for the defense of American merchant ships. The first vessel so protected was the SS *Dunboyne*, which received several .50-caliber machine guns and a seven-man Armed Guard detachment under a coxswain on 2 December, just before she sailed for Murmansk. The SS *Expositor* sailed for Murmansk early in 1942 with an Armed Guard crew of four seamen and a signalman under Lieutenant (jg) Robert B. Hicks.

When the program began in late 1941, guns were in short supply. Those ships not sailing in dangerous waters were not furnished with guns. Those sailing the most dangerous routes, such as to Murmansk, were given top priority. Still, even in late 1942 the shortage was still critical. The vice-chief of Naval Operations issued the following directive: "Ships sailing independently should be armed. Ships sailing in regularly made-up convoys, other than ships bound to North Russia or tankers en route to the United Kingdom, may sail unarmed if the urgency of delivery of their cargo warrants it." He further recommended that antiaircraft guns be removed from ships entering a port and placed on outgoing ships.

By the end of December, 1941, there were Naval Armed Guard crews on 14 American merchant ships. By the end of 1942, there were Armed Guard units on 1,000 American ships, almost all the Armed Guard crews commanded by junior grade lieutenants or ensigns of the Naval Reserve. In addition, there were Armed Guard contingents on some American-owned vessels under Allied colors, primarily Panamanian.

There is little question that ships were not armed adequately or in time. The United States had not been in the war six months, and the Merchant Marine was suffering losses that were proportionately far greater than those endured by any branch of the armed services. In those six months, 350 ships were lost and with them almost three thousand men.

In all, 6,236 merchant ships were armed during World War II. these included U.S. ships and certain Allied and neutral ships. Guns were the most important defense item; some fifty-three thousand of them were placed on Merchant ships. In addition to the guns, an attempt was made to add other defensive items to give merchant ships their best chance of survival such as degaussing, life saving equipment and extra radio equipment.

(Source: Bunker, *Liberty Ships*, 25–26, 51–57.) ■

U.S. Navy Armed Guard
"We aim to deliver!"

Editor's note: In 1942, at the age of 17, I joined the Navy. Eager to go to sea and get into the action, I volunteered for the Naval Armed Guard.

Following are two excerpts from my semi-autobiographical memoir, *Bluejacket Odyssey, 1942–1946—Guadalcanal to Bikini, Naval Armed Guard in the Pacific.* "Volunteer Duty" recounts my indoctrination into the U.S. Navy Armed Guard. "The Fatal Voyage of Task Unit 32.4.4" recounts my first voyage at sea in 1943 in the Liberty ship, SS *Nathaniel Currier.* (I would later make three more Pacific trips in the *Currier* to the Solomons, New Guinea and Hawaii.)

During the war, I served as a gunner in four Liberty ships. The following Table details the gun crew sizes and armament for these four Libertys. Note the smaller gun crew on the *Currier* in 1943. Also note the number of communications liaison people. This number was based on the voyage and destination; e.g., in convoys the master and C.O. required greater communication capabilities between ships. The merchant crew served as ammunition passers on the bigger guns early on and later also loaded the ammo drums for the 20mm gunners.

U.S. Navy Armed Guard—Crews and Ship Armament

	SS Nathaniel Currier 1943	SS David Belasco 1944	SS Thomas Nelson 1945	SS Yugoslavia Victory 1944
Armed Guard Crew (based on maiden voyages)				
C.O.	1	1	1	1
Gunners	13	24	24	24
Communications	2	3	2	1
Totals	16	28	27	26
Ship Armament				
20mm	9	8	8	8
3-inch/50-caliber	1	2	1	1
4-inch/50-caliber	–	–	1	–
5-inch/38-caliber	–	–	–	1

Source: Armed Guard Officer's Reports

Editor: From *Bluejacket Odyssey, 1942–1946:*

Volunteer Duty

It all started in boot camp. After learning there was a four to nine month wait for the service schools of my choice, Submarines and Quartermaster, I revised my preferred duty assignment to guns and sea duty. My counselor responded with, "If you volunteer for the Naval Armed Guard, you can go to gunnery school immediately and be at sea within six to eight weeks." Bingo!

Since I had never heard of the Armed Guard, I asked the counselor to explain. "The Armed Guard," he said "is a special arm of the U.S. Navy that defends cargo ships, troop transports, tankers and other support-type vessels from enemy air attacks and submarines. On average, there are about 15 gunners, one signalman and maybe a radio operator in each Armed Guard crew. The rest of the ship's company is made up of civilian Merchant Marine personnel.

"It's volunteer duty at this time," he added, "due to the extremely hazardous Murmansk run to Russia. Allied convoys run the gauntlet of German U-boats, aircraft, and surface raiders and about twenty percent of the ships never make it back. But if you like guns, are eager to see action, and want to go to sea almost immediately, it should be just the ticket." I signed up for the Armed Guard then and there.

Gunnery School, 18 Feb–18 Mar 1943

What followed were four concentrated weeks of Gunnery School at the U.S. Navy Destroyer Base, San Diego, Calif. We were told that what would ordinarily take three months to learn, we would learn in a four week, crash training program that included both anti-aircraft and surface target practice. At the end of four weeks, our training culminated in two days of gunnery practice at sea aboard the USS *Sacramento*, a World War I gunboat and more recently Pearl Harbor survivor.

Our Commanding Officer left us with these words: "I want all of you 'cannon cockers' to remember this: A gun out of action from neglect is little different from a gun that has been put out of commission by direct enemy action." We learned a lot in four weeks.

Treasure Island, Armed Guard Center (Pacific)

On 18 March 1943, all of the Armed Guard gun crews in San Diego that had completed training were transferred to the Armed Guard Center (Pacific), Treasure Island, San Francisco, California. We were a happy bunch as we boarded our train. Sea duty was right around the corner. We pulled into the Oakland train station early the next morning and transferred to gray Navy buses for the short trip to Treasure Island (TI).

As our bus headed up the eastern section of the San Francisco-Oakland Bay Bridge, the driver became our tour guide. "You're looking at TI down there on the right. It's a man-made island, and was the home of the 1939 World's Fair." Before the driver could answer many questions, the bus pulled over just inside the gate and let us out in front of a large former World's Fair building—now TI's administration headquarters.

We were greeted at the front door by a young ensign who took our orders and other paperwork. Lining us up, he said, "Welcome aboard," took muster, and then added, "Two tractor-trailer rigs from the transportation pool will come by for you in about ten minutes to take you to the Center, so pick out your sea bags and be ready to board."

The road from the administration building to the Armed Guard Center hugged the tree-lined western side of the island. A lieutenant greeted us as we fell in for muster. Welcoming us aboard, he turned to a second-class gunner's mate and said, "After muster, give them your ever-popular orientation tour of the Center and be back here in thirty minutes."

"Gun's" tour was quick, all right. As we followed him, he pointed out where we would eat, sleep, and get our mail. He also told us about Saturday inspections, linen exchanges, early morning calisthenics, port and starboard liberty sections, and more, all in less than twenty minutes. "How in hell can we remember all of that?" said a gunner behind me. "You've got to work at it, Sailor," "Guns" fired back. "From now on, when someone says 'now hear this' or 'listen up' within earshot, you better do just that. Case closed."

We then lined up at ease in front of the main Center building to hear the assistant Commanding Officer (C.O.), LCdr E. D. Flaherty, USNR. His speech, obviously given many times before, went like this:

> "Armed Guard personnel are assigned permanent duty station at one of three Armed Guard Centers located in Brooklyn, New Orleans, or here in San Francisco. In spite of the military's reputation to the contrary, Armed Guard assignments usually make geographical and economic sense. In other words, if you received your gunnery training in San Diego, you were probably assigned to us here at Treasure Island.

"All Armed Guard Centers provide many important services. For example, each Center will serve as a home base for gun crews awaiting their next ship assignments with ample opportunities for liberty, recreation, and entertainment. Provide ongoing refresher training in gunnery and communication skills as well as firefighting, abandoning ship, chemical warfare, lookout, recognition and reporting. Be there for each man's family when/if needed while he is away. Provide medical, dental, and religious services. Process mail, pay records, leave and shipping orders, and much, much more.

"Finally, it is the mission of this Armed Guard Center to assemble, equip, train, retrain, and furnish the finest Naval gun crews anywhere to all merchant ships originating trips from any/all West Coast ports."

We were then addressed by a personnel officer who gave us two well-received points of information: First, we were all being promoted to seaman first-class (S1/c); and second, we were granted liberty for the rest of the day.

The next afternoon, we began enhancing our skills. One group listened to a boatswain's mate explain how to abandon ship, while in a pitch-black room another petty officer was offering techniques for developing night vision. Meanwhile, still others honed their plane-recognition and reporting skills with the help of models and flash cards.

Most of this class work instruction was mandatory. If you spent any amount of time at the Center, you received training or refresher training in all of the above skills, plus first aid, chemical warfare, ammunition handling, firefighting, sound-powered phone techniques and, of course, gunnery exercises. Communications personnel also honed their skills but mostly in separate classes.

March 27, 1943, was the day I had been looking forward to for months. During morning muster, 15 names, including mine, were called out for sea duty. We were to be, in Navy jargon, "detached this date to the SS *Nathaniel Currier*," a brand new Liberty ship. Those curious about the destination were told to wait, with the reminder, "loose lips sink ships."

As the crew gathered, we introduced ourselves and soon discovered we would have thirteen gunners and two signalmen in our crew. Petty Officer Leo Russell, gunner's mate third-class, ("Guns" for short), and Eluterio Barela, signalman third-class, ("Flags" for short), were the only men with sea time. The rest of us had the same rating, seamen first-class.

The photographer arrived, lined us up two deep, and took our picture, a routine we were destined to repeat each time we were "detached" from TI.

The commanding officer for our gun crew, Lt (jg) Robert L. Miller, a recent "90-day wonder" graduate, arrived as the bus pulled up. "Guns" had already mustered the group. After a quick handshake with the C.O., we climbed aboard and headed for our ship. You could sense our excitement by our chatter as we crossed the Bay Bridge. Everyone was eager to do battle with the Japs, including Lt Miller. Like most of us, this would also be his first trip to sea.

As the bus took the off-ramp leading to the waterfront, we watched for Pier 3 and our ship. The San Francisco waterfront on the Embarcadero was a bustling, noisy, exciting place. Trucks, railroad engines and freight cars, cranes, forklifts, and longshoremen were everywhere. The Navy bus driver skirted in, out, and around dozens of trucks like he was cutting some cattle out of the herd. When he finally stopped, we were on Pier 3, about 20 yards from the bow of the *Currier*. President Roosevelt might have called the Liberty ship an "ugly duckling," but to me she was a beauty. She was my passage to adventure.

Guns and Quarters Assignments

We were a sight that afternoon as we marched single file up the gangplank with our sea bags over our shoulders. Our excitement was so high, we looked and acted like a bunch of city kids arriving at our first day of camp. Our average age couldn't have been over 19 or 20. Lt Miller (hereafter the

"C.O.") had toured the ship earlier with the Master, David Hassell (also called the Captain, Skipper or The Old Man) and knew his way around. The C.O. said, "Pick up your sea bags and follow me," and then led us to the fantail (stern) to discuss gun and quarters assignments. With steam-powered winches hoisting cargo up from the dock and lowering it into the holds, we had to pay attention—or pay the price.

"First," said our C.O., "let's decide on gun assignments since your gun station dictates where you will bunk. Do any of you have a preference?" I put up my hand immediately and asked for one of the bow 20-mms. "You've got it," he said. Others requested the 3-inch/50 caliber stern gun just above us and, in less than five minutes, all gun stations and quarters had been assigned.

Three gunners, along with gun captain "Guns" Russell, would man the 3-inch/50, and two other men would handle the two 20s on the stern. The six of them were assigned accommodations in the afterhouse. The rest of us would bunk in the gunners' accommodations located in the midships house. "Flags" Barela and Joe Bergin, a signalman striker (studying to earn a signalman's rating), were also quartered midships since their duties were largely on the bridge deck.

After showing us where to bunk, the C.O. gave us the rest of the morning to unpack, with orders to meet in the gunners' mess for chow at 1200.

We were pleasantly surprised by our relatively spacious quarters. There were 16 bunks in four midships compartments. (The extra bunks would be needed on later trips.) The double-decker bunks (or "racks") were comfort-able and we each had a locker. Furthermore, we had our own head just down the passageway.

At lunch, the C.O. laid out the rest of the day for us. First, there would be a tour of the ship led by Chief Mate Robert Yates. Then "Guns" and the C.O. would hold an indoctrination meeting on the fantail, where, among other things, liberty sections and port security watches would be discussed.

Ship's Tour

Chief Mate Robert Yate's tour was interesting, particularly to me since I had helped build these Liberty ships when I worked as a welder at the Kaiser shipyards in Vancouver, Washington, prior to joining the Navy. However, what I saw as a welder during the early stages of shipbuilding was far different from a completely outfitted ship like the SS *Nathaniel Currier*. Chief Yates explained that the *Currier*, classified as an EC-2 Liberty dry cargo carrier ("EC" for Emergency Cargo, "2" for large capacity), was built by Kaiser's Permanente Metals Corp., Yard No. 1 (Hull No. 529) in Richmond, Calif., and completed in March 1943.

Her overall length was 441 feet, 7 inches, with a beam of 56 feet, 10 inches, and a loaded draft of 27 feet, 7 inches. For propulsion, she had a single screw driven by a 2,500 horsepower steam reciprocating engine. Her cruising radius was 17,000 miles at a speed of ten to eleven knots. The ship's net tonnage was 4,380, deadweight tonnage 10,800, and displacement tonnage 14,100.* The ship flew the U.S. flag and was registered in San Francisco, Calif. The armament of the *Currier* consisted of one 3-inch/50 dual-purpose gun on the stern and nine 20-mm anti-aircraft cannons—three forward, four on the bridge, and two aft.

Our Armed Guard crew included our C.O., Lt (jg) Robert L. Miller, 13 gunners, and 2 communication liaison personnel, for a total of 16. The merchant marine crew consisted of the master, David W. Hassell, plus a deck department of 18, engineering department of 13, and a steward's department of 9, for a total of 41.

Our indoctrination meeting later that afternoon was short and sweet. The crew was divided into two liberty sections, port and starboard. Under normal circumstances, one half the crew would have liberty while the other

---

* Gross tonnage is the entire internal cubic capacity of the ship expressed in tons of 100 cubic feet each. Net tonnage is derived by subtracting from the gross tonnage the cubic capacity of certain internal spaces not available for carrying cargo such as machinery compartments and crew's quarters. Deadweight tonnage is the carrying capacity of a ship in long tons of 2,240 pounds each.

half shared the duty. The duty section handled gangway watch and any other posts our C.O. deemed necessary.

I was so fascinated with the cargo handling, it was difficult to concentrate on work that afternoon. The steam winches chattered loudly. Longshoremen shouted and cursed as they went about their jobs. The scent of the dock from coffee beans, hemp and copra meal evoked far away places with strange-sounding names.

The days flew by. On 2 April, installation of armament and loading of ammunition was completed. Then, on 3 April, the following arrived: 1 fire control phone system with 7 bridge phones (3 forward sets and 1 aft), 16 life jackets, 41 helmets (25 for the merchant crew ammo handlers), 16 sets of foul weather clothing, 7 sets special winter clothing (for lookouts), 12 sets of lookout goggles (6 light- & 6 dark-density), 61 gas masks (45 for the merchant crew), 3 binoculars, and 16 Army cots.

We also received 1 set of boxing gloves, 1 Chinese checker board, 1 sack of marbles, 1 chess set, 2 sets of checkers, 2 cribbage boards, 1 Acey-Deucy game, 2 sets of dominoes, 6 decks of playing cards, 2 decks of pinochle cards, 1 set of books for men at sea, 1 phonograph with records, 1 medicine ball, and 1 fishing kit.*

The five holds seemed to swallow an unlimited amount of general/military cargo consisting of drummed aviation gasoline and diesel oil, ammunition, small stores, beer and soft drinks, and miscellaneous items. We watched as the stevedore crews topped off each hold, hoisted the strongbacks (beams) and hatch boards into place, and covered the hatches with canvas and cross battens. Departure was close at hand. The C.O. confirmed this by canceling all liberty.

Then the stevedores loaded a deck load of construction equipment and landing barges on top of the hatches and on the main deck of the ship. Everything was secured with heavy cable and turnbuckles to avoid shifting at sea. Finally, a catwalk (a wooden walkway with railings) was

---

* From the "Armed Guard Center Report of Materials Furnished To Armed Guard Units."

built over the top of the barges and/or construction equipment fore and aft so we could get to our guns. Of course, the merchant mariners used these catwalks, too.

Later that afternoon, the master and our C.O. left the ship to get our sailing orders from the Port Director's office.

Sea Duty at Last

On 4 April 1943 at 1620, with pilot aboard, the *Nathaniel Currier* slowly inched away from the pier with the assistance of two tugboats, destination unknown. The C.O. promised to tell us where our first stop would be after we cleared the harbor. All Armed Guard were at their assigned gun stations for this momentous occasion.

As the pilot navigated the *Currier* between the other ships dotting the Bay and the submarine nets protecting the harbor near the Golden Gate Bridge, we saw fog rolling in. It turned chilly as we gained speed and the sun disappeared.

I felt a strange combination of apprehension and excitement. I was proud to be serving my country. However, even though we had our headsets on and there was some chatter, I think most of us were deep in thought: What lies ahead? Will we see action? Will we make it back? Why are we sailing alone instead of as part of an escorted convoy?

Leaving the Golden Gate, the ship began to pitch and roll just enough to remind us—as if we needed a reminder—that we'd better develop our sea legs, and fast. The pilot boat pulled alongside, bobbing like a cork, and the pilot climbed over the gunwale and descended the Jacobs ladder. In some ways, it was like cutting the umbilical cord to the U.S.A.

Editor: After leaving San Francisco on 4 April 1943, the SS *Nathaniel Currier* sailed independently to the South Pacific and arrived 27 April 1943 at Noumea, New Caledonia. On 9 June 1943, after riding the anchor for six long weeks, she joined a U.S. Navy Task Force Unit designated Task Unit 32.4.4. Not more than a week later, the *Currier* and the other ships in the unit found themselves in the center of action, and were subjected to two major Japanese attacks—one by air (the second biggest enemy air attack since Pearl Harbor) and the other by torpedoes.

Due to the classified nature of most information during the war, it wasn't until 50 years later, while doing research for *Bluejacket Odyssey,* that the details of what had happened during these two attacks were made known to me. I was also fortunate to be able to locate and interview many of my former *Currier* shipmates, as well as other members and survivors of T.U. 32.4.4, who never forgot those attacks as evidenced by their vivid recall in the interviews.

The following excerpt from *Bluejacket Odyssey* details the action of 16 and 23 June 1943, and illustrates how the U.S. Navy and U.S. Merchant Marine joined forces in T.U. 32.4.4 for what started as a logistical supply run in preparation for the Central Solomons invasion and ended with fighting off the enemy in two surprise attacks just days apart.

The Fatal Voyage of Task Unit 32.4.4

It's now 9 June 1943. We've been anchored off Noumea, New Caledonia since 27 April 1943. Everyone is broke and most of us have a bad case of "channel fever." So we're eager for a change when we weigh anchor and join six other ships in a U.S. Navy Task Unit designated T.U. 32.4.4.*

In addition to our merchant ship, SS *Nathaniel Currier*, there were three U.S. Navy cargo ships: USS *Aludra* (AK-72), USS *Celeno* (AK-76), and USS *Deimos* (AK-78). All four were EC-2 class Liberty ships built within weeks of each other under Maritime Commission contracts by

---

* Task forces are divided into task groups, with numbers following a decimal point; and task groups are divided into task units, with a number following second decimal point. T.U. 32.4.4 means the fourth Task Unit of the fourth Task Group of Task Force 32 of Admiral Halsey's Third Fleet.

Kaiser shipyards in Richmond, Calif. The difference between them was crew size and armament.

The AKs had a complement of about 200 officers and enlisted men to the *Currier's* 41 merchant mariners and our 16-man Armed Guard unit. Each AK's armament consisted of 5-inch/38-caliber and 3-inch/50-caliber guns on the stern and bow respectively, plus eight 20mm anti-aircraft cannons; whereas the *Currier* had one 3-inch/50-caliber on the stern and nine 20s.*

Our escorts were the destroyer USS *O'Bannon* (DD-450), fast transport USS *Ward* (APD-16), and minesweeper USS *Skylark* (AM-63). Additional protection was scheduled during the last two days of the trip north as we sailed through "Torpedo Junction," that part of the Coral Sea between the Solomon and the New Hebrides islands regularly patrolled by enemy submarines.

Convoy speed was set at 10 knots. Ships were grouped in convoys to maximize the defense capabilities of the escorts—radar, sonar, depth charges and guns. For security reasons, we bluejackets—and most officers for that matter—never knew where we were headed until we were well underway, and sometimes, not until our destination was in sight. In fact, most Pacific islands had code names. Furthermore, we seldom knew the names of the other vessels in a convoy. The Coast Guard ordered the name boards on the midships house reversed on all merchant ships and the U.S. Navy displayed hull numbers only on the bow.

The promised additional protection in the form of land- and carrier-based air cover was provided on 12–13 June as we sailed through "Torpedo Junction." At least half the gun crew was constantly at battle stations with lifejackets nearby. Some men slept by their guns all night.

---

* Caliber has two meanings when applied to naval guns. First, it refers to bore diameter, expressed in inches or millimeters (mm). Second, it expresses the ratio of the gun's length in inches divided by the bore diameter, i.e., you can find the barrel length of a gun by multiplying the bore diameter by the caliber of the gun.

Guadalcanal, Solomon Islands

On 14 June, we dropped anchor off Guadalcanal, ten months after the U.S. Marines had first landed on this mountainous island of the Solomons group. Enemy troops—stragglers who had missed the evacuation boats—were still being pursued in the distant hills by our soldiers. We soon realized our days of practice were behind us and that the next General Quarters (GQ) bell could be the real thing. In fact, we were introduced to the Japanese our first night off the 'Canal.

On 14 June at 2305, we experienced our first real GQ alarm. We all scrambled to our gun stations only to hear "Washing-Machine Charlie" off in the distance somewhere over Henderson Field. He putt-putted around for over 30 minutes, then dropped what sounded like a pretty small bomb, and took off in a northerly direction. That was it. No big deal, but he managed to cut into our sleep.

Bright and early the morning of 15 June, the First Special Naval Construction Battalion, a Seabee stevedore crew, came aboard to begin offloading. They rigged the booms with the help of the *Currier* deck crew, lowered the deckload of landing barges into the water, filled them with construction equipment, and all before lunch. By afternoon, they were offloading drummed aviation gas from the holds into two Navy LSTs (Landing Ship, Tank), one on each side of us. They finally knocked off about 1900.

Later, the Seabees worked far into the night. This meant sacrificing the safety of blackouts to expedite offloading. However, with radar and coastwatchers providing early warning signals, there was ample time to darken the ship. With every alert, landing craft and barges were under orders to cast off immediately. If it was daylight, they headed for the safety of the beach; at night, they simply scurried out into the dark and waited for the all-clear signal.

The Seabees were back on the job the next morning by 0700. Right after noon chow, "Sparks" Churchon received a Radio Guadalcanal Yellow alert signifying that Jap planes were headed our way from the northern Solomons. They were first spotted by a Coast Guard patrol plane. Sparks sounded the GQ alarm and all hands were soon at battle stations.

Japanese Air Attack, 16 June 1943

At 1350, we received a Condition "Very" Red signal with orders to get underway immediately. We watched impatiently as the *Celeno* immediately stood out towards Koli Point in a northeasterly direction, followed closely by the *Deimos*. The *Skylark* was already some 500 yards to the north in a screening position and the *Aludra* was slowly getting underway off Koli Point.

The two LSTs tied up alongside the *Currier*, the "353" and "398," seemed to take forever getting underway. In the meantime, Airsols' fighter pilots went into action. It was a confidence-builder for us newcomers watching them take off, one after another, to intercept the incoming force of Japanese bombers and fighters. There were Navy Wildcats and Hellcats, Army P-40 Warhawks and P-38 Lightnings and, last but certainly not least, Marine gull-winged Corsairs.

While we waited at battle stations, our imaginations ran wild. The chatter over the battle phones picked up in volume and intensity. You could hear both excitement and apprehension in every voice. To the few sailors in T.U. 32.4.4 who had already seen action, the wait was probably tolerable since they only concerned themselves with what the enemy would do; but those of us without experience were anxious about our own reactions as well as the enemy's actions.

> "I felt that I didn't know what I was gettin' into and, when the air raid hit, I wondered if I was gonna get out of it. It's surprising what'll go through a man's mind."
>
> —*Duane Curtis, Gunner,* Nathaniel Currier

C.O. Miller told everyone to "pipe down," but it did little good. He even tried "group therapy" on us, like how to get a laugh out of a stressful situation. I'm the first to admit that laughter relieves stress and we proved it that day with some very corny jokes as we watched and waited.

We were on the lookout for high-altitude dive-bombers and low-flying torpedo planes. Hundreds of watchers strained their eyes to the horizon

Airsols

The Solomon Island Air Force ("Airsols") was a heterogeneous mix of U.S. Army, Navy, and Marine Corps airmen, as well as the New Zealand Air Force. Marine, Navy, and Army fliers flew on missions together, lived through bombing raids together, and many died together aloft or in foxholes.

Airsols' fighter planes kept guard over ships off Guadalcanal and over convoys running north of Espiritu Santo. Its deep-chested Fortresses (B-29s) and Liberators (B-24s) pulverized enemy airfields; its PBY-5A "Black Cats," equipped with radar and landing wheels as well as pontoon hulls, conducted nighttime scouting and anti-submarine patrols, rescue missions, and bombing and gunfire spotting. Its PBY "Dumbo" rescue planes picked up shipwrecked mariners and bailed-out aviators, delivered rations to beleaguered coastwatchers, and rushed spare parts to the fighting front. And, to reduce the enemy's fondness for night air attacks, night fighter squadrons of Corsairs (F4U-2) and Vega Venturas (PV-1) were added to the mix of Airsols' firepower.

In June 1943, Commander Aircraft Solomon Islands (ComAirSols) was RAdm Marc A. Mitscher. (Command of Airsols rotated between the U.S. Army, Navy, and Marine Corps.) By spring 1943, Airsols had gained the advantage in quality aloft and sometimes in numbers, too. Many changes based on combat experience were made in older models of American planes—more power, more heavily armed and armored with longer ranges. New types were the F6F-Hellcat and the F4U Corsair fighters, and the B-24 Liberator, which was capable of carrying more bombs longer distances than the older B-17.

Just two of many Airsol pilots to distinguish themselves were Marine Medal of Honor winners Capt Joe Foss and Major "Pappy" Boyington. Both would become top Aces during the period of August 1942–April 1944; Foss with 26 Victories and Boyington with 28.

and directly above, but saw nothing. It was maddening. Where the hell were they? Our 3-inch/50-caliber gun crew on the stern was ready to reach out seven or eight miles to greet the raiders if they could only see a target. We later learned that many of the enemy planes were directly overhead at 18,000 feet, their well-camouflaged undersides invisible from the surface.

It wasn't until 1410, twenty minutes after receiving the "Red," that we were free from the two LSTs and our ship was able to move out and start zigzagging. The C.O. had just finished reminding us to keep a close watch for enemy planes that might sneak over the 'Canal's mountains when, at 1413, as the ship was making its first hard turn to starboard, all hell broke loose. Japanese "Val" dive-bombers and "Zero" fighters appeared from out of nowhere, coming in at all directions and angles.

C.O. Miller, "Flags" Barela, and signalman striker Joe Bergin tried to spot enemy planes and report them to us over the battle phones, but my loader, Dave Powers, and I had all we could do just to cover our own "zone of influence." Dave tapped me on the shoulder and pointed out approaching "bogeys" (unidentified aircraft). I swung around, ready to fire if they were Japs. It happened that fast.

From the Armed Guard Officer's Action Report, *Nathaniel Currier:*

> The *Currier* had just turned in a northeasterly direction when a Val dive-bomber appeared out of a low-hanging cloud over Guadalcanal headed for the stern of the ship at an angle of about thirty degrees. (Vals were easily identified by their non-retractable "pants down" landing gear.)
>
> Duane Curtis, manning the after starboard 20mm gun, immediately started shooting, and his line of fire was observed directly in front of the attacking plane. The pilot banked sharply to port to avoid Curtis' 20mm fire and dropped three bombs prematurely. One bomb missed abaft starboard; another directly astern missed by 40 or 50 yards; and the third missed by about 75 yards off the port quarter. Keith Sutton, the after port 20mm gunner, and Gerry Olson, the after port bridge gunner, also opened fire as the plane drew away; but no hits were observed.
>
> There can be little doubt that the combination of the hard right turn made by the Captain and the prompt and accurate fire laid down by Curtis, Sutton and Olson saved the ship from a bomb hit.

Immediately afterwards, three Japanese planes were diving on LST-340 about 300 yards west of the port bow of the *Currier*. The pilot of the leading plane, a Val, commenced his long, whistling dive on the target and dropped three bombs from a very low altitude, appearing to get one or two direct hits before banking away sharply abreast of our portside. Joe Jurgens and Gerry Olson, manning the forward and aft port bridge guns respectively, hit the plane with several long bursts that appeared to rake the entire length of the fuselage. Joe Skalenda, our bow gunner, also put several tracers through it. The plane began smoking heavily and crashed on the beach about 200 yards inshore. (The loud, tension-relieving cheers of our forward gun crews when that Jap plane hit the beach reminds me today of when the 49ers scored a touchdown in the last five seconds to win the Super Bowl.)

A second Val attacked LST-340 from the port bow with bombs and machine gun fire, narrowly missing the target. Then the plane was hit many times by both the "340" and *Currier* forward gunners as it passed overhead. We saw this plane crash some 500 yards off our starboard bow. However, our C.O. didn't see this one splash and refused to credit us with even a half-plane kill.

We starboard gunners got in some valuable practice on another Val bomber while LST-340 was under attack off our port side. "Flags" Barela reported this one from his spotter station on the flying bridge. I opened fire as the Nip was making his run on our starboard bow with his machine guns blinking. I remember thinking for the first time, hell, I might die at 17, and never get to own my own ranch, or raise a family. About the time my tracers began disappearing into the nose of his plane, he gunned his engine, banked sharply to port, and ran smack into a lead curtain put up by Gibe and Gassen on the starboard side of our bridge. The Jap pilot never released any bombs but he was soon greeted by a very daring U.S. Army P-38 flyboy who zoomed in out of nowhere for this easy kill of the cripple. As we watched him splash the Val some 1,000 yards off our starboard quarter, I wondered if we could have claimed the plane had it not been for the P-38 pilot's interception.

When the attack on the LST-340 ended, enemy bombers and fighters made the first of several passes at the *Celeno*, about 1,000 yards southwest of our port quarter. Each of the planes peeled off in succession with the sun behind them from a height of several thousand feet, dove on the ship, dropped bombs and/or strafed her in a stern-to-stem direction, then leveled off near the *Currier*. As each plane passed by, it was fired on by all *Currier* guns that could be brought to bear.

The first Val to attack the *Celeno* scored a direct bomb hit near the stern. All four of our port side 20s shot at this one. The second or third attacking plane hit the unfortunate AK somewhere aft of midships. It passed almost directly over the *Currier* at a height of about 500 feet. Our crew put several bursts into the plane as it came over, went into a glide, smoking heavily, and crashed into the sea about a mile off the starboard bow.

Another plane was hit by us as it traveled abreast of the *Currier's* port side, then made off trailing smoke and was promptly pounced on and splashed by a Marine Corsair pilot.

While the foregoing action was taking place, a single enemy fighter, a Mitsubishi Zero, was spotted by Dave Powers coming in on the starboard side about 150 feet above the water. I hesitated at first, thinking it must be one of our fighters. By the time I opened fire, and Gibe and Gassen joined in, that Zero wasn't more than 150 yards out. He bracketed the *Currier* with two light bombs, probably 100-pounders. One exploded about 100 feet to starboard and the other some 50 feet to port. It happened so fast, we only winged him.

Another plane, out of nowhere it seemed, was hit several times as it went by the starboard side. It, too, became a "smoker" before it passed out of range, but no one saw it crash. However, a member of the Seabee battalion, who observed the action from shore, told our C.O. several days later that the plane did crash about one mile inshore.

At the same time, two Val dive-bombers approached the bow in a low-level run. They were spotted by Skalenda, Haynes, and my loader, Dave Powers, about 1,000 yards away. We opened fire immediately and

The Enemy in the Air

Allied pilots found the Japanese airmen far superior to the stereo-types depicted by WWII U.S. journalists and cartoonists. In fact, the first American air crews to return from combat knew they had faced some of the world's most experienced combat pilots equipped with formidable airplanes. Early in the war, Japanese training of airmen was tough, reportedly far beyond the limits of U.S. Marine Corps boot training. But by the spring of 1943, their edge wore thin as they lost many of their most experienced pilots and flight commanders along with their aircraft. Even the most experienced pilots eventually came up against a losing roll of the dice. To make matters worse, every Japanese plane was highly inflammable for lack of self-sealing gas tanks. As Rear Admiral Samuel Eliot Morison put it, "The 'Val' was a slow and easy target for an American fighter plane or anti-aircraft bullet. 'Kate,' the torpedo-bomber, lacked speed and endurance compared with the American TBF (Avenger). 'Betty,' the twin-engine torpedo-bomber, was fast and long-winded but horribly quick to catch fire. Japanese Army planes, seldom seen in the Solomons, were subject to the same defects. And the enemy made no provision for pilot survival. Many an aviator prematurely joined his ancestors because he was unprotected by cockpit armor. There was no rescue organization similar to our 'Dumbo,' and aviators, like other Japanese fighting men, were indoctrinated to die rather than surren-der. An air squadron was often kept flying until completely wiped out, instead of some of the veterans being saved to instruct young aviators.

the planes banked off sharply at about 100 yards without dropping their bombs. All three forward 20s appeared to score hits as we bracketed the Vals, but they did not seem to be seriously damaged.

At about 1430, three Mitsubishi "Betty" twin-engine bombers—the only Bettys I remember seeing on 16 June—made a bomb run over the Guadalcanal base (now referred to in code as "Mainyard") escorted by two Zeros. I was amazed to see several American fighters wade into them ignoring A/A flak from both ship and shore batteries. They were well out of range of the *Currier*.

We fired on several other planes that had attacked shore installations or other ships from time to time as they passed overhead, most of them beyond the range of our 20mm guns. Several shells fired by our 3"/50 gun crew, captained by Leo Russell, GM 3/c, appeared to burst fairly close but no damage was observed.

Different Views of the 16 June 1943 Air Attack

USS *Deimos*. The crew of the *Deimos* had a different view of the battle:

> "We were unloading on some barges when they sounded GQ. One of the barges pulled away. It was 50 yards beyond us when it got one straight in the middle. There was nothing left of it. I saw the bombs coming and thought we were going to get them because they always look like they're coming straight at you. They went on over and caught the barge on the other side of us."
>
> —*Lester "Ray" Weathers, Boatswain's mate 2/c,* Deimos

> "We had just started unloading—the Seabees were unloading us—when the red alert came. Some of those Seabees didn't even wait for the landing craft to take them to the beach, they just started swimmin'."
>
> —*Robert E. Vorhies, Seaman 2/c,* Deimos

> "I remember looking over to the beach and seeing the *Celeno* on fire, the smoke coming out. How long the raid lasted I don't know. I know it seemed like an eternity to me. After it was over, I couldn't sit down, I couldn't lay down, I couldn't get still in any way. I know I was scared to death."
>
> —*Robert E. Vorhies,* Deimos

USS *Aludra*.   The *Aludra* was also discharging cargo when the alert came:

> "In addition to the thousands of barrels of high test gasoline down in those holds, we had 50 tons of dynamite and 14 tons of nitroglycerin caps. I've always remembered that because the chief said if we ever get hit, we can walk to Tokyo!"
>
> —*Roy Lucy, Radioman 3/c,* Aludra

> "I was on watch and Hopper was up there with me. All of a sudden, we saw our planes taking off from Henderson Field "en masse" and we got to talking about how the Japs were going to catch hell today, boy, because those bombers and fighters were just zooming out of there. Then the Japs hit all over us."
>
> —*William Earl Hartman, Chief Boatswain's mate,* Aludra

> "The first-class radioman, the Chief, and I were out on the port side of the bridge. Somebody had hung his helmet on one of those ribs sticking out. The Jap planes were shooting and we were underway by then. The ship hit a swell and rolled. That helmet came down, hit the deck, and it sounded exactly like the rat-a-tat-tat of a machine gun. All three of us went through that hatch at the same time. Don't ask me how we did it. Man, we were moving!"
>
> —*Roy Lucy, Radioman 3/c,* Aludra

USS *O'Bannon*.   The lead escort, USS *O'Bannon* (DD-450), LCdr Donald J. MacDonald, USN, Commanding, started the day patrolling as a unit in the outer anti-submarine screen 6,000 to 8,000 yards off Lunga Point, screening Task Unit 32.4.4. The Task Unit commander was in *Aludra*, the screen commander in *O'Bannon*.

From the *O'Bannon's* Action Report for Wednesday, 16 June 1943:

The *Aludra* and *Schley* (APD-14) were off Togoma Point, while the other three AKs were unloading between Lunga Point and the Tenaru river. Also in this area were several LSTs and many smaller craft. No other escorts were available at this time.*

Air Attack and Narrative:

At 1337 L (0237Z), 16 June 1943, considerable information commenced coming in over fighter control circuit stationing fighter groups. Bogies were reported at this time.

1346 condition red over Cactus was reported on Harbor circuit. All hands were called to General Quarters, speed increased to 25 knots, and course set to close cargo ships. Speed was shortly thereafter increased to 30 knots.

1346 the escorts were ordered by me to close cargo vessels and screen in accordance with our pre-arranged plan. This plan provided for one escort vessel in each quadrant distance 1,500–2,000 yards.

1347 condition red over Cactus received over fighter control circuit.

1349 the *Waters* (APD 8) was again ordered to close, which she did.

1355 Bogies were reported southwest of Cape Esperance-distance 25 miles. SUGAR CHARLIE radar picked up unidentified planes bearing 275 degrees T-distance 28 miles. Tracking was started.

1358 condition red reported existing over Tulagi.

1403 SUGAR CHARLIE radar reported unidentified planes bearing 353 degrees T-distance 7.5 miles.

1405 Bogies reported as closing on Henderson Field from southeast 15 miles. At this time our radar could not pick up enemy aircraft, having lost them in land mass.

---

* One of the APDs in this report was no doubt the *Ward* (APD-16), one of the three T.U. 32.4.4 escorts. —Ed.

1409 Bogies were reported over Henderson Field, Angels 15. This altitude was above the cloud banks which were directly overhead. We also had friendly fighters overhead. In fact, there were a number of friendly planes all around the area. The sun was bearing in direction of Savo Island at a position angle of about 50 degrees. Great stress was laid to watching up in the sun. The *O'Bannon's* position was on the port quarter of the formation, toward the sun.

1410 Bogies were reported over fighter number two. My radars were unable to pick them up. All guns that could bear were trained in this direction.

1410 The Commanding Officer saw a group of planes, possibly 12 in a Vee formation, appear in a hole in the clouds at an altitude that must have been about 15,000 feet. He could not identify them, but ordered Control to commence fire on them, giving bearing and approximate position angle. At practically the same moment, they began to peel off coming down in dives that were nearly vertical. Most of the group pulled out at about 500 feet and then attempted to strafe ships. Several never pulled out. I believe the LST that was damaged was hit by a crashed planed.

At about 1411, fire was commenced by this vessel by all guns including the machine guns and 1.1" on the starboard side at planes just pulling out of dives. Control was unable to get on planes until they were half way down in their dives. After following a few in, our 5" fire was finally raised to planes still overhead just about to dive.

The *Celeno* and the damaged LST were hit by what I believe were the first bombs dropped.

The Jap bombers were Aichi 99s with wheels down. They were carrying at least two bombs and possibly three apiece; one large bomb under the fuselage and 1–2 wing bombs. My Air Defense Officer reports seeing several Type Zero's with square wings in the melee strafing our shipping. This I believe is true because I saw several Jap single engine planes with wheels retracted strafing us.

Some of our fighters came in with the second attacking group. A P-40 and a P-38 were definitely identified and, unfortunately, they were shot at, but I do know the P-40 got through without crashing.

Bombs were dropped all around our formation by the first Jap group. There were 3 dropped in this vessel's vicinity, the nearest exploding about 100 yards on the starboard beam, two others fell about 200–300 yards on port bow.

All planes coming within range were taken under fire as fast as targets could be shifted. This vessel shot at approximately seven planes with its machine guns, and besides breaking up second attack by 5" fire, fired at several at low level. One plane being fired at by our machine guns was definitely seen to crash while at least two, and possibly four others, were seen to catch fire and start smoking while clearing the immediate vicinity.

By the gunfire of all vessels, it is believed that at least five planes were shot down, many of the planes being shot at by different vessels at the same time and possibly claimed by each.

1415 Firing ceased. The ship was still being maneuvered around as a unit of the screen for the cargo ships. One LST was on fire forward and burning fiercely. The *Celeno* had a fire aft, emitting great volumes of black smoke.

1420 Bogies were reported over Tulagi. *Skylark* was ordered from screen by me to protect the cripples, who were about 2,500 yards from beach never having really gotten very far before being hit.

1430 Several small craft from landing area came out to assist cripples.

1504 Message was received by me from the Shore Station that two submarine periscopes were sighted from Tulagi toward Lunga. This was passed by me to the *Strong* who was in that area and later at 1522 the *Waters* was ordered to proceed to that area and investigate.

1517 condition green over Cactus was announced on all circuits. . . .

Comments and Remarks:

It is believed that the big Jap air offensive of the 16th had as its objective, Blue Shipping in Guadalcanal area. If, in fact, submarines were present as reported on the 16th, and later on morning of 17th by an LCT and a plane, then no doubt the offensive was to have been a well coordinated attack, with the air flushing the shipping out for the Subs. The raid on Tulagi on the night of the 17th would bear this out. Or the Subs were being used solely for intelligence. So far there have been no attacks made by subs. Searches made by escort ships have all been negative.

The AKs and Merchant Ship did very well considering the short notice that was given. They should definitely be instructed to make maximum speed and radical changes of course if not closed up in formation where Unit Commander can exercise control. Both the LST and the *Celeno* were lagging well behind, only being clear of beach area by about 2,500 yards.

The shipping off Lunga Point was attacked by 18–24 Jap dive-bombers with several Zero's coming in to strafe. Some of our own fighters were staying outside of range to get them as they cleared, so that very few finally got away.

(Source: USS *O'Bannon*, Action Report for
Wednesday, 16 June 1943.)

USS *Celeno*.   The *Celeno* would be the only casualty in Task Unit 32.4.4 of this air attack. According to the *Celeno's* 22 June 1943 Action Report, she was about midway between Lunga and Koli Points, and one-and-a-half miles offshore, when, at 1410, eight enemy bombers and Zeros made the first of several dive-bombing and strafing runs on her.

Anthony "Tony" Gray had a 360-degree view of the action from his battle station on the flying bridge as the C.O.'s messenger:

"When we got the red alert, you're kind of wondering, where the heck are they? As I remember, they came in real high, in line with the sun. There were a few scattered clouds and all at once the devils were comin' right at us."

—*Anthony Gray, Quartermaster third-class, USS* Celeno

At approximately 1416, the first bomb made a direct hit forward of the No.7, 20mm platform, continuing on through the main deck and exploding below. (It also jammed the rudder full right, rendering it inoperative and, at the same time, flooded the shaft alley.) The second direct hit was in No. 5 hold. Exposed parts of the ship were raked from stem to stern by enemy strafing.

> "The ship bounced like a rubber ball, up and down. We knew we'd been hit because we could hear and see the flying debris, but I couldn't imagine that big ship going up and down like it was on one end of a teeter-totter."
> —*Anthony Gray, Quartermaster third-class, USS* Celeno

There were four near-misses: one on the starboard side abreast of No. 4 hatch, two by the port side of the forecastle abreast the 3-inch/50-caliber bow gun, and another very near-miss on the port side abreast the No. 3 hatch—all causing severe hull damage.

Fire broke out almost immediately in a deck load of gasoline and oil drums abreast of No. 5 hatch, and in No. 5 hold, which was nearly full of cargo. Before the fire could be brought under control, it had spread to No. 4 hold, also nearly full of cargo.

Fire and damage control parties worked with *Celeno's* guns booming and chattering around them, seemingly oblivious to flying shrapnel and strafing bullets.

> "It was shrapnel and strafing bullets that got our people on deck. Shrapnel did a bad number. Like on Chief Fry, a piece of shrapnel ripped his stomach open and his intestines were just hanging there. It was really a shock. Then there was the dead lying around on the deck. I mean, guys that 15 minutes before were racing up and down doing something. There they were stretched out."
> —*Anthony Gray, Quartermaster third-class, USS* Celeno

The gun crew manned all guns except No.7, 20mm, which was put out of action, and the 5"/38 that had received damage to its elevating and depressing gear. No shots were fired by the latter gun crew even though the Gunnery Officer, at main control, had given the order to "Commence Firing." The pointer on the 5"/38 and the gun captain left their posts before the first hit and went over the side into the water. They were picked up later by rescue boats. (Both men received general courts martial later on.)

Conning throughout the entire action was done by the C.O. from the flying bridge rather than from the safety of the enclosed wheelhouse where vision would have been greatly handicapped.* With the ship's rudder jammed to the right, it was only by skillful handling and the prompt assistance rendered by the *Rail* (AT-139), the *Vireo* (AT-144), and the LCT-322, that the *Celeno* was able to beach herself off Lunga River, Guadalcanal.

The shaft alley, steering engine room, and No. 4 and No. 5 holds were completely flooded, and the ship's counter at the main deck was under water. A limited amount of power was provided by the main engines up to the time of beaching at 1645.

From the *Celeno* Action Report of Division Officer Lt (jg) Edward O'Rourke:

> At 1425, the *Rail*, and later the *Vireo*, provided power and steerage from alongside the port and starboard quarters respectively to assist in fighting the fires.
>
> At 1535, the *Celeno* dropped anchor in 20 fathoms of water 800 yards off Lunga Point. At 1550 the all-clear signal was finally received from shore.
>
> At 1600, *Celeno* lifted anchor and made a run for the beach full speed with the *Rail* pushing on the port quarter until the *Celeno* was in 2 fathoms of water. At that point, the *Rail* ceased rescue operations.
>
> LCT-322 furnished personnel to fight the *Celeno's* fires and to evacuate her dead and wounded. Later she stood by to take

---

* "Conn" is being in control of a ship's movements, e.g., "The officer in control has the conn." —Ed.

the crew ashore. Boatswain Edward Mican also called on the 322 to "come up under the *Celeno's* starboard bow to take the starboard anchor as close to shore as possible. . ."

At 1706, by order of the C.O., the crew began disembarking the vessel with the exception of the ship's security watch.

(Source: USS *Celeno,* Action Report of Division Officer Lt (jg) Edward O'Rourke.)

On the lighter side, Tony Gray recalls:

"There was this rope hanging over the side and this sailor ran and grabbed that line—he wasn't going to take time to go down the cargo net—and the damn rope wasn't secured. It was kinda funny 'cause I saw him go over the rail with that rope and here comes the other end following behind him. I don't even know if he got hurt. The silly things you remember."

—*Anthony Gray, Quartermaster third-class, USS* Celeno

Due to flooding and settling, and with Nos. 4 and 5 holds partially filled with cargo, shoring and plugging of holds from inside the ship was impossible. The *Celeno* was credited with shooting down three enemy planes and three possibles. She had 15 men killed and 19 wounded in battle.

According to LCdr N. E. Lanphere, USNR, Commanding Officer, with the exception of two 5"/38 gun crew members who deserted their battle stations, ". . .the entire crew performed their duties in a most satisfactory manner. . . .Many of our men fought fire in the cargo, partly made up of ammunition and gasoline, after having received wounds from machine gun strafing, shrapnel, and from burning."*

The Commander Service Squadron, South Pacific Force, issued commendations to the *Celeno,* LCT-322, *Vireo,* and *Rail* ". . .for saving USS *Celeno,* which received extensive damage as a result of 2 direct hits and 4 near-misses from enemy bombers."

---

* USS *Celeno* Action Report, 22 June 1943.

USS LST-340.   The LST-340, crammed with soldiers and loaded with vehicles, was another major casualty of the 16 June 1943 raid. Ironically, she was only about 30 yards off the beach waiting for the Army Engineers to complete construction of an unloading ramp when the GQ bell shattered everyone's nerves.

At 1350, a group of nine enemy planes was observed overhead at about 20,000 feet. Suddenly all nine planes went into a diving attack and peeled off in groups of three. The first three dive-bombers headed straight for the 340 and dropped nine bombs of about 300 pounds each in sticks of three.

One of the planes that attacked from the port side registered a direct hit on the 340's main deck near the after cargo hatch on the port side. Two near misses from this same plane landed about 50 feet off the starboard side. Their explosions caused personnel at the waist guns and on the conning station to be drenched with water. This plane was hit by nearly a full drum of 20mm bullets and splashed on the starboard side. Another plane, attacking from the port bow, scored two near-misses on the port side, strafing the bow guns as it passed over the ship. The shrapnel from these near misses and the strafing put more than 100 holes in the port side of the hull. The plane was hit many times by the forward guns and crashed in the water on the starboard side after passing over the ship.

The direct bomb hit created a dreadful fire among the trucks, all with full fuel tanks and highly flammable loads, such as cans of oil and gasoline, wooden crates, trunks, bedding, and barracks bags. The explosion and fire cut the water main and all interior communication. Gun crews and all other personnel at battle stations continued the fight against the attacking planes in spite of the immense heat and frightful explosions.

James Stalp, Seaman 1/c aboard the 340, proved himself that day. Stalp was at his gun post in the bow of the ship when the bombs hit, knocking out the gunner's mate, wounding the ship's communications officer, and setting aflame the deck cargo of vehicles and gas. Stalp slung the officer over his shoulder and made his way through 100 feet of flaming deck cargo to the stern. Then he returned through the flames to his post where he found the gunner's mate had lost an arm. Stalp slowed the flow of blood with a tourniquet and lowered the man over the side. Next he threw overboard four 55-gallon drums of gas which were in the path of the oncoming flames. After that, he climbed down a hatch and came up with a wounded New Zealand soldier who had been pleading for help. Stalp lowered him over the side, too. Then he returned to his 40mm gun post to shoot down a Jap bomber. Stalp received the Silver Star for "diving into the roaring flames to rescue three of his shipmates."

With no water to fight fire and with the imminent danger of ammunition magazines exploding, the Army troops were ordered to abandon ship. Life rafts were cast loose and two ship's boats, which had been trailing astern, picked up the troops.

The auxiliary engine room had to be abandoned because a bomb fragment that penetrated started a gasoline fire. Shortly after the direct hit, the port engine went out of commission. About five minutes later, the main engine room reported it was impossible to remain any longer due to unbearable heat. But the skipper, Lt William Villella, refused to give up. He ordered his engineers, at the point of suffocation, to set the starboard engine at flank speed ahead and then abandon the engine room.

All personnel, other than the gun crews and repair party, were then ordered to abandon ship. Some swam ashore. Others were picked up by nearby boats.

Villella headed the ship toward the beach at Tenaru, maneuvering to take advantage of the wind to prevent the flames from spreading. About 500 yards offshore, the clutch on the starboard engine kicked out, but the 340 beached herself on her own momentum with a little help from the wind.

Flotilla 5 Commander, Capt G. B. Carter, directed two sister LSTs to give the 340 assistance. The few personnel still on board then went by boat to the LST-353 and directed her to the port side of the 340 where water was immediately played on the fire. Skipper Villella, spotting LST-398 nearby, boarded that ship and asked her C.O. to maneuver alongside the 340's starboard side where hoses could get at the flames.

"The heat was threatening to explode the ammunition magazine located below the stern deck. The commodore, skipper, and I tried to start two handy billy pumps in a last desperate attempt to flood the ammunition magazine, but failed. As far as we could tell, the three of us were the last to leave the ship. We left by way of a Jacob's ladder off the stern. By this time, the steel deck was so hot our shoes seemed to be on fire. We also had a real fear that the magazine would explode. Apparently, the magazine locker was sufficiently below the water line to maintain a cooler temperature. Anyway it did not explode. . . .

"Jap planes did try to strafe those of us in the water, but were driven off. Very shortly thereafter, an LST from our flotilla came along and picked us up. It also used its own fire fighting equipment to help fight the 340 fires."

—*Anthony Tesori, Gunnery Officer, USS LST-340*

USS *Celeno* Survivors.   The survivors of the *Celeno* spent two or three days on Guadalcanal living in tents and foxholes while a salvage crew made temporary repairs and pumped out the holds. Tony Gray, captain's messenger, recalls:

"We were then towed over to Tulagi where further repairs were made. The rudder and shaft were badly bent, so we couldn't move under our own power. After about a month, we were towed down to Espiritu Santo where the *Celeno* went into a floating dry-dock to check the repairs. The shipfitters replaced some of the temporary patches and, about 1 September, we left for the States on a towline from two seagoing tugs. We reached San Francisco 30 days later and went into a Mare Island dry-dock for a stem-to-stern overhaul."

—*Anthony Gray, Quartermaster third-class, USS* Celeno

Most of the *Celeno* crew received survivors' leave while the ship was under repair and being outfitted for troop handling. In December 1943, the ship loaded at Oxnard, Calif., with a Navy ACORN Construction Group and headed back to the Russell Islands in the Solomons. *Celeno* brought troops and cargo to Manus through the spring of 1944. She continued to operate throughout the Pacific until the war ended and was decommissioned at San Francisco on 1 March 1946 and transferred to the Maritime Commission. She received three battle stars for World War II service.

SS *Nathaniel Currier.* At 1559, the *Currier* received the all-clear signal from shore and returned to the anchorage. From the time the ship got underway until the all-clear message was received, the skipper kept the ship zigzagging in a radical pattern at flank speed with a skill that reflected a lifetime of experience.

A total of 2,103 rounds were fired from the 20s. Ten shells were fired from the 3"/50; one of which misfired. No damage was inflicted on the *Currier* by the enemy and there were no casualties, except for burns Grady Murphy received during the attack.

The C.O.'s report summarized the Armed Guard's defense of the *Currier* with these words:

> Two enemy planes were definitely destroyed by the fire from the guns of this ship, and two more were damaged: one was subsequently destroyed by a P-38 fighter plane, and the other possibly destroyed. Several other planes were hit, but no material damage can claim to have been done to them. At least three other bombers attacking this ship during the course of such raid were driven off.

Our gun crews were so busy shooting we had no time to count, but most of us felt the C.O. was low on all his tallies. The merchant seamen at the guns carried out their battle assignments quickly and efficiently, and without any confusion or signs of panic.

The casualty count and damage to U.S. ships would have been far worse had we not had the protection of the Solomon Island Air Force ("Airsols"). Their fighter pilots were absolutely fearless—and a bit too trusting of "AA" (anti-aircraft) gunners.

CinCPAC/POA Summary of Attack.   Admiral Chester W. Nimitz, Commander in Chief Pacific Fleet (CinCPAC) and of the Pacific Ocean Area (CinCPOA), directed all U.S. military forces in the North, Central, and South Pacific, and provided support to the Southwest Pacific forces of General Douglas MacArthur. In Adm Nimitz's June 1943 summary for the Joint Chiefs, he bottom-lined the 16 June 1943 action as follows:

> On 16 June, the largest enemy force since 7 April attacked our shipping in the Guadalcanal area. Enemy forces consisted of at least 60 VB (bombers), screened by a like number of fighters.
>
> One hundred four U.S. fighters were scrambled in defense, and 74 made contact with enemy. There were numerous U.S. ships in the transport areas off Lunga Point and in Tulagi. The attack lasted from 1315 to 1513 (-11).
>
> ComSoPac [RAdm Halsey] credits his VFs [fighters] and ships' A/A with the destruction of 107 enemy planes. Six of our VFs were lost, two pilots being recovered.
>
> During this attack the LST 340 received one hit which set fire to her cargo of trucks, gas, oil, etc., completely destroying it [the cargo]. LST 340, itself, though badly damaged, was beached and later salvaged.
>
> At 1410 *Celeno* (AK) received 2 hits, and the resultant fire destroyed most of her cargo, though the ship was likewise beached and later salvaged.
>
> (Source: CinCPOA, "Operations in Pacific Areas," June 1943.)

First "Special" Naval Construction Battalion

The first U.S. Navy stevedore battalion to arrive in the South Pacific—known as the First "Special" NCB—earned high praise on Guadalcanal for its professional cargo handling talents while offloading long-haul freighters and battle-loading the revolutionary new landing craft, or both.* The 1st Special NCB offloaded almost 6,700 tons of *Currier* cargo into or onto anything that would float (the new Flotilla 5 LSTs which had just arrived at Guadalcanal, the 70-ton barges made up of pontoon cells, the 45-foot LCMs) in only seven days, about 24 hours of which were lost due to air raids.† During the approximately eight days the *Currier* was standing off Guadalcanal, there were 13 air raids and/or red alerts. The Merchant Marine and Naval Armed Guard crews that manned the 6,000 plus long-haul carriers like the *Currier* were quick to recognize and appreciate the increased efficiency and shorter turnaround times.

Japanese Submarine Attack, 23 June 1943

On 22 June 1943 at 0945, Task Unit 32.4.4, composed of SS *Nathaniel Currier*, USS *Aludra*, USS *Deimos*, USS *O'Bannon*, USS *Ward*, and USS *Skylark*, got underway.

From the USS *O'Bannon* Action Report for 22 June 1943:

> Preliminary Information—Task Unit 32.4.4. . .departed Guadalcanal via Lengo channel. . .for points south via route Careen.

---

* The revolutionary new landing ships and craft would soon prove invaluable as medium- to short-haul carriers of troops, war materiel, and supplies between advance bases like Noumea, Espiritu Santo, and Guadalcanal, and new amphibious operations such as the upcoming New Georgia campaign. —Ed.

† Much of the *Currier's* cargo was offloaded into the new Flotilla 5 LSTs for (as we learned later) Operation Toenails, the invasion of New Georgia in the Central Solomons starting 21 June 1943; no doubt the reason why the enemy mounted such an all-out raid on 16 June 1943, the second biggest enemy air raid since Pearl Harbor. —Ed.

Commander Task Unit 32.4.4 was LCdr Collins, USNR, the Commanding Officer of the USS *Aludra*. The Commanding Officer of the *O'Bannon* [LCdr Donald J. MacDonald] was the senior officer of the escort ships.

After clearing the Channel the *Aludra* was the guide followed by the *Nathaniel Currier* at a distance of about 700 yards; the *Deimos* was 1,000 yards on the *Aludra's* starboard beam. The formation of the AKs and the merchant ship remained as mentioned above throughout the day and night.

Narrative—Speed of auxiliary ships was approximately 10 knots, we were zigzagging in accordance with plan #38 so the speed made good over the ground was approximately 9 knots. All screening vessels were patrolling station radically at speeds up to 14 knots. . . .

At 0445 L (1745Z) the formation was steaming on course 124 degrees at base speed of 10 knots, zigzagging in accordance with plan #38. The moon was full and directly overhead, the sky was completely overcast, the sea was choppy, the wind was force about 3 from southeast. The indirect illumination caused by the overcast sky with a full moon above, caused our ships to stand out very clearly at a range of 4.000 yards.

It was at this time [0443] that two explosions, which seemed almost simultaneous, were felt by this vessel. The Officer of the Deck reported that the *Skylark* had changed course to Port and had just dropped depth charges. The Commanding Officer upon looking over the situation immediately realized that the auxiliary ships had been torpedoed. Radar screen showed nothing, nor had they shown anything during the night other than our own ships.

(Source: USS *O'Bannon*, Action Report for 22 June 1943.)

The *Currier* gun crew had been at battle stations all night because we were headed south back through Torpedo Junction. At 0443, Joe Skalenda, our bow-lookout, sighted a torpedo wake and got everyone's attention when he shouted, "Torpedo off port bow!" Our bridge lookouts also spotted the torpedo streaking toward us. Of course, there wasn't time to change course or maneuver. I no sooner picked up the fast-moving line of phosphorescent bubbles than it disappeared under our bow, only to emerge to starboard racing off through the early morning darkness.

USS Aludra *and* USS Deimos *Sink*

We had barely absorbed the shock of this close call when the *Aludra* and *Deimos*, steaming abreast of each other just ahead, were both hit by torpedoes on the port side less than 30 seconds apart.

From the *Nathaniel Currier's* Action Report of 17 July 1943:

> The ships had been zigzagging all night and, at the time of the attack, had gone on the left leg of the convoy. This brought the three cargo vessels in a V-shape or triangular formation about eight hundred yards apart with the *Currier* the last ship in the convoy.
>
> Within a few seconds after the attack, Captain Hassell took charge of the bridge and the ship continued for several miles at flank speed in company with one of the escorting destroyers [*Ward*], using a radical zigzag pattern. A sharp lookout was kept in all sections, but the submarine was never sighted and no further attacks were made.
>
> Captain Hassell requested permission to return to render assistance to the damaged ships, but he was ordered to continue away from the point of the attack, which order he carried out. No shots were fired, and when last sighted, both ships which had been hit were afloat.
>
> (Source: SS *Nathaniel Currier*,
> Action Report dated 17 July 1943.)

The *O'Bannon* Action Report covering the 23 June 1943 sub attack, dated 17 July 1943, continues:

> [The *O'Bannon's* course]. . .was changed to starboard and a circle commenced to try and locate submarine on starboard

side. Communications could not be established over TBS [Talk between ships] with other friends, so the Commanding Officer was not aware at this time from which side the torpedoes had hit. A search to starboard was immediately made for the submarine although survivors in boats began flashing SOS over blinker lights. No attempt was made at this time to pick up survivors.

At 0529 L [local time] (1829 Z [Greenwich Mean Time]) a surface radar contact was made on bearing 033 degrees T[rue], distance 13,800 yards; speed was immediately increased to ultimate 30 knots and course changed to run down contact. It was at first thought that this might be the submarine, upon drawing closer, two contacts were definitely established and at 0600 communications were established with YPs 514 and 518.* They were requested to come back and pick up survivors while this ship continued submarine hunt.

After the YPs were in the area, the Commanding Officer of the *O'Bannon* directed the *Skylark* and YPs to pick up survivors while the *O'Bannon* continued circling and to hunt for the submarine. Sunrise was at 0629. It was not until 0645 that communications were established with any of our ships over the TBS.

The *Currier* and the *Ward* stood on ahead on base course swinging clear of the crippled ships and, after getting about 10,000 yards away, were directed by me to proceed at best speed toward BUTTON [Espiritu Santo]. We were not able to establish definitely from which side the ships had been hit until 0720 and this was over the TBS at which time Commander Task Unit 32.4.4 said that they had been hit on the Port side of base course. . .

Rescue Operations: The *O'Bannon* continued to search for the submarine except as indicated below; to put a boat in

---

* These distinct patrol craft (a.k.a. YPs, "Yippies," "Yard Patrol Craft," "Cactus Navy," "Yard Birds," "Tuna Boats," or "Pineapple Navy") were small and slow, displacing between 50 and 150 tons. Mostly fishing boats from Hawaii or patrol craft from Hawaiian Sea Frontier Forces, they were converted for military use. Wooden-hulled and lightly armed, they were used as tugs, dispatch boats, rescue craft, troop and supply ferries, and transports for minor amphibious assaults.

the water and send a doctor to the *Skylark* at 0728. At 0743 YP 514 reported sound contact off port bow and this vessel proceeded in that vicinity to search. Contact was false and nothing further was developed.

At approximately 0900 a PBY approached and circled the formation. He was directed to go out to circle 25 miles and work in. Shortly thereafter, another PBY closed the formation and he circled the area, assisting in the hunt. A Flying Fortress closed the Unit and looked over the situation and then departed.

Sinking of the *Aludra:* At 0933 the *Aludra* sank. At 1024, YP 518 came alongside and transferred the Commanding Officer of the *Deimos* with 7 other *Deimos* officers and 41 enlisted men to this vessel.

At 1028, YP 518 and 514 were directed to make final sweep for survivors.

At 1055 this vessel went alongside the *Skylark* and transferred two containers of blood plasma.

At 1105 all ships made a complete sweep of the entire area and after ascertaining that there were no more survivors in the water, the Commanding Officer of the *O'Bannon* directed *Skylark* and the two YPs to proceed to Button at best speed.

Sinking of the *Deimos:* At 1200, after circling the *Deimos*, verifying that no contact in the area prior to sending salvage party aboard, it was noticed that the *Deimos* was settling by the stern fairly rapidly so that her after gun was just going underwater.

After talking over the situation with the Commanding Officer of the *Deimos* and ascertaining the damage which had been done and her chances for salvage, it was decided that salvage would be impossible, so the *Deimos* was sunk by gunfire at 1233.

T.U. 32.4.4 Search continues: After the *Deimos* was sunk, a thorough [*O'Bannon*] search was started for any remaining survivors and also for the submarine. At 1400 radar contacts on unidentified aircraft bearing 060 degrees T, distance 10 miles began to come in. From 1400 until 1518 radar contacts were maintained on four different unidentified aircraft. One closed the range to 8 miles but was not identified visually. The others circled at ranges of 12 and 15 miles.

At 1830, just at dusk, this vessel was again back in the area of the empty life rafts and life boats that were still floating. At 2027 L (0927 Z) a black cat [Allied aircraft] circled overhead and gave us the proper reply. At 2046 a flare was dropped to the North of us; course was changed to north and speed increased to 30 knots to run down the vicinity of the flare. It was thought at first that the black cat had a contact and was illuminating it. After steaming on this course for 40 minutes with no radar contact and not being able to establish communications with the black cat plane over the common frequency, course was changed to rendezvous with the *Currier* and *Ward* which was accomplished the next morning at dawn.

(Source: USS *O'Bannon*, Action Report covering
23 June 1943 sub attack, dated 17 July 1943.)

The Casualty Report from the *Aludra's* medical officer revealed that two crew members died of injuries on 23 June and were buried at sea the following day. Twelve crew members were wounded; four were transferred to Base Hospital #3. The casualty report for some unknown reason didn't mention the military passengers who were killed.

The *Skylark,* (Lt Roy H. Jones, Commanding) and two YPs, the 514 and 518, rescued the *Aludra* and *Deimos* survivors.

USS Skylark

The *Skylark's* War Diary for 23–24 June 1943 describes the recovery action:

> 0630 Received orders to pick up survivors, DD450 screening.
> 0635 Alongside first raft with nine men, none injured.
> 0652 All men aboard from second and third life rafts (17 men).
> 0710 Recovered two men clinging to wreckage, one injured.
> 0715 Four more men singly, two injured.
> 0730 One man recovered injured.

0735 *Aludra* sank, bow down. Recovered eighteen men, none injured.

0742 Twenty-nine men picked up from life boat, one seriously injured.

0754 Recovered twenty-one men aboard, two badly injured.

0755 Received the doctor from *O'Bannon*. YP514 and YP518 joined the search for survivors.

08–12: 0803 Recovered seventeen men from life raft, two injured.

0813 Recovered eleven men from life raft, one injured.

0826 Recovered three men from life raft, none injured.

0843 Recovered nine men from life boat, none injured.

0847 Recovered five men from life boat, none injured.

0847–1049 Continued to search the area for survivors.

1049 Doctor reported need of plasma and proceeded on a course in order that DD 450 could pass supplies by line.

1107 Medical supplies aboard by line from DD450 and searching the area was complete.

(Source: USS *Skylark*, War Diary for 23–24 June 1943.)

Leonard D. Honeycutt joined the *Skylark* in Noumea on 6 June 1943, his 18th birthday. Here's how he remembers the rescue operation:

"Until I joined the Navy, I'd never even seen anyone seriously ill in my life, much less dead, and here we were bringing all these men aboard, some alive, some wounded, and some dead. It was still dark and we were pulling them aboard, covered with oil, black from head to foot. We had the mess tables and decks filled with people. It was total chaos. We had our doctor there as well as one from the *O'Bannon*. I guess I was pretty much in shock because we had to stack the dead on the fantail for some time. We used our berthing compartments for the survivors and we stayed topside. Of course we were sleepin' topside anyway because of the heat."

—*Leonard D. Honeycutt, USS* Skylark

Editor's note: To those who survived the attacks on the USS *Aludra* and USS *Deimos,* it was a morning they would long remember. Here is a sampling of their recollections from interviews conducted by the editor in the 1990s:

"The aft mast came flying down, but thank God, it missed everybody. Within minutes, the Captain ordered 'abandon ship' over the loud speaker. . . .I abandoned ship twice. The first time, I slid down a line to my life raft, but the fellows were yelling 'there's no more room.' So I went back up the rope, hand over hand, to the deck and ran up to the bow where there were still several men and the Captain. But there were no more life rafts available. So the skipper said, 'Throw the hatch covers over the side and get on them. So I abandoned ship, again, only the hatch covers didn't float so well and got all tangled up. All we could do was stay in the water and hang on to them. The fellows in the boats and rafts kept telling us to 'watch out for sharks'. . .which didn't make us feel very secure."

—*Merle Luther, Shipfitter 2/c, USS* Aludra

"My abandon ship station was right there alongside the gun. It was my job to cut the rafts loose, but after the torpedo hit, we were taking water in the bow and the fantail was up in the air. We were empty, so you're talking about 30 feet. The screw was goin' round as we circled; it wouldn't stop. The chief machinist mate went down and shut the engines off 'cause I wouldn't cut the rafts loose until the screw stopped. It was cutting guys in half. When the engine stopped, I got a 4-inch mooring line, put a figure-eight in it, and dropped it over the side. That's the way about 18 of us went down to the raft so we wouldn't have to jump."

—*Eugene M. Hopper, USS* Aludra

"Four of us were on the life raft about 17 hours. It was after dark when I heard this diesel engine running and thought we'd had it 'cause we figured it was an enemy sub that had surfaced in the darkness and was running on the surface looking for survivors. It circled, then approached. All of a sudden, out of the night, we hear, 'Ahoy there!' You talk about relief. We couldn't answer, you know, and pretty soon here comes this little 'ole white yippie boat, a converted San Diego tuna boat, and they took us aboard. They'd been searching all day for survivors. . .and the way I heard it, we were the last ones to get picked up. There were sharks there, you damn betcha there were sharks. The able-bodied tried to protect the wounded as best they could."

—*Bill Hartman, USS* Aludra

"They were shooting at the sharks from the *O'Bannon,* using rifles, .45s, and Tommy guns. We lost some of our crew. We lost a third-class signalman named Franklin. He was a great guy, regular Navy. And we lost a machinist mate, second-class, and a striker. They were both down in the engine room. We had about 35 passengers of Army, Navy and Marines, all headed Stateside on emergency leave or for some other reason. They were asleep on top the Nos. 1 and 2 holds, so we lost almost all of them. We picked some of them up, but they died. They were wounded going into the water. We took them to the *O'Bannon* and a lot of them died."

—*Roy Lucy, USS* Aludra

"I was on the flying bridge behind the stack—why, I don't know—lookin' off to port when I saw the phosphorescent wake. They make a helluva wake especially when it's that dark. I saw that and I knew immediately it was a torpedo. So I let out a yell, 'Torpedo!' and just flopped down. As I flopped down, I could see the *Aludra* going up. Then we got a dull thud, and then, wham! I asked later why there were two explosions. I didn't know it, but they tell me those torpedoes carried a penetrating cap, so the first thud was the cap knockin' a hole in the hull."

—*Bernard Barker, USS* Deimos

"I was standing out on deck. I saw the ship *Aludra* alongside of us get hit. All I heard was a big boom. The next thing I remember. . .seconds later, we must have been hit because I found myself scrambling over twisted steel beams, I suppose hatch beams, and where I ran to, I don't even know."

—*Pat Paones, USS* Deimos

"I was sittin' in the little cantina having a cup of coffee and all of a sudden GQ sounded. I got up to start for my battle station when, whambo, right next to me, that torpedo hit and just blasted the hell out of things. Damn near blew me overboard. I went right through them black-out curtains and hit the rail—not the rail, but the chains. All I got out of the whole mess was a broken thumb."

—*Mike Hosier, USS* Deimos

"We were goin' to have beans and cornbread for breakfast. Those beans had been simmering all night long. I had a gas mask, lifejacket, and helmet under my arm when they woke me and said, 'Cookie, it's time to start breakfast.' I remember walkin' into the galley and layin' my lifejacket on the peelin' table we used to prepare vegetables. Then I got a big 'ole pan and headed for the forward storeroom right beneath the 3"/50 where we stored cornbread and other dry produce. There were two watertight doors and, if I'm not mistaken, six dogs on each hatch, and as you go through, you dog them behind you. Well,

I went through the two, got my cornmeal, came back out and dogged the doors behind me. . . .

"There was a meat block just outside the ice box. I set that cornmeal on the meat block, pulled the plunger on that big 'ole ice box door, opened it, pulled off my old cook's hat, and, just as I bent over, I hear the explosion. At first I thought, my god, what's happened? I thought maybe we collided 'cause we were runnin' pretty close together. I ran for that plunger and when it didn't open I thought, oh, my god! I picked up a couple of boxes or crates or something and I ran at that door, and when I hit it with my shoulder, it swung open. . . .

"I looked down the ladder and saw that stream of water comin'. I ran up that ladder to get my lifejacket. But somebody had taken it. I remember runnin' forward. My division officer said, 'Vorhies, get to your abandon ship station.' I don't know what I said to him but I kept runnin'! That's when I jumped off the bow of that ship. It seemed like 30 days before I hit water. I remember reaching for my legs and I can't feel a thing. My God, what's happened, what's happened, I wondered. . . .

"I remember goin' by that hull and seein' the oil splattered around where the torpedo had entered. I could hear that water making kind of a sucking sound. I finally got hold of a boat skid and hung on to that for I don't know how long. Withers, he was a first-class cook, got a hold of me and got me to a donut raft. It was for 16 people and there were 27 of us hanging on it. Bowie, he was a mess cook for the officer's wardroom, the back of his head was blown out and you could see the inside of his head."

—*Robert E. Vorhies, USS* Deimos

"There was so much oil on the main deck, I went up to the boat deck. A pharmacists' mate had somebody in his arms, rocking him, trying to get him to come to or whatever. I asked him if he needed any help and he said, 'No, go ahead.' So I went up this twisted old ladder to the captain's promenade. I was going back into the main radio shack when the communications officer came out and said, 'I've taken care of all the secret stuff. I deep-sixed all the coded stuff. So go abandon ship.'"

—*Jay S. Rider Jr., USS* Deimos

"I went topside and helped load a couple whaleboats. Then I jumped over the side when the skipper gave three calls to abandon ship, then two calls, then every man for himself! I went over the side and hung on to the side of a whaleboat. Somebody puked in my face. I let go and got on this boat skid with Morris D. Martin; he was yelling at me. I remember another guy, a teeny black guy named Ferguson. He was rattling around about something and offered free rides to San Francisco for ten bucks or something. Everybody got a big bang out of it."

—*Bernard Barker, USS* Deimos

"Our guy knocks the pin out so the raft can drop into the water, but somebody forgot to secure the painter [line] to the ship. I look out and there's the goddamn raft back there about a quarter mile. I went over the side on a cargo net, got into the water, and someone picked me up. I think it was Lt Bailey."

—*Mike Hosier, USS* Deimos

"We all had bunker fuel in our hair, in our mouth; we were covered in it. There was a young fellow, a cook, and his side was laid open. You could see his ribs. One of those big old hatch covers had hit him. He was pretty good. He didn't make much noise. We rode around and picked up a few people. Those destroyers, like the *O'Bannon*, would come up and slow down. We'd row like hell to get to them and they'd take off. I can't blame them because that Jap was still out there."

—*David Haugh, USS* Deimos

"There was an electrician and a shark come up and tore his whole arm off."

—*Pat Paones, USS* Deimos

"Oh, God, there were lots of sharks but we never had any of them attack. We were sure we'd get eaten up by sharks if the damn Japs didn't get us. Our rescue ship, the *Skylark,* shot at quite a lot of them with their 30-caliber machine guns."

—*Walter P. Ballow, USS* Deimos

"I saw plenty of sharks. In fact, after I was picked up, there was this guy out there hanging onto a gas drum. When the *Skylark* backed down to get him, the sharks ate him before you could blink."

—*Lester "Ray" Weathers, USS* Deimos

"Some of those YPs were tuna boats from San Pedro with big reefers on them so they could carry fresh food up to the 'Canal. Finally one of them pulled up and we got aboard. We kind of overwhelmed them because they had a small crew and small ship, but they were wonderful. They helped pick up quite a few survivors. They turned over their bunks to us. I climbed in one all oily. Those poor guys probably ended up throwing all their bedding away. I didn't even go out on deck to watch the *O'Bannon* sink the *Deimos.* I wasn't about to lose my bunk."

—*David Haugh, USS* Deimos

"While we were in the water, the *O'Bannon*—they used to call her the 'Little Helena'—was running around dropping depth charges. We were picked up by a YP and transferred to the *O'Bannon* later. When we boarded the *O'Bannon*, each crew member grabbed a survivor and gave us clothes and stuff. We stayed there all day trying to find that sub. The Skipper was really hot."

—Bob Parker, USS Deimos

"The *O'Bannon* came over and picked us up. It was light by then. We climbed up a net, two of us. They took us to the mess hall and we got under a table. I remember the doc reaching down, putting cotton to my face, and wiping it off. I don't remember getting clean clothes. They were operating on guys on the table."

—Richard T. Rogers, USS Deimos

"They put me in a bunk on the Yard Patrol. Oh, Lord, I couldn't move. My legs were paralyzed. It happened when I jumped. I either hit something, debris in the water, or maybe it was the way I hit. I remember them burying six of the boys they picked up. Some of them had their lifejackets on and their heads were down, just their bottoms bobbing up. They just reached down and bow-hooked them. There was a chaplain aboard who gave the burial services. I remember they were wrapping them in canvas and shoving them overboard. Now who they were, I don't know."

—Robert E. Vorhies, USS Deimos

On June 24 at 0635, the O'Bannon picked up the *Ward* and the *Currier* on her radar and joined formation taking station in screen at 0714. These remnants of Task Unit 32.4.4 sighted Espiritu Santo Island at 1705 bearing 115 degrees T., distance about 25 miles. The *Skylark* and YPs 514 and 518 joined formation at 2048 and took position astern.

Most survivors boarded attack transport *John Penn* (APA-23) for the short trip south to Noumea, home of Admiral Halsey's headquarters and "rest camp." Here is a sampling of recollections from various survivors:

"After being put ashore on Espiritu Santo, the gentle Red Cross folks gave us a little ditty bag with toothbrush, soap, comb, razor, and a little bit of clothing, like a couple pair of skivvies and a pair of shoes. Damn little. Most spent two or three days there, others a week, living in tents furnished with Army cots. The showers were outside, the roads muddy, and the U.S. Marine chow wasn't great—but we were out of range of land-based Jap bombers."

—*Kenneth F. Keller, USS* Deimos

A few bluejackets drew assignments on New Caledonia—a good climate and out of range of Japanese land-based bombers:

"At first, they put me on a tank farm. A captain came to talk to me and, when he learned I had shipyard experience, he transferred me to the ship repair base. I was there 13 months."

—*Pat Paones, USS* Deimos

"I got assigned to a naval repair base in Noumea and was there 'til July '44."

—*Edval Helle Sr., USS* Deimos

Several men were transferred to a Naval Mobile Hospital in Auckland, New Zealand:

"We were sent on the USS *Crescent City* to MOB6 Hospital in Auckland for about six months. We didn't even know what a mobile hospital was. I remember Captain Stelle of MOB6 pinning a purple heart on my chest the day after he restricted me for two weeks for 'AOL'—absent over leave. It was real tough duty. The gals used to trip you, then beat you to the deck. I had a hard time making my money, liberty, and beer come out even."

—*Bob Parker, USS* Deimos

"A lieutenant commander, a doctor at the hospital said, 'Don't worry, Hosier, you're never going to see sea duty again. You're going back to the States.' I didn't even make it to San Francisco. I was assigned to the USS *Sitka* (AKA-113).

—*Mike Hosier, USS* Deimos

Most T.U. 32.4.4 survivors were back in action within two weeks.

CinCPOA Summary of Attack

Admiral Nimitz summarized the submarine attack in his June 1943 report to the Joint Chiefs of Staff:

> 43. Loss of USS *Aludra* and USS *Deimos*. On the night of 22–23 June (L) T.U. 32.4.4, composed of USS *Aludra*, USS *Deimos*, (AKs), SS *Nathaniel Currier* (XAK), escorted by *O'Bannon* and *Ward* (DDs) and *Skylark* (AM), were enroute from Guadalcanal for ports south, speed 10 knots.
>
> At about 0445 (L), in Lat. 11-35, Long. 162-08 E, with the convoy zigzagging, with full moon directly overhead, both *Aludra* and *Deimos*, then abreast of each other at 1,000 yards, were hit by torpedoes almost simultaneously.
>
> The *Currier* and *Ward* stood on; *Skylark* picked up survivors, assisted shortly by YPs in the vicinity; while *O'Bannon* made search, but without success. No contacts were made either by sound or by radar (with which all escort vessels were equipped), either before or after the attack, except for one doubtful radar contact at 10,000 yards about an hour before by *Skylark*, which through inexperience of personnel was not developed.
>
> The Escort Commander (C.O., USS *O'Bannon*) believed that the Task Unit had been shadowed for some time and that the submarine came up from astern on the port side on the surface, without detection by the screening vessels, and made her final attack submerged.
>
> 44. Unfortunately, the Escort Commander was unable to determine on which side the vessels had been hit, and hence

made his initial search to starboard, whereas they had both been hit on the port side. Inability to establish TBS communication between vessels was a considerable handicap in getting information.

Both vessels were abandoned soon after being hit. The *Aludra* sank at 0933 (L). At 1200 the *Deimos* was seen to be settling rapidly, and after consulting with her Commanding Officer and deciding that salvage was impossible, the Escort Commander had her sunk by gunfire at 1233.

There were several casualties due to the explosion of the torpedoes, but all survivors are believed to have been rescued.

The same CinCPOA report included this observation under "Comments and Conclusions":

> 62. Signaling Direction of Submarine Attack. When a convoy is attacked by a submarine, it is obviously of the highest importance for screening vessels to know immediately the direction from which torpedoes were fired, so as to lose no time in making effective search and attack. Yet it appears possible (case of *Aludra* and *Deimos,* Para. 44) for Escorts to be uncertain about this even after vessels of the convoy have been hit, if it is at night or in thick weather. Escort Commanders should make sure that all vessels of a convoy understand both the necessity and the method for transmitting this information promptly, even if all electric power has been lost.
>
> (Source: CinCPOA report to the Joint Chiefs of Staff, June 1943.)

(Source: McGee, *Bluejacket Odyssey, 1942–1946,* Chap 3–8:41–177.) ∎

Editor: In conclusion, the ill-fated convoy, Task Unit 32.4.4, composed of four Liberty ships and three escorts, left Noumea on 6 June 1943 for Guadalcanal. Two weeks later, there was only one Liberty left, the SS *Nathaniel Currier,* and our escorts.

An estimated 1,250 crew members manned the seven ships. The *Celeno* suffered the heaviest casualties: 15 KIA (Killed In Action), 19 WIA (Wounded In Action), and 2 MIA (Missing In Action). The *Deimos:* 6 to 8 KIA. The *Aludra:* 2 KIA, 12 WIA, MIA unknown; she also lost an estimated 25 military passengers.

The U.S. Navy had 160 AKs and 108 AKAs in its Auxiliary Fleet during WWII.* All but three AKs—*Aludra, Deimos* and *Serpens* (AK-97)—survived the war, The *Aludra* and the *Deimos* each earned one battle star for their brief but courageous World War II service.†

Later, the SS *Nathaniel Currier's* skipper, D. W. Hassell, sent a very complimentary letter to the commanding officer of the Naval Armed Guard Center on Treasure Island when we got back. His final paragraph quoting the Seabees makes me particularly proud:

> "It is my belief that the reason we sustained no casualties or damage was the volume and accuracy of the barrage put up. Officers and enlisted personnel of the Seabee battalions in the Cactus-Ringbolt area [Guadalcanal] repeatedly asserted that they had never seen a merchant ship put up such a volume of fire as this ship did."

The *Currier* gun crew received a commendation from the Chief of Naval Personnel for the 16 June 1943 enemy action. It reads, in part:

---

* Morison, *Ships and Aircraft of the United States Navy 1940–1945,* Vol. 15, 79–83.

† *Dictionary of American Naval Fighting Ships.*

"A report of the experience reveals that this
ship and the areas about her were subjected to a
vicious attack by a formation of enemy dive-bombers.
Disregarding the danger from falling bombs and flying
shrapnel, the Navy gun crew fought back gallantly, setting up an accurate and sustained barrage of shellfire,
which shot down two planes, inflicting severe damage
on two others, and aided in driving off the rest."

Summary and Conclusions

Editor's note: Bruce L. Felknor was a radioman in the merchant
marine during World War II. He provides several thought-pro-
voking observations in the following summary and conclusions
in the Epilogue from his book, *The U.S. Merchant Marine at
War, 1775–1945.*

Of the 250,000 merchant mariners that sailed during the war, 6,845
were killed in various ways—shot, bombarded, drowned, incinerated, or
vaporized. When the survivors got home, any big reception they received was
from their individual families. No parades down Fifth Avenue and no GI Bill.

Of the 144,970 Armed Guard that served on the same merchant ships
during the war, 1,810 were killed or missing in action and presumed dead,
14 were made prisoners of war.

Fifty-three years after the last World War II military homecoming
parade, the Pentagon and Congress, in two separate actions in 1988
and 1998, reversed decades of denials and granted veterans status to
oceangoing merchant mariners who served in World War II. The initial
court decision came in a class action brought in 1986 by four merchant
marine veterans, after six years of unavailing appeals to the Civilian/
Military Service Review Board of the Department of Defense. One of

the quartet was Lane Kirkland, a deck officer through the war, and then president of the AFL-CIO, whose maritime unions paid the costs of the eight year legal battle. U.S. District Judge Louis F. Oberdorfer ordered the Pentagon review, and the resulting reversal was implemented at last on 19 January 1988. In subsequent legislation a decade later, merchant seamen who served between 15 August 1945 and 31 December 1945 were also granted veteran status.

This did not provide them with a GI Bill of Rights or other substantial benefits, but it did honor their war service and entitled them to an American flag for their caskets. It also enabled them to join existing veterans' organizations, and to organize several of their own, notably the American Merchant Marine Veteran Association and the U.S. Merchant Marine Veterans of World War II. A number of states authorized modest bonuses for merchant marine veterans, generally for those who resided in the state before and returned as residents after their war service.

Looking Ahead

The Armed Guard disbanded at the end of WWII, as it did at the end of WWI, since there was no need for its special service in peacetime. The merchant marine shriveled to its prewar status. Surplus ships were sold; 1,113 of them to foreign operators. Its postwar fate had certain similarities to what happened after the Civil War and WWI; the number of ships and jobs inevitably declined.

But more important merchant marine factors were technological advances and economic considerations. Ships grew larger, faster, and fewer. Crews got smaller and pay better. Unions were smaller and richer. Vessels under the U.S. flag plummeted in number from about 5,600 oceangoing ships at VJ-Day to about 400 fifty years later.

Interactions between the military and the merchant marine have changed as dramatically as the technology. And there have been revolutionary changes in the wartime problem of safety of ships and mariners from enemy action.

Technological Changes

The size, speed, maneuverability, cargo-carrying facilities, and cargo-handling equipment of ships have undergone revolutionary change since 1945. Container ships started the revolution: Their cargo is in what amounts to over-the-road trailer bodies; they are offloaded onto railroad flatcars, or flatbed trailers, and driven to their destination. Today, they are ubiquitous on American highways.

But for all the increase in speed, passenger shipping has not been able to compete with airlines in business and point-to-point, non-business travel. The passenger liner has become the cruise ship, and sea travel and shore stops are the vacation.

Accompanying these developments have been colossal increases in size. The largest modern freighters are more than twice the length of a Liberty ship (1,000 feet versus 441 feet with a beam of 175 feet versus 59 feet), and their deadweight tonnage, one million, is nearly a hundred times that of the "Lib." Speeds range up to 30 knots and more. Crew size in the modern giants is half that of a World War II freighter or tanker in American-flag ships; in Japan, that figure is one-quarter. Satellites have enabled global positioning systems that make navigation electronic, quick and easy.

Economic Changes

These physical, mechanical, and electronic changes have precipitated some great economic changes and accompanied others. As fewer seafarers (incidentally including a slowly increasing number of women, from captain to able-bodied or "AB") run bigger and faster ships, salaries and overtime pay have skyrocketed on U.S. ships. This is a tribute to the maritime unions and their congressional allies, but these tremendous increases also reflect years of double-digit inflation in the mid-1970s.

The higher technology of modern ships has increased the educational requirements for ships' officers, and it still takes a captain, a chief engineer, and three mates or deck officers and three assistant engineers (and a steward and some cooks) to run a merchant vessel. The U.S. Merchant

Marine Academy and a few other schools have risen to that challenge and turn out superbly qualified marine officers, far more than there are ready berths in U.S. ships. These officers are in demand on foreign ships, where the jobs really are, but at lower salaries.

Radio officers face a declining prospect, as modern electronic communication has taken on more and more of a "plug-and-play," do-it-yourself character. Many captains now handle the radioman's responsibilities, almost in spare time. Telegraph keys have gone the way of the pterodactyl—to the museum.

The boatswain and the electrician survive. But the new ships require only a few ABs and oilers, and only one or two wipers and ordinary seamen. Ships' carpenters are no more. Only the messboy has thrived in the bottom ranks, because even small and elite crews have to eat—but more and more, they do so from buffet tables.

U.S. shipping companies that remain in business enjoy more congenial relations with the unions than in the World War II era and before. This is partly because of, and partly the result of, effective lobbying both interests have done on behalf of continuing maritime subsidies (now outright grants in exchange for companies' making ships available to the military in emergencies).

Meanwhile, the "flight from the flag" in the U.S. shipping industry continues, as more U.S.-owned ships are registered under foreign flags and manned with foreign or mixed U.S./foreign crews.

Military-Merchant Marine Relations

All military transportation operations have been consolidated under the U.S. Transportation Command, under which the Military Sealift Command (MSC) carries by far the greatest volume of cargo, and in ships manned by merchant crews. This has made it easier for congenial naval-civilian relations at the upper levels, and at least in peacetime there is no naval presence whatever at the individual ship level. The likelihood of an armed guard presence on merchant ships in a future war seems to be very much in limbo for the foreseeable future.

In a future war the kind of military-civilian and intramilitary disputes and disjunctions that sank so many ships and killed so many merchant seamen early in World War II virtually disappears, for the head of the Military Sealift Command is necessarily one of the most competent sea transport executives to be found, and the vital sea-transport decisions will fall to him or her, and not to a future Admiral King or any other fleet, force, or theater commander.

In the [first] Persian Gulf War, the Military Sealift Command carried 85 percent of all dry-cargo military supplies to the theater, with a dispatch and a generally high level of efficiency. This was accomplished by seven of its eight Fast Sealift Ships, which carried what it would have taken 120 World War II freighters to transport. These vessels are essentially container ships, modified to allow them to carry a mix of container and roll-on, roll-off cargo.

There are two other major elements of the MSC. The Afloat Prepositioning Force has thirteen Maritime Prepositioning Ships to carry combat equipment and supplies for the U.S. Marine Corps, and twelve other vessels to supply army and air force needs (seven freighters for ammunition and other supplies, four tankers, and one ship carrying a complete field hospital.)

At the time of the Gulf War, the Ready Reserve Force (RRF) consisted of ninety-four vessels under the control of the U.S. Maritime Administration, MARAD in "Federalese." Two-thirds of these ships are designated as ready for activation within five days and the others in ten to twenty days. "Flat racks" and "sea sheds" can be applied to these ships to accommodate "unit equipment;" that is, tanks, self-propelled guns, and vehicles.

In actual service in the Gulf War, forty-nine of the lot were break-bulk freighters, eleven were tankers, and the remainder vessels of various specializations from roll-on, roll-off freighters to crane ships. The Military Sealift Command is authorized to charter ships from U.S. owners whether they operate under the U.S. flag or a foreign "flag of convenience," and it also can charter foreign-owned, foreign-flag ships.

One of the thorniest problems confronting the whole military sea transport enterprise is manpower. The Maritime Administration anticipated that the pool of merchant seafarers qualified to operate deep-draft ships would number some 11,000 by the year 2000, down from 48,000 in 1980.

Safety of Ships and Crews

At the beginning of the twenty-first century, a sea war like either of the world wars does not seem a realistic prospect. If a superpower adversary does emerge, nuclear submarines and long-range or carrier-based bombers again will be offensive and defensive instruments. However, to anticipate this is akin to the old generals' game—approaching a next war by studying how to win the last.

Nations must of course be prepared for such eventuality, but in the world of the twenty-first century, the rogue microstate, the terrorist country or religion, the renegade North Korean or Soviet with plutonium to go, is a constant threat. In a world of supertankers and superfreighters, the truck bomb or the suitcase nuclear bomb are more deadly than a torpedo and can be placed and detonated for pennies instead of billions.

(Source: Felknor, *The U.S. Merchant Marine at War, 1775–1945*, Epilogue, 331–335.) ∎

New York navy yard workers arm merchant ships, circa 1941–42. A 5-inch/51-caliber WWI vintage surface gun is being lowered into position on the fantail of the freighter. (National Archives)

Merchant Marine officer signals full speed ahead on bridge engine order telegraph. (Naval Historical Center)

A pre-sailing convoy conference. Ship masters and involved Naval officers listen as the convoy escort Commander explains that his warships have orders to "shoot out unauthorized lights if necessary." Note the expressions on the men's faces. (Naval Historical Center)

U.S. Navy Armed Guard gunnery school gunboat, San Diego, Calif. (Naval Historical Center)

Naval Armed Guard gunnery practice on a 3-inch/50-caliber gun with dummy shells. (U.S. Navy)

Fantail 5-inch/38-caliber on a Victory ship in San Francisco Bay. (U.S. Navy)

"Traveling sailsmen" at Naval Armed Guard Center (Pacific), Treasure Island, Calif. (U.S. Navy)

LCdr E. D. Flaherty conducts Armed Guard awards ceremony, Treasure Island, Calif. (U.S. Navy)

The Kaiser-managed Richmond Shipyards, Todd-California Corporation (later the Permanente Metals Corporation). Many Libertys, including the four EC-2 Libertys that would be part of U.S. Navy Task Unit 32.4.4, were built within weeks of each other at this shipyard in Richmond, Calif. (Kaiser Industries)

A typical Liberty ship underway, SS *George H. Dern*, 1943. Note absence of deck load. (Courtesy William F. Hultgren)

President Franklin D. Roosevelt aboard a ferry off Bremerton, Washington, 1942. The President was likely inspecting shipyards. Identified include VAdm Charles S. Freeman *(back seat)*, the President *(front seat)*, and Mr. John Boettiger *(at President's elbow)*. (Naval Historical Center)

Naval Armed Guard at sea. A 3-inch/50-caliber gun crew at battle station, 1945. (William L. McGee)

Signalmen ("Flags") on the job. (Naval Historical Center)

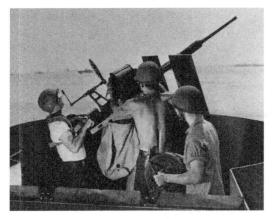

Naval Armed Guard crew practice on their 20mm, AA gun. The canvas bag beneath the magazine is to catch empty shell casings. (National Archives)

A 20mm, AA crew stands alert to counter enemy air attack onboard a Liberty ship in convoy. Note the simple ring sight. (Naval Historical Center)

King Neptune's Court aboard the SS *Thomas Nelson*, 1945. "Davey Jones" (center) with his bodyguards "Vacek" and "Wohleb" has just emerged from the deep blue sea with an ultimatum in hand for all lowly "Pollywogs" crouching subserviently on No. 5 cargo hatch. This initiation extended over two days. (Courtesy Charles C. Espy, Lt (jg), USNR, C.O. Armed Guard contingent, *Thomas Nelson*)

Task Unit 32.4.4 was made up of four EC-2 class Liberty ships: SS *Nathaniel Currier,* USS *Celeno,* USS *Deimos,* and USS *Aludra.* They were all built under Maritime Commission contracts within weeks of each other by Kaiser Permanente Metals Corporation, Yard No. 1, Richmond, Calif. *Pictured here,* merchant ship SS *Nathaniel Currier.* (Naval Historical Center)

U.S. Navy cargo ship, USS *Celeno* (AK-76). (Naval Historical Center)

U.S. Navy cargo ship, USS *Deimos* (AK-78) (ELSILRAC Enterprises). Not pictured, USS *Aludra,* (AK-72)

T.U. 32.4.4 had three escorts. Pictured here, destroyer USS *O'Bannon* (DD-450). (ENSILRAC Enterprises)

Minesweeper USS *Skylark* (AM-63). (ENSILRAC Enterprises) Not pictured, the third escort, fast transport USS *Ward* (APD-16).

Tulagi Island (foreground), 18 miles north of Guadalcanal, was the capital of the British Solomon Islands. (National Archives)

Japanese air attack on Guadalcanal, 16 June 1943. This appears to be anti-aircraft fire directed at a "Val" dive-bomber. (National Archives)

USS LST-340 burning after she was hit by an enemy bomb. She was run ashore off Lunga Point and her fires were extinguished after considerably damaging her and her cargo. Note the trucks burning on deck. Photograph was taken 15 minutes after the hit, 16 June 1943. (Marine Corps photo)

LST-340 continues to burn as LST-353 (right) moves alongside to assist in firefighting, 16 June 1943. (Courtesy Ralph K. Brown)

USS *O'Bannon* (DD-450) laying a smoke screen, as seen from her own bridge, in the Solomons, June 1943. (Naval Historical Center)

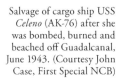

Salvage of cargo ship USS *Celeno* (AK-76) after she was bombed, burned and beached off Guadalcanal, June 1943. (Courtesy John Case, First Special NCB)

LST-340 salvage crew examines the smoldering aftermath on 17 June 1943. The "340" was the first LST casualty in the Pacific. (Naval Historical Center)

Chapter 6
U.S. Army Transportation Corps

Editor's note: This chapter addresses the U.S. Army's sea-going transportation problems and their solutions during World War II. The construction, acquisition and maintenance of Army vessels—such as transports, cargo vessels, and tug boats—were seldom covered by the consumer-oriented media during World War II. This chapter addresses this neglect with answers to many questions this writer/editor had been searching for.

Special thanks are due the following authors for providing photographs for this chapter from their books: David H. Grover, *U.S. Army Ships and Watercraft of World War II,* and Charles Dana Gibson and E. Kay Gibson, *Over Seas—U.S. Army Maritime Operations, 1898 Through the Fall of the Philippines.* The Gibson's are widely recognized as authorities on the history of the "U.S. Army's navy."

The chapter opens with an excerpt from *United States Army in World War II, The Technical Services—The Transportation Corps: Responsibilities, Organization and Operations* (hereafter

Principal sources for this chapter are Chester Wardlow, *United States Army in World War II, The Technical Services—The Transportation Corps: Responsibilities, Organization, and Operations* (1951); and David H. Grover, *U.S. Army Ships and Watercraft of World War II* (1987).

The Transportation Corps). The original text is heavily docu-
mented with notes, most of them citing communications of
various types and the agency housing the cited documents at
the time of publication. For this excerpt, the editor has selectively
included notes of interest to the reader. The notes and a list of
abbreviations used in the notes are at the end of the chapter.

The Transportation Corps

When in December 1941 the United States was plunged into a global
war with unprecedented transportation implications, the Army's plan
for dealing with transportation matters was essentially what it had been
in peacetime. There had been some expansion of personnel and facilities
during the prewar emergency, but the organizational set-up was basically
the same as that which had existed during the 1930's. There was a lack
of integration and some disagreement as to where certain responsibilities
rested. A long step toward correction of this weakness was taken in March
1942 when a transportation service under a chief of transportation was
established. Further progress was made when the Transportation Corps
was created in July 1942, and again when the corps' responsibilities were
considerably expanded a few months later. . . .

The Early Months of World War II

The first three months of the war brought about marked changes
in the management of transportation. New agencies were set up by the
President to exercise more complete control over the employment of the
nation's transportation resources. The Army's machinery for handling its
transportation requirements was completely reorganized. The relationships between the Army and the new civil transportation agencies were
tentatively worked out.

The heavy movements of men and supplies which became necessary immediately after the Japanese attack on our Pacific outposts put
the entire transportation system to a severe test. In some respects the

demands of a two-ocean war were met promptly and efficiently. In other respects there were handicaps which could be overcome only gradually. In the former class was the rail movement of about 600,000 troops with their organizational equipment during the first five weeks of war.[1] The excellent working relationships which had been established between the Quartermaster General's Commercial Traffic Branch and the Association of American Railroads' Military Transportation Section paid off handsomely during this period. Allowing for minor delays due to lack of experience on the part of transportation officers with some of the troop units, inadequate loading facilities at certain camps, and the necessity of drawing railway equipment from distant areas to meet the requirements of large organizations moving out of western stations, the rail results were gratifying. The situation in regard to shipping and port operations was less propitious. There were not enough vessels available and many of those on hand had to be taken out of service temporarily for arming. The Atlantic coast ports were embarrassed by the large amount of lend-lease freight which had to be transshipped in addition to military supplies. The Army's port of embarkation at San Francisco, although an expansion of facilities had been started a year earlier, was not prepared to handle smoothly the large movements of troops and materiel which were rushed to the Pacific bases.

The President was deeply concerned lest we fail to achieve the most effective utilization of our inadequate shipping resources, and shortly after Pearl Harbor he announced the creation of a Strategic Shipping Board, to act under his supervision. The board consisted of the Chairman of the Maritime Commission, the Army Chief of Staff, the Chief of Naval Operations, and Mr. Harry Hopkins. Its function was to establish policies for and plan the allocation of merchant shipping to meet military and civilian requirements and to coordinate the shipping activities of the agencies represented in its membership. The President stated that it was his intention to review the "recommendations" of the board with its members.[2] The Chief of the Transportation Branch, G-4, was designated to represent the Chief of Staff on this board.

The effectiveness of the Strategic Shipping Board was limited because of differences of opinion between the Army, the Navy, and the Maritime Commission regarding the utilization of the merchant fleet and because of the absence of authority, short of the President, to resolve such differences. Accordingly, steps were soon taken with a view to the establishment of an agency with broader powers over shipping than those possessed by the Maritime Commission. Such an agency was needed not only to insure the effective use of the American merchant marine for our own requirements, but also to enable the United States to enter into a cooperative shipping arrangement with Great Britain, which already had placed all British-controlled merchant ships under the management of the Ministry of War Transport.[3] The result was the creation of a War Shipping Administration (WSA) by executive order of the President, issued 7 February 1942. Although the authority vested in WSA exceeded that which the Army had contemplated, officers of G-4 at once undertook to establish a working relationship with the new agency.

> **The effectiveness of the Strategic Shipping Board was limited because of differences of opinion between the Army, the Navy, and the Maritime Commission . . .**

The War Shipping Administrator, Rear Adm. Emory S. Land, suggested that the Strategic Shipping Board be used as a channel for informing his office of the "joint objectives" of the Army and the Navy in regard to merchant shipping. The War Department, however, took the attitude that the order establishing WSA contemplated a direct relationship between that agency and the Army, and that in issuing it the President had abrogated his letter setting up the Strategic Shipping Board. Moreover, the functions to which the War Shipping Administrator referred fell naturally within the scope of the Joint Chiefs of Staff organization which was being developed at that time. The Strategic Shipping Board was not dissolved, but it functioned in a very limited way thereafter.

The President also recognized the necessity of getting the maximum service out of domestic transportation facilities, and on 18 December 1941 he established the Office of Defense Transportation, with broad powers to coordinate and regulate the railway, highway, and inland waterway carriers. The Under Secretary of War proposed that representatives of both his office and G-4 be appointed to maintain liaison with ODT. This dual representation was opposed by G-4, and eventually it was arranged that a single Army representative would be designated by the Assistant Chief of Staff, G-4; that the Office of the Under Secretary would coordinate its interest in transportation matters through that representative; and that a member of the Office of the Under Secretary might accompany the War Department representative to meetings convened by the Director of Defense Transportation, in order to be informed regarding proposed policies and procedures that might affect the responsibilities of the Under Secretary. The Chief of the Transportation Branch, G-4, was designated War Department liaison officer with ODT. . . .

The necessity of moving large numbers of troops and great quantities of construction materials and military supplies overseas as rapidly as ships could be found to transport them called for a prompt increase in the Army port establishment. This meant expanding existing ports of embarkation by constructing and leasing new pier and warehouse facilities and enlarging troop staging areas. It also meant increasing the number of Army-operated ports. . . .

Before we had been in the war a full month, disturbing congestion had developed at the principal ports, New York and San Francisco, and it soon appeared also at Philadelphia and New Orleans. During 1941 the Army had established a release system for the control of its own portbound shipments. Immediately after Pearl Harbor, Army regulating stations were established at strategic points on the transcontinental rail lines for the purpose of holding or diverting shipments destined to Pacific coast ports, as port or other conditions might dictate. Additional holding and reconsignment points were authorized to provide intransit storage for supplies moving toward the South Atlantic, Gulf, and Pacific seaboards. Additional commercial traffic agencies were established at principal ports. It was soon evident, however, that the situation could not be met with anything short of an overall traffic control system, covering not only military but also lend-lease and commercial shipments and capable of holding shipments at the source or of taking any other action that might be necessary to protect the ports from having to receive more freight than they could properly handle. The War Department, the War Shipping Administration, and the Office of Defense Transportation discussed this problem at length during the winter of 1941–42, with the result that the general principles of a system which would operate under a Transportation Control Committee and make extensive use of the machinery already established by the Army were agreed on in mid-March. The development of details was undertaken promptly. . . .

Recognizing the need for technical advice and direction of the highest order in connection with the operating phases of the Army's transportation task, the Quartermaster General took steps during the winter months of 1942 to acquire the service of men of broad transportation experience.[4] Leading executives from the commercial field were engaged to head the activities relating to water, rail and motor transportation, traffic control, and intransit storage, and these men became full-time members of the Army transportation staff. . .

Aside from the lack of sufficient equipment and facilities to accomplish the transportation task which confronted the Army, the greatest handicap was the lack of integration in the headquarters organization. The Quartermaster General was responsible under the law and the regulations for accomplishing the movement of troops and materiel. The Transportation Branch, G-4, was responsible for the supervision of these operations, and considered itself responsible in the last analysis for their success. In its effort to make sure that no undertaking failed for lack of preparation and direction, the Transportation Branch sometimes encroached on the Quartermaster General's domain. This was notably true in regard to ports of embarkation, which were responsible to G-4, but which at the same time required technical supervision from the Quartermaster General's staff of experts in connection with the operation of both shore facilities and floating equipment. The Chief of the Transportation Division, OQMG, expressed the following opinion: "The real weakness of our transportation setup is that the entire job, inland, terminal, and oversea is not the direct responsibility of one operating organization."

This weakness was recognized in the General Staff also. Accordingly, when the War Department was reorganized under the wartime powers of the President, effective 9 March 1942, and a Services of Supply was established to relieve the General Staff of the supervision of supply and administrative services, one of the components of SOS was a transportation organization which absorbed the transportation functions previously performed by G-4 and the Quartermaster General, and relieved the Under Secretary of the work which had been assumed by his transportation staff. This was a long first step in the direction of integration in Army transportation administration. It is noteworthy that the step was taken boldly early in the war, and was not the result of slow evolution as in World War I. It is noteworthy that the new transportation organization was placed on the supply or technical service level, rather than in the General Staff as in World War I.

Transportation Service Established

"Transportation and traffic control" were among the responsibilities assigned to the Services of Supply (later renamed Army Service Forces) in the reorganization of the War Department in March 1942. For the performance of these responsibilities General Somervell, commander of SOS, created a Transportation Division, to which he assigned the staff and the functions previously assigned to the Transportation Branch of G-4 (except the Motor Section), the Quartermaster General's Transportation Division, the ports of embarkation including their staging areas, the regulating stations, and the holding and reconsignment points.[5] In his initial directive General Somervell designated as Chief of Transportation Col. Charles P. Gross, who had been Chief of the Transportation Branch, G-4, and Gross was promptly promoted to brigadier general.[6] Concurrently, Brig. Gen. Theodore H. Dillon, who had been Chief of the Transportation Division, OQMG, was designated Deputy Chief of Transportation.

On the day he assumed office the Chief of Transportation announced the initial organization of the Transportation Division. It consisted of two groups of units, designated respectively the functional staff and the operating branches. The functional staff included the Deputy Chief of Transportation, who was to act as the principal coordinating agent of the division, and a number of units which were to deal with the various aspects of administration and the supervision of operating activities. The several operating branches were to deal with the more technical aspects of transportation and with the execution of troop and supply movements.

This organizational set-up, having been hastily and experimentally accomplished, was subject to early revision. In April 1942 the name of the Transportation Division was changed to Transportation Service, and concurrently the staff units and the operating branches were redesignated divisions. . . . A number of new units were set up to deal with rapidly expanding aspects of the work and that clearer definition was given to the functions of the Deputy Chief of Transportation and the Executive Officer. The Organization of the Office of the Chief of Transportation, as it had developed up to 30 June 1942, is shown in Chart 1.

Although the headquarters organization expanded in most directions between its establishment and 31 July 1942 when the Transportation Service became the Transportation Corps, it lost control of the administration of priorities and the assignment of space for the air movement of Army personnel and freight. . . .

Adequate provision had not been made for the procurement and training of military personnel to perform transportation tasks, though a large increase of such personnel would soon be required. . . .With a view to correcting this situation, a number of recommendations were presented to the Chief of Staff. It was proposed that the Transportation Service be constituted a separate corps paralleling in a general way

CHART 1—ORGANIZATION OF THE OFFICE OF THE CHIEF OF
TRANSPORTATION: 30 JUNE 1942

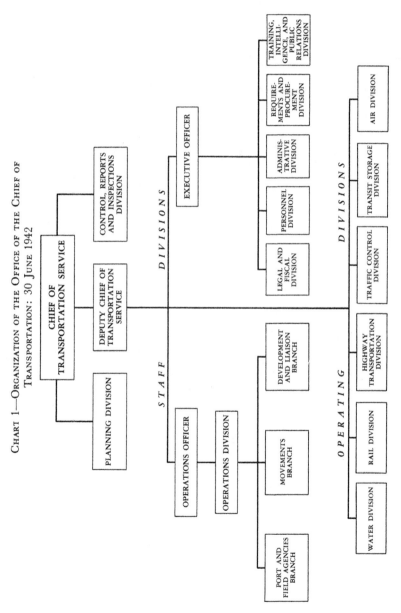

Source: Administrative Log of the Transportation Corps, prepared in the Historical Unit, OCT, July 1945, period 1, exhibit 1–F.

the Corps of Engineers and the Quartermaster Corps, and that the Transportation Corps have a distinctive insignia. It was proposed that the Transportation Corps have its own replacement training center and officer candidate school; that officers of the Transportation Corps be assigned as transportation officers at posts, camps, and stations, and on the staffs of tactical units; and that port battalions, port headquarters and headquarters companies, and railhead companies, then designated Quartermaster units, be redesignated Transportation Corps units. It was proposed also, in view of the urgent necessity for rapid expansion of the staff, that the restrictions on recruitment of military personnel from civil life be relaxed in favor of the Transportation Corps, and that the corps be authorized to acquire officers and enlisted men having transportation experience, although they already were in service with other branches of the Army.

Transportation Corps Established

The main proposal to establish a transportation corps was approved by the Chief of Staff. . . .Creation of the Transportation Corps was announced on 31 July 1942, effective as of that date. The new corps was placed under a Chief of Transportation, who was charged with "the direction, supervision, and coordination of all transportation functions of the War Department, and with the operation of field installations pertaining thereto." All duties previously assigned to the Army Transportation Service [ATS] were transferred to the Transportation Corps, and the former designation was ordered discontinued. All officers and warrant officers who were serving with the Transportation Service on the date of its discontinuance were detailed to duty with the Transportation Corps, and enlisted men who were assigned to the Transportation Service were transferred to the Transportation Corps. . . .The Quartermaster troop units known as port headquarters and headquarters companies, port battalions, railhead companies, and aviation boat companies were transferred to the Transportation Corps and appropriately redesignated.

The Field Establishment

Ports of Embarkation

An Army port of embarkation is a highly complex institution, especially during wartime. It is far more than a shipping terminal. . . .[It] is a military command with jurisdiction over the shipping, storing, staging, and other facilities necessary to the performance of its mission, most of which lie within the geographic limits of a municipality. Ports of embarkation within the continental limits of the United States were under the command of the Chief of Transportation in World War II. Although ports in areas outside the United States ordinarily were under the command of theater commanders, the regulation provided that the War Department might place such ports under the control of the Chief of Transportation, and this was done in the case of certain Canadian and Alaskan ports.

The term "port of embarkation" has been used loosely to designate all port installations under the command of the Chief of Transportation, but more precisely such installations were of three types. Strictly speaking, *ports of embarkation* were installations which performed all or most of the Army's port functions and handled both passenger and freight traffic. *Subports of embarkation* were operated under the supervision of ports of embarkation, and in practice they were of less importance from the standpoint of volume of traffic and variety of activities. *Cargo ports of embarkation* also were operated under the supervision of ports of embarkation, and were set up to handle cargo primarily. By placing subports and cargo ports under the supervision of the larger ports of embarkation, a saving was made in overhead personnel, while at the same time the smaller installations were given the benefit of expert direction. The regulations also provided for *mobile ports of embarkation,* which were troop units organized primarily to operate oversea ports but which were sometimes used at domestic ports prior to assignment to the theaters.

On the Atlantic seaboard, at the outbreak of war in September 1939, the Army was operating one port of embarkation, located at New York [City]. During the ensuing two years of preparatory rearmament, a port of embarkation was established at New Orleans and a subport at Charleston, S.C. . . .

On the Pacific coast the only Army port installation in operation in September 1939 was at San Francisco. During 1940 the quartermaster depot at Seattle was expanded to handle the growing traffic with Alaska, and in 1941 a subport was established there.

After our entry into the war, Seattle became an independent port of embarkation; a subport was established at Los Angeles under the jurisdiction of San Francisco, which later became an independent port of embarkation; a subport was set up at Portland, which retained that status throughout the war and functioned under the supervision first of San Francisco and then Seattle; subports to operate under the supervision of Seattle were set up at Prince Rupert, British Columbia, and at the Alaskan ports of Juneau, Excursion Inlet, and Skagway. The installation at Prince Rupert was established for the dual purpose of lessening the load on the port of Seattle and the railroads serving it and of shortening the sea route to Alaska. The installations at Juneau and Skagway served as discharge points for traffic destined to Army posts in those areas and as transshipment points for freight destined to more distant parts of Alaska. The Excursion Inlet subport was set up solely as a transshipment facility. Juneau, Excursion Inlet, and Skagway served as northern terminals for a barge line which the Transportation Corps operated out of Seattle and Prince Rupert over the inside passage, for the purpose of reducing the demand for deepwater ships in the Alaska service.. . . .

Los Angeles eventually was given independent status as a port of embarkation, and Portland was placed under the supervision of Seattle because of its proximity to the latter port and the heavy traffic which San Francisco was required to handle. Thereafter the commander of the San Francisco Port of Embarkation commanded only the Army port installations in the San Francisco Bay area.

At the close of the war the Transportation Corps was operating eight ports of embarkation, three cargo ports, and two supports, through which traffic was being moved regularly to oversea destinations. The relative importance of the thirteen installations, as measured by the number of passengers and the tons of cargo embarked during the period December 1941–August 1945, inclusive, is shown in the following tabulation:

Port	Number of Passengers	Measurement Tons of Cargo
All Ports	7,293,354	126,787,875
Boston Port of Embarkation	740,705	8,927,363
Searsport Cargo Port	—	470,584
New York Port of Embarkation	3,172,778	37,799,966
Philadelphia Cargo Port	—	5,893,199
Hampton Roads Port of Embarkation	725,880	12,521,868
Baltimore Cargo Port	—	6,504,029
Charleston Port of Embarkation	35,495	3,215,981
New Orleans Port of Embarkation . .	166,696	7,240,687
Los Angeles Port of Embarkation . . .	188,270	8,644,847
San Francisco Port of Embarkation . .	1,657,509	22,735,244
Seattle Port of Embarkation	523,290	10,204,760
Portland Subport	51,827	1,689,075
Prince Rupert Subport	30,904	940,272

For the handling of this large traffic and the performance of related functions the Army utilized both owned and leased facilities. At the beginning of the emergency the government-owned properties included the large Army bases at Boston, Brooklyn, Newark, Philadelphia, Newport News, Charleston, and New Orleans, all of which had been projected during World War I, and the smaller terminal at Fort Mason, San Francisco.[7] While the public and privately owned terminals on the Atlantic and Gulf coasts were considered adequate, the shipping facilities on the Pacific coast were a cause of concern. Accordingly, early in 1941 the Army acquired terminal properties at Oakland and Seattle and immediately began to improve them. Later, when establishing subports at Prince Rupert and

Juneau, the Army found it necessary to construct piers and warehouses, because the existing facilities were exceedingly limited. Excursion Inlet was an entirely new port. . . .

The largest port installation was at New York. In December 1944 the Army was using a total of 28 piers with berths for 100 oceangoing vessels, 4,895,000 square feet of transit shed space, 5,500,000 square feet of warehouse space, and 13,000,000 square feet of open storage and working space. The next largest installation was at San Francisco where the Army used 20 piers with 43 berths for oceangoing vessels, 1,984,000 square feet of transit shed space, 2,867,000 square feet of warehouse space, and 7,640,000 square feet of open space. At that time the staging areas connected with the New York Port of Embarkation had active space capable of accommodating 78,099 persons (station complement and intransit troops), and the staging areas of the San Francisco Port of Embarkation had a total active capacity of 34,338 persons. . . .

The operating divisions were those which were concerned directly with the means of transportation and the movements of troops and materiel. The *Water Division* was responsible for the loading and discharging of transports, the employment of crews and stevedores, the operation, maintenance, repair, and conversion of transports and harbor boats, and the operation and maintenance of piers, docks, wet storage basins, and marine repair shops.

The *Port Transportation Division* was responsible for controlling the movement of passengers and freight into the port of embarkation, effecting movements of passengers and freight between facilities of the port of embarkation, and coordinating all such movements with arrangements made by the other operating divisions for the loading and unloading of transports.

The *Overseas Supply Division* received and edited requisitions from the oversea commands for which the port had primary supply responsibility, forwarded extract requisitions to the proper sources of supply, scheduled the inland and oversea movements of such supplies in accordance with shipping schedules and oversea requirements, and kept the oversea commanders informed as to the status of their requisitions.

The *Troop Movement Division* arranged for the orderly movement of transient military personnel through the port, supervised the processing of such personnel at staging areas, prepared embarkation schedules and billeting plans, and coordinated the work of all other divisions affecting such movements.

The *Initial Troop Equipment Division* controlled the flow through the port of equipment and supplies accompanying troops and also materiel shipped separately but consigned to specific units overseas, and it supervised port activities pertaining to the clothing and individual equipment of transient military personnel.

The chiefs of these divisions constituted the *Operations Council,* which met from time to time with the Deputy Port Commander to plan for port operations and discuss the problems involved. (See Chart 3, Typical Organization for Ports of Embarkation.). . . .

In wartime other activities took on increased importance, and closer coordination with water transportation was necessary.

Although the port commanders clearly were responsible for the operation of ships and shipping terminals at their installations, during the early part of the war they were in some instances embarrassed by the traditional independence of the Army Transport Service superintendents who were immediately responsible for these activities. This independence had developed during peacetime when ATS overshadowed all other phases of Army port operation. In wartime other activities took on increased importance, and closer coordination with water transportation was necessary. General Gross first attacked this problem in July 1943 by calling attention to the fact that ATS operations were completely under the control of the port commanders. Soon thereafter, in order to further emphasize this relationship, he announced the abolition of the term Army Transport Service and the substitution of the title Water Division to designate that phase of port operation. After visiting ports in some of the theaters, he requested that this change be brought to the notice

CHART 3—TYPICAL ORGANIZATION FOR PORTS OF EMBARKATION, APPROVED BY THE
CHIEF OF TRANSPORTATION, ARMY SERVICE FORCES: 1 JULY 1945.

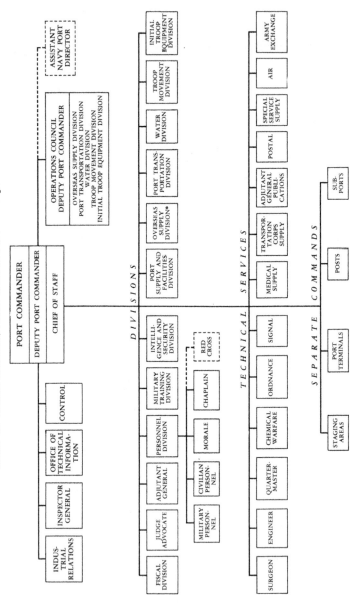

*The Overseas Supply Division exercises supervision over the Technical Services in connection with overseas supply matters.

Source: *Report of the Chief of Transportation, Army Service Forces, World War II,* 30 November 1945, p. 64.

of the oversea commanders in order that it might be made effective at ports under their control. . . .

Because efficient port operation was essential to the orderly flow of men and materiel to the oversea commands, General Gross selected the port commanders with great care. He saw that executive ability was the prime requisite for the head of so large and complex an installation. Expert assistants were provided in all technical branches, and the essential task of the port commander was to coordinate and control their activities and to plan for the development of personnel and facilities adequate for future military needs. The port commanders also had to maintain successfully the vital relationships with the service commands, with local representatives of the Navy, the War Shipping Administration, the British Ministry of War Transport, the Office of Defense Transportation, and the carriers, and with the oversea theaters. Eventually all commanders of ports of embarkation (not subports or cargo ports) were general officers, and the commanders of the two largest ports were major generals.

TABLE 2—PERSONNEL EMPLOYED AT PORT
INSTALLATIONS: 31 DECEMBER 1944

Port	Total	Military	Civilian	Other
All Ports...	171,099	62,646	77,986	30,467
Boston Port of Embarkation...........................	12,558	4,881	4,570	3,107
Searsport Cargo Port..............................	850	186	128	536
New York Port of Embarkation........................	55,791	22,616	25,344	7,831
Philadelphia Cargo Port............................	4,836	937	969	2,930
Hampton Roads Port of Embarkation...................	17,053	7,498	4,620	4,935
Baltimore Cargo Port..............................	3,291	444	969	1,878
Charleston Port of Embarkation.......................	9,068	2,737	5,850	481
New Orleans Port of Embarkation [a]..................	12,077	2,584	5,861	3,632
Los Angeles Port of Embarkation......................	8,513	2,715	3,499	2,299
San Francisco Port of Embarkation....................	27,142	9,154	17,024	964
Seattle Port of Embarkation..........................	14,006	5,266	7,159	1,581
Portland Subport.................................	1,487	683	601	203
Prince Rupert Subport.............................	4,079	2,726	1,263	90
Juneau Subport...................................	348	219	129	....

[a] Figures (for New Orleans) do not include personnel employed by port commander for operation of unit training center at Camp Plauché and TC School.

Source: Based on statement prepared in Office of Dir of Pers OCT, 23 Feb 45, OCT HB PE Gen Pers.

The Chief of Transportation was responsible in the zone of interior for the "direction, supervision, and coordination of all transportation by common carrier. . .for the War Department."[8] It was his task to make sure that movements of troops and supplies were started and deliveries effected according to the requirements of the military program. . . .

While ports of embarkation and the transportation zones embraced the field agencies which were concerned directly with transportation and traffic, the Chief of Transportation's field establishment included a number of other activities. Those activities were concerned with the training of Transportation Corps personnel and the design, procurement, and distribution of Transportation Corps materiel.

Editor's note: The Army historians go on to cover Transportation Zones, Other Field Agencies, Supervision by Headquarters, and Demobilization Planning and Adjustments. Due to space limitations, these field agencies will not be profiled here. Interested readers may find this information in the source publication. Continuing from Wardlow, *The Transportation Corps:*

The Critical Role of Shipping

Throughout the war the demand for ships exceeded the supply, with the result that from first to last ocean transportation was a persistent and sometimes a serious limiting factor to be dealt with in planning strategy and preparing for combat operations. This was true despite the fact that the submarine, which in the early stages seriously threatened our lines of communications, eventually was curbed and that the shipping losses suffered by the Allies were more than offset by the magnificent American shipbuilding achievement.* In a war of such great proportions, the task of moving men and supplies between the zone of interior and the theaters of operation, and within the theaters, created a need for vessels which

---

* See the chapter, "Ships for Victory." —Ed.

never was wholly satisfied. A careful coordination of military plans with anticipated shipping capabilities was therefore necessary. Even then, new developments frequently created unforeseen demands. This latter fact is illustrated by a statement of the British Prime Minister to the House of Commons late in February 1945. He said: "The reason why shipping is so tight at present is because the peak period of the war in Europe has been prolonged for a good many months beyond what was hoped last autumn, and meanwhile the peak period against Japan has been brought forward by American victories in the Pacific.[9]

At the outbreak of World War II the oceangoing merchant shipping of all nations, counting vessels of 1,000 gross tons or more, totaled 13,004 vessels of 59,078,000 gross tons, or 81,359,000 deadweight tons.[10] This represented a tonnage increase of more than 50 percent over the vessels of comparable size under all flags at the beginning of World War I. The volume of shipping registered under the flags of the principal maritime nations on 1 September 1939 is shown below, and it is noteworthy that the United States and the British Empire between them controlled about 45 percent of the total deadweight of 81,359,000 given above for all nations:

Nation	No. of Vessels	Gross Tons	Deadweight Tons
British Empire	3,424	18,028,953	24,174,000
United States.	1,432	8,514,879	12,154,000
Japan	1,180	5,102,346	7,145,400
Norway	1,072	4,499,086	6,931,200
Germany	858	3,923,353	5,186,700
Italy	679	3,227,902	3,978,800
France.	563	2,704,300	3,019,500
Netherlands.	542	2,687,119	3,427,100
Sweden	484	1,311,763	2,033,100
Greece	436	1,697,988	2,791,000
Denmark	379	1,041,756	1,575,800
USSR.	354	1,135,783	1,597,900

Although the United States ranked second among the maritime nations of the world in September 1939, it began feeling the effects of a shipping shortage long before it was forced to abandon the role of nonbelligerent. The war in Europe stimulated a demand for vessels throughout the world, with the result that American operators reached out into new services and foreign purchasers and charterers actively entered the market for American bottoms. The President's policy was to help the democracies with shipping as well as with supplies and equipment. The accelerated importation of strategic raw materials, for immediate use in the manufacture of munitions and for stockpiling against the day when the sources of those materials might be cut off, created additional demands for oceangoing vessels. On top of this came the increased transportation needs of the armed forces, which were engaged in building up oversea bases and otherwise preparing for eventualities.[11] . . .

Early Military Requirements

The outbreak of war in Europe necessitated early adjustments in the Army's ocean transportation program. For several years prior to 1939 the Army Transport Service (ATS) had operated six transports—four troopships and two freighters. Early in 1939 two additional troopships had been acquired as replacements for two which were outmoded and scheduled for decommissioning. . . . At the end of 1939, the Army was operating seven troopships and three freighters. . . .

Action to increase the Army transport fleet substantially came late in 1940. A report was submitted by G-4 to the Chief of Staff in mid-November, showing the anticipated shipping requirements and capabilities, and recommending the acquisition of additional vessels. Within a few weeks an enlarged program was submitted, calling for the purchase and conversion of three passenger liners and one freighter, the charter and conversion of seven passenger ships and four freighters, the purchase of two small transports for use by the Alaska and Puerto Rico commands, and the reconditioning of existing transports to enable them to meet the requirements of the steamboat inspection service. The Secretary of War requested the President to authorize him to incur obligations totaling $17,508,800 for these purposes at once, stating that he did not consider it feasible to wait for Congressional action because of the backlog of traffic and the increasing scarcity of ships. The President indorsed this letter, "approved subject to O.K. by Budget Director." The latter official gave his approval.

By early 1941 the seriousness of the world shipping shortage had been deeply impressed on all concerned and the need for a more closely knit national program was apparent. In February the President took specific steps to deal with the situation. First, in a note addressed jointly to the Secretary of War, the Secretary of the Navy, and the Chairman of the Maritime Commission, he pointed out that the shortage was likely to increase in months to come and directed that the Army and the Navy take over "a minimum number of merchant ships" for their own use and insure that these ships "not be kept idle." A few days later the President instructed the Chairman of the Maritime Commission to coordinate the employment of American shipping carefully in order to obtain maximum utilization, to coordinate the acquisition and creation of additional ships and shipping facilities, and to aid the Office of Production Management by expediting the shipment of materials essential to its program. . . .

Following up the action which he had taken earlier in the year, the President in July 1941 requested that the Army, the Navy, and the Maritime Commission make a joint investigation to determine whether the vessels operated by the military services were being utilized with maximum efficiency. The War Department pledged its full co-operation in such an investigation and submitted a list of its transports showing their current employment." This report apparently satisfied the President and the Maritime Commission.

In reviewing the situation for the Chief of Staff in September 1941, the Assistant Chief of Staff, G-4, expressed no concern over the Army's shipping position. He stated that the "Army's main fleet" (presumably the ATS) consisted of 31 vessels—16 troop transports and 15 freighters; that in addition to the traffic handled by these Army vessels, a large amount of commercial space had been used, and that the Maritime Commission had met all requests for such space promptly. His statement indicated that the Army Transport Service then had a capacity of 18,000 troops and 177,000 measurement tons of cargo; that the Naval Transportation Service had a capacity of 35,000 troops and 273,000 tons of cargo; that in an all-out effort the Maritime Commission could make available ships with capacity for 96,400 troops and 1,852,000 tons of cargo. . . .*

The effort to reinforce the Philippines during the fall of 1941 was beset with numerous problems which brought into sharp focus the Army's unreadiness to provide and move overseas large emergency shipments of troops and materiel. This effort involved the equipment of the Philippine Army and the equipment and reinforcement of the United States garrison. . . .In order to expedite the movement of about 20,000 troops to the Philippines, six commercial passenger liners were chartered to supplement the seven Army transports which could be made available for the purpose, and there was delay in arranging waiver of the inspection regulations so that the maximum number of troops could be carried on the chartered ships.

When word of the Japanese attack was received six troopships and nine cargo ships were at sea bound for Manila. None reached its destination. Acting under radio instructions, four of the troopships which had sailed recently from San Francisco returned to that port; the remainder headed for other friendly ports, and all but one cargo ship arrived safely. . . .

Preparations for Amphibious Operations

The Army's difficulties in obtaining sufficient shipping to service its oversea bases properly were intensified by the necessity of providing vessels for use in joint Army-Navy exercises and in preparing for joint operations against enemy opposition. The arrangements for such exercises and operations brought to light many points of physical unpreparedness, a lack of understanding between the Army and the Navy regarding responsibility for

---

* For more on the Naval Transportation Service, see the chapter, "Naval Transportation Service in World War II." —Ed.

the provision of transports and landing boats, and the absence of adequate doctrine and procedures.

For the joint exercises which were held on the Pacific coast in January 1940, the San Francisco Port of Embarkation was responsible for assembling the Army transports which were to be used, installing special equipment on them, loading ship stores and supplies for the troops, and handling the embarkation of troops at two ports on Puget Sound. In his report covering the operation, the port commander stated that the War Department had sent him no instructions until he had asked for them, and that the Fourth Army, from which the troop units had been drawn, had provided no basic loading plan by which he could be guided. Among the conditions requiring correction, as listed by the War Plans Division after an analysis of all reports submitted after these exercises, were the transport masters' unfamiliarity with convoy procedure, lack of up-to-date drawings of the transports, lack of proper facilities on the transports for radio and visual signaling, unsuitability of the transports for "combat loading," insufficiency and unsuitability of the boats available for landing operations, and lack of adequate training in loading and unloading personnel and equipment.[12]

The reports on these joint exercises and subsequent discussion brought out other points of unpreparedness. There was a difference of opinion as to who should control the combat loading of transports, the port commander or the commander of the landing force. The pertinent regulation gave the commander of troops the final decision, and the Quartermaster General considered this the proper arrangement since the problem was essentially a tactical one.[13] The suggestion was offered that a stevedore battalion should be activated to facilitate operations at ports of embarkation and debarkation when such exercises were being conducted, but G-3 considered this impracticable since it would necessitate the in-activation of other units and the matter was not pursued further. . . .*

---

* For more on the Naval Construction Battalions, see the chapter, "Builders at the Front." —Ed.

The fact that the Navy was responsible for providing transports for joint operations against enemy resistance did not mean that the ATS was unaffected by the preparations for such operations. Early in 1941, in order to avoid the necessity for improvising emergency expeditionary forces after the demand had arisen, certain units were selected for organization into three task forces and planning was begun to place them in a state of readiness for oversea service. The Navy, after estimating with Army assistance the snipping required for moving these forces, found that it would not be able to obtain all of the needed vessels from the Maritime Commission and proposed that it take over three of the Army's troopships. The final result of this proposal was that in late May the Army was directed by the President to arrange for the transfer of six of its troop carriers to the Navy, including the largest of its fleet, the *Manhattan* and the *Washington.* In substitution for these ships, the President directed the chairman of the Maritime Commission to turn over to the Army seven smaller passenger vessels. In the same letter he directed the Maritime Commission to turn over to the Navy five passenger ships and fourteen cargo ships. Among the passenger ships thus placed under Navy control was the *America,* the largest vessel under the American flag.

Three of the ships transferred from the Army to the Navy were converted into combat loaders. In July 1941 the Navy proposed that it also be permitted to convert ten of the Army's remaining transports to combat loaders according to Navy standards, so that they would be ready if and when needed. The Quartermaster General pointed out that this would impair the vessels' effectiveness on the regular routes where they were sorely needed, and G-4 registered a strong protest on the ground that the proposal involved taking the Army's best passenger ships out of service for a period and reducing their capacities by conversion in order to provide against the "improbable contingency" that they might be required for special operations. The Chief of Staff nevertheless approved a recommendation of the Joint Planning Committee that the ten Army transports be converted, with the understanding that the conversion schedule would be so arranged that Navy transports would be available to the Army during the conversion period, if required.

In support of its July proposal to convert ten additional Army transports, the Navy had stated that, from its own fleet and such vessels as could be obtained from the Maritime Commission, it had been able to provide only seventeen combat loaders, whereas twenty-seven were needed in order to handle two divisions and have three vessels in reserve. In October the Navy raised its requirements to thirty-six vessels, and the Joint Board directed the Joint Planning Committee to make a study of the situation. Our entry into the war and the emergency actions which followed that event removed the necessity for this study.

While losing its struggle to prevent a large number of Army troopships from being converted to combat loaders (in which status they were likely to be withdrawn from troop service at any time for combat operations), G-4 was overruled also in its opposition to a Navy proposal that the large Navy troopships *West Point (ex-America)*, *Wakefield (ex-Manhattan)*, and *Mount Vernon* (ex-*Washington*), be converted into airplane carriers, for in September 1941 the Secretary of War approved a Joint Board report which favored such action. The conversion work on these vessels did not get under way promptly, however, and was destined not to be accomplished. After our entry into the war, the Army requested that those vessels continue as regular troopships in view of the extreme need for greater troop capacity and especially the need for fast transports. Plans then were adopted for providing airplane carriers, as well as additional combat loaders, by converting vessels of other types. . . .

In October the Navy raised its requirements to thirty-six vessels . . .

The correspondence and reports concerning joint exercises during 1940–41 and the negotiations in regard to vessels required for planned expeditionary forces indicate how inadequate were the preparations for carrying on amphibious operations up to the time of our entry into the war, and emphasize the magnitude of the task which lay ahead of the armed services in preparing themselves for the successful execution of the many joint actions that would be required both in Europe and in the Pacific.

Central Control of Ship Employment

Because of the persistent scarcity of bottoms to carry out Allied military designs, it was necessary that the available shipping be employed in the most effective manner. As already indicated, that necessity was forecast well before the United States entered the war, and early in 1941 the President took steps to place the greater portion of the American merchant fleet under the control of one agency, the Maritime Commission. There remained, however, the problem of determining how ships in the pool should be used to best serve the national interest. During 1941 and the early months of 1942 this problem remained unsolved. The Maritime Commission, and the War Shipping Administration after its establishment early in February 1942, were confronted with the difficult task of allocating vessels to meet the needs of the Army and the Navy and fulfilling lend-lease commitments, while at the same time maintaining what were considered essential commercial services. That was a task which under the circumstances could not possibly be performed to the satisfaction of all parties. The deficit in ships had to be distributed; there was no alternative.

It was the hope of the President that the Strategic Shipping Board, which he established soon after we entered the war, would be an effective instrument for planning ship allocations. It failed to accomplish that purpose, however, because of the differing views held by the participating agencies— the Army, the Navy, and the Maritime Commission. The Army submitted its requirements to the Maritime Commission and later to the War Shipping Administration but received no better assurance than that every possible effort would be made to meet them. The President gave specific directions from time to time regarding the utilization of ships, and at that period there seemed to be no other means of resolving differences between the several claimant agencies than by appeal to the Chief Executive.

Aside from ships to carry out immediate tasks, the Army's great need was for a long-range plan for the distribution of shipping to enable it to determine in advance, and with reasonable assurance of fulfillment, the number of troops and the tons of cargo it would be able to move overseas during the ensuing year. As a step in that direction, a plan for the distribution of cargo shipping during the remainder of 1942 was worked out early in March, in conferences between representatives of the Army, the Navy, the Lend-Lease Administration, and the War Shipping Administration. This preliminary step in long-range planning was followed by the development of more permanent procedures. . . .

The Combined Shipping Adjustment Board, a high-level civilian agency responsible directly to the President and the Prime Minister, was established in January with branches in Washington and London.[14] Its function was to propose such exchanges of British and American shipping as would produce the best over-all results, taking into account civilian and lend-lease requirements as well as military needs. The Combined Chiefs of Staff, which began functioning in February, dealt primarily with the military aspects of shipping, but in its estimation of military requirements and its effort to propose sources from which those requirements could be met, CCS necessarily took into consideration the possibility of reducing civilian and lend-lease shipping services. The effective utilization of shipping was an inevitable subject for consideration at the recurrent meetings of the President, the Prime Minister, and the heads of other Allied governments for the determination of strategy, on which occasions both the civilian and the military aspects were reviewed.

The shipping which served the Allies, excluding those vessels which were more or less permanently assigned to the armed services, was operated in two large pools, one under control of the War Shipping Administration and the other under the control of the British Ministry of War Transport. The pools included not only the merchant fleets of the Allied countries but as much neutral tonnage as could be chartered and such enemy vessels as had been interned or captured. Exchanges of shipping between the British and American pools usually did not involve changing flags or operating controls but merely the assignment of the use of a vessel or vessels for a voyage or a period. The United States, however, transferred many vessels to the flags and the controls of other nations, chiefly the United Kingdom and the Soviet Union.[15]

On 1 January 1942, a few weeks after the entry of the United States into the war, the oceangoing merchant shipping available to the Allies totaled 44,390,000 deadweight tons. By 30 June 1945 the total had increased to 88,035,000 deadweight tons, of which 52,648,000 were available to the United States and 35,387,000 to other United Nations, principally the British Commonwealth. Of the total for 30 June 1945, 66,228,000 deadweight tons were accounted for by dry cargo and passenger vessels and 21,807,000 deadweight tons by tankers.

The Joint Chiefs of Staff, the American component of the Combined Chiefs of Staff, had an important role in determining the employment of shipping.

The Joint Chiefs of Staff, the American component of the Combined Chiefs of Staff, had an important role in determining the employment of shipping. In regard to strategic and logistic matters, of which shipping was at all times an essential element, JCS performed the dual function of planning and controlling the American military operations and representing the American interests in the combined deliberations. JCS determined the employment of the shipping which was made available to the American armed forces and estimated the volume and types of shipping which future operations would require.

Despite the inevitable conflict of interests between the Army and the Navy, JCS dealt with the shipping aspects of its work in an effective manner. The fact that the President was represented on JCS by Admiral William D. Leahy, Chief of Staff to the Commander in Chief of the Army and Navy, facilitated decisions and meant that it was not often necessary to call on the Chief Executive himself to settle differences relative to the utilization of shipping. . . .

The Joint Military Transportation Committee dealt with long-range programs for the utilization of shipping, usually making its estimate for six-month periods but keeping those estimates constantly under review and revision. . . .

Supplementing their role in connection with the distribution of shipping, the Joint Chiefs of Staff took an active hand in improving the utilization of vessels in the theaters. Long delays in discharging cargoes in some of the oversea areas and the freedom with which certain theater commanders retained transoceanic ships for use in intratheater operations appreciably reduced the number of bottoms available for outward loading from the United States and thus accentuated the effect of the shipping shortage on all military programs.

Late in 1944, when the accumulation of shipping in oversea ports became so serious as to call for Presidential intervention, JCS took drastic action to reduce the congestion which already existed and established rules which were intended to prevent the recurrence of such a situation. . . .

The Army and the Navy negotiated numerous agreements outside the Joint Chiefs of Staff, which affected the employment of the ships under their control. Since the two services worked side by side in the theaters, coordination was necessary to avoid needless duplication and resultant waste in their supply and shipping operations. This was particularly true in the Pacific where the Navy's logistic responsibilities were larger then elsewhere. An effort for coordination, which General Gross fully endorsed and supported, brought success in some directions and frustration in others.

The first significant agreement entitled "Joint Logistics Plan for the Support of United States Bases in the South Pacific" was adopted in July 1942.[16] Its purpose was to reduce the waste which had resulted from the maintenance of wholly independent supply systems in the South Pacific Area, where joint bases were set up during the early months of the war. Supplies which were in common use were broken down into categories, and responsibility for each category at each base was assigned either to the Army or the Navy. The commander of the South Pacific Area (a naval officer) was given control of all United States shipping assigned to the area and over-all responsibility for the distribution of supplies within the area. A Joint Purchasing Board was established at Wellington to procure such supplies as were available in New Zealand and Australia, and thus to reduce the weight of the requisitions sent to the zone of interior and the amount of shipping utilized in filling them. That agreement served as a prototype for arrangements affecting other areas. . . .

A further and broader agreement was signed, the purpose of which was to "insure coordinated logistical effort and procedure in each command area. . .involving joint Army-Navy operations in which unity of command and responsibility has been established to the end that the combined personnel, equipment, supplies, facilities, shipping and other services of the Army and Navy are most effectively utilized and adequately provided."[17]. . .

The Chief of Transportation informed the commanders of the several ports of embarkation that while the principles of the Basic Logistical Plan were especially applicable to the Pacific they were to be applied to some extent to other ports, and directed the Army port commanders to initiate conferences with the corresponding naval commanders in order to implement the agreement. . . .

In May 1943 the Basic Logistical Plan was supplemented with an agreement which directed that a single joint priority list be prepared for personnel moving to all areas of the Pacific, and that standing operating procedures be established for the implementation of the priority lists contemplated by both the original and the supplementary agreements.[18] Soon thereafter a general plan for the administration of joint priorities for personnel moving from west coast ports to the Central, South, and Southwest Pacific Areas was adopted. The Chief of Transportation then proposed more detailed joint procedures for cargo as well as personnel movements, including strong central control of shipping, but after consideration of the proposal the Navy stated that it considered such further action unnecessary.[19]. . .

The Joint Army-Navy-WSA Ship Operations Committee, which was set up informally at San Francisco early in 1943, undertook to coordinate the shipping activities of the three agencies in order to obtain the best possible utilization of ships sailing from the Pacific coast in accordance with determinations of the Joint Chiefs of Staff and to control the use of port facilities. . . .

Despite the limitation placed on their authority relating to ship operations, the west coast joint committees performed a useful function in connection with the movement of troops and supplies to the Pacific. Their role in regard to the administration of priorities and the utilization of port facilities was an important one. The San Francisco committee, which had the central role, included the commandant of the Twelfth Naval District (later the Pacific Coast Coordinator of Naval Logistics), who acted as chairman, the commander of the Army port of embarkation, and the west coast representative of the War Shipping Administration. . . .

During the spring of 1945, in anticipation of the surrender of the German forces and the intensification of the war against Japan, the Navy proposed that a joint conference be held to discuss supply and shipping problems in the Pacific.[20] The designation of General Douglas MacArthur as commander of all Army forces in the Pacific (CINCAFPAC) and Admiral Chester W. Nimitz as commander of all Navy forces in the Pacific (CINCPAC)

During the spring of 1945, in anticipation of the surrender of the German forces and the intensification of the war against Japan . . .

presented a new command set-up which necessitated new arrangements in regard to ocean transportation. In addition to representatives of the Navy Department, the Army Service Forces, and the Army Air Forces, representatives of the land, sea, and air commands in the Pacific were invited to the conference. The discussions were held in Washington, 1–5 May 1945, under the chairmanship of Admiral Royal E. Ingersoll, Commander, Western Sea Frontier. According to a report filed with the Assistant Chief of Staff, G–4, agreement was reached on all matters except the control of shipping.

The Navy plan presented at the conference was that all shipping matters should be dealt with by a joint organization to be established by General MacArthur and Admiral Nimitz. The Army, recalling its unsatisfactory experience in the Pacific Ocean Areas where a joint logistics staff had existed, contended that such an arrangement would be unduly cumbersome and slow. The Chief of Transportation and other Army representatives at the conference proposed that the Army and the Navy commands in the Pacific make their shipping arrangements separately—which it was believed would be more satisfactory and entirely practical in most instances—and that joint control be established only when the exigencies of joint operations or other circumstances rendered such control necessary. The discussion brought out the fact that the Seventh Fleet, serving in the Southwest Pacific under an Army commander, had complete independence in logistical matters until early 1945, and that afterward the Army commander had reviewed the Seventh Fleet requests for supplies in the light of the over-all capacity of the ports but had not undertaken to control its shipping operations. By way of contrast, it was stated that shipping for the supply of Army forces in POA west of Hawaii had been completely under Navy control. The conference ended without either service modifying its position on the point at issue.

Early in June the Navy placed the question of control of shipping in the Pacific formally before the Joint Chiefs of Staff.[21] It recommended that CINCAFPAC and CINCPAC be directed to set up a joint agency for the coordination and control of all merchant-type shipping except assault craft. A meeting between CINCAFPAC and CINCPAC had been held on Guam, 1–4 June 1945; during which the shipping problem had been discussed and estimates of shipping requirements to February 1946 had been prepared. The Army Chief of Staff requested the opinion of CINCAFPAC with regard to the joint agency recommended by the Navy, and was informed by General MacArthur that he was opposed to the arrangement since it would deprive the Army of control of the shipping serving its forces. While he recognized the need for Army-Navy co-operation, General Mac-Arthur favored separate shipping responsibilities; he recommended that his intra-theater shipping requirements be submitted directly to the War Department and that vessels to meet those requirements be allocated to him and be operated under his control. The Navy proposal had not been acted on by the Joint Chiefs of Staff when hostilities ended.

TABLE 4—EMPLOYMENT OF OCEAN-GOING PASSENGER AND DRY-CARGO SHIPPING
UNDER U.S. CONTROL ON SELECTED DATES: 1943–1945 [a]

(Thousand Deadweight Tons)

Employment	1 Jan 43	1 Jan 44	1 Jan 45	1 Jul 45
Total..	12,318	25,820	36,022	39,967
U.S. Army..	4,521	10,765	17,330	13,609
U.S. Army Owned & Chartered...........................	835	1,552	1,154	1,989
WSA Allocations to U.S. Army..........................	3,686	9,213	16,176	11,620
U.S. Navy..	2,182	4,028	8,016	11,649
U.S. Navy Owned & Chartered...........................	1,029	2,133	4,230	4,386
WSA Allocations to U.S. Navy..........................	1,153	1,895	3,786	7,263
Other U.S. Traffic....................................	4,434	8,265	5,724	8,982
Allocated to U.S. Lend-Lease..........................	2,776	5,674	3,462	4,953
Allocated to Civilian Needs..........................	1,658	2,591	2,262	4,029
Foreign Control.......................................	165	1,591	3,490	3,699
Lend-Leased to British................................	0	1,059	2,919	2,872
Lend-Leased to USSR...................................	165	532	571	827
Under Repair or Laid-up...............................	1,016	1,171	1,462	2,028

[a] Includes merchant-type vessels of 1000 gross tons or more. Naval auxiliaries are excluded, but merchant-type vessels converted to assault vessels (AKA's and APA's) are included. WSA allocations are shown according to allocations for outbound voyages.

Source: WSA Shipping Summary, September 1945, p. 38.

The intricacy of the problems involved in the exercise of centralized control over the employment of U.S. shipping, as well as the Army's interest in the proper solution of these problems, are best understood when the volume and distribution of such shipping are visualized. Table 4 shows the disposition, according to outbound allocations, of the oceangoing passenger and dry cargo vessels under U.S. control at the beginning of 1943, 1944, and 1945, and in mid-1945.

As of 1 January 1945, when the campaign against Germany was at its height, out of a total of 36,022,000 deadweight tons, 17,330,000 tons (48.1 percent) were at the disposal of the Army, and 8,016,000 tons (22.3 percent) were at the disposal of the Navy. Six months later, with Germany defeated and the concentration of strength in the Pacific well begun, the Army's percentage had shrunk and the Navy's had increased.

The latter fact, however, must be interpreted in light of the arrangement under which vessels for both Army and Navy use in the Pacific Ocean Areas were allocated to the Navy. In other words, the shift of allocations from the Army to the Navy does not imply a corresponding change in the actual utilization of shipping.

Tankers are not included in Table 4. Bulk shipments of petroleum products to meet the Army's oversea requirements were transported by the Navy. On 1 July 1945, out of a total of 14,582,000 deadweight tons of oceangoing tank vessels in the service of the United States, 9,143,000 deadweight tons, or 62.7 percent, were owned or chartered by the Navy or were allocated to the Navy by the War Shipping Administration.

Editor's note: The Army historians go on to cover The Submarine Threat in the Battle of the North Atlantic, The Shipbuilding Achievement, Central Control of Ship Employment, Coordination of Port Utilization, and Coordination of Ship Repair and Conversion. However, due to space limitations, these subjects are not included here. Continuing from Wardlow, *The Transportation Corps:*

Relations with Other Ship-Operating Agencies

A large percentage of the vessels utilized by the Army were operated by or under the control of other agencies. On 31 July 1945, for example, out of a total of 1,706 oceangoing vessels in the service of the Army, only 186 were operated by the Army. The remainder were operated by agents of the War Shipping Administration or by the U.S. Navy or were included in the pool of foreign vessels controlled by the British Ministry of War Transport. The maintenance of smooth working relations with these agencies was therefore an important aspect of the Army's transportation task.

The total of 1,706 vessels in Army service at the end of July 1945 embraced all vessels of 1,000 gross tons or over which were carrying Army personnel to at least 50 percent of their passenger capacity, or were carrying at least 5,000 measurement tons of Army cargo.[22] This total included 261 vessels which were classified as troopships because they had permanent accommodations for 500 or more troops, and 1,445 which were classified as cargo ships although some of them carried limited numbers of troops. This fleet provided 620,355 permanent troop spaces and had a total cargo capacity of 16,192,700 measurement tons. Seventeen of the troopships and 78 of the cargo ships were under foreign registry.[23]

Relations with the War Shipping Administration

The Army was dependent on the War Shipping Administration for vessels to carry the bulk of its oversea traffic, and during the winter of 1945 it was using almost 50 percent of the dry cargo and passenger shipping controlled by that agency. While a limited number of vessels was made available to the Army by WSA under various forms of charter or on permanent allocation, most of them were allocated for the voyage only and therefore were subject to reallocation when they returned to the United States. The WSA pool of cargo vessels had to meet demands from other sources, and in view of the almost continuous over-all shortage of shipping the question of priorities frequently was an acute one. Naturally there were many problems of policy and procedure to be worked out between the Chief of Transportation and WSA, in order that the Army might receive the numbers and types of vessels which it required at the places where they were needed.

The Army had concurred in the establishment of an agency to control the employment of U.S. shipping, but it had not visualized such broad authority in the hands of a civilian official as was given to the War Shipping Administrator.* Military leaders recognized that an agency of this type was necessary to insure that American vessels were operated in the national interest and to facilitate collaboration with the British Ministry of War Transport in the effective utilization of all vessels under Allied control.

---

* Rear Admiral Emory S. Land, USN (Ret), served as head of both the Maritime Commission and War Shipping Administration during World War II, and spearheaded the construction of the most massive fleet in history, the amazing total of more than 5,600 ships totaling over 56,000,000 tons. —Ed.

But the Army officers most directly concerned believed that since military victory was the objective and shipping was essential to that victory, the military authorities should have the deciding voice in determining what portion of the merchant marine was to be assigned to military uses. Other agencies and individuals had different views, however, and the end product varied considerably from the Army's conception.

An understanding of the circumstances under which the War Shipping Administration was created is aided by taking a quick look at the British Ministry of War Transport (BMWT). During the early part of the war in Europe the control of British transportation was divided between two agencies; the Ministry of Transport, which had existed in peacetime, responsible for inland transportation; and the Ministry of Shipping, established in September 1939, responsible for ocean transportation. In May 1941 these hitherto independent agencies were combined to form the Ministry of War Transport in an effort to achieve closer coordination between the inland carriers, the ports, and the steamship lines, and more efficient utilization of all. The Minister of War Transport, Lord Leathers, was responsible directly to the Prime Minister, and the means under his control had to be employed in the manner that would best meet both civilian and military requirements.

Immediately after our entry into the war the President established the Office of Defense Transportation, with authority over the rail, motor, and inland waterway carriers, and in so doing departed from the British example of a single transportation agency. In creating the War Shipping Administration some weeks later the Chief Executive followed the British example of vesting a broad control over shipping in a civilian agency. In practice, however, WSA did not exercise as complete control over port operations and the loading of ships as did the BMWT, a matter which will be presented more fully hereafter.

When it became apparent that the Strategic Shipping Board, which President Roosevelt had established immediately after our entry into the war, would not be able to solve the problem of shipping allocations by agreement among the three agencies represented in its membership (the

Maritime Commission, the Navy, and the Army) a number of alternatives were put forward.

A plan which originated in the Navy proposed the establishment of a shipping coordinator with cabinet rank. That plan was not acceptable to the Army, which objected to placing the Army-owned transports and the Army ports of embarkation under the absolute control of such an official.[24] The Army proposed instead that a "central shipping administration" be established, with the chairman of the Maritime Commission as administrator, to function under the general supervision of a board consisting of the administrator and representatives of the Army, the Navy, and the Office of Production Management; that all transoceanic vessels, except those of the armed services, be pooled "under the exclusive direction" of the new agency; and that the central shipping administration "be guided by the decisions of the Army-Navy Joint Board with respect to the movement of troops and supplies for the Army and the Navy and in the allocation of the necessary shipping to initiate and maintain such military and naval operations as may be adopted."

A plan which originated in the Navy proposed the establishment of a shipping co-ordinator with cabinet rank.

An informal expression of opinion by a representative of the Maritime Commission indicated that their office was favorably disposed toward the latter arrangement and also that it was willing to undertake the manning and operation of the vessels necessary to carry the troops and supplies of the Army, if called on to do so.[25] The Army and the Navy then agreed on a plan conforming to the Army's contention that ship allocations should be in accordance with joint decisions of the armed services, and they submitted a draft of an executive order embodying that idea.[26] Rear Adm. Emory S. Land, who was chairman of the Maritime Commission and slated to head the new agency also, objected to this subordination of his authority, and Mr. Harry Hopkins likewise opposed it on the ground that lend-lease might not receive sufficient consideration. The President supported these views and accordingly the final draft of the executive order, which was prepared in the Bureau of the Budget, gave the War Shipping Administrator sole direction of the new agency and made him directly responsible to the President.

The War Shipping Administrator's duties included control of the "operation, purchase, charter, requisition, and use" of all oceangoing vessels under the flag or control of the United States, except combatant vessels of the Army, the Navy, and the Coast Guard, fleet auxiliaries of the Navy, transports owned by the Army and the Navy, and coastwise vessels controlled by the Office of Defense Transportation. He was charged with the allocation of vessels under his control for use by the Army, the Navy, other federal departments and agencies, and the governments of the United Nations. He was directed to "comply with strategic military requirements" in allocating vessels, to collaborate with existing military, naval, and civil departments and agencies of the government in order to secure the most effective utilization of shipping in the prosecution of the war, and to be guided by schedules transmitted to him by the chairman of the War Production Board prescribing the priorities of movement of cargoes essential to the war production effort and the civilian economy.

> **He was charged with the allocation of vessels under his control for use by the Army, the Navy, other federal departments and agencies, and the governments of the United Nations.**

Broadly speaking, the plan contemplated that WSA would concern itself with the utilization of vessels in service, while the Maritime Commission would devote its main effort to the construction of new tonnage.

The War Shipping Administrator considered it essential that the operating relationships of his office with the transportation offices of the Army and the Navy, under the general terms of the executive order, should be defined in some detail. To that end, he first worked out an understanding with the Navy and then approached the Army on the subject. After about a month of negotiation, agreement was reached and a memorandum on interdepartmental relationship was signed on 13 June 1942 by General Somervell on behalf of the Army and by Mr. Lewis W. Douglas, the Deputy Administrator, on behalf of WSA.[27]

The memorandum provided that the Army would operate its owned vessels, keeping the War Shipping Administration informed regarding their employment and making them available to WSA on the homeward voyage when military requirements permitted. WSA troopships assigned to the Army were to be handled through existing operating organizations (WSA agents) in accordance with existing charters, and their homeward employment was to be determined by WSA subject to the requirements of the Army's troop movement schedule. WSA freighters were to be assigned on a voyage basis; they were to be loaded outbound by the Army and revert to WSA upon completion of discharge at oversea ports.

The memorandum provided that additional piers and terminals might be placed under the control of the Army when necessary to carry out strategic movements; that Army terminals would be made available to WSA, and WSA terminals to the Army, when not needed by the controlling agency; that when commercial terminal facilities were taken over by the Army it would, insofar as practicable, continue to use the same contracting stevedores and terminal operating personnel; and that the Army and WSA would confer regarding the purpose and the terms of occupancy in connection with the acquisition of piers and terminals by the Army.

The memorandum further provided that except in emergencies WSA would be the sole contracting agent of the Army for the purchase, charter, or requisition of oceangoing vessels; that Army and WSA representatives in Washington and at the ports would maintain close liaison in an effort to interchange cargo and obtain "full and down" loadings; and that the conversion and alteration of ships to fit them for Army use would be accomplished by WSA, or the Army, or by the two agencies jointly, as might be arranged. In the last paragraph of the agreement, each party foreswore any "intention or ambition" to absorb the functions of the other "by use of its requisition powers or otherwise.". . .

On 31 December 1942 Mr. Douglas presented to Admiral William D. Leahy, on behalf of the War Shipping Administration, a plan under which allocated ships would be loaded in accordance with a "mutually satisfactory program" and military technicians would be on hand to give advice whenever military cargo was being loaded by WSA operators.[28] Although Admiral Leahy thought the proposal went far toward resolving the difficulty, General Gross commented that it was based on a complete acceptance of the WSA interpretation of the executive order of 7 February 1942 and expressed the view that "there cannot be divided responsibility for the success of the military effort."

A few days later, in a personal letter to Mr. Douglas, General Marshall referred to a "serious" and, he thought, "profitable" conversation at luncheon; stated that the Army's purpose in supporting the creation of WSA was to make available the maximum number of ships in a pool for allocation to the various uses; asserted that the Army had understood at that time that there was no intent to change the then effective practice of loading ships; remarked that he had made special inquiry regarding the shipping personnel utilized by the armed services and had found an "impressive list" of men drawn from civil life, who could scarcely have lost their judgment and skill through donning a uniform; and commented that the method of procedure adopted by WSA in this affair "was bound to cause grave difficulties, animosities and delays." On the same day Secretary Stimson advised Admiral Land that the matter was under discussion with the President. . . .

In the spring of 1943 Army shipping operations, along with those of the Navy, were attacked from another quarter and on a broader basis. The CIO maritime unions, charging inefficiency in the handling of American cargoes, proposed that all operations, including warehousing, terminal management, and stevedoring, be centralized under the War Shipping Administration and that the formulation and administration of policies governing those activities be vested in tripartite bodies representing labor, management, and government.

In rejecting the proposal as "wholly unwise," WSA cited, among various considerations, the long-established transportation services and large marine organizations of the Army and the Navy, the abandonment of which in the midst of war would create greater problems than already existed.[29] The Senate Special Committee Investigating the National Defense Program (Truman Committee), while recognizing that there were inefficiencies in the wartime use of shipping, substantially supported the WSA position. . . .

The pooling of cargo in order to obtain more complete utilization of ship capacity, which was one of the principal arguments offered in favor of bringing the loading of both military and lend-lease cargoes under WSA control, had been given attention by the Army during 1942, but with only partial results. . . .

In connection with sailings from the Pacific coast the War Shipping Administrator proposed a co-operative arrangement to bring about quicker turnarounds as well as fuller ships, an arrangement which included utilization of the Joint Army-Navy-WSA Ship Operations Committee then being organized at San Francisco.[30] General Gross agreed to the proposal with certain reservations. He wanted it clearly understood that ship allocations to the Army would be made by WSA as in the past and not by the Pacific coast joint committee, which he considered only a local organization to insure better use of the shipping which had been allocated for loading on the west coast. He also stated that Army cargo could not be scattered widely over commercial piers and would not be delivered to such piers until the vessels on which it was to move actually had been assigned. Understanding on these points was followed by better understanding on the general question.

General Gross agreed to the proposal with certain reservations.

On 19 February 1943 the Army informed the War Shipping Administration that "as . . . in the past" it would call on WSA for space to lift less-than-shipload lots, in order to take advantage of deck loading on WSA vessels and to utilize earlier WSA sailings for high priority items; also that the Army would "continue" to offer space in ships which it operated, or which were allocated to it, for bottom and filler cargo to be supplied from lend-lease shipments. Although the Army communication indicated, and quite accurately, that no new principle was being invoked, the actual pooling of cargo was increased considerably during the months which followed. This was particularly true of cargo interchanges between the Army, the War Shipping Administration, and the British Ministry of War Transport for sailings to the United Kingdom. . . .

One of the first problems which had to be worked out after the establishment of the War Shipping Administration was the development of a satisfactory method for the allocation of shipping to the several uses. . . . This task soon was undertaken by the Joint Military Transportation Committee, in collaboration with WSA. Meantime WSA developed its machinery for establishing long-range requirements, making long-range allocations of blocks of tonnage to meet those requirements, and eventually nominating specific vessels for specific voyages. In May 1942 Mr. Douglas, as Deputy War Shipping Administrator, took charge of these activities.[31]

After the WSA had received an indication through the Joint Chiefs of Staff regarding the amount of shipping needed for Army movements during ensuing months and had determined the number of ships it could allocate, it remained for the Chief of Transportation to inform WSA as to the vessels required for loading at the respective ports in the immediate future and to obtain from WSA the nomination of specific vessels to meet these requirements. . . .

Despite the careful attention given to the matter, monthly deficits continued to occur. The obvious explanation was that cargo ships did not become available for allocation as anticipated in the long-range planning. The less apparent explanation was that while the planners took into reasonably accurate account the progressive reduction in ship losses and the increase in construction, they did not fully foresee the extent to which vessels would be held in the theaters for use in local operations and on account of discharging delays.[32] . . .

Troopship Allocations

The allocation of troopships was on a different basis. In the early months of the war the Army applied to the Maritime Commission and later to the War Shipping Administration for the allocation of troop-carrying vessels to meet specific requirements in much the same manner as it applied for cargo vessels. The Army then controlled the vessels only on the outward voyages, and the ships reverted to WSA after completing discharge at oversea ports. Later, because of the urgent need for getting the vessels back to their home ports without the delays incident to loading return cargo, the Army requested that troopships be allocated for the round voyage. This arrangement, which apparently became effective late in 1943, ostensibly applied only to the faster troopships which had small cargo capacity. In effect, however, all WSA troopships, except the temporarily converted freighters, were allocated for round voyages, since their employment was governed solely by troop movement requirements.

When nonmilitary passengers and cargo were available for homeward voyages they were lifted by arrangements between WSA representatives and Army transportation officers at the oversea ports, but with the understanding that the voyages would not be delayed. Since there was a substantial amount of such traffic, detailed regulations were published covering the movement of nonmilitary passengers on WSA vessels, both outbound and inbound. . . .

The principal financial arrangements were as follows: When title to a vessel was transferred from WSA to the Army, no charge was made for the vessel or for any conversion effected by WSA prior to transfer in order to make the vessel suit the Army's need, but the Army bore the cost of subsequent alterations and the cost of operation, maintenance, and repair.

When vessels were assigned permanently by WSA under bareboat charter or similar arrangement the Army paid no charter hire, and the arrangements regarding conversion, operation, maintenance, and repair were the same as in the case of vessels transferred outright. . . .

While firm in his insistence on centralized control of ship allocations, General Gross favored direct dealings and full cooperation between the local representatives of the War Shipping Administration and the Transportation Corps in matters affecting the loading, discharging, operation, and repair of vessels. In addition to participating in numerous joint committees at the ports, the personnel of the two agencies worked in close coordination in the day-to-day handling of the affairs of the ships with which both were concerned.

Relations with the Navy

The relations of the Army and the Navy in connection with ship operations would have been comparatively simple had the prewar plan been carried into effect. Joint Army and Navy Basic War Plan, rainbow 5, contemplated that in case of war the Army would continue to operate ports of embarkation but that the Navy would "provide sea transportation for the initial movement and the continued support of the Army and Navy forces oversea," and in so doing would man and operate the Army transports. That arrangement was set aside, however, and the maintenance of separate ocean transport services gave rise to numerous problems in connection with the joint use of troop and cargo ships and the convoying and routing of merchant vessels.

The question of placing the Army transports under Navy manning and operation was actively considered during the year preceding our entry into war. In November 1940 G-4 suggested that this be done without waiting for an actual state of war, but the War Plans Division and the Quartermaster General did not concur.[33]

In April 1941, actuated by the U.S.-British staff conversations which were concluded during the preceding month, the Navy proposed that the subject be discussed by representatives of the two departments. The Army assented, with the understanding that if such an arrangement should be made, the Army would retain control over the missions and the movements of the vessels.[34] Agreement was reached substantially on that basis, and since the Navy believed that it could accomplish the manning in from 30 to 45 days, a schedule was prepared which would have placed all Army troopships and freighters under Navy operation by the end of July. The Navy did not accomplish the task as had been anticipated, however, and by November had placed crews on only seven Army transports; G-4 then expressed doubt as to the Navy's ability to give satisfactory service to the Army, because of the subordination of this service to other Navy interests.

On the day after the Japanese attack on Pearl Harbor, representatives of the armed services and the Maritime Commission discussed the subject and decided that the Army and the Navy should continue their separate transport services, subject to the Navy's preponderant interest in ships in the Pacific. The Navy, confronted with a heavy demand for crews for combatant vessels, soon proposed removing its personnel from six of the seven Army transports and retaining the operation of only one, which was being converted to a combat loader. It also proposed turning over to the Army the *LaFayette (ex-Normandie)* which was then undergoing conversion to a troop transport. To this the Army agreed, anticipating no difficulty in providing civilian crews for these ships, in addition to approximately 140 other vessels then in its service.[35]

The entire question was reopened almost immediately, however, when the Army undertook to bring the Joint War plans into harmony with these informal arrangements. The Navy then advised that, after further consideration, and with the consent of the Army Chief of Staff, it would continue to man the six Army transports; also that it would man the *LaFayette* when that vessel was ready for service.[36] Late in February 1942 the Chief of Naval Operations requested the concurrence of the Army Chief of Staff in a memorandum to be submitted to the Joint Board, which proposed not only placing all Army transports under Navy operation but also making the Navy responsible for arranging with the War Shipping Administration for the allocation of such additional ships as were required for military purposes. General Marshall did not concur; rather, he contended that the establishment of WSA by executive order of 7 February 1942 had abrogated that feature of the Army-Navy joint action agreement and had provided for Army control of its own transports and for allocation of WSA vessels directly to the Army.[37]

Late in 1942, when the general question of more effective coordination between Army and Navy oversea supply operations was being considered, the subject of unified operation of the transport fleets again came to the fore, together with consolidation of other transportation functions. . . .

Underlying the differences of opinion, which produced a stalemate in the effort to achieve a unified transportation system, were fundamental differences in the logistical systems of the Army and the Navy. The entire system of naval logistics at that time was decentralized: the Naval Transportation Service dealt only with ocean transportation; the movement of supplies to the ports and within the country was a function of the Bureau of Supplies and Accounts.* Because of the dispersion of procurement and shipping responsibilities, Navy headquarters had no adequate facilities for making accurate estimates of its shipping requirements.[38] The Army's transportation system was more closely integrated: the Chief of Transportation had supervision of both inland and transoceanic transportation, had a close liaison with the technical or supply services of the Army and the headquarters organization of the Services of Supply (later Army Service Forces), and actually controlled the movement of both troops and supplies through the Traffic Control Division in his office and the Oversea Supply Divisions at the ports of embarkation. The Army based its effort to centralize control of transportation and supply movements for the armed services on its own experience. The Navy shrank from the adoption of such a plan, because that would have required extensive adjustments in its logistical organization and methods.[39] Beyond the organizational and procedural differences, however, there was a natural and evident reluctance on the part of each service to place complete control of any important phase of its logistical operation in the hands of the other.

Although the efforts to bring the ocean transportation systems of the Army and the Navy under a single operating management did not succeed, the Navy provided crews for certain Army transports and operated them on missions established by the Army. In other respects also the Army Transportation Corps and the Naval Transportation Service complemented and assisted each other in an effort to increase the efficiency with which

---

* See Chapter 3, "The Naval Transportation Service in World War II." —Ed.

the men and materiel of the armed services were moved between the zone of interior and the theaters and within the theaters.

Soon after our entry into the war the Army arranged that the Maritime Commission should construct fifty troop transports for its use.[40] Up to the end of 1942 the Transportation Corps had planned to man the vessels with civilian crews, but since it was anticipated that they would be utilized extensively in forward areas the Under Secretary of War proposed that consideration be given to the advisability of manning them with naval personnel.[41] The views of the commanding general of the New York Port of Embarkation were sought on the general question of replacing civilian with naval crews, and he strongly favored the latter on grounds of discipline, continuity of service, and co-operation between vessel crews and gun crews.[42] Similar inquiries sent to the theater commanders brought replies which predominantly favored naval crews, although the Army commanders in the Central and the Southwest Pacific saw no advantage in naval as compared to civilian manning.

Early in 1943 the Navy, having learned through "informal conversations" that it might be called on to man the new troopships, requested the Army to advise it in this regard as soon as practicable, in order that it might begin to assemble personnel and arrange with the Maritime Commission for crew accommodations according to Navy standards to be installed while the vessels were under construction.[43] This request brought into active discussion a matter in which the Transportation Corps had a keen interest—the larger crews carried by Navy-manned transports and the consequent danger of reduced troop capacity on the new vessels.[44] The Army's reply to the Navy indicated that existing plans for the new transports called for Army manning, but apparently hinted that these plans were subject to change. The Navy at once began to study the possibility of restricting the size of its crews on the vessels in question.

A concrete proposal on this subject was submitted to the Navy in April by General Somervell, who in so doing referred to a "suggestion made by the Navy that the new Army transports be crewed by the Navy." The proposal stipulated that the Army should have control over the missions and the schedules of the vessels and over their loading and unloading, as in the case of the several old Army transports already manned with naval personnel; that the vessels should be returned to transport service promptly after completion of any task force operations to which the Joint Chiefs of Staff might assign them; and that the size of the Navy crews should be limited so as not to impair their capacities as transports.

The Navy agreed in principle to these stipulations, but indicated that it would be the judge as to what size crews were required for the services to be rendered. General Somervell accepted this condition, but expressed the view that the determination of such matters should be "a command decision with all phases of the shipping problem in mind," rather than a technical decision by a bureau with professional reputation to consider. In this, as in other aspects of shipping, Somervell and Gross felt that the Navy held too rigidly to its technical standards, considering the scarcity of bottoms. . . .

The Office of the Chief of Transportation and the Naval Transportation Service conferred in preparing sailing schedules and in establishing the availability of ships for repairs. . . .

Both the Army and the Navy procured a large amount of equipment which had to be towed to the theaters, such as barges, small tugs, cranes, car floats, and floating power plants. In addition to the oceangoing tugs owned by the Army, the Navy and the War Shipping Administration had craft of this type. Some of these large tugs were intended for use in the theaters, but others returned to home ports after delivering their tows. Early in 1944, in order to bring this traffic under better regulation, the three agencies agreed to prepare joint priority lists.[45]. . .

The joint logistical operations of the Army and Navy, including their joint use of ships, created a demand for greater uniformity in shipping procedures. The first real progress in that direction came with the publication of "United States Army and Navy Shipping Procedures" in March 1945. . . .It provided that a central record control unit, to facilitate the execution of the plan, should be set up at each United States port and in each theater, jointly whenever practicable. Up to the end of the war, joint units, known as Army-Navy Shipping Information Agencies (ANSIA), had been established at San Francisco, Los Angeles, Seattle, and Boston. . . . [Army historians go on to cover inter-agency relationships: Naval Convoy and Routing Arrangements, and Relations with the British Ministry of War Transport.

Operation of the Army's Large and Small Vessels

Although the Army operated a small percentage of its oceangoing vessels, the wartime Army-operated fleet was a big and varied one. On 1 August 1945 there were 186 vessels (1,000 tons gross or larger) under full Army management. These vessels were manned, supplied, maintained, and scheduled by the Transportation Corps. On the same date, the Transportation Corps had differing degrees of operating responsibility for more than 12,000 smaller boats.

Of the 186 oceangoing vessels, 40 were owned by the Army, 144 were under bareboat charter, and 2 were loaned by the War Shipping Administration.[46] Among these vessels were 51 Army transports (troopships and cargo ships), 26 hospital ships, 55 interisland vessels, 17 floating warehouses, 12 repair ships, 7 spare parts depot ships, 2 cable ships, 1 news transmission ship, and 15 training ships. Of the total, 89 were assigned to ports of embarkation in the zone of interior, 4 were undergoing conversion, and 93 were assigned to oversea commands. The making of such assignments was a responsibility of the Chief of Transportation, and transfers between ports or between oversea commands required his prior approval except in emergencies. The Chief of Transportation delegated the control of assignments and reassignments to the chief of his Water Division.

Military, naval, and civilian personnel were used in operating the Army's oceangoing vessels. With the possible exception of a few ships assigned to oversea theaters and concerning which full information is not available, the crews on these vessels were civilians, divided into the usual deck, engine, steward, and administrative departments, serving under a civilian master. The medical staffs were military personnel provided by the

Surgeon General. The Armed Guard gun crews were naval personnel. The signal sections which handled radio communications embraced military, naval, and civilian personnel. In addition, the troop transports had military complements under transport commanders to deal with passenger matters. The cargo transports had cargo security officers (later known as ship transportation officers). The floating warehouses, spare parts depot ships, and repair ships had military personnel to perform the specialized tasks for which the ships were equipped.

Civilian Crews on Oceangoing Vessels

During peacetime when seamen were plentiful, the Army Transport Service was able to maintain a rather independent position in regard to terms of employment, but this condition changed as the United States approached a state of war. Rates of pay and manning scales were subject to approval by the Secretary of War.[47] During the early emergency period wage increases were recommended by the Quartermaster General as necessary to enable the ATS superintendents to obtain crews for the growing transport fleet, but they lagged behind those granted by civilian ship operators. When civilian operators began paying bonuses during the months just prior to Pearl Harbor, ATS undertook to do likewise, but, because of the complicated bonus system and the many areas of Army operation, there was considerable confusion, and full conformity with civilian practices was difficult.[48] Payment for overtime, a growing practice among civilian operators, could not be made on Army vessels without the approval of the Secretary of War, and there was some uncertainty as to the legal authority for such payment.

There also were differences between Army and commercial practices in regard to conditions of employment. The Army ran its vessels on an open-shop basis and employed union and nonunion men without preference. It thoroughly investigated complaints and endeavored to administer crew matters with full justice to the men but refused to recognize union grievance committees as agencies for adjusting differences between masters and crews. From the union standpoint, these were disadvantages.

On the other hand, as civil service employees, the crews on Army transports enjoyed certain advantages which were not general in the maritime industry, such as those relating to annual and sick leave, the benefits of the Civil Service Retirement Act, and the benefits of the U.S. Employees Compensation Act. During the emergency period prior to Pearl Harbor, with the Army's shipping operations expanding rapidly, the seamen's unions complained frequently about the disadvantages suffered by their members on Army vessels, but they continued to give the ports of embarkation their full support in the procurement of crews.

After our entry into the war, the unions increased their efforts to obtain full acceptance by the Army of the terms and conditions of employment which were in effect with civilian operators. After the establishment of the Maritime War Emergency Board in December 1941, the Army endeavored to conform to the decisions of the board regarding bonuses, war risk insurance, and compensation for loss of personal property. Although there was the customary lag in making those decisions effective, the unions had no serious cause for complaint in such matters. But the Army's position on overtime, closed shop, and the recognition of grievance committees still gave rise to union complaints. In August 1942 a situation arose in the Gulf of Mexico which brought the matter to an open issue. The New Orleans Port of Embarkation reported that during the process of taking over the vessels *Yarmouth, Evangeline and Florida* from private operators, the crews, which at first appeared satisfied with the terms offered by the Army, were persuaded by representatives of one of the unions to leave the ships. After about a week of effort by Army officials, some of the original crew members returned to the vessels. The remaining positions were filled with newly recruited union and nonunion seamen.

Soon after this incident, Mr. Edward F. McGrady, labor relations consultant to the Secretary of War, called a series of conferences which were attended by representatives of General Somervell, General Gross, and the unions. While the discussions were in progress, General Gross informed Mr. McGrady that the Transportation Corps was having no difficulty in obtaining crews for its vessels under the existing policy and urgently recommended that the War Department continue to adhere to that policy.[49] He maintained that the ATS should not change its attitude with regard to grievance committees since it had to be free to operate its vessels "under strict military control." With regard to the unions' demands for the payment of overtime, he stated that there was "pending legislation" which, if enacted, would enable the Army to promulgate such regulations as it might deem necessary on the subject.[50]

The result of these conferences was the issuance of a statement of War Department labor policy for [ATS] vessels.[51]. . .This statement of policy met the more critical points of the unions' complaints. . . .

During the remainder of the war the relations of the Transportation Corps and the seamen's unions were on a mutually cooperative basis. There were problems of a local nature, but no serious threats of strikes or other crises. When the rapid increase in the merchant fleet, the competition of less hazardous jobs ashore, and the operation of the Selective Service Act made the task of obtaining full crews increasingly difficult, the unions, when called upon, provided men to the extent of their ability. The relations between the Transportation Corps and the organizations of licensed marine officers also were orderly throughout the war, and there were no serious disputes or strikes. . . .

The Army supported a Maritime Commission proposal which resulted in the passage of Public Law 524, 77th Congress, and in accordance with that law it recommended from time to time to the Merchant Marine Medal Awards Committee that the Merchant Marine Distinguished Service Medal be presented to deserving seamen. . . .

Any employee or group of employees who believed they had a grievance, upon termination of the voyage in the United States, could present the complaint to the commander of the vessel's home port, directly or through representatives. If the port commander's settlement was not satisfactory, the complainant could take the matter up with the Secretary of War through the Chief of Transportation. . . .

Crew discipline was a matter of constant concern to the Army because of the casual types of seamen which had to be employed, [as well as] the relative inexperience of many masters and mates, and the unusual conditions encountered in wartime. The problem was particularly acute at those oversea ports where seamen were required to assist in loading and unloading cargo, or to perform other unusual tasks because of the lack of local longshoremen or equipment. At many such ports civil courts were nonexistent or ineffective.

Accordingly in October 1942 the commanders of theaters of operations, defense commands, service commands, and ports of embarkation were informed that the military tribunals of the United States had jurisdiction over the crews of merchant vessels, not only Army transports but other American and foreign vessels operating within a base or military area, or carrying materiel or personnel in connection with U.S. military operations. These commanders were instructed to exercise necessary authority whenever military considerations required. . . .

The ship transportation agent was charged with the care and issue of supplies, the care and disbursement of funds, the performance of the duties of baggage-master and civilian personnel officer for the ship, and the preparation of papers and reports required by law or by Transportation Corps regulations. He was responsible to the master and the home port commander in all matters except funds, for which he accounted directly to the Fiscal Director of the Army Service Forces. On cargo vessels the transportation agent usually handled all the work of the administrative department himself, but on troop transports he had as many as six assistants.

> Editor's note: The Army historians go on to cover vessel Maintenance and Voyage Repairs, Supplies for Vessels, and Food Service on Transports and Hospital Ships. Due to space limitations, these sections have been omitted in this excerpt. Continuing from Wardlow, *The Transportation Corps:*

Armament and Gun Crews

Although the question of guns and gun crews for Army vessels had been before the War Department and the Navy since November 1940, adequate preparation had not been made when the Japanese attacked Pearl Harbor.[52] Consequently, in the early weeks of the war, considerable confusion attended both the installation of armament and the provision of gun crews, or armed guard as the Navy called them.*

Initially it was understood that the Navy would provide the armament and that the Army would provide detachments from the Coast Artillery Corps to man the guns.[53] It developed that the Navy, which was responsible for arming privately owned American merchant vessels and which also armed numerous foreign vessels, was short of equipment, and the Army undertook to make up the deficit so far as its own transports were concerned.[54] Army sources were unable to furnish the prescribed equipment in many instances and some vessels were not capable structurally of taking normal armament; therefore considerable improvisation was necessary in order that ships might sail without delay and with a reasonable degree of protection. The Western Defense Command reported that the necessity of providing armament for vessels sailing from the Pacific coast had created a serious shortage of weapons in that command.[55]

In the midst of the confusion regarding the installation of armament, the Navy, without warning to the Army, decided to man the guns which the Navy had installed on Army vessels, with the result that both Army and Navy gun crews were assigned to certain ships.[56] The Army requested that the Navy order be rescinded and that Navy crews be withdrawn pending further consideration of the matter. The Navy Department complied but instructed its personnel at the ports that in the future Navy Armed Guard crews would be furnished wherever Navy guns were installed. At San Francisco, where the situation was particularly acute, the Army port commander found it expedient to place mixed gun crews on some vessels. G-4 directed that this practice be discontinued; that insofar as the Navy

---

* The gun crews serving on WSA-allocated merchant ships (transports, freighters and tankers) were not armed guards with sidearms. They manned the anti-aircraft, 20mm cannons, and dual-purpose 3-inch/50-caliber and 5-inch/38-caliber guns. See Chapter 5, "U.S. Merchant Marine and U.S. Navy Armed Guard." —Ed.

could provide full crews it should be permitted to do so but that otherwise the Army should provide full crews.[57]

In July 1942 the Army, which by then had placed gun crews on more than seventy vessels, inquired as to the possibility of the Navy's assuming the entire responsibility and was informed that since the shortage of naval Armed Guard had been relieved, such guards could be provided for all Army transports. The War Department then directed that the Coast Artillery detachments be replaced by Navy personnel as rapidly as this could be accomplished.

The relationship between the naval Armed Guard and the civilian officers on Army transports caused some concern. In December 1942, the commander of the San Francisco Port of Embarkation reported that this relationship long had been a matter of controversy, with resulting lack of discipline.

In reply the Chief of Transportation pointed out that their respective jurisdictions were adequately defined in the regulations. He indicated that the Navy regulation, which was incorporated by reference in a recently issued Army Regulation (AR 55-330, paragraph 5, 1 December 1942), made the commander of the Armed Guard subject to the orders of the master in all matters pertaining to the internal organization of the ship, including matters of conduct, dress, and leave. The military discipline of the Armed Guard, on the other hand, was to be administered by its commander, and the members of the Armed Guard were not to be required to perform any duties except their military duties.

The Chief of Transportation also explained that the commanding officer of troops, who had been mentioned in the San Francisco report, had no authority whatsoever over the Armed Guard, and stated that it was not considered advisable to suggest such an arrangement to the Navy. He further stated that the Navy Department informally had recognized that, in view of the paramount position of the master affecting the internal organization and safety of the ship, in an extreme case of disobedience on the part of the commander or members of the Armed Guard, the master might be justified in taking action on the spot to the extent of placing the recalcitrants in confinement.

Other reports regarding jurisdictional and disciplinary disputes arising between officers of the civilian crews and the Armed Guard were received by the Chief of Transportation, but they were not numerous. On the other hand, the personal relationships between civilian seamen and the enlisted men of the Armed Guard frequently were troubled.

During the early part of the war, according to a Navy source, 30 percent of the Armed Guard officers reported friction. The dissimilar responsibilities of these groups, the disparity in the rates of compensation, and the differing conceptions of their responsibilities toward the ships on which they served were basic causes of antagonism. Nevertheless, as time went on and civilian and naval personnel became accustomed to working side by side, the relationship improved.

Radio Service and Radar

Under the regulations, the radio operators on the Army's oceangoing vessels might be either enlisted men assigned by the Signal Corps or commercial operators employed by the home port commanders.* But the regulations also provided that instructions regarding the use of radio equipment aboard the transports would be issued by the Chief of Naval Operations, and a Navy directive promulgated soon after our entry into the war provided for the assignment of Navy communication liaison groups.[58] These groups normally would consist of a commissioned officer, three radiomen, and three signalmen. In view of the scarcity of trained naval radio personnel, however, it was provided that when Signal Corps or commercial operators were retained, they would be counted as members of the communication liaison groups, provided at least one Navy radioman was assigned to each transport.

Although this Navy directive required only that one Navy radioman be installed on each Army vessel, reports from San Francisco and Seattle disclosed that the Twelfth and Thirteenth Naval Districts were assigning

---

* All U.S. Navy Armed Guard contingents included one or two communications personnel (a signalman or radioman, or both) as well as the gun crews of 16–26 men. —Ed.

more. Because of limited accommodations on the vessels and the number of naval personnel assigned, it was necessary sometimes to remove the Signal Corps personnel. The Army ports of embarkation indicated that they had found the Signal Corps operators fully competent to handle radio communications according to Navy requirements and that the assignment of naval operators was a waste of manpower.

After consideration of these arguments, the Chief Signal Officer and the Chief of Transportation concurred in the view that, since Navy radio procedure was used on Army transports and only Navy radio stations were authorized to communicate with the transports, it was desirable that Navy radiomen be carried and that they be permitted to stand watch. Nevertheless, a revision of the Navy directive issued soon thereafter explicitly stated that Navy personnel would be assigned only to complete communication personnel complements, not to replace Signal Corps and commercial operators.[59]

The Navy directive contemplated that, as it became available, naval communication personnel would be placed not only on Army vessels but on all U.S. merchant vessels of 1,000 gross tons or more. This did not eventuate, however, and in May 1944 a new plan was agreed on by the Navy, the Army, and the War Shipping Administration.[60] It provided that "the present practice" of assigning Army radio technicians to Army transports would be continued. WSA vessels carrying 250 or more troops were to be assigned either Army or Navy radiomen, according to the service to which the vessels were allocated when the assignments were made, and Army and Navy personnel were not to be assigned to the same vessels at the same time. All WSA cargo vessels were to be assigned commercial radio operators, regardless of their allocation. The Navy directive on this subject stated that when commercial operators were not available Navy operators would be assigned to cargo ships; it also stipulated that Navy radio personnel might be assigned to any vessel at the discretion of the Chief of Naval Operations.

In June 1943 it was arranged that emergency radio rooms would be installed on the troop transports which were being provided for Army use by new construction and by the conversion of existing cargo vessels. The emergency rooms were located in the after parts of the ships within the hulls, where they would be least subject to damage by enemy action. The radio equipment installed in them did not have the range required for the regular radio installations on transports but was adequate for emergency purposes. These rooms were intended for use only when the regular communications equipment was out of service.

Although earlier efforts had been made to have Army troop transports provided with radar equipment for aiding navigation, this was not accomplished until 1945, and installations had been made on only a few of the transports when the war ended. The provision of seaborne radar equipment rested entirely with the Navy, for under a 1942 agreement between the Army and the Navy the Signal Corps confined its activities to air and ground equipment. . . .

In January 1945 the Navy announced a plan to establish pools of radar equipment under the control of the commanders of the Eastern and Western Sea Frontiers for installation on fast, independently routed Army and WSA transports, the entire program to be limited to 150 sets of equipment and 450 men. In April further details as to the execution of the plan were announced. By 7 July, however, radar installations had been completed on only six Army transports; installations on sixteen others were under way or had been arranged. . . .

The Transportation Corps renewed its effort to have radar installed on all War Shipping Administration troop transports allocated to the Army and informed the ports of embarkation that if WSA should refuse to bear the cost of installation, the Army would do so. Coordination of the installation program was assigned to the Chief Signal Officer, who designated the signal officers at the ports of embarkation as local coordinators.

Assignment of Small Boats

The Army required small boats and other floating equipment for many purposes. The types with which the Chief of Transportation was concerned included tugs, barges, lighters, floating cranes, fireboats, launches, marine tractors, and dories for harbor use; tugs, barges, patrol boats, passenger and cargo vessels for coastwise and interisland service; rescue and airplane retrieving vessels for the Army Air Forces; mine laying and target vessels for the Coast Artillery Corps.[61] These units were under 1,000 gross tonnage and 200 feet length; they included both self-propelled and nonpropelled types. As a class they were known as "small boats"; sometimes they were referred to as Harbor boats, but that designation was not accurate, since many types were built expressly for coastwise and interisland service.

In December 1940 the Army had a total of 386 such boats. By the end of the war the fleet under the control of the Chief of Transportation had grown to 12,466 vessels.[62] Of the latter number, 3,413 were assigned to commands in the zone of interior, 7,791 had been dispatched or were assigned to oversea commands, 67 were assigned to lend-lease purposes, 995 were in the zone of interior awaiting assignment, and 200 had been reported as available for disposition. These figures relate only to vessels subject to assignment by the Transportation Corps; they do not augment Navy-procured landing craft, amphibious trucks, specialized vessels procured by the Board of Engineers for Rivers and Harbors, or vessels acquired by the theater commanders from oversea sources. . . .

Manning of Small Boats

Early in 1943 it was apparent that extraordinary means would have to be employed to provide crews for the several thousand units of floating equipment for which the Transportation Corps had contracted. In May the Water Division estimated that 10,000 marine officers and seamen would be needed for the small boats that would be delivered in the United States during the next twelve months, and at about the same time General MacArthur indicated that 4,000 would be required for boats being built in Australia.

Several methods were adopted to provide this personnel. Since it was becoming increasingly difficult to engage civilian crewmen and since military crews were desirable for certain types of vessels which served in the forward areas, the Transportation Corps began the training of harbor craft companies at the Charleston Port of Embarkation in March 1943, and later in the year moved this activity to Camp Gordon Johnston, Carrabelle, Fla., where it could be conducted on a broader scale. A total of 12,782 officers and men were trained under this program in the zone of interior, and companies embracing more than 3,000 were activated overseas. During the summer of 1943 an intensive campaign to recruit civilian marine personnel was launched, in which 40 government and private agencies and 44 marine publications were called upon for aid. Concurrently a Marine Officer Cadet School was established at St. Petersburg, Fla., and schools to provide additional training for civilians already holding licenses in the deck and engine departments were opened at the ports of embarkation at New Orleans, New York, and San Francisco. . . .

The schools at New York and San Francisco, which were in operation only about one year, provided final training and tests for young civilian marine officers who were shipped overseas from those ports. All civilian training activities were under the general supervision of the Industrial Personnel Division in the Office of the Chief of Transportation. . . .

The delivery pools, or harbor boat cadres, not only provided reservoirs from which crews could be drawn as required but also afforded an opportunity for training men who were not fully qualified when they were employed. Though these cadres were utilized principally in providing delivery crews, when occasion required they were drawn on also for permanent crews. . . .

In the spring of 1943, the Southwest Pacific Area, which already had a large number of vessels employed in intra-theater services, reported that great difficulty was being experienced in administering the complicated system of war bonuses applicable to the seamen who signed the usual ship's articles. Also the theater was losing the services of many experienced men who desired to return to the United States after a period in foreign waters, some claiming that the home ports from which they shipped had not made it clear that their vessels would remain overseas. These difficulties existed not only in connection with the crews of small boats but also with crews of the Army-operated oceangoing vessels permanently assigned to the theater.

In order to meet the problem a new form of individual contract was developed, calling for one year of service overseas and providing for a flat payment of 100 percent of the base wage in lieu of all bonuses. This additional payment approximated the average bonus payments to seamen serving overseas under ship's articles. The individual contract gave a clearer definition of the employee's rights and responsibilities than did the ship's articles. It expressly stated that the employee was eligible for treatment by the Medical Corps and thus cleared up a disputed point which had given trouble in the past. The contract form soon was revised to provide for service over a mutually agreed period, rather than for a year. Although this type of contract had been devised particularly for SWPA, it was suitable for and was extensively used in the employment of marine personnel to serve in other theaters. . . .

Civilian officers and crewmen on small boats had the same status under civil service as did the crews on the Army's oceangoing vessels. They were not required to undergo competitive examinations, their appointments were not subject to prior approval by the commission, and their compensation was not governed by the Classification Act. They enjoyed all the privileges of civil service employees, including the leave and retirement features. Other benefits provided for in Transportation Corps Marine Personnel Regulations were equally applicable to them. . . .

(Source: Wardlow, *The Transportation Corps: Responsibilities, Organization, and Operations*, Chap 2:28–55; Chap 4:95–134; Chap 5:135–185; Chap 6:186–227; and Chap 7:228–261.) ∎

U.S. Army Ships and Watercraft of World War II

Editor's note: David H. Grover graduated from the U.S. Merchant Marine Academy in 1945. That same year, he served as third mate on an Army troopship. Forty years later, he researched and wrote his comprehensive work, *U.S. Army Ships and Watercraft of World War II,* about the Army's "fleet." The complete 280-page book includes informative tables for designated vessel types, numerous lists of ship names or numbers by specific categories, plus hundreds of photographs. Highlights of Grover's text and three informative tables follow.

During World War II, the trade journals of the maritime and ship-building industries contained almost as many references to the acquisition, construction, and repair of Army ships as to those of the Navy. However, the popular press of the day was much less aware of, or interested in, Army ships. Articles did appear from time to time in a "believe-it-or-not" vein to the effect that the Army had a surprisingly large fleet of vessels, but a general public awareness of the nature, size, and variety of the Army's fleet, as well as the rationale for its existence, never developed during that time.

This lack of awareness was almost as widespread within the armed forces as it was within the general public. Unfortunately, little has been done through the ensuing years to explore and explain to the public and to the military community the circumstances surrounding the Army's role in the operation of ships and other watercraft. This section will describe the size and nature of the Army's waterborne activities during the years 1941 through 1945.

In spite of the problems encountered in assembling this kind of information, the collected data appear to make a good case for the size and significance of the Army's involvement with ships and watercraft in World War II. The total was at least 127,793 pieces of floating equipment.

This total is made up as follows:

Army Floating Equipment in World War II

Ships Over 1,000 Gross Tons

Troopships, owned/bareboat chartered	80
Troopships, allocated	114
Troopships, foreign-flag, allocated	18
Cargo ships, owned/bareboat chartered	83
Cargo ships, time or voyage chartered	32
Cargo ships, non-Maritime Commission type, allocated	195
Cargo ships, Maritime Commission type, allocated	102
Cargo ships/troopships, Victory ships, allocated	107
Cargo ships/troopships, Liberty ships, allocated	748
Cargo ships, unclassifiable, allocated	3
Cargo ships, Southwest Pacific Area and Philippines	75
Hospital ships	31
Aircraft repair ships	6
Hopper dredges	33
Port repair ships	10
Marine repair ships	6
Spare-parts ships	7
Cable ships	3
Communication ship	1
Tankers	6
Coastal cargo ships	4
Cargo ship, bareboat chartered, Panama Canal Company	1
Total	1,665

Vessels Under 1,000 Gross Tons

Coastal cargo ships/FS boats	511
Coastal cargo ships, Philippines	36
Ferries	11
Coastal tankers	121
Tugs, all types	4,343
Small cargo vessels	289
Minecraft	361
Landing craft	489
Tenders	251
Military dredge tenders	7
Cable vessels	2
Communication ships	3
Rescue and patrol craft	516
Aircraft retrieval vessels	11
Target vessel	1
Launches and small craft	4,697
Inland waterway vessels: Corps of Engineers	532
Inland waterway vessels: Panama Canal Company	193
Sailing vessels	5
Total	12,379

Barges and Non-Propelled Craft

Barges, all types and purposes	8,596
Pontoon sections/units	16,787
Total	25,383

Amphibious Assault Craft	Total	88,366
	Total	127,793

By clustering these units somewhat differently, and by deleting the ponton totals, the list can be made roughly comparable to that of the Navy.

Army		Navy*	
Over 1,000 tons	1,665	Large combatants	1,388
Under 1,000 tons, seagoing	1,225	Large landing craft	4,436
Under 1,000 tons, harbor	11,154	Patrol/minecraft	1,792
Named/numbered vessels	14,044	Yardcraft	4,070
		Named/numbered vessels	13,734
Barges	8,596		
Amphibious assault craft	88,366	Small landing craft	60,974
Total vessels	111,006	Total vessels	74,708

Source: Grover, *U.S. Army Ships and Watercraft of World War II* (1987) xi–xii.

*Source of Navy data: Morison, *History of United States Naval Operations in World War II*, Vol. 15, *Supplement and General Index* (1962); with yardcraft data from Fahey, *Ships and Aircraft of the U.S. Fleet* (1945).

Observations based on the data in the above table:

- The totals show that, while the Navy had significantly more large ships than did the Army, the Army's greater number of harbor craft and amphibious craft produced a grand total of vessels that was almost 50 percent greater than that of the Navy.
- In terms of shipping space, the deadweight capacity of dry cargo and passenger ships owned by, chartered to, and allocated to the Army during the peak of shipping activity was 17.3 million tons; the comparable figure for the Navy was 8.0 million tons. Clearly, the Army afloat was primarily a transportation organization, while the Navy was primarily combatant.

Definition and Designation of Army Ships and Watercraft

The vessels described in this section qualify as Army vessels in one of several ways:

- Most of the vessels, particularly the smaller craft, were owned by the Army.
- A second group of ships was chartered by the Army, generally for moving troops and cargo but occasionally for other purposes, such as cable laying.
- A third group of ships was allocated to the Army by the War Shipping Administration.

To understand why the Army operated such an extensive fleet during World War II, seemingly in competition with the Navy, it is useful to review briefly the background of this apparent rivalry. Under the provisions of the prewar document, "Joint Army and Navy Basic War Plan—Rainbow Five," the Navy was to man and operate the transports of the Army if the United States became a belligerent. In the spring of 1941 under orders from President Franklin D. Roosevelt, the Army began turning over its large troopships to the Navy.

It soon became apparent, however, that the Navy was not in a position to provide crews for a large number of merchant-type vessels because of the heavy demand for combatant crews. At this point the Coast Guard was called upon to crew several of these large ships, including the *Leonard Wood, Hunter Liggett,* and *Joseph T. Dickman.*

Shortly after Pearl Harbor, the Army and Navy agreed that the Army would man and operate the remaining vessels that it owned or controlled under bareboat charter. The War Shipping Administration would then allocate additional vessels as the Army might require.

The War Shipping Administration (WSA) was much like a spin-off agency of the U.S. Maritime Commission. The latter agency, created by the Merchant Marine Act of 1936, was charged with the stewardship of federally owned vessels (except for World War I vessels that were still the responsibility of the United States Shipping Board at that time). In the late 1930s and early 1940s the Maritime Commission was primarily concerned with the procurement, rather than the operation, of government-owned vessels. During the military buildup of 1941 when the demand for ships far exceeded the supply, it struggled to allocate ships to both the Army and Navy.

Prior to the creation of the War Shipping Administration the President had created the Strategic Shipping Board with Army, Navy, and Maritime Commission membership. It functioned briefly as a ship allocation agency, but soon the need for a larger and stronger organization was apparent. On 7 February 1942, the WSA came into existence through Executive Order 9054. The new agency was assigned those Maritime Commission functions that dealt with the requisition and operation of vessels, while the Commission retained responsibility for new construction. The same man, retired Admiral Emory S. Land (USN), served both as chairman of the Maritime Commission and as administrator of the WSA.

After the creation of the WSA, Army Chief of Staff General George C. Marshall took the position that the executive order had abrogated the provisions of the earlier war plan that gave the Navy exclusive control of transports. For the balance of 1942, the Army and Navy maneuvered politically for control of troopships, with the Navy even proposing that the three largest ships be converted into aircraft carriers. But at the end of this period, the situation generally remained about as it had been at the time the WSA was created, with the Army retaining control of those ships it owned or had chartered, and other newly built ships being operated by the WSA through general agents or by the Navy.

During this period of political maneuvering, efforts were made to achieve an agreement under which either the Navy or Army would control all military shipping, an arrangement that was recognized as being more efficient than the operation of two fleets. But the two departments could not agree on how this proposal could be implemented. The WSA continued to allocate ships to both services, and later in the war the two services traded ships back and forth on a reasonably amicable basis.

Inasmuch as most Army vessels were smaller craft serving the marine terminals—such as tugs, launches, and barges rather than oceangoing ships—there was no competition with the Navy in operating this large group of vessels. These Army-owned craft supported the operation of military ports, a responsibility not shared by the Navy.

Although the term "Army" as used throughout this text normally refers to the operating armed forces of the United States Army, it also includes certain other components of the Army that operated inland waterway fleets, notably the civil works section of the Corps of Engineers and the Panama Canal Company, which was a non-Army component of the War Department.

Designations of Army ships have never been as clear-cut as have those of the Navy. In general, a ship owned by, or under bareboat charter to, the Army was designated by the letters USAT, for U.S. Army Transport, preceding the ship's name. Ships allocated to the Army or under voyage or time charter retained their civilian designations as steamships (SS) or motorships (MS). Mine planters of the Coast Artillery Corps were designated with AMP for Army Mine Planter preceding the vessel's name. Vessels of the Corps of Engineers similarly used the letters USED for U.S. Engineers Department in conjunction with vessel names or numbers. In peacetime, smaller launches frequently had QM or QMC for Quartermaster Corps preceding their numbers.

Transports

A transport, as the term was used in the U.S. Army, was an ocean-going vessel used to move personnel, or cargo, or both. This usage contrasted with that of the Navy, in which the term applied only to ships moving personnel.

It is difficult to know which ships to include when counting the transports of the Army within both the general fleet and the Southwest Pacific Area fleet. Authoritative sources differ on the exact number of such ships, and even as to what criteria should be used in identifying vessels as "Army" ships.

The most liberal ship-counting system, in terms of the types of management control it encompassed, was that of the Vessel Operations Analysis Branch of the Water Division of the Office of the Chief of Transportation. This system used ten types of management control in categorizing 1,621 ships that were "in service or assigned to the service of the Army as of 23 June 1944." The ships were distributed as follows:

Control Status	Passenger	Freight	Refrigerator	Tanker	Total
Owned by Army	40	12	2	3	57
Bareboat charters to Army.	33	58	2	0	93
Time charters to Army . . .	0	2	0	0	2
Voyage charters to Army. .	0	2	0	0	2
Owned by Navy	18	5	1	0	24
Chartered by Navy	12	16	0	0	28
Loaned to Navy by WSA. .	17	0	0	0	17
Allocated to Army by WSA	129	1,131	4	0	1,264
British Control.	21	0	0	0	21
U.S. Commercial	7	9	14	83	113
Total.	277	1,235	23	86	1,621

Classification of "Army" vessels was also made by vessel type. The following table was prepared in the Water Division of the Office of Chief of Transportation near the end of the war:

Vessels in Army Service, 31 July 1945

Design Type Maritime Commission	Number of Troopships	Number of Freighters
Liberty		822
Liberty, passenger	12	
Liberty, special-purpose		20
Liberty, hospital	6	
Liberty, enlarged		79
Liberty, tank transport		8
Liberty, boxed aircraft transport . .		21
Victory	19	95
Victory, enlarged		27
C1	13	95
C2	16	65
C3	37	9
C4	35	
P2	15	
S4	6	5
N3		24
R2		4
Non-Maritime Commission by Nationality		
USA	61	93
Panama		4
Britain	5	46
Honduras		4
Netherlands	9	14
Norway	1	15
Other	2	5
Hospital Ships	24	
Totals	261	1,445
Grand Total: 1,706		

Significant differences in totals between these two tables can be attributed to the widely separated dates on which the tallies were taken and to different ways of counting ships.

Both of these tables suggest that it is possible to be too generous in counting "Army" vessels, particularly in adhering to the definitions used in this section. Naval vessels and British ships are a case in point. No justification seems to exist in this current study to count such vessels as part of the marine operations of the United States Army. However, ships of certain other countries may be an entirely different matter.

During most of WWII the governments of Norway, the Netherlands, Belgium, Denmark, France, and Yugoslavia were in exile. The ships of these nations were generally requisitioned by the WSA when available and integrated into the pool of American shipping. Italian vessels were seized during the war as they became subject to American authority. Ships of Central American nations such as Panama and Honduras were often owned by American interests, and thus were available for allocation. A few ships of Latin American nations were acquired through charter. Because of the special circumstances prevailing for all these ships, it is more logical to count these vessels as available for Army service.

Although authoritative sources differ as to how many vessels were actually in Army service during the war, there has been general agreement that only about 185 ships of more than 1,000 gross tons were under direct operational control of the Army at the end of the war. The remaining ships were allocated from the pool of ships controlled by the WSA. As the discrepancies in totals would indicate, the term "in Army service" meant different things to different people, even within the Army Transport Service and its successor, the Transportation Corps.

The concept of allocation of ships by the WSA is the key to understanding the problem of counting transports. Under the arrangement that existed after February of 1942, the WSA requisitioned all private ocean-going ships in the United States and also took title to all new vessels coming out of the Maritime Commission's construction program. It then assigned most of its ships to private operators who, as general agents, actually manned and operated the vessels under the direction of the WSA. It also allocated vessels directly to the Army and Navy, and to private firms who operated the vessels for these services. The wartime volumes of the "Record" of the American Bureau of Shipping show only a hundred or so ships directly allocated to Army operation at any given time, although according to the total number of ships reported "in Army service" by various authorities, there must have been between 1,200 and 1,500 ships allocated to Army use during the peak months of wartime shipping.

One of the underlying problems in identifying Army transports grows out of the difference in the way the Army and Navy handled their allocated ships. The Navy had a clear-cut method of identifying which vessels it considered to be part of its fleet, whether owned, chartered, or allocated. But the Army's allocated ships resembled other merchant vessels more than they did military vessels, and their civilian crews looked just like crews of Army-owned ships, chartered ships, and merchant ships. Aside from a few show-place USAT ships, the vessels themselves, in their drab wartime gray, differed little in appearance from all other merchant ships of that era. The ultimate decision as to what ships were Army ships must be left to the service itself.

Amphibious Landing Vessels

From the beginning of its involvement in overseas wars the Army faced the responsibility of landing troops on foreign shores. In World War I American troops were able to debark at well-developed European ports, sparing the Army the challenge of amphibious landings. But as World War II became imminent, it was clear to military planners that the United States was unprepared to put troops ashore in substantial numbers other than by pierside debarkation.

Prewar exercises demonstrated that neither the Army nor the Navy had the equipment or capability to land troops effectively over a beach.

Shortly before the war both services were engaged in trying to develop suitable landing craft. Much of this effort, influenced by British experience in 1940 and 1941, was focused through Higgins Industries in New Orleans, with each service working independently of the other.

During this period the Army produced two basic sizes of rigid-hull landing craft: the 36-foot CL (landing craft) which corresponded roughly to the Navy's evolving LCVP, and the 45- and 50-foot TKL (tank lighter) which resembled the LCM that the Navy was developing at the same time.

The CL was first produced by Higgins Industries for the Army in 1940, and the first versions of the TKL appeared in mid-1941, a product of American Car and Foundry in Wilmington, Delaware. By mid-1943 the exclusive responsibility for landing craft procurement and operation had been given to the Navy, so the Army's supply of these vessels was turned over to the Navy. No further construction contracts were issued by the Army for rigid-hull landing craft.

Ironically, even though the Army was cut off from developing amphibious vessels after the middle of the war, at about that same time the Corps of Engineers moved heavily into amphibious warfare with the creation of amphibious engineer battalions. Using equipment furnished largely by the Navy, these units participated in the assault phases of a number of landings in the Pacific Theater.*

Grover's Observations and Conclusions

The United States Army afloat was simply too unique, too complex, and too enmeshed in tradition to permit an examination of its extensive operations to conclude without some final observation.

Demonstrably, the years 1941–45 were the halcyon days of marine activity for the Army. But the service unification that was implemented in 1949, abetted by technological change, initiated the quick and irreversible disintegration of the Army's fleet of ships and watercraft, perhaps forever.

---

* For an in-depth biographical history of the revolutionary World War II landing craft and their crews, the reader is referred to William L. McGee, *The Amphibians Are Coming! Emergence of the 'Gator Navy and its Revolutionary Landing Craft.* —Ed.

What happened in World War II can best be regarded as an historical aberration—a zenith of immense proportions attained in the life of a military organization, followed by a rapid demise of that organization.

Considering the modest proportions of the Army afloat in the 1930s and the virtual disappearance of the waterborne Army in the 1950s, it is sometimes difficult to recall that the 1940s represented a period of marine activity of staggering proportions.

Quite possibly, even without service unification, the ultimate postwar outcome—the virtual disappearance of the Army's marine activities—would have been the same. Each of the major waterborne functions of the Army was destined to be outmoded by technology. The non-transport functions—in which the sea was an incidental setting for the task to be carried out—were particularly vulnerable to technological change:

- Planting of controlled mines in harbors has been outmoded by the new technology of coastal defense: radar, sonar, rocketry, and ASW warfare.
- Rescuing of downed aviators by crash boat has been relegated to a secondary role by the use of helicopters.
- Communicating military messages by submarine cable has become a redundant back-up system to electronic media and satellites.
- Bridging rivers with pontons has been replaced for all but the widest streams by mobile extension bridges.*

In the case of waterway maintenance functions, political rather than technological change deprived the Army of most of the vessels needed to do the job, even though the Army was left with the responsibility for seeing that the work was done.

In yielding the transport function, the Army had more to lose than with these other non-transport functions. The troop transport was more than the

---

* Ponton is the Army's term and spelling for a float that supports bridges or serves as a causeway or barge. Pontoon is the Navy's spelling. —Ed.

application of military technology; it was a way of life. The troopship had always been the foundation of the overseas movement of troops, the "raison d'être" of a water transportation organization within an Army. But it had been much more: a hallowed military tradition, a Spartan but romantic interlude in the lives of men, and a symbol of overseas dominion. Perhaps we Americans have not shared in the Kiplingesque awe of troopships felt by the British, but we have certainly had warm feelings about the great old ships that have carried American soldiers to and from what were perceived to be just wars and justified occupations abroad.

Considering the capacity and speed of transport aircraft, it is unlikely that troopships will ever again be needed to haul troops great distances to combat zones or peacetime garrisons. The troopship is no longer on the tide for "Tommy Atkins," and the world will never be quite the same.*

While no one can fault the Army for the changes that have taken away its marine operations—whether brought about by technology, political decisions, or military unification—what is regrettable is the Army's indifference to its once-great marine past. Against significant odds the Army in World War II developed a remarkable capability for vessel operations within five major branches of arms, often overcoming a second-class status assigned to it as a perceived intruder attempting to become one of the sea services.

Accepting the awareness that it is all virtually gone should make the Army no less proud of the fact that the vessel fleet existed on the scale that it did. But the Army does not seem proud; indeed, it does not care. Research efforts in behalf of this book [reference is to Grover's book] were repeatedly greeted with disinterest by the higher echelons of Army history and public affairs offices.

Let us hope that military historians eventually will rediscover the reality that the largest armada of World War II vessels belonged to the United

---

* "Tommy Atkins" (often just "Tommy") is a term for a common soldier in the British Army and is particularly associated with World War I. German soldiers would call out to "Tommy" across no man's land if they wished to speak to a British soldier. In more recent times, "Tommy Atkins" or "Tom" is occasionally still heard, especially with regard to paratroopers. —Ed.

States Army. While the surviving vessels and crew members are still with us, much more needs to be done to preserve the outstanding record of that fleet of vessels and the men who sailed in them.

(Source: Grover, *U.S. Army Ships and Watercraft of World War II*, xi–xvi, 3–5, 149–154, 253–254.) ■

Abbreviations Used in Endnotes for Chapter 6

Abbreviations were used extensively in the notes for *United States Army in World War II, The Technical Services—The Transportation Corps.* Insofar as practicable, these abbreviations conform to War Department Technical Manual, TM 20-205, Dictionary of United States Army Terms, issued 18 January 1944.

AAF	Army Air Forces	Bd	Board
ACofS	Assistant Chief of Staff	BMWT	British Ministry of War Transport
ACofT	Assistant Chief of Transportation	Bn	Battalion
		BPE	Boston Port of Embarkation
Adm	Administration or Administrative		
		Br	Branch
Adv	Advisory	BuPers	Bureau of Personnel (Navy)
AFPAC	U.S. Army Forces, Pacific		
		BuShips	Bureau of Ships (Navy)
AFWESPAC	U.S. Army Forces, Western Pacific	BUSHIPS	Chief, Bureau of Ships (Navy)
AG	Records of the Adjutant General's Office	C	Chief
		CCS	Combined Chiefs of Staff
AGF	Army Ground Forces	CE	Corps of Engineers
AGO	Adjutant General's Office	CG	Commanding General
		Chm	Chairman
AR	Army Regulations	CINCAFPAC	Commander in Chief, U.S. Army Forces, Pacific
ASF	Records of Army Service Forces headquarters		
		CINCPAC	Commander in Chief, U.S. Pacific Fleet
ASF MPR	Records of Army Service Forces Monthly Progress Report	CINCPOA	Commander in Chief, Pacific Ocean Areas
ASW	Assistant Secretary of War	Cir	Circular
		Civ	Civilian
ATS	Army Transport Service	CMTC	Combined Military Transportation Committee

CNO	Chief of Naval Operations	G-l	Personnel Division, War Department General Staff
CO	Commanding Officer		
CofEngrs	Chief of Engineers	G-2	Military Intelligence Division, War Department General Staff
CofOrd	Chief of Ordnance		
CofS	Chief of Staff		
CofT	Chief of Transportation Corps	G-3	Organization and Training Division, War Department General Staff
Com	Committee or Commission		
Comdr	Commander	G-4	Supply Division, War Department General Staff
Comdt	Commandant		
COMINCH	Commander in Chief, United States Fleet		
		Gen	General
Coml	Commercial	gf	General files
Conf	Conference	GHQ	General Headquarters
Cons	Construction	GO	General Order
CSAB	Combined Shipping Adjustment Board	GSUSA	General Staff, U.S. Army
DCofS	Deputy Chief of Staff	HB	Historical Branch, Office of the Chief of Transportation
DCofT	Deputy Chief of Transportation		
DF	disposition form, also used for comments and instructions	Hist	Historical
		Hq	Headquarters
		HR	House of Representatives
Dir	Director		
Dist	Distribution or District	Incl	Inclosure
Div	Division	Ind	indorsement, used within the War Department as a substitute for separate memoranda
DWT	Deadweight tons or tonnage		
Emb	Embarkation		
EO	Executive Order	Int	Intelligence
Equip	Equipment	JAG	Judge Advocate General
ETO	European Theater of Operations		
		JAGD	Judge Advocate General's Department
ETOUSA	European Theater of Operations, U.S. Army		
		JB	Joint Board (Army and Navy)
Exec	Executive		

JCS	Joint Chiefs of Staff	Mvmt	Movement
JLC	Joint Logistics Committee	NATO	North African Theater of Operations
JMTC	Joint Military Transportation Committee	NATOUSA	North African Theater of Operations, U.S. Army
JPC	Joint Planning Committee	NTS	Naval Transportation Service
Ltr	letter, used chiefly for correspondence between the War Department and other departments and agencies	OCMH	Office of the Chief of Military History
		OCofEngrs	Office of the Chief of Engineers
		OCS	Office of the Chief of Staff
Mar Com	Maritime Commission (also "MC")	OCT	Records of the Office of the Chief of Transportation
Memo	memorandum, used for correspondence within the War Department, and sometimes with other governmental agencies, notably the Navy	OCT HB	Records of the Historical Branch (at one time called Historical Unit) of the Office of the Chief of Transportation
		Opn	Operation
Mil	Military	OQMG	Office of the Quartermaster General
Msg	message, used when it is not clear by what means an electrically transmitted message was sent	Ord Dept	Ordnance Department
		Org	Organization or Organizational
MT	Measurement ton— 40 cubic feet	OSW	Office of the Secretary of War
Mtg	Meeting		
MTO	Mediterranean Theater of Operations	OWM	Office of War Mobilization
MTOUSA	Mediterranean Theater of Operations, U.S. Army	P&O	Records of the War Plans Division of the General Staff, and its successors, the Operations Division and the Plans and Operations Division
MTS	Military Transportation Section, Association of American Railroads		

PE	Port of Embarkation	Trans Br G-4	Records of the Transportation Branch of G-4, prior to March 1942
Pers	Personnel		
Plng	Planning		
POA	Pacific Ocean Areas	TWX	teletype message
Prod	Production	TZ	Transportation Zone
Prog	Progress	USA	United States Army
QMC	Quartermaster Corps	USASOS	U.S. Army, Services of Supply
QMG	Quartermaster General		
		USCG	U.S. Coast Guard
Rad	radiogram	USF	U.S. Fleet
Rec	Record	USN	U.S. Navy
Reg	Regulation	USW	Under Secretary of War
Req	Requirements		
Rpt	report, which reviewed a specific subject or the developments during a given period	VCNO	Vice Chief of Naval Operations
		WDCSA	Chief of Staff
		WDGAP	Personnel Division of the General Staff
S	Senate	WDGDS	Supply Division of the General Staff; WPD, War Plans Division of the General Staff
Secy	Secretary		
SN	Secretary of the Navy		
SOS	Services of Supply		
Sv	Service	WDGS	War Department General Staff
SvC	Service Command		
SW	Secretary of War	WDMB	War Department Manpower Board
SWPA	Southwest Pacific Area		
T/O	Tables of Organization	WESPAC	Western Pacific
TAG	The Adjutant General	WPB	War Production Board
TC	Transportation Corps	WPD	War Plans Division, War Department General Staff
Telg	telegram		
Tng	Training	WSA	War Shipping Administration
Tr	Troop		
Traf	Traffic	WSF	Western Sea Frontier (Navy)
Trans	Transportation		
		ZI	Zone of interior

Endnotes for Chapter 6

1. *Biennial Rpt, CofS USA, 1943*, p. 8.
2. Ltr, the President to SW, 8 Dec 41, AG 334.8 Strategic Shipping Bd. Presumably Hopkins was to act as personal representative of the President in this as in so many other matters.
3. When establishment of CCS was being discussed, Gen Marshall pointed out that U.S. could support the proposal only in principle, because centralized control of U.S. shipping had not yet been accomplished. See arcadia Proceedings, 10 Jan 42, p. 4.
4. Memo, C of Trans Div OQMG (Dillon) for ACofS G-4, 4 Feb 42, sub: Trans Org; Memo, ACofS G-4 for Dillon, 6 Feb 42. Both in ASF Hq QMG. When this exchange took place G-4 (Somervell) believed that QMG had done well in obtaining strong men as advisers, but needed more of that type on his operating staff.
5. Memo, CG SOS for C's of Supply Arms and Svs, etc., 9 Mar 42, sub: Initial Directive for Org of SOS, par. 14c (3). Although not expressly mentioned, commercial traffic agencies were transferred to Transportation Division. The Motor Section of the Transportation Branch G-4 had been dealing principally with organizational equipment, rather than with commercial motor transportation, which accounts for its not being transferred.
6. lbid., par. 12f (7). Although from April to July 1942 Gross officially was known as Chief of Transportation Service, the title Chief of Transportation is used uniformly in this history.
7. For data concerning seven Army bases on eastern seaboard see *Report of the Chief of Transportation Service,* 1920, pp. 33–38. Except for part of the Brooklyn base, all facilities were leased to commercial operators between the wars. During WWII, TC utilized all except the Newark base, which was used by AAF.
8. AR 55–5, par. 3a, 5 Oct 42.
9. Quoted by Acting Secy State Joseph C. Grew, in "Our Global War," *Department of State Bulletin,* March 4, 1945, p. 329. In this address Mr. Grew said, "There is . . . a serious shortage of shipping. There has been ever since the beginning of the war and there probably will be a shortage until some months after the final defeat of the enemy."
10. Statistical study, Merchant Fleets of the World, as of 1 Sep 39, prepared by Div of Economics and Statistics, Mar Com, 24 Aug 45. Vessels on Great Lakes and inland waterways, icebreakers and other specialized types excluded.

[11] See *United States Maritime Commission Report to Congress for the Period Ended October 25, 1940*, pp. 1–2, 24–25; . . . *Period Ended October 25, 1941*, pp. 1–2, 34–36. Hereafter cited as *Mar Com Rpt.*

[12] Memo, WPD for CofS USA, 11 Jun 40, sub: Joint Army-Navy Exercises (WPD 4232-4), AG 354.21(9-29-39), Sec 3. Combat loading involved stowing organizational equipment and supplies in the ships so that they might be unloaded quickly and in the order needed.

[13] Memo, ACofS G-4 for TAG, 21 Jun 40, sub: Rpt on Army Participation, etc., G-4/30557-ll; lst Ind, QMG for TAG, 23 Jul 40. Both in AG 354.21 (9-29-39), Sec 3. AR 30-1190, par. 3b, 23 Jul 32.

[14] Memorandum of Organization, 19 Feb 42, signed by Admiral Emory S. Land and Sir Arthur Salter, members of Washington branch, states purpose, policies, and principal tasks of CSAB, OCT 334 CSAB. Members of London branch were W. Averell Harriman for U.S. and Lord Leathers for UK.

[15] "WSA Announces Charter Pool to Supply Allies with Ships," *Journal of Commerce* (New York), July 30, 1943. WSA Shipping Summary, 30 Jun 45, p. 16, shows total of 427 U.S. vessels lend-leased to other countries, including 325 to UK and 98 to USSR. The number increased subsequently.

[16] Plan signed by Admiral Horne and General Somervell, 15 Jul 42, OCT HB Topic Army-Navy Joint Logistics.

[17] Agreement, Basic Logistical Plan for Command Areas Involving Joint Army and Navy Operations, promulgated by TAG USA, 7 Mar 43, and by CinC U.S. Fleet, 8 Mar 43.

[18] Agreement, CofS USA and COMINCH, 26 May 43, sub: Joint Priority List for Pacific Shipments, OCT HB Topic Army-Navy Joint Logistics.

[19] Memo, CofT for Dir NTS, 1 Jul 43, sub: Joint Troop and Cargo Movements West Coast, OCT HB Topic Army-Navy Joint Logistics.

[20] JCS 1259/4, 3 Apr 45, sub: Command and Operational Directives for the Pacific.

[21] JCS 1286/6, 5 Jun 45, sub: Joint Agency for Coordination of Shipping, within Pacific.

[22] ASF MPR, Sec. 3, 31 Jul 45, p. 66. Total of 1,706 vessels in Army service was peak or near peak for war period. ASF Statistical Summary, World War II, p. 145, shows 1,765 vessels in Army service in December 1944. Due to new and more restrictive method of counting adopted early in 1945, it is doubtful whether figures are strictly comparable. For new basis of counting see Memo, Water Div for Contl Div OCT, 28 Mar 45, OCT HB Water Div Misc.

[23] Statistical table, Water Div, Vessels in Army Service, 31 Jul 45, OCT HB Water Div Vessel Opns Analysis.

[24] Memo, ACofS G-4 for CofS USA, 28 Dec 41, sub: Admiral Turner's Proposed JB Action, G-4/33920.

[25] Memo, C of Trans Br G-4 for ACofS G-4, 1 Jan 42, sub: Opn of Water Trans, Trans Br G-4/560 Mar Com.

[26] Bureau of the Budget, *The United States at War,* pp. 149–50.

[27] Memorandum Covering the Interdepartmental Relationship Between the Army and the War Shipping Administration to Form a Basis for Full and Complete Cooperation in Connection with the Purchase, Charter, Use and Operation of Vessels and Terminal Facilities, transmitted with Ltr, Douglas to Somervell, 13 Jun 42, OCT HB Wylie WSA.

[28] Memo, Admiral Leahy for General Marshall and Admiral King, quoted in JCS 173/3, 1 Jan 43.

[29] Ltr, WSA to Sen Harry S. Truman, 8 Apr 43, and attached WSA reply to unions, OCT HB Mar Com Opns; "CIO Ship Operations Plan May Be Revived in Congress."

[30] Memo, n.d., sub: Program to Speed up Turnarounds of Ships Operating in S and SW Pacific, submitted to Army by WSA; Ltr, CofT to WSA, 18 Jan 43.

[31] Memo, ACofS G-4 for Mr. Hopkins, 24 Feb 42, sub: Allocation of U.S. Shipping for 1942, G-4/29717-116.

[32] Memo, CofT for Plans Div ASF, 20 Apr 44, sub: Priority of Ships for Pacific Theaters, OCT 563.5 POA.

[33] Memos, ACofS G-4 for DCofS USA (Moore), 26 Nov 40 and 7 Dec 40, sub: Opn of ATS by Navy; Memo, QMG for ACofS G-4, 3 Dec 40, QM 570 T-W-C (Army Transports).

[34] Memo, C of Trans Br G-4 for ACofS G-4, 7 Apr 41, OCT HB Wylie Navy Crews for Army Transports; sub: Manning Army Vessels with Navy Crews, G-4/29717-51.

[35] Memo, CNO USN for CofS USA, 9 Jan 42, sub: Removal of Navy Crews from Army Transports.

[36] Memo, ACofS G-4 for CofS USA, 17 Jan 42, sub: Change in Joint Action on Water Trans, OCT HB; Memo, CNO for CofS USA, 26 Jan 42, G-4/29717-51; Memo, CNO for BUSHIPS, etc., 27 Jan 42, G-4/29717-51. Four of the six Army transports were turned back to the Army later in the war. The giant *LaFayette,* following serious damage by fire during conversion, capsized at her pier in New York harbor and never returned to service.

[37] Memo, CNO for CofS USA, 26 Feb 42, and Incl; Memo, CofS USA for CNO, 27 Feb 42, sub: Opn of Army Transports.

[38] See Duncan S. Ballantine, *U.S. Naval Logistics in the Second World War* (Princeton, 1949), pp. 70–80, 90–94, 101–08, 119, 124–28. Memo, Somervell for Horne, 1 Apr 43, sub: Increasing the Powers of the Naval Trans Sv, OCT 020 Joint Trans Sv–Army and Navy.

[39] For Army views on duplications and conflicts arising from separate Army and Navy transportation operations see joint Memo, Wylie, McIntyre, and Meyer, for Finlay Exec OCT, 19 Apr 44.

[40] CCS 56/1, 6 Mar 42, par. 7; Memo, Mvmts Div OCT for Col. Wylie, 2 Sep 42, sub: Ships under Cons for Army, OCT HB Wylie Staybacks. Of these troopships 30 were converted cargo ships (C-4 type) and 20 were wartime passenger ship designs (P-2 type). Other cargo ship conversions were arranged later.

[41] Memo, USW for CG SOS, 1 Jan 43, and Reply, 2 Jan 43, AG 231.8 (12-29-42) (1). Navy had proposed and Army had agreed to install features which would make these vessels more readily adaptable for combat loading.

[42] Memo, Gross for Somervell, 29 Dec 42, sub: Disadvantages of Civ Crews, OCT HB Gross Crews.

[43] Memo, VCNO for CofS USA, 15 Jan 43, sub: Army Transports—Manning by Navy, OCT 231.8 Army Vessels.

[44] General Wylie presented comparisons indicating that both operating and gun crews on Navy-manned transports were much larger than on similar Army transports, and that larger reserves of stores were carried. Larger naval crews are explained as necessary on transports operating in Pacific forward areas to avoid delays in unloading at ports where there were no shore gangs and delays on account of needed repair at ports where there were no shore repair facilities. Naval transports subject to use in assault operations naturally carried larger gun crews than vessels in regular transport service.

[45] Memo of Agreement, 28 Jan 44, sub: Joint Priority Lists for Ocean Towing Operations, ASF Hq Shipping 1944; Joint Memo, Dir NTS, CofT, and WSA for their representatives at Pacific ports, 7 Mar 44, OCT HB Water Div Towing.

[46] AG 560 (3 Aug 45) OB-S-SPTWO-M, 13 Aug 45, sub: Monthly List of U.S. Army Transports, etc.; AR 55–515, par 4, 1 Sep 42, sub: TC Charters of Vessels; AR 55–305, 10 Oct 42, sub: TC Water Trans Gen.

[47] OQMG Cir 1–15, 1 Jul 37, pars. 166 and 167, as amended 23 Feb 39, sub: Regulations Governing Civilian Employees.

[48] Ltr, C of Trans Br G-4 to Secy of Sailors Union of the Pacific, 27 Jan 42, OCT HB Wylie Staybacks.

[49] Memo, 22 Aug 42, sub: Protest of Seafarers International Union, OCT 545.02 Army Vessels.

[50] Bill to authorize payment of overtime had been drafted in OCT in June 1942, but Gross had decided not to press it then. Memo, Pen Div OCT for Water Div OCT, 13 Jun 42, OCT 231.8 Army Vessels.

[51] Memo, CofS SOS for TAG, 29 Oct 42, AG 570.1 (10-29-42); WD Memo W620-4-42, 31 Oct 42, sub: WD Labor Policy Governing Vessels Operated by WD, in AG 570.1 (10-29-42).

[52] Ltr, Acting SN for SW, 13 Nov 40; 2d Ind QMG, 25 Nov 40; Memo, ACofS G-4 for CofS USA, 30 Nov 40; Memo, SW for SN, 3 Dec 40, sub: Degaussing and Arming Army Transports.

[53] Memo, C of Trans Br G-4 for Port Comdrs, 19 Dec 41, sub: Arming Transports and Chartered Vessels.

[54] Memo, C of Trans Br G-4 for ACofS G-4, 22 Dec 41, OCT HB; Ltr, SN to Chm of Mar Com, 3 Feb 42, sub: Arming Foreign Vessels, G-4/29717-50.

[55] Memo, ACofS G-4 for CG's NYPE and SFPE, 23 Dec 41, sub: Army Transports; Memo, CG WDC for CG GHQ, 31 Jan 42, sub: Armament for Ships; Memo, C of Trans Br G-4 for CG SFPE, 17 Feb 42.

[56] Memo, C of Trans Br G-4 for CG SFPE, 8 Jan 42, sub: Gun Crews, G-4/29717-51; Memo, CofS USA for CNO (Stark), 10 Jan 42, G-4/29717-51; Telg, Nav Dept to Naval Dists, etc., 17 Jan 42, OCT HB Wylie Armament.

[57] Memo, CG SFPE for C of Trans Br G-4, 21 Jan 42, sub: Arming Vessels; Memo, C of Trans Br G-4 for CG SFPE, 4 Feb 42.

[58] Memo, CNO for Naval Dists, etc., 24 Jan 42, sub: Com Liaison Groups—U.S. Flag Merchant Vessels and U.S. Army Transport Vessels, OCT 221 Army Vessels.

[59] Memo, VCNO for Dir BuPers and Naval Dists, 30 Mar 43, sub: Com Liaison Pers, OCT 221 Army Vessels.

[60] Memo, CNO for Naval Dists, 6 May 44, AG 220.3 (22 May 44); WD Memo W55–44, 23 Jun 44, sub: Assignment of U.S. Army Radio Technicians or Navy Radiomen.

[61] AR 55–510, par. 1, 9 Oct 42, sub: Harbor Boat Service. General characteristics of vessels shown in Report of Army Small Boat Construction, 1 July 40 to 31 May 45, issued by WD, 18 Dec 45.

[62] Gross final rpt, p. 72. Classification by designs and assignments is shown in statistical table, Harbor Boats in Service, in Storage, and Intransit, 1 Aug 45, OCT HB Water Div Small Boats.

Coastal freighters of F, FP and FS type. Pictured here, F-129 coastal freighter, Manila, Philippine Islands, August 1946. The crew is probably Philippino. (Photographs for this chapter courtesy of David H. Grover; Charles Dana Gibson and E. Kay Gibson)

FP-172 coastal freighter.

FS-240 coastal freighter.

Australian-type coastal freighters used in New Guinea.

Y-P Army coastal tanker, length 180', gross tons 630, engine 2 6-cyl dies/480 hp.

General Charles R. Krauthopf, unnumbered LT-size tug.

LT-454 oceangoing steel-hulled tug, 143' in length, Diesel-electric engine 1,500 HP.

State of Virginia (ex-Chesapeake Bay steamer), bareboat-chartered troopship, September 1942. Length 320', gross tons 1,783, engine recip/2,850 hp.

USAT *Kilauea* being decommissioned in Hawaii, September 1945.

The 1,362-ton USAT *Taku* served in Alaska before and during World War II. In 1942 at Yakutat, she towed the burning USAT *Clevedon* out of the harbor before that ship exploded. (U.S. Army Military History Institute)

Southern Seas (ex-*Lyndonia*). Once a luxury 1920s yacht, she served as the station ship for Pan American Airways in New Caledonia during 1940–41 before being acquired by the Army Corps of Engineers. After being put aground in 1942, she was salvaged by the Navy who operated her until she was wrecked in a typhoon in 1945.

Chapter 7
U.S. Coast Guard-Manned
Vessels in World War II

The Coast Guard's participation in amphibious activity during World War II was perhaps the most important war-related job the service performed. Incredibly, the Coast Guard fully manned 351 naval ships, including 76 LSTs (Landing Ship, Tank), 21 cargo and attack-cargo ships, 75 frigates, and 31 transports. In addition, the Coast Guard manned more than 800 cutters and 288 ships for the U.S. Army, as well as thousands of amphibious-type assault craft.

In the ships and craft of the amphibious forces, the Coast Guard discharged its most important role during the war—getting the men to the beaches and providing support. The largest Coast Guard-manned ships were the transports, and they played a vital role in landing operations. Just as vital, and generally overlooked, was the absolutely critical small-craft operations. The LCVPs (Landing Craft, Vehicle Personnel), LCMs (Landing Craft, Mechanized), Higgins Boats, LVTs (Landing Vehicle, Tracked) and others carried assault troops from the offshore transports and brought in reinforcements and supplies.

Principal sources for this chapter are three publications of the Office of the Coast Guard Historian: Robert M. Browning Jr., "The Coast Guard and the Pacific War" (1995); Robert Erwin Johnson, "Coast Guard-Manned Naval Vessels in World War II" (1993); and Robert L. Scheina, "The Coast Guard at War" (1987); and Winn B. Frank, "Farewell to the Troopship," *Naval History* (January/February 1997).

The handling of these small craft in the surf is a specialized skill, and it was not common among men in the Navy. Not so for men in the Coast Guard. Many of the coxswains had learned this skill from handling boats in the surf at lifesaving stations. In fact, Coast Guard coxswains from lifesaving stations were the most seasoned smallboat handlers in government service.

As only experienced men could successfully maneuver landing craft through strong currents, reefs, sand bars and heavy surf, their contributions to amphibious operations is immeasurable. This experience was particularly important during the training exercises before the early amphibious operations. The Coast Guard's "surfmen" acted as mentors to the Navy coxswains trying to learn the nuances of controlling smallboats in the surf.

Coast Guard Participation in the Solomons Campaigns

Guadalcanal.　On September 27, 1942, a group of diminutive landing craft sped toward the beaches of Guadalcanal. Huddled on shore, and fighting for their lives, were about 500 men of Colonel Lewis B. "Chesty" Puller's 1st Battalion, 7th Marines.

Earlier that day, the same group of landing craft had put the Marines on the beach; now they were returning to extract them. As the LCVPs and LCMs reached the shore, Coast Guard Signalman 1st Class Douglas Munro steered his LCVP between the evacuating Marines and the Japanese. By interposing his craft between the men on the beach and the enemy, Munro allowed the landing craft to safely evacuate all the Marines, including the wounded.

As the last men climbed aboard, Munro steered his craft away from the beach. When almost clear, Japanese gunfire struck Munro and killed him instantly. Munro was posthumously awarded the Medal of Honor. Given the Coast Guard's lifesaving tradition and the tremendous part the Coast Guard played during World War II, it is fitting that the Coast Guard's only Medal of Honor winner was not only involved with a rescue but also an amphibious operation.

The Coast Guard's first major participation in the Pacific war was at Guadalcanal and Tulagi, the first major Allied offensive of the war. Here the service played an important part in the island landings. Nineteen of the 23 naval transports attached to the campaign's task force were either manned by the Coast Guard or carried Coast Guard members. The Coast Guard's primary role at Guadalcanal, and in almost every subsequent campaign, was to facilitate the landing of troops and supplies.

The Coast Guard continued its supporting role as the Allies moved north and west from Guadalcanal. In June and July 1943, the Army and Marines made landings at several [Central Solomons] points on Rendova, New Georgia, and Vangunu islands. Five transports with partial Coast Guard crews participated in the month-long operation.

Vella Lavella.   Vella Lavella, just 40 miles from New Georgia, was the next link in the chain to be attacked. It lay on the other side of the fortified and well-garrisoned island of Kolombangara. In a tactic repeated throughout the war, the Americans bypassed Kolombangara and landed on Vella Lavella.

On August 15, the partially-manned Coast Guard LST-334 and the fully-manned LST-167 participated in the landings. For weeks both assisted with the supply of the troops ashore.

On September 24, LST-167 departed Guadalcanal and beached at Ruravai, Vella Lavella. Three Japanese dive-bombers appeared as the last piece of equipment rolled off the ship. The LST's 20 anti-aircraft guns blazed away at the three planes as they rolled into their attack. The planes released their bombs and as they pulled out of their dive, one burst into flame and another began trailing smoke.

Despite accurate and intense anti-aircraft fire, two bombs struck LST-167. One penetrated the main deck, exploded, and the blast blew through the side of the ship. A second also went through the main deck and exploded on the tank deck, setting fire to 1,000 gallons of gasoline and 250 drums of oil that had yet to be unloaded.

The explosions caused an intense and lethal fire and forced most of the crew to abandon ship. Two officers and eight men died in the attack and an additional five men were listed as missing. It took a week for American and New Zealand troops to secure Vella Lavella.

Bougainville Island.   Bougainville Island, 75 miles northwest of Vella Lavella and the most northwestern of the Solomon Island chain, was the Allies' next objective. The goal was to secure a portion of the island and build a base to strike at the Japanese stronghold of Rabaul. On October 31, the amphibious forces assembled off Guadalcanal. Nine of the 11 transports attached to the operation had Coast Guardsmen aboard. The initial landing force consisted of more than 14,000 men.

The Coast Guard-manned *Hunter Liggett* (APA-14) served as the flagship of the amphibious forces and carried more than 1,800 men. On November 1, the invasion force arrived off the island and the boats of the transports went into the water with incredible efficiency.

The *Hunter Liggett* led the transport column and opened fire on Cape Torokina with its 3-inch guns. With virtually no confusion, the first wave hit the beach about 40 minutes after the transports arrived. In Empress Augusta Bay nearly 8,000 Marines went ashore in the first wave. Against light opposition, the men landed on 12 predetermined beaches that stretched for more than four miles. The steep beaches, combined with moderate surf, caused nearly 90 landing craft to broach or swamp. Over a period of a couple of weeks more than 33,000 men landed and 23,000 tons of supplies went ashore. Coast Guard-manned LSTs helped move supplies ashore and evacuate the wounded. By the end of the year the island was virtually in Allied hands.

Coast Guard-Manned Vessels

Coast Guardsmen manned both combatant and non-combatant naval vessels. Some combatants never fired an offensive shot in anger whereas many non-combatants were ordered into harm's way with relatively little defensive fire power.

Non-Combatants

AP Transports.   The first three transports to be commissioned in 1941, the USS *Leonard Wood* (AP-25), USS *Joseph T. Dickman* (AP-26) and USS *Hunter Liggett* (AP-27), were turbine-powered, 535-footers of

World War I design, while the USS *Wakefield* (AP-21) had been launched as the liner *Manhattan* in 1931. At 705 feet, the *Wakefield*, commissioned in June 1941, was the largest ship ever manned by the Coast Guard and one of the fastest. Geared turbines drove it at 20 knots sustained speed.

All immediately began naval training. Active service for the *Wood, Dickman* and *Wakefield* came during the autumn of 1941 when, together with three Navy-manned transports, they embarked some 20,000 British troops at Halifax, Nova Scotia, for transportation to the Near East by way of the Cape of Good Hope.

Arriving at Cape Town on December 8, they were diverted to Bombay and Singapore because of Japan's belligerence. The *Wakefield* had discharged its troops at Singapore and was refueling there on January 30, 1942, when Japanese bombers attacked waterfront facilities. A bomb exploded in its sick bay, killing 5 men and wounding 15; nonetheless, the ship embarked approximately 500 women and children and took them to Bombay where the ship was repaired sufficiently to steam to New York. Upon their return to the United States, the *Wood* and the *Dickman* underwent further conversion to enable them to conduct assault landings.

The *Liggett* was similarly refitted, but the *Wakefield* was apparently thought unsuitable for this purpose, so it did not receive the extra davits for small landing craft that distinguished the vessels reclassified as attack transports (APA) in 1943.

The *Liggett* continued to support the advance in the Solomon Islands, ending its combat service with the Bougainville invasion in November 1943. The *Liggett* then ferried battle casualties to San Francisco and, after overhaul, spent the remainder of the war as an amphibious-training ship operating out of San Diego.

The *Wood* and the *Dickman* had longer combat careers. Both had important roles in Operation Torch landing troops in the vicinity of Casablanca, Morocco, in November 1942, and in the Sicily invasion in July 1943.

The *Wakefield* was almost lost to fire in September 1942 while in a New York-bound convoy. Naval escorts removed her passengers and crew and placed a salvage detail aboard. Towed to Halifax, she was declared a constructive total loss, but was completely rebuilt in Boston and recommissioned by a Coast Guard crew in February 1944. The *Wakefield* spent the remainder of the war transporting troops in the Atlantic and Pacific theaters. (See Table I for other AP vessels manned by the Coast Guard.)

Table I, Coast Guard-Manned Vessels

P2-SE2-R1

Maritime Administration Design (Admiral Type)

Length:	608 feet
Beam:	75.5 feet
Speed:	19 knots
Troops:	4,650–5,000

Admiral W.L. Capps (AP-121)

Admiral E.W. Eberle (AP-123)

Admiral C. F. Hughes (AP-124)

Admiral H.T. Mayo (AP-125)

P2-S2-R2

Maritime Administration Design (General Type)

Length:	622.5 feet OA
Beam:	75.5 feet
Speed:	20.6 knots
Troops:	Approximately 5,500

General William Mitchell (AP-114)

General George M. Randall (AP-115)

General M.C. Meigs (AP-116)

General W.H. Gordon (AP-117)

General W. P. Richardson (AP-118)

General William Weigel (AP-119)

General J. C. Breckinridge (AP-176)

C4-S-A1

Length:	523 feet
Beam:	71 feet
Speed:	17 knots
Troops:	3,000–3,800

General R.L. Howze (AP-134)

General W.M. Black (AP-135)

General H.L. Scott (AP-136)

General A.W. Greely (AP-141)

General C.H. Muir (AP-142)

General H.B. Freeman (AP-143)

General H.F. Hodges (AP-144)

General A.W. Brewster (AP-155)

General D.E. Aultman (AP-156)

Source: L. A. Sawyer and W. H. Mitchell, *From America to United States* (London: World Ship Society, 1979); Arnold Kludas, *Great Passenger Ships of the World* (Wellington: Patrick Stephens, 1977).

The APs in Table I performed a very valuable logistical service but were never intended to engage in combat. All were commissioned in 1944 or 1945; most had busy careers, crossing the oceans repeatedly with thousands of troops embarked, often without escort because their speed made it difficult for an enemy submarine to get a torpedo-firing solution.

The *General William Mitchell* (AP-114) may serve as an example of these ships' service: In some 20 months, this P-2 transport made 10 transoceanic voyages traversing more than 165,000 miles and carrying more than 80,000 passengers.

AK Cargo Ships.   The Coast Guard also provided crews for 16 Navy cargo ships; all but one, the smaller *Enceladus* (AK-80), were Liberty ships. These 11-knot cargo carriers served in the Pacific.

The USS *Alberio* (AK-90) and the USS *Eridanus* (AK-92) made repeated [long haul] supply runs between San Francisco and the South Pacific. The others spent their entire wartime careers shuttling supplies and men among island bases. Some took part in invasions despite their auxiliary designation.

The USS *Serpens* (AK-92), veteran of 19 months of South and Southwest Pacific service, exploded and sank January 29, 1945, while loading depth charges in Lunga Roads off Guadalcanal. There were only two survivors from the 198 men of the crew who were aboard at the time. Fifty-seven members of an Army stevedore unit also died in the explosion. The commanding officer and seven others were ashore when their ship sank. The *Serpens* disaster, which was not attributed to enemy action, resulted in the Coast Guard's greatest loss of life incident in World War II.

AO Tankers.   Eighteen gasoline tankers, most of which were commissioned in 1944, were manned by Coast Guardsmen. These small 220-foot, 10-knot ships supplied gasoline and lube oil to combatants operating in the Pacific

Combatants

APA Attack Transports.   Six APAs of the Maritime Commission C-3 type were manned by the Coast Guard upon commissioning in 1942 and 1943. One or more of these vessels participated in every major amphibious operation carried out by the United States during World War II.

As stated earlier, the Coast Guard was represented in the invasion of Guadalcanal in the Solomon Islands on August 7, 1942, by the USS *Hunter Liggett* (APA-27) and by landing craft crews in 18 of the 22 Navy-manned transports participating. The landings were enlivened by Japanese bombers, one of which crashed into a nearby transport, causing a fire that resulted in its loss. As partial recompense, the *Liggett's* gunners claimed four aircraft shot down. On the morning of August 9, the *Liggett* joined other vessels in picking up survivors from the heavy cruisers—three American and one Australian—sunk in the Battle of Savo Island.

The first of the smaller attack transports, the *Arthur Middleton* (APA-25), seemed likely to have the shortest career, for while landing troops at Amichitka in the Aleutians on January 12, 1943, it was forced aground by a williwaw. Finally refloated almost three months later, the *Middleton* was towed back to the United States for repairs. Thereafter, the ship redeemed itself by participating in seven amphibious operations: Tarawa, Kwajalein, Eniwetok, Saipan, Leyte, Lingayen Gulf and Okinawa.

Its sister ship, the *Samuel Chase* (APA-26), began with Operation Torch, putting troops ashore at Algiers, and followed with the Sicily, Salerno, Southern France, and Normandy invasions before going to the Pacific in 1945.

Four other Coast Guard-manned attack transports were ready for service early in 1944. One of them, the USS *Bayfield* (APA-33), landed its troops on Utah Beach, Normandy, on D-Day and spent 19 days there, sending supplies ashore and providing medical treatment for battle casualties. It had similar functions during the invasions of Southern France and then went to the Pacific to take part in the conquest of Iwo Jima.

The USS *Cambria* (APA-36) landed troops at Majuro in the Marshall Islands in January 1944, without opposition, and then at Eniwetok, Saipan,

Leyte, Lingayen Gulf and Okinawa. It emerged from all unscathed, unlike its sister, the USS *Cavalier* (APA-37), which began its combat career at Saipan, took part in the Leyte invasion, and while landing troops at Lingayen Gulf, sustained casualties from shore fire. She was supporting Army forces on Luzon when, on January 30, 1945, a Japanese torpedo crippled her. The *Cavalier* was towed to Leyte and then to Pearl Harbor. Hostilities ended before she was ready for sea again.

The USS *Callaway* (APA-35) landed troops of the 4th Marine Division at Roi-Namur, Kwajalein, and followed with the Emirau, Saipan, Palau and Leyte invasions. En route to Lingayen Gulf in January 1945, its task force came under repeated kamikaze attack, and one Japanese fighter crashed into the *Callaway's* superstructure just abaft the navigation bridge. Twenty Coast Guard sailors and 11 Navy men, members of the transport division commander's staff, died or suffered fatal injury in the resulting blaze, which rendered four landing craft useless. Nonetheless, the *Callaway* kept its place in the formation and landed troops on schedule. After repairs at Ulithi, the embarked troops were assigned to floating reserve at Iwo Jima, the attack transport's last invasion.

AKA Attack Cargo Ships.   The attack transports were not the only Coast Guard-manned participants in most assault landings. Beginning in 1943, five of the somewhat smaller C-2 type vessels were commissioned as attack cargo ships with Coast Guard crews.

Although these, too, transported soldiers and Marines, they devoted a greater portion of their space to the supplies and gear necessary to support the troops engaged in various amphibious operations. They spent more of their time between invasions shuttling supplies among island bases in their capacity as cargo ships.

Landing Ships and Craft.   While attack transports and attack cargo ships could carry troops to invasion shores, they had to debark troops into small landing craft to be ferried ashore. By early 1943, oceangoing vessels capable of beaching themselves and retracting after landing troops and equipment were leaving builders' yards in sufficient number that the Navy designated Coast Guard crews to help man units of the two larger types.

The LST (Landing Ship, Tank) and the LCI (Landing Craft Infantry) were unlike the larger amphibious-force ships. These unglamorous vessels never received names, just numbers, but their contribution to the Allied offensives in almost every theater of operations was invaluable.

Initially, the Coast Guard was asked to provide crews for 61 LSTs, flat-bottomed ships, 328 feet, fitted with ballast tanks that could be pumped out to reduce their draft when beaching with a bow ramp that opened so that vehicles could be driven off the tank deck.

The LCIs were 160-foot vessels with a ramp on each side of the bow that could be lowered to permit infantrymen to debark after beaching. Faster and more maneuverable than the LSTs, they were uncomfortable at sea with almost 200 soldiers aboard.

LST participation in an invasion was rarely the simple beaching, landing of equipment and men, and retracting. Invasion convoys were often subjected to air attack while in passage, and after an LST's initial beaching, it was sometimes ordered to pull alongside a larger vessel offshore to embark more cargo or troops, or both, to be landed on the beach. This sequence was often repeated a number of times in the course of a single amphibious operation.

In addition, beaching on coral reefs in the Pacific was likely to be especially tricky, because the landing ship might find itself impaled on a coral head when it came time to retract. For example, the Coast Guard-manned LST-203 had to be abandoned after broaching on a coral reef in the Ellice Islands, October 1, 1943.

Also, two other Coast Guard LSTs were lost: LST-69 was one of six destroyed by explosion and fire while loading ammunition in Pearl Harbor, May 21, 1944. None of its crew died in the catastrophe, but 13 were seriously injured. Japanese bombers damaged LST-167 irreparably during the Vella Lavella invasion September 25, 1943. The latter's casualty list—7 men killed, 23 wounded, of whom 3 died of their wounds, and 5 men missing—was the largest suffered by a Coast Guard-manned landing ship or craft.

The Coast Guard-manned bobtail flotilla of 24 LCIs received its baptism of fire in the Sicily invasion, July 9, 1943.

On LCI-90, eight men were burned seriously, one fatally, when a kamikaze crashed into the conning station off Okinawa, June 13, 1945, but the ship survived, making off under its own power.

Escort Duty

Since its cutters had been serving as convoy escorts almost from the beginning of America's involvement in World War II, it was to be expected that the Coast Guard would provide crews for some of the many escort vessels being built for the Navy during the war.

Corvettes.   First of these were eight corvettes, 208-foot vessels built in Canada and commissioned between November 1942 and August 1943. All were principally employed escorting coastal convoys between New York and Guantanamo Bay, Cuba.

Destroyer Escorts.   Meanwhile, the Navy had begun a major program of destroyer-escort building, which ultimately produced some 500 ships. Thirty of these DEs, all of the 306-foot-long, Fairbanks Morse-diesel type with reduction gears, were commissioned by Coast Guard crews during the autumn of 1943. Following shakedown cruises and antisubmarine-warfare training, all were assigned to transatlantic-escort duty, taking convoys from the American East Coast to ports in the United Kingdom and to the Mediterranean.

While the threat of U-boats and, to a lesser degree, air attacks posed the greatest dangers, the sea could also be considered an enemy. Sea conditions in the North Atlantic during the winter were among the most severe encountered anywhere, and the DEs were notoriously "lively" in a seaway.

"I never questioned the seaworthiness of those ships (after the first winter storm)," said the CO of the *Pettit* (DE-253). "I think everyone on board, however, wondered if they could hang in, or literally hold on, for the 14-day trips." Hold on they did, while escorting 24 convoys across the Atlantic.

Most of the Coast Guard-manned DEs continued to escort convoys to and from Europe or Africa until the European war ended in May 1945. Then, after overhaul and further training, 23 of the ships were ordered to the Pacific. However , only the 6 sent to Adak in the Aleutians had any opportunity for active service before Japan's surrender; they escorted convoys in the North Pacific and served with the 9th Fleet in its campaign against the Kurile Islands.

Frigates.   The insatiable demand for antisubmarine vessels in 1942 led the Navy to utilize merchant shipyards for their construction. Shipyards in California and on the Great Lakes received contracts for 69 of these ships in 1942; ultimately, 96 were built, 21 of which were transferred to the Royal Navy. They were laid down as gunboats (PG) and later redesignated frigates (PF). The Coast Guard was made responsible for manning 75 of them.

Eighteen of the California-built frigates reported to the 7th Fleet in the Southwest Pacific in 1944, where they were joined by four of their Great Lakes sisters. For the remainder of the year, they escorted convoys, made antisubmarine patrols, and occasionally provided fire support for American and Australian troops advancing westward along the northern coast of New Guinea.

PCs and SCs.   Smallest of the Navy's escort vessels manned by Coast Guardsmen were 10 submarine chasers—four of the 173-foot steel PCs and six of the 110-foot wooden SCs. Despite their size, several had more impressive records than many of the larger vessels.

PC-469 engaged U-154 in a five-hour battle in the Caribbean Sea in November 1942, damaging the enemy and emerging unscathed. It went on to serve as control vessel at Iwo Jima and Okinawa, sinking two suicide motor boats and driving off a third in May 1945, and shooting down two Japanese aircraft six weeks later.

PC-545 and PC-556 took part in the Sicily and Southern France invasions, and the first was at Anzio as well, sinking an enemy motor torpedo boat.

Summary

- Coast Guard-manned ships sank 11 enemy submarines and Coast Guard aircraft sank one. Most of these U-boats were destroyed in 1942 when the issue of who would win the Battle of the Atlantic was still very much in doubt.
- Coast Guard personnel manned amphibious ships and craft from the largest troop transports to the smallest attack craft. These landed Army and Marine forces in every important invasion in North Africa, Italy, France and the Pacific. Also, due to their experience in handling surfboats, Coast Guardsmen helped train members of the other military services in the use of amphibious craft.
- Coast Guardsmen patrolled beaches and docks, on foot, on horseback, in vehicles, with and without dogs, as a major part of the nation's anti-sabotage effort. Once this threat abated, the Coast Guard manned 351 naval ships and craft and 288 Army vessels.
- Coast Guard cutters, boats and aircraft rescued more than 1,500 survivors of torpedo attacks in areas adjacent to the United States. Cutters on escort duty saved another 1,000, and more than 1,500 were rescued during the Normandy operation by sixty 83-foot patrol craft specifically assigned for that duty.
- During World War II, 231,000 men and 10,000 women served in the Coast Guard. Of these, 1,918 died, a third losing their lives in action. The Service sustained its first casualties on December 8, 1941 when the *Leonard Wood* (AP-25) was bombed by Japanese aircraft at Singapore. One Coast Guardsman died as a prisoner of war, having been captured at Corregidor. Almost 2,000 Coast Guardsmen were decorated, one receiving the Congressional Medal of Honor, six the Navy Cross, and one the Distinguished Service Cross.
- The Coast Guard manned 351 naval vessels in the course of World War II, those serving numbering 48,622 at war's end.

The "surfmen" assigned to vessels manned by the Navy, to serve in landing craft and as mentors for landing craft crews while the Navy was learning the techniques of amphibious warfare, must not be forgotten. Their contribution to victory was second to none, far out of proportion to their numbers.

On January 1, 1946, the Coast Guard returned to the Treasury Department. Admiral Russell R. Waesche, the Coast Guard commandant, had hoped that U.S. Navy crews would replace Guard personnel aboard these ships when the Coast Guard was returned to Treasury Department control. The Navy, however, was facing its own demobilization problems, so the Coast Guardsmen ultimately decommissioned most of the vessels in which they were serving.

(Source: R. M. Browning Jr., "The Coast Guard and the Pacific War"; R. E. Johnson, "Coast Guard-Manned Naval Vessels in World War II"; R. L. Scheina, "The Coast Guard at War"; and W. B. Frank, "Farewell to the Troopship," *Naval History*.) ∎

U.S. Coast Guard landing craft practice invasion maneuvers in Chesapeake Bay. (U.S. Coast Guard)

U.S. Coast Guardsman directs traffic on beach at Guadalcanal as landing craft unload supplies and equipment from AKs. (U.S. Coast Guard)

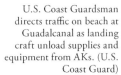

Coast Guardsmen and Marines proudly display a Japanese flag they picked up during the capture of Engebi Island, Eniwetok Atoll, 19 February 1944. (National Archives)

Bombs for Tokyo guarded by U.S. Coast Guard patrol. (U.S. Coast Guard)

U.S. Coast Guardsmen patrol the docks to discourage would-be saboteurs during World War II. (U.S. Coast Guard)

Part IV

IN CONCLUSION

"The strategical concepts of 'offshore toeholds' and 'leapfrogging'
would be employed in upcoming operations."

*—Rear Admiral Richmond Kelly Turner, USN,
Commander Amphibious Task Force 62*

Chapter 8
Filling the Pipeline

Editor's note: The following summary of the "Big Lift" during World War II is excerpted from a report prepared by Vice Admiral Emory Scott Land, USN, "The United States Merchant Marine at War: Report of the War Shipping Administrator," dated 15 January 1946, and submitted to President Harry S. Truman. It should be noted that the report covers all theaters of operation.

During World War II, the United States fighting team was made up of three major entities: the fighting forces overseas, the production army at home, and the link between them—the difference between victory and defeat—the United States Merchant Marine.

The United States Merchant Marine possessed the largest number of merchant ships in the Allies' pool of shipping and was the greatest single strategic factor in the defeat of the Axis powers. American sea power kept the Allies supplied with the raw materials and products essential to victory.

In the European theater, Germany launched a U-boat fleet to choke off supplies from Britain and Russia. The antisubmarine warfare carried on by British and Anglo-American navies forced Germany into a long war she could not sustain. The *coup de grace* was given by the combined air fleets and the Russian steamroller, both of which owed their power to the stream of supplies carried in American ships.

In the Pacific theater, the role of our Navy against Japan was reversed. It fought an offensive war and succeeded in closing Japan's sea lanes and sinking her merchant fleet while ours sailed in comparative security.

Our fighting forces were never knocked off an important beachhead, nor—thanks to the merchant fleet—did we fail to develop each landing with a steadily increased flow of supplies that enabled our armies to meet their objectives.

For the U.S. Army, the high point was on the beaches of Normandy and Okinawa; the Air Force, in the great sky battle over Regenberg; the U.S. Navy, in the Battle of Midway; and the U.S. Marine Corps, atop Mount Surabachi. For the Merchant Marine, the stuff of legends was the Murmansk run. The ships ran innumerable gauntlets of air, surface, and submarine attacks ranging around the globe, from the Red Sea and the Indian Ocean to the mid-Atlantic and the Mediterranean, and the kamikaze attacks in the Pacific. But none of these combined all elements of danger as did the Murmansk run.

The most direct route to Russia was through the Denmark Straits between Iceland and Greenland, around the North Cape of Norway and into Murmansk. Through icy, fog-bound seas, their flanks exposed to the dive bombers, surface raiders, and submarines moving out from the Nazi-held fjords of Norway, the slow gray convoys kept moving. Nor was there sanctuary at their destination, for every hour on the hour, the *Luftwaffe* blasted delays in the grim business of unloading the ships in the ice-cluttered harbor of Murmansk. Yet the cargoes were delivered. The Murmansk run exemplified the high price of victory.

Through the first part of 1943, casualties among the sea-going force were greater proportionately than in all branches of the armed services combined, except the U.S. Marine Corps. Unreported thousands of our seamen and officers were injured under attack or suffered the nightmare of waiting aboard boats and rafts for rescue. Of American merchant vessels over 1,000 gross tons, 733 were sunk. A total of 6,700 merchant seamen and officers were dead and missing; 581 were made prisoners of war.

The cold evaluation in dollars and cents of the cost of building and operating our wartime merchant fleet reached a grand total of more than $22,500,000,000.

The Cargo Lift

The final measure of accomplishment of the Merchant Marine during the war is the amount of cargo transported. Since the war had to be planned on the amount of shipping available within certain dates, fluctuations in cargo were an index to the progress of the war from Pearl Harbor to Tokyo Bay. The total dry cargo and bulk liquid shipments* rose rapidly from 44,117,000 tons in 1942, to 62,113,000 in 1943, 78,553,000 in 1944, and 83,469,000 in 1945. During the last year of the war, this meant an average rate of delivery of 8,500 tons of cargo every hour of every day and night.

The total cargo lift from the United States between December 7, 1941 and the capitulation of Japan was 268,252,000 long tons, of which 203,522,000 were dry cargo and 64,730,000 were petroleum products and other bulk liquids carried in tankers.* Approximately 75 percent was carried by ships of the WSA-controlled fleet.

Ships of America's merchant fleet also carried the great majority of the 7,129,907 Army personnel and 141,537 civilians moving overseas between December 7, 1941, and November 30, 1945, and the 4,060,883 Army personnel and 169,626 civilians returning to the United States within the same dates.

The Wartime Fleet

The unprecedented growth of the United States merchant fleet was the primary reason for the WSA's ability to meet the tonnage demands

---

*   Data not available on amount of bulk liquid cargo carried by WSA tankers for Army and Navy.

of the war. Upon America's entry, the fleet, augmented by foreign vessels acquired by negotiation, requisition, and seizure in American ports, totaled about 900 dry-cargo vessels of 6,700,000 deadweight tons and some 440 tankers of 5,150,000 deadweight tons. The curve rose rapidly. At the end of 1942, there were 1,639 ships in WSA operation; in 1943, 2,847; and in 1944, 3,744. By the end of the war with Japan, the WSA-controlled fleet numbered 4,221 with a deadweight tonnage of 44,940,000.*

The race between ship construction and sinkings by the enemy was won by the Allied convoy system and naval superiority in combating the submarine menace, and an unprecedented shipbuilding technique. WSA losses, including marine casualties during 1942, were equivalent to 39 percent of new construction in that year. This was reduced to 11 percent in 1943, less than 8 percent in 1944, and 4 percent in 1945.

What We Shipped and Where It Went

Cargo ranged in size from pins and ball bearings to locomotives and landing craft; from drugs, medicines, hospital supplies, and clothing to explosives and fire fighting equipment; from foodstuffs to agricultural machinery and Army tanks—the tools of destruction and construction, the means to help sustain the war overseas, the implements and materials that are basic to the support of civilian populations. Some of the commodities were stowed compactly in the holds of ships, others required space out of all proportion to their weight, and were carried on the decks of cargo vessels and tankers.

Planes, tanks, trucks, and other vehicles require enormous quantities of fuel and lubricants to keep them in operation. Exclusive of shipments for the Army and Navy, we sent overseas from January 1943 through August 1945, 18,907,089 tons of gasoline, 7,235,999 tons of gas oil, and more than 667,979 tons of lubricants. In all, petroleum and its products

---

*   For details on vessel types, see Chapter 1, "Ships for Victory." —Ed.

totaling some 35,109,145 tons comprised 99 percent of the total bulk liquid shipments; inedible oils and chemicals made up the remaining 326,204 tons.

Cargoes were carried across every ocean into practically all inhabited areas of the world, along many sea lanes never before used, to old established ports and to wartime destinations which were ports in name only. The distribution in 1944 indicates the proportion of dry cargo each major area received: 15 million tons to the United Kingdom and Continent of Europe; 13 million tons to the Pacific areas; 8 million to the Mediterranean area; 6 million to South American and the Caribbean; 5 million to the U.S.S.R., and 3 million to India and Ceylon.

The Big Customers

There were five major accounts: the Army, the Navy, the lend-lease program, civilian exports to Allied Nations, and shipments to Latin America and other countries. Imports included strategic materials for war industries and essentials for civilian use. Each of these programs was essential to winning the war, and the problem of meeting the cargo needs of each, without jeopardizing the other and with the amount of shipping available, was the principal task of the War Shipping Administration.

Aid To Our Allies

The gallant stand of Great Britain and Russia in the months before Pearl Harbor and in the early days of our participation was of incalculable value to the United States in gearing up its war machine. As the war proceeded, it was necessary to increase the flow of supplies and equipment. Vessels of various nations carried these lend-lease cargoes, but the bulk was transported overseas in WSA-controlled ships: in 1942, 39 percent of all shipments for lend-lease and civil requirements; in 1943, 53 percent; in 1944, 62 percent; and in the first ten months of 1945, 58 percent.

In 1943, WSA ships made 2,876 sailings with lend-lease supplies. Of the total, 2,267 sailings were for Great Britain, her colonies and dominions, 328 for Russia, and 281 for other lend-lease countries. The improvement in antisubmarine warfare was especially helpful. In 1942, an average of 12 percent of ships carrying lend-lease for Russia were sunk, principally along the dangerous Murmansk run, but by the end of 1943, barely one percent of such vessels were lost.

Although the principal function of the WSA in the lend-lease program was the delivery of war materials, there was another and highly important phase: the servicing, supplying, and repair of ships belonging to foreign governments who had lend-lease agreements with the United States, and the allocation of ships to replace their excessive war losses. The WSA transferred 509 vessels to serve under Allied flags. These were principally Liberty-type and prewar ships. Of the total, 341 went to the United Kingdom, 93 to Russia, 23 to Norway, 14 to Greece, 13 to France, 7 to Belgium, 6 to Netherlands, 6 to Poland, 4 to Chile, and 2 to China.

Latin America

Latin America's participation in the war further emphasized the economic and social ties between them and the United States. Dry cargo exports in WSA ships for both the lend-lease program and civilian commodities totaled 10,242,000 long tons in 1942, 16,221,000 in 1943, 16,485,000 in 1944, and an estimated 21,733,000 in 1945. Tanker exports in the same categories amounted to 4,246,000 in 1942, 6,370,000 in 1943, 13,874,000 in 1944, and an estimated 9,389,000 in 1945.

War Sinews From Abroad

To keep war production at peak efficiency, the Merchant Marine had to bring home essential raw materials in great amounts. Commodities were brought into the United States from every continent. Bauxite, copper, coffee, sugar, nitrates, manganese, and other essentials came from South American and Caribbean ports; burlap was brought back from India and Ceylon; wool from Australia; hides and skins, cocoa beans, sisal and henequen from

Africa; and chrome came from Turkey via the Red Sea and from North and Transpacific Russia.

The Big Lift

During the war years, the War Shipping Administration allocated as much as three-quarters of its tonnage to Army and Navy cargoes. The armed services were always the Number One customers of the Merchant Marine. The first two years of the war saw the buildup of the military powerhouses of Africa, the United Kingdom, and the South and Southwest Pacific. This process called for a steady stream of cargo ships. During 1942 and the early part of 1943, the WSA merchant fleet devoted 41 percent of its capacity to Army cargo and 13 percent to the Navy. This ratio changed slightly toward the end of 1943, when WSA ships were devoting 49 percent of their capacity to the Army and 10 percent to the Navy.

Invasion of the Mediterranean area was the first large-scale action engaged in by ships of the WSA fleet. Hundreds of merchant vessels were in the initial attacks on North Africa and the landings on Sicily. Seizure of these areas created another problem for the WSA operations staff. The campaigns of our armies in that area called for the diversion of a large fleet of merchant ships for initial attacks and required a sufficient number of vessels to maintain the stream of men and supplies moving in as the invasion developed. This withdrew from other world services a sizable proportion of our cargo fleet. Fortunately, success in North Africa came ahead of schedule and large numbers of ships again were available for multiple tasks in other oceans.

Toward the end of 1943, we built up in the British Isles the greatest invasion force ever assembled. The great convoys, some with as many as 167 ships, shuttled across the Atlantic bearing essential cargoes.

In the southwest Pacific area, the situation was different. The circuitous route necessary during the early days of the war to send supplies to General MacArthur in Australia greatly cut down the tonnage an individual vessel could deliver in a given period of time. Ships diverted to that area for shuttle runs between Australian ports and New Guinea and inter-island services were sometimes detained for months.

In 1944, 74 percent of WSA tonnage was allocated for the Army and Navy, compared with 59 percent so employed toward the end of 1943. Ships allocated to the Army alone comprised about 60 percent of the WSA fleet, while the dry-cargo tonnage allocated to the Navy amounted to 14 percent.

In 1944, the Allies took Sicily, went into the Italian boot, and hammered at the Casino gateway to Rome. The beaches at Anzio were occupied with substantial losses. General Eisenhower returned to England and opened wide the valve on the great flood of American troops and gear needed to build up overwhelming power for the assault on the Normandy coast. The vast war raging along the Russo-German front from the Baltic to the Black Sea called for more and more shipments of American war materiels for Russian armies.

And in the Far East, the tempo increased. At the start of the year, the incredibly difficult Burma campaign was in its opening phases, and General MacArthur established a firm hold on eastern New Guinea. On the eastern sea approaches to Japan, Admiral Nimitz began investment of the Marshall Islands. The long stretches of the Pacific were now American highroads to numerous powerful bases where supplies were assembled to attack the Philippines and the home islands of Japan. Our forces were successfully installed on the northern flank, the Aleutians. All of these movements needed steady maintenance of supplies by the merchant fleet.

By mid-1944, the war reached maximum fury.

By mid-1944, the war reached maximum fury. The greatest sea-borne invasion in history crossed the English Channel on June 6. In the van were 32 American merchant ships to be sunk off the beachhead to form a breakwater. They were manned by more than 1,000 merchant seamen and officers who volunteered for the hazardous duty. They sailed from England through mined waters, filed into position off the Normandy beach under severe shelling from German shore batteries, and were sunk by the crews to form the artificial harbor. Behind this breakwater, prefabricated units were towed to handle the subsequent debarkation of men and equipment.

Ten oceangoing tugs operated by the WSA and manned by merchant crews assisted in the famous MULBERRY operation by towing the harbor units into position. From D-day until the last tug departed the Channel area, they towed 182 units. This project stands as one of the most remarkable water-born engineering accomplishments of all time. Later, the English Channel was nicknamed by the merchant crews "Liberty Lane" because of the number of these cargo ships shuttling between England and France. In all, 150 American merchant vessels were operated by the WSA in this cross-Channel service.

By June 1944, in the Central Pacific, the Marianas were attacked and Saipan fell; Tinian and Guam in July; in the southwest Pacific, General MacArthur bypassed strong Japanese forces by the capture of Hollandia on New Guinea and was looking northward toward the Philippines. The second invasion of France from the south was mounted, and our forces raced up the Rhone Valley to join with those from the Normandy break-out.

The weight of shipping needed in the assault of western Europe was tremendous: on January 1, 1944, 1,970,000 deadweight tons were employed by the Army in the United Kingdom-Continent area. By September this had increased to 6,508,000 deadweight tons, largely in shuttle service. In the western Mediterranean, Army tonnage increased from 3,118,000 on July 1, to 5,658,000 on November 1, most of which had been built by the Maritime Commission since the war began.

In the latter part of the year, the full flood of shipping poured into the rapidly moving forward drives in the Central Pacific, into the Philippines, and to sustain the great battle of France and the Low Countries. By November, the port of Antwerp, vital to the supply of the northern armies, was in our possession. In the south, Toulon and Marseilles were used while facilities in Antwerp were improved, even in the face of a constant rain of V-bombs. By the end of the year, interior lines of supply connecting the Allied armies with the ports were functioning, and merchant vessels were discharging materiel for use in the final assault across the Rhine into Germany itself.

Bombers now mounted the assault on the Japanese homeland from bases on the Marianas, and the signal was given by the combined Chiefs of Staff to General MacArthur to hit the Philippines at Leyte. The buildup of his supplies and the seaborne invasion of that island was made possible by the thousands of tons of war materiel carried by hundreds of WSA cargo ships. By the end of 1944 American invasion fleets steamed for Manila.

As this great expansion of power was taking place in the Pacific during the year, more and more WSA tonnage was allocated for the Army and Navy. On January 1, 1944, 2,301,000 tons; on December 31, this had increased to 4,526,000 tons. Tonnage placed at the disposal of naval needs was primarily for use in the central Pacific where, from January 1 to December 31, allocations were increased from 570,000 deadweight tons to 2,629,000 tons.

The year 1945 saw our maritime power at its peak. The nation's gigantic wartime shipbuilding program and the development of convoy operations, the perfection of antisubmarine warfare devices and techniques, and the training of Navy personnel to man them, and to serve aboard the merchant vessels as gun crews, all combined to put overwhelming strength into overseas operations of the United States Merchant Marine. By June, the WSA-controlled fleet numbered 4,125 Vessels, with a deadweight tonnage of 44,435,000. Ship sinkings, which during the years 1943 and 1944 showed a steady decline, were consistently lower during that period. The terrific power shown by our Navy in the Pacific cleared the sea approaches to our forward-moving forces.

With the sustained airborne blows at Japan from the hard-won fields on Okinawa and Iwo Jima, and the hammering the enemy received from the great naval fleets ranging the shores of her home islands, followed by the atomic bombing of Hiroshima and Nagasaki, the WSA made ships ready for the occupation forces and materiel taken by General MacArthur into the beaten enemy territory.

The men in command of the armed services had high praise for the Merchant Marine:

> Fleet Admiral Ernest J. King, Commander in Chief of the United States Navy and Chief of Naval Operations:
>
> "During the past three-and-one-half years, the Navy has been dependent upon the Merchant Marine to supply our far-flung fleet and bases. Without this support, the Navy could not have accomplished its mission. Consequently, it is fitting that the Merchant Marine share in our success as it shared in our trials.
>
> "The Merchant Marine is a strong bulwark of national defense in peace and war, and a buttress to a sound national economy. A large Merchant Marine is not only an important national resource; it is, in being, an integral part of the country's armed might during time of crisis. During World War II, this precept has been proven.
>
> "As the Merchant Marine returns to its peacetime pursuits, I take pleasure in expressing the Navy's heartfelt thanks to you and through you to the officers and men of the Merchant Marine for their magnificent support during World War II. All hands can feel a pride of accomplishment in a job well done.
>
> "We wish the Merchant Marine every success during the years ahead and sincerely hope that it remains strong and continues as a vital and integral part of our national economy and defense."
>
> General Dwight D. Eisenhower, Supreme Commander of the Allied Expeditionary Force, ETO:
>
> "Every man in this Allied command is quick to express his admiration for the loyalty, courage, and fortitude of the officers and men of the Merchant Marine.

We count upon their efficiency and their utter devotion to duty as we do our own; they have never failed us yet and in all the struggles yet to come we know that they will never be deterred by any danger, hardship, or privation. When the final victory is ours there is no organization that will share its credit more deservedly than the Merchant Marine."

General Douglas MacArthur, Commander, Allied Forces SowesPac:

"I wish to commend to you the valor of the merchant seamen participating with us in the liberation of the Philippines. With us they have shared the heaviest enemy fire. On this island I have ordered them off their ships and into fox holes when their ships became untenable targets of attack. At our side they have suffered in bloodshed and death. The high caliber of efficiency and the courage they displayed in their part of the invasion of the Philippines marked their conduct, throughout the entire campaign in the southwest Pacific area. They have contributed tremendously to our success. I hold no branch in higher esteem than the Merchant Marine services."

The War's End

The end of hostilities did not mean the cessation of WSA activities. The final month of 1945 found the merchant fleet operating at a rate never before reached in wartime. During December 1945, there were 1,200 sailings as against 800 in the busiest months of the war. The reasons were the final liquidation of our wartime military operations and the increase of our responsibilities to provide relief for liberated nations.

Even before V-E day, work began on converting cargo ships and preparing passenger vessels to bring home the men of the Armed Services.

A total of 546 such vessels comprised the WSA troop return fleet. Ninety-seven Victory ships were converted to troop carriers with a capacity of 1,500 men each. More than 300 converted Liberty ships were in the fleet, in addition to numerous large converted dry-cargo vessels.

This fleet, operated in a common pool of WSA, Army, and Navy vessels, by December 1 brought back about three-and-a-half million men from overseas. From V-E day to V-J day, practically the whole troop-return responsibility was on the WSA, which accomplished better than 85 percent of the troop return up to September 1, 1945. The remainder was for the most part carried on British vessels, including the liners *Queen Mary* and *Queen Elizabeth*.

From V-E day on, the number of ships sailing with relief cargoes of food, clothing, medical supplies and other supplies increased. A great number of these carried goods under the United Nations Relief and Rehabilitation Administration program. Others were destined for Allied military authorities in charge of relief for civilian populations in certain areas. To a large extend, the relief program filled shipping space previously used for lend-lease cargoes.

(Source: Land, "The United States Merchant Marine at War: Report of the War Shipping Administrator," 1–32, 77–78.) ∎

Convoy of cargo ships, circa 1943. (Naval Historical Center)

Action in the North Atlantic, circa 1942. (Naval Historical Center)

Convoy in heavy weather. (National Archives)

A Merchantman steams through stormy north Atlantic seas, as seen from the escort USS *Greer* (DD-145), June 1943. (Naval Historical Center)

U.S. Merchant tanker *Camden* sinking under tow on 10 October 1942. On 4 October 1942, the *Camden* was attacked by the Japanese sub I-25 off Coos Bay, Oregon. (Naval Historical Center)

Convoy. (National Archives)

Chapter 9
Lessons Learned

The Amphibious forces learned a good deal from the August 1942 landings at Tulagi and Guadalcanal, and they continued to learn a great deal during the long, hard six months' struggle to maintain logistic support for these two important toe-holds in the Southern Solomons. By January 1943, marked changes had occurred in their thinking about the techniques of support through and over a beachhead, and the new amphibious craft which were finally becoming available.

RAdm G. K. Fort, Commander Landing Craft Flotillas, submitted a report to RAdm Richmond Kelly Turner following the 1943 Central Solomons New Georgia campaign highlighting further lessons learned in logistics support, night landings, shore party bottlenecks, force requirements, and several other areas. Capt G. B. Carter, ComLSTFLOT 5, made additional recommendations based on later combat experience in the Northern Solomons.

Space limitations prohibit a full discussion on the many lessons learned by the crews of the pioneer amphibious landing ships and craft but, suffice it to say, they paid off in spades during the remaining two years of the war. However, please know that the lessons learned that follow cover all areas of

Excerpted from William L. McGee, *The Solomons Campaigns, 1942–1943—From Guadalcanal to Bougainville, Pacific War Turning Point* (2002).

an amphibious operation—not just the new landing craft—a "checklist," if you will, that includes previously mentioned lessons as well.

Logistics Support

The Navy had been much condemned for its inadequacies in logistic support during the first months of WATCHTOWER. Unlike the Guadalcanal Operation, there were 1st, 2nd, 3rd and 4th Echelon logistic support movements set up for the TOENAILS Operation, and a dozen support echelons had sailed in the first 15 days.

RAdm G. K. Fort, Commander Landing Craft Flotillas, made a report to RAdm Turner on the performance of landing craft in which was written these heartening words:

> It appears for the first time in modern warfare that supplies have arrived with or immediately behind the Assault Troops. A good example is the airstrip at Segi. There, bulldozers were clearing a strip forty (40) minutes after the first echelon LST had beached. The flow of supplies to the front has been greater than the Advanced Bases could handle. All have requested that the flow of supplies be reduced.*

Enemy action, groundings, and modified plans had forced many changes in the ships and landing craft originally designated for specific supporting echelon tasks. The important lesson from all this was that in order for logistic support to be delivered by amphibious ships and craft on time, a large excess of ships and craft is required over the computed space requirements for the total of personnel and tons of equipment to be moved.

For the Central Solomons TOENAILS Operation, 36 LSTs, 36 LCIs, 72 LCTs and 28 APcs had been scheduled to be available. Fortunately, plans

---

* Commander Landing Craft Flotillas to COMPHIBFORSOPAC FE 25-2/A3/Ser 002 of 13 Jul. 1943, subj: Performance of Landing Craft.

were not based on this number as only 12 LSTs, 26 LCIs, 43 LCTs and 16 APcs were in the area on 30 June 1943. This number was barely adequate.*

CINCPAC had preferred that the large transports not be employed for the assault landings in TOENAILS because of the lack of strong air cover over the landing areas and a decent respect for Japanese air capabilities.

The Bougainville Operations again demonstrated that the over-water movement and landing of the first echelon of troops is only the initial step in a continuous amphibious series, all of which are integral parts of the same venture. Success of the venture depends upon the ability to deliver safely not only the first, but also the succeeding echelons of troops, engineers, ancillary units, equipment and operating and upkeep supplies and replacements. The aggregate of personnel and cargo for the later movements is far greater than that carried initially. Each movement requires protection, and losses in transit from the logistic bases to the combat position must be kept low enough to be acceptable. It is particularly true that when small vessels are used, an uninterrupted stream of them must be maintained.

The first movement for the seizure of a position, the exploitation on shore of that position, and the long series of succeeding movements of troops and materiel, together form a single operation. All parts must be accomplished under satisfactory condition if the whole operation is to be successful.

Landing Ships and Craft

The personal worry bug to be overcome by every amphibian, coxswain, officer-in-charge, or commanding officer, was the coral shelf and the many coral heads off the few and generally narrow beaches. In due time, these coral heads would be dynamited. The beaches would be augmented with landing piers, which would be coconut log bulkheads backed up by crushed coral. But the first few days in poorly or uncharted waters were real tests.

---

* CTG 31.1 Loading Order 14-43, 12 Jul. 1943.

When the first surge of TOENAILS was over, it was apparent from the reports that both landing ships and craft had turned in better than satisfactory performances. RAdm Fort:

> The LCTs had been the most useful of all types. However, low speed (6 knots) limits their daily staging in combat areas to about 100 miles per night. . . .It is still advisable to have them underway only at night. Against a head sea, their speed is greatly reduced, sometimes to two knots. . . .The crews and officers have been standing up well in spite of operating two out of every three days.
>
> Some LSTs have transported 400 men each for short periods. . . .LCTs have carried as many as 250 men overnight, but in exposed positions. . . .
>
> The LCIs carry about 170 combat troops. . . .For unopposed short runs of a few hours, 350 men have been transported on a single LCI. . . .They are ideal for night landings on good beaches. . . .
>
> The APcs, besides having proved useful as escorts, have been used to transport small groups of men. . . .*

Captain Grayson B. Carter, ComLSTFLOT 5, made several innovative recommendations following the New Georgia campaign. Here are two of the most successful:

> Employ trailers to roll on/roll off cargo such as ammo, boxed rations, and fuel to expedite the unloading process on unfriendly beaches. Pending the procurement of the perfect trailer, Cmdr Cutler [ComLSTGRP 13] obtained from the United

---

* Commander Landing Craft Flotillas, letter, 13 Jul. 1943.

States Army depot at Noumea, and brought up to Guadalcanal 22 October some 85 vehicles that would fit into LSTs without too many 'holidays.' One LST would take in 33 of these jury-rigged trailers, as Carter called them, and that gave the LST a relatively large pay load. Trailers made for quick turnaround as well, for they could be parked ashore until the soldiers got around to unloading them, and could be picked up empty later. Trailer loading was first tried in the second echelon to Bougainville with limited success; but after much practice, and with an improved model designed for such work, it became doctrine for sending LSTs into beaches where air attack was expected.

Increase the original LST armament by about 200%; e.g., replace the 3"/50 and single 40-mm guns with 40-mm quad mounts, power driven and director-controlled, supplemented with more 20-mm guns. Experience in the New Georgia campaign showed that an LST needed more armament than her original complement to repel air attack, and Carter's flotilla went up to Bougainville loaded for bear, with three to five 40-mm, eleven to eighteen 20-mm, four to eighteen .50-caliber machine guns and one three-inch 50-caliber gun apiece.

Transports and Cargo Ships

The first lesson the transport boat crews learned at Guadalcanal was that they were going to have to get used to being shot at. One coxswain reported:

> After getting the ramp up, we backed down as far as we could so as to keep the ramp between us and the line of fire. When we started around a little knoll, which was lined with trees, we were fired at

> from these trees. We spotted the flash from a gun up
> in one of these trees. I picked up the Marine's Risen
> gun and blasted the flash and the Jap fired again and I
> got a better bead on him, and fired again and he came
> tumbling down like a bird.*

The second lesson the big ship to shore "heavies" learned at Guadalcanal was they just had to have more people in their ships and craft. These amphibious ships did not have enough officers and men to continuously unload over a 72-hour period. It was both good and bad fortune that the Japanese made three air raids and threatened another during the first 48 hours of unloading. For these gave many of the boat crews a breathing spell, and also supplied an urgency to the need to get the unloading job done.

Beach Troubles

Another lesson the amphibians learned at Guadalcanal was that the logistic support of the troops over the beaches in the first 24 hours had to be both beefed up and streamlined. The captain of the *Hunter Liggett* reported:

> After dark conditions reached a complete impasse. It
> is estimated that nearly one hundred boats lay gunwale to
> gunwale on the beach, while another fifty boats waited,
> some of these, up to six hours for a chance to land. . . .
> No small share of the blame for this delay, which
> prolonged by nearly twenty-four hours the period when
> the ships lay in these dangerous waters, would seem to
> rest with the Marine Corps personnel and organization.
> The Pioneers, whose function it was to unload the boats
> and keep the beach clear, were far too few in numbers.

---

* USS *President Adams* Action Report, 25 Aug. 1942, Encl. (A), Report of G.I.D. Sporhase, BM2c.

As a result much of this work was accomplished by boat crews, and stores which they landed at low water were frequently damaged or destroyed by the rising tide before the Pioneers removed them to safety.*

Over at Tulagi, according to the transport *Neville's* War Diary:

It was not until about midnight that the first word had been received to send the important food rations and ammunition ashore and from then till daylight it went slowly due to insufficient personnel to unload and conflicting orders as to where to land the stores.†

Not all the beach trouble was caused by inadequate Pioneer parties. Often it was the transports and cargo ships overloading the landing craft:

A considerable number of landing boats, chiefly ramp lighters, were stranded on the beach, adding to the confusion. These ramps [boats] had been loaded too deeply by the head, and could not be driven far enough up on their particular beach to keep from filling and drowning the engine when the ramp was lowered.‡

RAdm Turner after the landing wrote:

There were two primary reasons for failure to completely unload. First the vast amount of unnecessary impediments taken, and second a failure on the part of the 1st Division to provide adequate and well organized unloading details at the beach.

---

*   *Hunter Liggett* War Diary, 7 Aug. 1942.
†   *Neville* War Diary, 9 Aug. 1942.
‡   *Hunter Liggett* War Diary, 8 Aug. 1942.

The Shore Party had been much condemned for its inadequacies on 7 August 1942 at Guadalcanal. Much effort had gone into making more definite its duties and increasing the number of warm bodies to carry out these duties during the next three months. On 16 October 1942, COMPHIBFORSOPAC issued a new "trial operating procedure" for the Shore Party. But in November 1942, the Commander Transport Division Eight still wrote: "The bottleneck of unloading is still the Shore Party. . . .At Aola Bay, the Shore Party was 800 strong (200 per ship); plus 400 Army, 100 Marines and 100 ACORN personnel. . . .Unloading boats on a beach is extremely strenuous physical labor and the Shore Party must be organized into reliefs if the unloading is to extend over 12 hours."*

Further increases in personnel as well as cleaner command lines were again tried in TOENAILS (Central Solomons). They paid off.

Night Landings

Night landings on foreign shores look very good on paper and over the long history of amphibious operations have been resorted to many times; e.g., the North Africa invasion on 8 November 1942.

RAdm Turner took a dim view of night landings prior to TOENAILS, but had not closed his mind to their use. He was willing to experiment on a small scale. So the Eastern Force scheduled a night landing at Wickham Anchorage and the Western Force scheduled night landings for the Onaiavisi Entrance Unit and for the Advance Unit on Rendova.

One lesson which RAdm Turner stated he had vividly relearned during the TOENAILS Operation was the great hazard of night operations. In

---

* COMTRANSDIV Eight to COMPHIBFORSOPAC, letter, Nov. 1942.

fact, his lack of success with them soured him on night landings for any large contingent of amphibians for the rest of the war.

Diversionary Landings

The 7 October 1943 landing in the Northern Solomons on Choiseul Island by the 2nd Marine Parachute Battalion under the command of LtCol Victor Krulak as a diversion for the Treasury landings and for the Bougainville operation to come was a swift and vigorous activity that surprised the enemy while creating the impression that a much larger force was at work.

Offshore Toeholds

During the New Georgia amphibious operation, an operational technique was developed which carried through the Central Pacific campaigns and on into the planning for the final attack on the Japanese homeland. This technique was pointed towards seizing toeholds on nearby islands close to, but not so well defended as the main objective, and making a key part of the major assault on the main objective direct from these toeholds rather than from far across the sea. They also provided a place from where artillery support could be supplied on a round-the-clock basis.

Bypassing Enemy-held Islands

Perhaps of equal or even greater importance than the strategic advantages gained by the campaign of Vella Lavella and Kolombangara (Central Solomons) were the lessons learned. The principle of seizing unoccupied territory for the development of an airfield—soon to be repeated in the Bougainville operation—was worked out in this campaign.

The success of the operation clearly demonstrated the soundness of the strategy of bypassing enemy strongholds, then blockading and starving them out. This operational pattern, later repeated so often in the Central and Southwest Pacific, was rehearsed successfully for the first time in the

Central Solomons. In view of the successes achieved and lives saved, no more popular strategical concept came out of the Pacific War than that of bypassing or leapfrogging Japanese-held islands and letting the Japanese threat "die on the vine," while our forces directed their efforts at the enemy closer to the Japanese homeland.

The popularity of this strategy has led to many claims as to who was the originator. According to VAdm George Dyer, who read thousands of dispatches relating to the Pacific War while doing research for his excellent book, the first dispatch in which he saw the expression used was in a dispatch of VAdm Halsey's (COMSOPAC's 110421 of July 1943) addressed to RAdm Turner asking for his comments and recommendations on the concept.

Force Requirements

There was one sobering lesson from TOENAILS which carried forward into future planning of assault and follow-up forces for the island campaigns of the Pacific. It was expressed in a COMINCH planners memorandum of 6 August 1943:

> At the termination of Japanese resistance in Munda, there were seven regimental combat teams, totaling more than 30,000 troops in our assault forces. No information differing from our initial estimate of 4,000 to 5,000 troops on Munda, to which reinforcements were believed to have been added for a time, has been received.
>
> However, of the Japanese on Munda only 1,671are known to be dead and 28 captured. The overwhelming superiority of our forces in numbers and equipment had to be applied for 12 days despite air bombing and naval bombardment support before a force not more than one-seventh its size had been overcome. If we are going to require such overwhelming superiority at every point

where we attack the Japanese, it is time for radical change in the estimate of the forces that will be required to defeat the Japanese now in the Southwest and Central Pacific.*

Neutralization of Enemy Airfields

Enemy airfields on Bougainville beyond and to the rear of the Allied beachhead at Torokina point had been neutralized or weakened to such an extent by the end of November 1943, that they held no immediate threat to the Allied landing operation. American air supremacy made Japanese counter landings and reinforcements near impossible while reinforcement by land routes from southern Bougainville presented grave difficulties. However, in order to exploit the advantages achieved, the defense perimeter had to be expanded, airstrips completed, and an advance naval base established. Furthermore, the beachhead would have to be supplied and reinforced by echelons following a course within close range of several enemy airfields. These airfields would have to be kept neutralized as well as a constant guard maintained against enemy surface forces.

Gunfire Support

WATCHTOWER and TOENAILS were poor operations for training gunfire support ships, and for bettering the judgment of either planners or operators in the fine art of first-rate gunfire support against a well-defended coral atoll. However, based on experience gained primarily during the North African invasion by the amphibious forces of the Atlantic Fleet, a completely revised chapter on Naval Gunfire in FTP 167 ("Landing Operations Doctrine") was promulgated by COMINCH on 1 August 1943 and distributed to the Fleet.

This newly issued chapter provided that the Naval Gunfire Annex to an operational order issued by a Commander Naval Attack Force would:

---

*   Captain Clarence E. Olsen, USN, to ACS (Plans), memorandum, 6 Aug. 1943.

. . .contain the directions for furnishing naval gunfire support for the Landing Force. Its preparation is a
joint function of the Staff of the Commander Attack
Force and the Staff of Commander Landing Force.

The detailed instructions provided that:

The staff of the Marine Division Commander
[should] outline on the map prepared for the operation the probable target locations and probable enemy
dispositions in the area to be attacked. The assignment of fire missions is a function of the Staff of the
Commanding General, Marines. The Combined
Staffs of the Commander Naval Attack Force and
Commanding General, Marines now prepare the plan
of naval gunfire. Upon approval, this plan is authenti-
cated and issued as the Naval Gunfire Annex.

Close fire support was supplied by destroyer *Monssen* (DD-436) for
steep-hilled Gavutu and Tanambogo with 92 rounds of 5-inch from 500
yards. This gunfire was particularly effective at Tanambogo the second day
after a 200-round, five-minute bombardment from a respectable 4,000
yards had proven ineffective the first day.* This close fire support by the
Monssen was the first really "close up" use of the 5-inch naval gun from a
thin-skinned naval ship to blast Japanese defenders from caves and well-
prepared defense positions.

One marked improvement in gunnery did result from TOENAILS,
where it had been learned that high-capacity ammunition with thinly-cased
shells was inadequate to pierce Japanese defense structures. However, if
armor-piercing projectiles were used, an appreciable angle of fall had to

---

* USS *Monssen* War Diary, 7 Aug. 1942.

be provided by increasing the gun range and reducing the powder charge, otherwise the AP projectile would ricochet without exploding.

Advances in Operation Planning

Vice Admiral Spruance's GALVANIC Operation Plan represented a distinct advance over the plans issued for WATCHTOWER and TOENAILS, which RAdm Turner, Commander Assault Force, previously had fought under.

Vice Admiral Spruance's plan provided the following advances in doctrine:

(1) That a ship-based commander—Commander Central Pacific Force—with a determination to be in the objective area, retained immediate personal operational control over the operation.

(2) For the coordination of the various Central Pacific task forces under one commander in the operating or objective area should a Japanese surface or carrier task force show up to threaten or attack the amphibious forces.

(3) In advance, the conditions for the essential change of command from the Amphibious Task Force Commander to the Landing Force Commander at each assault objective.

(4) In advance, the command responsibility for the development of the base facilities at the objective to be seized.

(5) For support aircraft at each assault objective to be under the control of the Amphibious Task Force Commander. These aircraft had a capability for dawn or dusk search of the sea area approaches to the assault objective areas, should the need arise.

(6) For the reconnaissance aircraft to be at the outer limits of their searches at sundown in lieu of arrival back at base at sundown.

The Defense Force and Shore-Based Air Force was new in concept, developing out of the experience at Guadalcanal. Its missions included defending and developing the positions captured, including the construction and activation of airfields on the atolls of Makin, Tarawa, and Apamama. All this was to be done to give air support to the Central Pacific campaign.

On 25 October 1943, CINCPAC modified his Operation Plan so that command would pass from the Commander Attack Force to Commander Landing Force in accordance with the following procedure:

> At each atoll, as soon as the Landing Force Commander determines that the status of the landing operations permits, he will assume command on shore and report that fact to the Commander Attack Force.

This changed the previous directive under which the Commander Landing Force would announce he was ready to assume command ashore, and the Commander Attack Force would direct him to do so.

An additional change made by CINCPAC at the same time provided for an orderly change of responsibility for the defense and development of atolls or islands captured. This had been sadly lacking in the operation orders for WATCHTOWER and TOENAILS:

> Commander Central Pacific Force will determine and announce when the capture and occupation phase is completed, whereupon Commander Defense Force and Shore Based Air will assume his responsibility for the defense and development of positions captured.

This superseded the provision:

> Commander Central Pacific Force will determine when the capture and occupation phase is completed and will then direct command of all forces ashore at objectives pass from Commander Assault Force to Commander Defense Force and Shore Based Air.

RAdm Turner supported both of these changes, and inaugurated the second one.*

Amphibious Force Command Flagship

RAdm Turner had come out of the South Pacific with the very definite belief that the commander of an amphibious task force should be provided with a flagship which did not have to carry troops and their logistical support to the assault landing, and which had adequate working and sleeping accommodations for his staff. Additionally, the flagship had to provide adequate accommodations for the Amphibious Corps Commander, the Landing Force Commander and the Commander of the Support Aircraft and the numerous personnel of their staffs, as well as provide multiple communication facilities adequate for the escalating requirements of three or four commanders aboard the same ship during the early hours of an assault landing.

Since there was no ship currently afloat in the United States Navy to meet such requirements, a transport hull with a wholly new topside design was necessary. This ship was to be called a headquarters ship, although its official title would be Amphibious Force Command Flagship. The USS *Appalachian* (AGC-1) was the first of 15 built in 1943–1944 on Maritime Commission C-2 hulls with an average displacement of 7,431 tons. (She would arrive in the Pacific in late 1943.)

Solomons Observations and Conclusions

Now for a few final observations:

- American planners would have to improve their ability to estimate the enemy's strength and defenses, and the U.S. Navy would have to improve its ability to stop nighttime Japanese troop movements.

---

* COMFIFTHPHIBFOR, letter, OSA/A16-3/Ser 0023 of 19 Sept. 1943, with endorsements thereon by COMCENPACFOR and CINCPAC, subj: Recommended changes in command arrangements, CINCPAC Operation Plan 13-43.

- The strategical concepts of "offshore toeholds" and "leapfrogging" would be employed in upcoming operations.
- The risk the United States incurred in the South and Southwest Pacific by dispensing its forces and conducting two strategic offenses, Solomons and New Guinea, brought substantial rewards.
- Words fail to convey the demands placed on the men who served at the front or to praise their efforts sufficiently. However, a special tribute is due the Seabees, Army and Marine Engineers, Marine Pioneers, Coast Guard, and other extensions of the "Pacific Express"—like the Marine's Fifth Field Depot, another logistics organization which started as the 4th Base Depot in the Solomons.
- Thanks to our newfound air supremacy and the new Allied airfields in the Central and Northern Solomons, the U.S. was now in position to drive the Japanese fleet out of Rabaul. The successful isolation of Rabaul—the ultimate objective of Operation CARTWHEEL—would be the beginning of the end.

The invasion of New Georgia signaled a new phase in the Pacific war; the beginning of an American strategic offensive. The struggle for control of the Solomons was a critical turning point in the war. It also provided—in spite of different opinions along the way—that joint naval, land, and air operations improve with experience.

During the Central and Northern Solomons Campaigns, the measure of the war with Japan changed dramatically. The invasion of New Georgia in June 1943 had signaled a new phase of the war, the beginning of a sustained American strategic offensive. Less than a year later, the failed Japanese counterattack on Bougainville and CARTWHEEL'S successful isolation of Rabaul heralded the beginning of the end—the eagerly awaited American return to the Philippines. The Solomons Campaigns constituted a major step toward that goal.

(Source: McGee, *The Solomons Campaigns, 1942–1943*, 543–562.) ∎

❖ ❖ ❖

The Southern Solomons advance bases on Guadalcanal, Tulagi, and the Russell Islands, as well as Espiritu Santo and Noumea, were used as staging areas or ports by the Amphibious Forces for the remainder of the war. For example, LST-582 battle loaded equipment and troops for the Philippines in January 1945 and in March 1945 she loaded Marines and headed for the Okinawa invasion. *Pictured here*, USS LST-582 headed for the Russell Islands from Pearl Harbor. Church service being held on forward ramp by Lt Howard Hazlett, XO, October 1944. (Photographs for this chapter courtesy of Robert E. Novak)

USS LST-582 with combat troops and equipment headed for Lingayen Gulf, Luzon, Philippines, January 1945.

Combat load of 1st Marine Division aboard USS LST-582 headed for invasion of Okinawa in some rough weather, March 1945.

Beached at Purvis Bay, Florida Islands, to take on supplies, March 1945. Sign on beach reads, "Admiral Halsey says, 'Kill Japs, kill Japs, Kill more Japs!' You will help kill the yellow bastards if you do your job well."

Appendix

U.S. Merchant Ship Casualties in the Pacific Ocean Areas
7 December 1941—10 August 1945

Abbreviations and codes used in columns:

Column A — Asterisk (*) following vessel name = WSA (War Shipping Administration) or U.S. Maritime Commission owned

Column B — Gross Tonnage definition: The total cubic measurement of the permanently enclosed internal capacity of a vessel, in units of 100 cubic feet to a ton.

Column D — Cargo abbreviations: Ammo=Ammunition, DG=Drummed Gas, Equip=Equipment, Veh=Vehicle, DLS= Diesel, Mil = Military

Column E — Attack Locations: The nearest port or land mass

Column F — Attack Methods codes: AR=Air raid, AT=Aerial torpedo, GF=gun fire, Kaiten torpedoes=Human-manned torpedoes carried on the decks of Japanese submarines and ships, K=Kamikaze, M=Mine(s), SGF=Surface gunfire, ST=Sub torpedo, SID=Self-imposed damage

Column G — Attack Damage codes: HD=Heavy damage, LD=Light damage, TL=Total loss, S=Salvaged, SI=Self-imposed damage

Column H — Personnel Aboard codes: MM=Merchant Marine, AG=Naval Armed Guard, P=Passengers (other than troops), T=Troops, CB=Construction Battalion Stevedores

Column I — Casualties codes: K=killed, drowned or dead of wounds, W=Wounded, POW=Prisoner of War

Column J — Armament abbreviations: cal.=caliber, mm=millimeters, 3", 4", or 5"=diameter of the larger gun bores, MG=machine gun

Sources: Robert M. Browning Jr., *U.S. Merchant Vessel War Casualties of World War II* (Annapolis: Naval Institute Press, 1996), Captain Arthur R. Moore, *A Careless Word...A Needless Sinking* (Kings Point, NY: American Merchant Marine Museum at the U.S. Merchant Marine Academy, 1983).

	A	B	C	D	E	F	G	H	I	J
Date	Vessel	Gross Tonnage (000)	Operator	Cargo	Attack Locations	Attack Methods	Attack Damage	Personnel Aboard MM/AG/P/T/CB	Casualties	Armament
1941										
7 Dec	President Harrison	10.5	American President Lines	none	China	SID	HD	MM154/P1	K3	Unarmed
8 Dec	Capillo *	5.1	American Mail Lines	Genl	Philippines	AR	HD	MM40		Unarmed
10 Dec	Sagoland	5.3	Madrigal & Co.	Flour	Philippines	AR	Sunk	Unknown		Unarmed
11 Dec	Lahaina	5.6	Matson Navigation Co.	Genl	Hawaii	GF	Sunk	MM34	K4	Unarmed
12 Dec	Vincent	6.2	United States Lines	Genl	22.40S/ 118.13W	GF	Sunk	MM36		Unarmed
12 Dec	Admiral Y.S. Williams	3.2	American Trading Co.	Rubber & Tin	China	SID	Salv.	MM34	K1	Unarmed
13 Dec	Manatawny	5.0	Madrigal & Co.	Genl	Philippines	AR	Sunk			Unarmed
17 Dec	Manini	3.2	Matson Navigation Co.	Genl	Hawaii	ST	Sunk	MM33	K2	Unarmed

Date	Vessel	Gross Tonnage (000)	Operator	Cargo	Attack Locations	Attack Methods	Attack Damage	Personnel Aboard MM/AG/P/T/CB	Casualties	Armament
		A								
19 Dec	*Prusa*	5.1	Lykes Brothers	Genl	Hawaii	ST	Sunk	MM34	K9	Unarmed
20 Dec	*Emido*	6.9	Socony-Vacuum Oil Co.	None	Calif.	ST	HD	MM36	K5	Unarmed
23 Dec	*Montebello*	8.3	Union Oil Co. of California	Crude Oil	Calif.	ST	Sunk	MM38		Unarmed
24 Dec	*Absaroka*	5.7	McCormick SS Co. Div.	Genl	Calif.	ST	Salv.	MM34	K1	Unarmed
29 Dec	*Don Jose*	10.9	Madrigal & Co.	Genl	Philippines	AR	HD	Unknown	Unknown	Unarmed
31 Dec	*Ruth Alexander*	8.1	American President Lines	Genl	1.0N/119.10E	AR	Sunk	MM49	K1	Unarmed
1942										
1 Jan	*Malama*	3.3	Matson Navigation Co.	Mil	26.21S/153.24W	AR from Japanese merchant cruisers	Sunk	MM33/P5	K2	Unarmed
19 Feb	*Mauna Loa*	5.4	Matson Navigation Co.	Genl	Australia	AR	Sunk	MM37/P7		Unarmed
19 Feb	*Don Isidro*	3.3	De La Rama SS Co.	Mil	Timor Sea	AR	Sunk	MM68/P16	K14	Unknown

Date	Vessel	Gross Tonnage (000)	Operator	Cargo	Attack Locations	Attack Methods	Attack Damage	Personnel Aboard MM/AG/P/T/CB	Casualties	Armament
19 Feb	Admiral Halstead	3.3	Pacific Lighterage Corp.	DG	Australia	AR	HD	NA		Unarmed
19 Feb	Portmar	5.6	Calmar SS Co.	Troops/ Supplies	Australia	AR	HD	MM34/P300	K3/W12	Unarmed
19 Feb	Florence D	2.6	Cadwallader-Gibson Lumber Co.	Mil	10.56S/ 130.07E	AR	Sunk	MM37/P8	K4	Unarmed
5 May	John Adams *	2.3	Sudden & Christensen	DG	New Caledonia	ST	Sunk	MM40/AG11	K5	1-4", 4-50 cal.
7 Jun	Coast Trader	3.7	Coastwise Line SS Co.	Newsprint	Calif.	ST	Sunk	MM37/AG19	K1	2-37mm, 4-50 cal., 2-30 cal.
14 Jul	Arcata	2.7	WSA	Ballast	Wash.	GF	Sunk	MM29/P3	K8/W1	Unarmed
21 Jul	Coast Farmer	3.3	WSA	Genl	Australia	ST	Sunk	MM36/AG5	K1	2-MG
22 Jul	William Dawes	7.2	WSA	Ammo +	Australia	ST	Sunk	MM40/ AG15/ P5	K5	1-4", 1-3", 6-MG

Date	Vessel	Gross Tonnage (000)	Operator	Cargo	Attack Locations	Attack Methods	Attack Damage	Personnel Aboard MM/AG/P/T/CB	Casualties	Armament
4 Oct	Camden	6.6	Shell Oil Co.	76K DLS Fuel	OR/WA Coast	ST	Sunk	MM39/AG9	K1	1-4", 4-30 cal. MG
5 Oct	Larry Doheny	7.0	Richfield Oil Corp.	66K DLS Fuel	Oregon	ST	Sunk	MM34/AG10	K6	1-5", 2-30 cal. MG
26 Oct	President Coolidge	21.9	WSA	Genl	Espiritu Santo	M	Sunk	MM290/AG51/T5050	K5	1-5", 4-3", 12-20mm
8 Nov	Edgar Allen Poe *	7.2	Weyerhaeuser SS Co.	Mil	New Caledonia	ST	Salv.	MM40/AG13/P18	K2	1-4", 1-3", 6-MG
1943										
18 Jan	Mobilube	10.2	Socony-Vacuum Oil Co.	Ballast	33.57S/157.10E	ST	Salv.	MM45/AG11	K3	1-4", 4-50 cal. MG
22 Jan	Peter H. Burnett *	7.2	American President Lines	Wool	32.54SS/159.32E	ST	Salv.	MM40/AG26/P8	K1	1-5", 1-3", 4-20mm, 4-50 cal. MG
23 Jan	Stephen Johnson Field *	7.2	American-Hawaiian SS Co.	Mil	Milne Bay, New Guinea	AR	HD	MM42/AG18	K1	1-4", 1-3", 6MG

Date	Vessel	Gross Tonnage (000)	Operator	Cargo	Attack Locations	Attack Methods	Attack Damage	Personnel Aboard MM/AG/P/T/CB	Casualties	Armament
30 Jan	*Samuel Gompers* *	7.2	Weyerhaeuser SS Co.	Chrome ore	New Caledonia	ST	Sunk	MM43/AG17	K4	1-3", 5-20mm, 2-30 cal. MG
10 Feb	*Starr King* *	7.2	McCormick SS Co.	Mil	Australia	ST	Sunk	MM37/AG16/P2		1-5", 4-20mm, 2-30 cal.
1 Mar	*Gulfwave*	7.2	WSA	Ballast	Fiji	ST	HD	MM39/AG15		1-4", 4-50 cal., 1-20mm
27 Apr	*Lydia M. Child* *	7.2	McCormick SS Co.	Genl	Australia	ST	Sunk	MM42/AG21		1-3", 5-20mm, 4-50 cal. MG
30 Apr	*Phoebe A. Hearst* *	7.2	American President Lines	Mil	Pago Pago	ST	Sunk	MM40/AG16		1-3", 9-20mm
2 May	*William Williams* *	7.2	Isthmian SS Co.	Ballast	Fiji	ST	HD	MM40/AG16	W1	1-3", 5-20mm
17 May	*William K. Vanderbilt* *	7.2	Isthmian SS	Ballast	Fiji	ST	Sunk	MM41/AG16	K1	1-3", 5-20mm

Date	Vessel	Gross Tonnage (000)	Operator	Cargo	Attack Locations	Attack Methods	Attack Damage	Personnel Aboard MM/AG/P/T/CB	Casualties	Armament
		A	B	C	D	E	F	G	H	I	J
18 May	H.M. Storey	10.8	WSA & USN	Ballast	New Hebrides	ST	Sunk	MM48/AG15/P2	K2	1-4", 6-20mm, 2-50 cal.
11 Aug	Matthew Lyon	7.8	Dickman, Wright & Pugh	None	Solomons	ST	HD	MM41/AG18	W1	1-3", 9-20mm
13 Aug	M.H. De Young *	7.2	R. A. Nicol & Co.	Construction Equip	Tongotabu	ST	HD	MM42/AG25/P28	K4	1-3", 9-20mm
31 Aug	W.S. Rheem	10.9	WSA	86,500 barrels Navy special fuel	Samoa	ST	HD	MM49/AG25		1-4", 9-20mm
11 Oct	George H. Himes *	7.2	Shepherd SS Co.	Munitions/Lumber	Guadalcanal	AT	HD	MM41/AG27/CB20		2-3", 8-20mm
11 Oct	John H. Couch *	7.2	Weyerhaeuser SS Co.	Oils/Gas	Guadalcanal	AT	Sunk	MM42/AG26/CB100	K3	2-3", 8-20mm
11 Nov	Cape San Juan *	6.7	American-Hawaiian SS Co.	Genl/Troops	Fiji	ST		MM60/AG42/T1348	K130	1-4", 4-3", 8-20mm

1944

Date	Vessel	Gross Tonnage (000)	Operator	Cargo	Attack Locations	Attack Methods	Attack Damage	Personnel Aboard MM/ AG/ P/T/CB	Casualties	Armament
		A	B	C	D	E	F	G	H	I	J
24 Jan	John Muir*	7.2	Alaska Packers, Inc.	Lumber/Veh	New Guinea	AR	LD	MM42/ AG28/ CB40	W3	1-5", 5-20mm
29 Jan	George Sterling*	7.2	Waterman SS Co.	Mil	New Guinea	AR	LD	MM44/AG26	K2/W1	2-3", 8-20mm
31 Jan	Stephen Crane*	7.2	Isthmian SS Co.	Mil	New Guinea	AR	LD	MM33/ AG29/ P40	K1/W22	1-5",1-3", 8-20mm
19 Mar	Oriental*	6.2	Seas Shipping Co.	Mil	New Hebrides	M	LD	MM53/ AG28/ P5		1-5",4-3", 8-20mm
18 Apr	John Staub*	7.2	Alaska SS Co.	Oil/Gas	Aleutians	M	Sunk	MM42/ AG27/ P1	K65	2-3", 8-20mm
2 Jul	Jean Nicolet*	7.2	Oliver J. Olsen SS Co.	Mil	Ceylon	ST	Sunk	MM41/ AG28/ P30	K76/ 3POW	2-3", 8-20mm
1 Aug	Extavia	6.6	American Export Lines Inc.	Genl/Troops	Solomons	M	LD	MM73/ AG81/ T845		1-4",4-3", 8-20mm
26 Sep	Elihu Thompson*	7.2	De La Rama SS	Genl/Troops	New Caledonia	M	HD	MM42/ AG33/ T211	K32	1-4", 1-3", 8-20mm

Date	Vessel	Gross Tonnage (000)	Operator	Cargo	Attack Locations	Attack Methods	Attack Damage	Personnel Aboard MM/AG/P/T/CB	Casualties	Armament
		A	B	C	D	E	F	G	H	I	J
30 Sep	Carl G. Barth *	7.2	Olympic SS Co.	Genl	Admiralties	AR	LD	MM52/AG26/P118	W6	1-5", 1-3", 8-20mm
24 Oct	Augustus Thomas *	7.2	Coastwise Line	Mil	Leyte Gulf, P.I.	AR/K	HD	MM41/AG27/P480		2-3", 8-20mm
24 Oct	David Dudley Field *	7.2	Isthmian SS Co.	Mil/Troops	Leyte Gulf, P.I.	RS	HD	MM40/AG30/T10/CB50	W4	2-3", 8-20mm
25 Oct	Adoniram Judson *	7.2	W. R. Chamberlin & Co.	Genl	Philippines	AR	LD	MM43/AG28/CB+	K2/W2	2-3", 8-20mm
25 Oct	John W. Foster *	7.2	Inter-Ocean SS Corp	Mil/Troops	Leyte Gulf, P.I.	AR	LD	MM41/AG27/P170/CB30	W11	2-3", 8-20mm
27 Oct	Benjamin Ide Wheeler *	7.2	American-Hawaiian SS Co.	Mil/Troops	Leyte Gulf, P.I.	AR/K	HD	MM43/AG27/T500	K2/W3	2-3", 8-20mm
28 Oct	Cape Romano *	5.1	Lykes Brothers	None	Leyte Gulf, P.I.	AR	LD	MM47/AG26/P2	W4	1-4", 1-3", 8-20mm
28 Oct	United Victory *	7.6	American President Lines	Ammo	Peleliu	SGF	LD	MM57/AG27/CB100		1-5", 1-3", 8-20mm

Date	Vessel	Gross Tonnage (000)	Operator	Cargo	Attack Locations	Attack Methods	Attack Damage	Personnel Aboard MM/AG/P/T/CB	Casualties	Armament
	A	B	C	D	E	F	G	H	I	J
29 Oct	John A. Johnson *	7.2	American Mail Lines	Mil	Hawaii	ST	Sunk	MM41/ AG28/ P1	K10	2-3", 8-20mm
3 Nov	Matthew P. Deady *	7.2	American-Hawaiian SS Co.	Mil/Troops	Leyte Gulf, P.I.	AR/K	HD	MM37/ AG27/ P300	K28/W77	1-4", 1-3", 8-20mm
4 Nov	Frank J. Cuhel *	7.2	Black Diamond SS Co.	Mil/Troops	Leyte Gulf, P.I.	GF	LD	MM42/ AG28/ T500	W3	1-5", 1-3", 8-20mm
4 Nov	Cape Constance *	6.7	Grace Lines	Genl	Leyte Gulf, P.I.	AR/K	LD	MM51/ AG28/ P1	W1	2-3", 8-20mm
12 Nov	Leonidas Merritt *	7.2	United States Lines	Bridge parts	Leyte Gulf, P.I.	AR/K	HD	MM43/ AG28/ CB50	K3/W36	2-3", 8-20mm
12 Nov	Thomas Nelson *	7.2	Calmar SS Co.	Mil/Troops	Leyte Gulf, P.I.	AR/K	HD	MM38/ AG28/ T578	K136/ W88	1-4", 1-3", 8-20mm
12 Nov	Jeremiah M. Daily *	7.2	American South African Line	Mil/Troops	Leyte Gulf, P.I.	AR/K	HD	MM39/ AG29/ T557	K106/ W43	1-5", 1-3", 8-20mm
12 Nov	William A. Coulter *	7.2	Hammond Shipping Co.	Genl	Leyte Gulf, P.I.	AR/K	LD	MM41/AG27/ P4	W9	1-4", 1-3", 8-20mm

Date	Vessel	Gross Tonnage (000)	Operator	Cargo	Attack Locations	Attack Methods	Attack Damage	Personnel Aboard MM/ AG/ P/T/CB	Casualties	Armament
12 Nov	Morrison R. Waite *	7.2	Coastwise Pac-Far East Line	Vehicles/ Troops	Leyte Gulf, P.I.	AR/K	HD	MM39/ AG29/ T600	K41/ W43	1-4", 1-3", 8-20mm
12 Nov	Alexander Majors *	7.2	Isthmian SS Co.	Vehicles/ Troops	Leyte Gulf, P.I.	AR/K	HD	MM41/ AG26/ T13	K2/ W16	1-5", 1-3", 8-20mm
14 Nov	Floyd B. Olson *	7.2	Oliver J. Olson Co.	Lumber/ Steel	Leyte Gulf, P.I.	AR/K	LD	MM43/ AG28/ CB40		2-3", 8-20mm
18 Nov	Nicholas J. Sinnott *	7.2	James Griffith & Sons	Genl/ Troops	Leyte Gulf, P.I.	AR	LD	MM40/ AG26/ T8		2-3", 8-20mm
18 Nov	Gilbert Stuart *	7.2	American Mail Lines	DG/Troops	Leyte Gulf, P.I.	AR/K	HD	MM39/ AG29/ CB23+	K6/W11	1-4", 1-3", 8-20mm
19 Nov	Alcoa Pioneer	6.7	Alcoa SS Co.	Gasoline	Leyte Gulf, P.I.	AR/K	HD	MM46/ AG28/ P2	K6/W13	1-4", 1-3", 8-20mm
19 Nov	Cape Romano *	5.1	Lykes Brothers	None	Leyte Gulf, P.I.	AR/K	LD	MM46/ AG26/ P2		1-4", 1-3", 4-20mm

Date	Vessel	Gross Tonnage (000)	Operator	Cargo	Attack Locations	Attack Methods	Attack Damage	Personnel Aboard MM/AG/P/T/CB	Casualties	Armament
		A								
20 Nov	*Fort Dearborn* *	10.4	Deconhil Shipping Co.	Ballast	Caroline Is.	AR	LD	50/27/P5	W4	1-5",1-3", 8-20mm
23 Nov	*Gus W. Warnell* *	7.2	J. H. Winchester Co.	Mil	Leyte, P.I.	AT	TL	MM41/AG27/ T15	W17	1-5",1-3", 8-20mm
26 Nov	*Howell Lykes* *	8.2	Lykes Brothers	Water	Leyte, P.I.	AR	LD	MM79/ AG41/ T58	W2	1-4",4-3", 8-20mm
29 Nov	*William C. C. Claiborne* *	7.2	Mississippi Shipping Co.	Genl	Leyte, P.I.	SGF	LD	MM42/ AG28/ P1	W4	1-4",1-3", 8-20mm
5 Dec	*Antoine Saugraine* *	7.2	Agwilines	Mil	Leyte, P.I.	AT	Sunk	MM42/ AG26/ T376	W4	1-4",1-3", 8-20mm
5 Dec	*Marcus Daly* *	7.2	Sudden & Christensen	Mil	Leyte, P.I.	AR	HD	MM40/ AG27/ T1200	K65/W49	2-3",8-20mm
5 Dec	*John Evans* *	7.2	General Steamship Corp.	Mil	Leyte, P.I.	AR	LD	MM43/AG26	W4	1-5",1-3", 8-20mm
10 Dec	*Marcus Daly* *	7.2	Sudden & Christensen	Mil	Tarragona Gulf, Leyte	AR/K	HD	MM38/ AG26/ T124/60 CB	W8	2-3", 8-20mm

Date	Vessel	Gross Tonnage (000)	Operator	Cargo	Attack Locations	Attack Methods	Attack Damage	Personnel Aboard MM/AG/P/T/CB	Casualties	Armament
10 Dec	William S. Ladd *	7.2	Weyerhaeuser SS Co.	Ammo	Leyte, P.I.	AR/K	Sunk	MM41/AG29/CB50	W6	2-3", 8-20mm
21 Dec	Juan De Fuca *	7.2	Weyerhaeuser SS Co.	Lumber/Equip	off Panay Island	AR/K	HD	MM41/AG27/T65	K2/W17	2-3", 8-20mm
25 Dec	Robert J. Walker *	7.2	McCormick SS Co.	none	Australia	ST	Sunk	MM42/AG26/P1	K2	1-5", 1-3", 8-20mm
26 Dec	James H. Breasted *	7.2	American President Lines	Genl	anchored off Mindoro, P.I.	SGF	Sunk	MM42/AG27	W1	1-5", 1-3", 8-20mm
28 Dec	William Sharon *	7.2	United Fruit Co.	Genl	Mindoro, P.I.	AR/K	HD	MM40/AG29/P1	K11/W11	2-3", 8-20mm
28 Dec	John Burke *	7.2	Northland Transportation Co.	Ammo	Mindoro, P.I.	AR/K	Vaporized	MM40/AG28	K68+	2-3", 8-20mm
29 Dec	Francisco Morozan *	7.2	Isthmian SS Co.	none	Mindoro, P.I.	AR	LD	MM38/AG29/P1	W3	2-3", 8-20mm
30 Dec	Hobart Baker *	7.2	General SS Co.	Steel	Mindoro, P.I.	AR	Sunk	MM38/AG26	K1/W3	2-3", 8-20mm

Date	Vessel	Gross Tonnage (000)	Operator	Cargo	Attack Locations	Attack Methods	Attack Damage	Personnel Aboard MM/AG/P/T/CB	Casualties	Armament
31 Dec	Juan De Fuca *	7.2	Weyerhaeuser SS Co.	Lumber/Equip	Mindoro, P.I.	AT	Salv	MM41/AG27		2-3", 8-20mm
1945										
1 Jan	John M. Clayton *	7.2	American-Hawaiian SS Co.	Genl	Mindoro, P.I.	AR	Salv	MM42/AG26/P21	K6/W8	2-3", 8-20mm
4 Jan	Lewis L. Dyche *	7.2	Inter-Ocean SS Co.	Explosives	Mindoro, P.I.	AR/K	Vaporized	MM41/AG28	K69	2-3", 8-20mm
11 Jan	Pontus H. Ross *	7.2	Moore-McCormick SS Co.	Mil	Hollandia, New Guinea	Kaiten torpedoes	LD	MM42/AG27/P1	W6	1-5", 1-3", 8-20mm
12 Jan	Elmira Victory *	7.6	Alaska SS Co.	Ammo	Philippines	AR/K	LD	MM56/AG27/P6	W6	1-5", 1-3", 8-20mm
12 Jan	Otis Skinner *	7.2	American-Hawaiian SS Co.	Explosives	Philippines	AR/K	LD	MM43/AG27/P1	W2	2-3", 8-20mm
12 Jan	Edward N. Westcott *	7.2	Agwilines	Veh +	Luzon, P.I.	AR/K	LD	MM41/AG25/T365	W11	2-3", 8-20mm

Date	Vessel	Gross Tonnage (000)	Operator	Cargo	Attack Locations	Attack Methods	Attack Damage	Personnel Aboard MM/AG/P/T/CB	Casualties	Armament
12 Jan	Kyle V. Johnson *	7.2	Watermen SS Co.	Veh +	Philippines	AR/K	HD	MM43/AG29/T506	K130	1-5", 1-3", 8-20mm
12 Jan	David Dudley Field *	7.2	Isthmian SS Co.	Mil	Philippines	AR/K	LD	MM40/AG30/P10/CB50	W8	2-3", 8-20mm
6 Feb	Peter Silvester *	7.2	Pacific Far East Line	Mil	Australia	ST	Sunk	MM42/AG26/T107	K33	1-4", 1-3", 8-20mm
22 Mar	Ransom A. Moore *	7.2	J. H. Winchester	none	Philippines	AR	LD	MM39/AG27		1-5", 1-3", 8-20mm
31 Mar	John C. Fremont *	7.2	American President Lines	Mil	Manila, P.I.	M	HD	MM33/AG27/P1	W5	1-4", 1-3", 8-20mm
6 Apr	Logan Victory *	7.6	American-Hawaiian SS Co.	Explosives	Okinawa	AR/K	Sunk	MM56/AG27/CB15	K16	1-5", 1-3", 8-20mm
6 Apr	Hobbs Victory *	7.6	Sudden & Christensen Inc.	Ammo	Okinawa	AR/K	Exploded	MM56/AG27/CB15	K13	1-5", 1-3", 8-20mm
12 Apr	Minot Victory *	7.6	American Mail Lines	Mil	Okinawa	AR/K	LD	MM57/AG27/P9	W5	1-5", 1-3", 8-20mm

Date	Vessel	Gross Tonnage (000)	Operator	Cargo	Attack Locations	Attack Methods	Attack Damage	Personnel Aboard MM/AG/P/T/CB	Casualties	Armament
27 Apr	Canada Victory *	7.6	Alaska SS Co.	Ammo	Okinawa	AR/K	Sank	MM43/ AG27/ CB15	K3/W5	1-5", 1-3", 8-20mm
28 Apr	Bozeman Victory *	7.6	Alaska SS Co.	Ammo	Okinawa	SGF+	LD	MM59/ AG27/ CB13	W6	1-5", 1-3", 8-20mm
30 Apr	S. Hall Young *	7.2	American-Hawaiian SS Co.	Mil	Okinawa	AR/K	HD	MM38/ AG12/ P25	W1	2-3", 8-20mm
1 May	Henry L. Abbott *	7.2	Alaska Transportation Co.	Mil	Manila, P.I.	M	HD	MM43/ AG27/ P1	K2	2-3", 8-20mm
3 May	Edmund F. Dickens *	7.2	Pacific Atlantic SS Co.	Genl	Manila, P.I.	M	LD	MM43/AG27		2-3", 8-20mm
3 May	Sea Flasher *	8	Isthmian SS Co.	Genl	Okinawa	SGF	LD	MM61/ AG43/ T1609	K7/W47	1-5", 1-3", 8-20mm
18 May	Cornelius Vanderbilt *	7.2	Alaska SS Co.	Gas/Ammo	Okinawa	AR	LD	MM38/ AG27/ CB108	K1	1-5", 1-3", 8-20mm
25 May	William B. Allison *	7.2	Waterman SS Co.	Genl	Okinawa	AT	HD/TL	MM40/ AG28/ CB150	K7	2-3", 8-20mm

Date	Vessel	Gross Tonnage (000)	Operator	Cargo	Attack Locations	Attack Methods	Attack Damage	Personnel Aboard MM/ AG/ P/T/CB	Casualties	Armament
28 May	Mary A. Livermore *	7.2	Isthmian SS Co.	Genl	Okinawa	AR/K	HD	MM41/AG27/ CB75	K10/W6	1-4", 1-3", 8-20mm
28 May	Brown Victory *	7.6	Alaska Packers, Inc.	Gas/Veh	Okinawa	AR/K	LD	MM56/ AG27/ P1	K4/W18	1-5", 1-3", 8-20mm
28 May	Josiah Snelling *	7.2	Sudden & Christensen	Genl	Okinawa	AR/K	LD	MM39/ AG14/ P32/ CB90	W25	2-3", 8-20mm
11 Jun	Walter Colton *	7.2	Williams Dimond SS Co.	Genl	Okinawa	AR/K	LD	MM41/ AG29/ CB11	W3	1-5", 1-3", 8-20mm
25 Jul	John A. Rawlins *	7.2	Matson Navigation Co.	Genl	Okinawa	AT	HD-TL	MM39/ AG28/ CB191	W3	1-4", 1-3", 8-20mm
27 Jul	Pratt Victory *	8.2	Waterman SS Corp.	Genl	Okinawa	AT	HD	MM55/ AG27/ CB28	W3	1-5", 1-3", 8-20mm
8 Aug	Casimir Pulaski *	7.2	United Fruit Co.	Veh	Manila, P.I.	M	LD	MM42/AG28	W2	2-3", 8-20mm
10 Aug	Jack Singer *	7.2	American West African Lines	Genl	Okinawa	AT	HD-TL	MM39/AG29	W1	2-3", 8-20mm

Abbreviations

The military has a language all of its own. This list includes most of the commonly used World War II acronyms, code words and abbreviations, as well as ship, landing craft, and aircraft designations. Certain acronyms are written either in a combination of capital and lowercase letters ("BuDocks") or in all capital letters ("BUDOCKS"). Military ranks are abbreviated in the same manner ("Cmdr" or "CMDR") and with or without a period at the end ("Cmdr.", "Cmdr"). These reflect changes in military writing style from time-to-time.

1. World War II Acronyms, Code Words and Abbreviations

AA	Anti-aircraft	ANZAC	Australia New Zealand Area
AAA	Anti-aircraft Artillery		
AAF	United States Army Air Force	AR	Action Report, also Army Regulation
ABDA	American-British-Dutch-Australian	Arty	Artillery
		ATS	Army Transport Service
ACORN	Code word for an advanced base.	BAR	Browning Automatic Rifle
Adm	Admiral	BGen	Brigadier General
AFPAC	U.S. Army Forces, Pacific	BLT	Battalion Landing Team
AGF	Army Ground Forces	BMWT	British Ministry of War Transport
AirSols	Air Solomons Command		
		Bn	Battalion
		Btry	Battery

Bu	Bureau	CLEANSLATE	Code word for the occupation of Russell Islands
BuDocks	Bureau of Yards and Docks		
BuOrd	Bureau of Ordnance	CMC	Commandant of the Marine Corps
BuPers	Bureau of Personnel		
BuSandA	Bureau of Supplies and Accounts	CNO	Chief of Naval Operations
		CO	Commanding Officer
BuShips	Bureau of Ships	Co	Company
CA	Coast Artillery	Col	Colonel
CACTUS	Code word for Guadalcanal	ComAirSoPac	Commander Aircraft (land-based) South Pacific Force (COMAIRSOPAC)
Cal	Caliber		
'Canal	Slang for Guadalcanal		
CAP	Civil Air Patrol	ComAirWing I	Commander, 1st Marine Air Wing
Capt	Captain		
Cardiv	Carrier Division	ComAmphib ForSoPac	Commander, Amphibious Force, South Pacific
CARTWHEEL	Code word for Solomons-Bismarcks operation area in the South Pacific		
		COMGEN FIRSTMARDIV	Commanding General First Marine Division
CBMU	Construction Battalion, Maintenance Unit (Navy)		
		ComGenSoPac	Commander General, United States Army South Pacific Force
CCS	Combined Chiefs of Staff		
Cdr, Cmdr	Commander	COMINCH	Commander in Chief (President)
CE	Corps of Engineers (Army)	COMNAVBAS	Commander Naval Base(s)
CEC	Civil Engineering Corps (Navy)	COMPHIFOR SOPAC	Commander, Amphibious Forces South Pacific
CG	Commanding General		
CIC	Combat Information Center	COMSERSOPAC	Commander, Service Force South Pacific
CinCAFPac	Commander in Chief, U.S. Army Forces, Pacific (CINCAFPAC)	ComServonSoPac	Commander, Service Squadron, South Pacific Force
CinCPac	Commander in Chief, U.S. Pacific Fleet (CINCPAC)	ComSoPac	Commander, South Pacific Force
CinCPOA	Commander in Chief, Pacific Ocean Areas (CINCPOA)	ComSowesPac	Commander, Southwest Pacific

Cpl	Corporal	GO	General Order
Crudiv	Cruiser Division	GQ	General Quarters
CT	Combat Team	GSUSA	General Staff, United States Army
CTF	Commander, Task Force		
		GT	Gross tons or tonnage
CTG	Commander, Task Group	HMAS	His Majesty's Australian Ship
CTU	Commander, Task Unit	HMNZS	His Majesty's New Zealand Ship
CUB	Code word for an advanced base unit consisting of all the personnel and material necessary for the establishment of a medium-sized advanced fuel and supply base. (The little brother of LION.)		
		HMS	His Majesty's Ship
		Hosp	Hospital
		HQ	Headquarters
		IJA	Imperial Japanese Army
		IJN	Imperial Japanese Navy
		Inf	Infantry
		Info	Information
DP	Dual Purpose	Insp	Inspection or Inspector
DRYGOODS	Code word for assembly of supplies for New Georgia Offensive	Int	Intelligence
		Is	Island
		JAG	Judge Advocate General
DWT	Deadweight tons or tonnage	JB	Joint Board
		JCS	Joint Chiefs of Staff
Emb	Embarkation	Lant	Atlantic (Fleet)
Ens	Ensign	LCdr, LCmdr	Lieutenant Commander
EO	Executive Order	LCol	Lieutenant Colonel
Equip	Equipment	LION	Code word for a large advanced base unit consisting of all the personnel and material necessary for the establishment of a major all-purpose naval base. (The big brother of CUB.)
ESF	Eastern Sea Frontier		
Estab	Establishment		
ETO	European Theater of Operations		
Exec	Executive		
ExO	Executive Officer		
FA	Field Artillery		
FAdm	Fleet Admiral	LT	Long ton, 2,240 pounds
Flex	Fleet Landing Exercise		
Flot	Flotilla	Lt	Lieutenant
FMF	Fleet Marine Force	LtCol	Lieutenant Colonel
Gen	General	Lt (jg)	Lieutenant, junior grade (Navy)
GHQ	General Headquarters		

MAC	Marine Amphibious Corps	NTS	Naval Transportation Service
MAG	Marine Aircraft Group	OB	Order of Battle
MAINYARD	Code word for the advance base on Guadalcanal.	Off	Officer
		OIC	Officer in Charge
Maj	Major	ONI	Office of Naval Intelligence
MajGen	Major General	OOD	Office of the Deck
Mar Com	Maritime Commission	OPD	Operations Division, War Department General Staff
MARAD	Maritime Administration		
MarCor	Marine Corps	OPlan	Operations Plan
MAW	Marine Aircraft Wing	Opn	Operation
MD	Marine Detachment	OPNAV	Chief of Naval Operations
MI	Military Intelligence		
MIA	Missing in Action	OQMG	Office of the Quartermaster General
Mil	Military		
mm	Millimeter	Ord Dept	Ordnance Department
MOB	Mobile	Org	Organization or Organizational
MSC	Military Sealift Command	PAD	Pontoon Assembly Depot
MSgt	Master Sergeant	PE	Port of Embarkation
MSTS	Military Sea Transportation Service (later Military Sealift Command)	Pers	Personnel
		Pfc	Private, First Class (PFC)
MT	Measurement ton, 40 cubic feet	Phib	Amphibious
		Pion	Pioneer
MTO	Mediterranean Theater of Operations	Pl	Platoon
		Plt Sgt	Platoon Sergeant
Mvmt	Movement	POA	Pacific Ocean Area
NAD	Naval Ammunition Depot	POW	Prisoner of War
		PTO	Pacific Theater of Operations
NAS	Naval Air Station		
NATO	North African Theater of Operations	Pvt	Private
		QM	Quartermaster
NCB	Naval Construction Battalion	QMC	Quartermaster Corps
		QMG	Quartermaster General
NGF	Naval Gunfire	R and R	Rest and Relaxation, or Recuperation
NOB	Naval Operating Base		
NSD	Naval Supply Depot		

RAAF	Royal Australian Air Force	TF	Task Force
RAdm	Rear Admiral	TG	Task Group
RAF	Royal Air Force	Tng	Training
RAN	Royal Australian Navy	TOENAILS	Code word for New Georgia Operation
RCT	Regimental Combat Team	Traf	Traffic
Rdr	Raider	Trans	Transportation
Reg	Regulation	TSgt	Technical Sergeant
Reinf	Reinforced	TU	Task Unit
Req	Requirements	TZ	Transportation Zone
RINGBOLT	Code word for the Tulagi Operation	UDT	Underwater Demolition Team
RLT	Regimental Landing Team	USA	United States Army
RN	Royal Navy	USAFISPA	United States Army Forces in the South Pacific Area
RNZAF	Royal New Zealand Air Force	USASOS	United States Army Services of Supply
RNZN	Royal New Zealand Navy	USAT	United States Army Transport
SECNAV	Secretary of the Navy (SN)	USCG	United States Coast Guard
Secy	Secretary	USED	United States Engineers Department
SFCP	Shore Fire Control Party	USF	United States Fleet
Sgt	Sergeant	USMC	United States Marine Corps (also United States Maritime Commission)
SoPac	South Pacific Area, South Pacific Force (SOPAC)		
SOS	Services of Supply	USN	United States Navy
SoWesPac	Southwest Pacific Area (SWPA)	USNR	United States Naval Reserve
Sqn	Squadron	USS	United States Ship
SS	Steamship, prefix to a merchant ship name; also Submarine	USSBS	United States Strategic Bombing Survey
		VAdm	Vice Admiral
SSgt	Staff Sergeant	VCNO	Vice Chief of Naval Operations
SW	Secretary of War		
TBS	Talk Between Ships (Voice radio)	VF	Navy Fighter Squadron
TC	Transportation Corps	VMF	Marine Fighter Squadron

VMSB	Marine Scout-Bomber Squadron	WO	Warrant Officer
		WPB	War Production Board
VP	Navy Patrol Squadron	WSA	War Shipping Administration
VS	Navy Scouting Squadron		
		WSF	Western Sea Frontier
WATCHTOWER	Code word for the Guadalcanal operation	XO	Executive Officer
		YR	Yard Repair (floating repair shop)
WD	War Diary		
WESPAC	Western Pacific	ZI	Zone of interior
WIA	Wounded in Action		

2. U.S. Naval Vessel Designations

Large Ship-to-Shore Cargo Ships & Transports

AK	Cargo Ship	APA	Attack Transport
AKA	Attack Cargo Ship	APc	Coastal Transport
AP	Transport		

Small Ship-to-Shore Landing Craft

LCC	Landing Craft, Control	LCS(S)	Landing Craft, Support (Small) (Mks I-II)
LCM	Landing Craft, Mechanized (Mks II-IV)		
		LCV	Landing Craft, Vehicle
LCP(L)	Landing Craft, Personnel (Large)	LCVP	Landing Craft, Vehicle, Personnel
LCP(R)	Landing Craft, Personnel (Ramp)		
LCR(L)	Landing Craft, Rubber (Large)	LVT	Landing Vehicle, Tracked (Mks I-IV)
LCR(S)	Landing Craft, Rubber (Small)		
		LVT(A)	Landing Vehicle, Tracked (Armored), (Mks I-IV)

Shore-to-Shore Amphibious Landing Ships & Craft

LCT	Landing Craft, Tank (Mark V & VI)	LCI (R)	Landing Craft, Infantry (Rocket)
LST	Landing Ship, Tank	LSM	Landing Ship, Medium
LCI (L)	Landing Craft, Infantry (Large)	LSM(R)	Landing Ship, Medium (Rocket)
LCI (G)	Landing Craft, Infantry (Gunboat)	LC (FF)	Landing Craft, Flotilla Flagship
		LCS (L)	Landing Craft, Support (Large)
LCI (M)	Landing Craft, Infantry (Mortar)	LSV	Landing Ship, Vehicle
		LSD	Landing Ship, Dock

Other

AE	Ammunition Ship
AF	Stores Ship
AFD	Auxiliary Floating Dock (mobile floating drydocks)
AGC	Amphibious Force Command Ship
AH	Hospital Ship
AMP	Army Mine Planter
Amph	Amphibious
AO	Oil Tanker (Navy: oiler)
AOG	Gasoline Tanker
APD	Fast Destroyer Transport
AR	Repair ship
ARD	Auxiliary Repair Dock (floating drydocks)
ARL	Landing Craft Repair Ship
AS	Submarine Tender
ATF	Ocean Tugs, Fleet
BB	Battleship

CA	Heavy cruiser
CB	Large Cruiser
CL	Light Cruiser
CL(AA)	Light Cruiser (anti-aircraft)
CV	Aircraft Carrier
CVE	Escort Carrier
CVL	Light Carrier
DD	Destroyer
DE	Destroyer Escort
DMS	Destroyer Minesweeper
DUKW	Amphibious truck
Jeep	Small amphibious vehicle
PC	Patrol Craft (Submarine chaser, steel hull)
PCE	Patrol Craft Escort
PT	Motor Torpedo Boat (also MTB)
SC	Submarine chaser (wooden hull)
SM	Submarine Minelayer
YMS	Motor Minesweeper
YP	Patrol Vessel

3. Aircraft Designations of the U.S. Navy, Marine Corps and Army

Note: Numerals in parentheses indicate number of engines

A-20	Boston, Army (2) light bomber; A-29 Hudson, Army (2) light bomber
B-17	Flying Fortress, Army (4) heavy bomber; B-24—Liberator, Army (4) heavy bomber (called PB4Y by Navy)
B-25	Mitchell, Army (2) medium bomber; B-26—Marauder, Army (2) medium bomber
B-29	Superfortress, Army (4) heavy bomber
Black Cat	PBY equipped for night work
C-47	Skytrain, Army (2) transport
Dumbo	PBY equipped for rescue work
F4F	Wildcat; F4U—Corsair; F6F—Hellcat; all Navy (1) fighters
P-35, P-36, P-39, P-40	Army (1) pursuit fighter planes
P-38	Lightning, Army (2) fighter; P-39—Airacobra; P-40—Warhawk, Army (1) fighters

P-47	Thunderbolt; P-61—Black Widow, Army (2) fighters
PBM-3	Mariner, Navy (2) patrol bomber (flying boat)
PBY	Catalina, Navy (2) seaplane; PBY-5A—amphibian
PV-1	Ventura, Navy (2) medium bomber
SBD	Dauntless, Navy (1) dive-bomber
SB2C	Helldiver; Navy (1) dive-bomber
SOC	Seagull, Navy (1) scout-observation float plane
TBD, TBF	Devastator, Avenger, Navy (1) torpedo-bombers
VB	Bomber Squadron
VF	Fighter Squadron
VT	Torpedo-bomber Squadron. M is inserted for Marine Corps Squadron.

4. Japanese Aircraft Designations, circa 1942–1943

Betty   Mitsubishi Zero-1, Navy (2) medium bomber

Emily   Kawanishi Zero-2, Navy (4) patrol bomber (flying boat)

Fran   Nakajima P1Y, Navy (2) land all-purpose bomber

Hamp   Mitsubishi Zero-2, Navy (1) fighter

Helen   Nakajima, Navy (2) medium bomber

Irving   Nakajima J1N, Navy (2) night fighter

Jake   Navy (1) float plane

Jill   Nakajima B6N, Navy (1) torpedo-bomber

Judy   Aichi D4Y, Navy (1) dive-bomber

Kate   Nakajima 97-2, Navy (1) high-level or torpedo-bomber

Oscar   Nakajima Army (1) fighter

Pete   Sasebo, Zero-o, Navy (1) float plane

Sally   Mitsubishi 97, Army (2) medium bomber

Tojo   Nakajima, Army (1) fighter

Val   Aichi 99-1 Navy (1) dive-bomber

Zeke   Mitsubishi Zero-3, Navy (1) fighter (called "Zero" in 1942–43)

Glossary of Military and Mariner Terms

According to terminology taught at the United States Naval Academy: One does not ride "on" a car. One does not live "on" a house. Thus, one does not serve "on" a ship—but rather "in" a ship.

Abaft	Nautical preposition meaning aft of, or toward, the stern.
Abeam	Beside a ship. An object in the sea beside a ship is said to be abeam of it, or off the port or starboard beam.
Able seaman	The next grade above the beginning grade of ordinary seaman in a merchant ship deck crew.
Aft	Toward the stern (not as specific as abaft)
All hands	The entire ship's company.
Allocation	A term developed as a result of the War Shipping Administration program for assignment of vessels under its jurisdiction.
Amidships	An indefinite area midway between the bow and the stern.
Armament	The weapons of a ship.
Athwart	Across; at right angles to.
Auxiliary	Extra, or secondary, as in "auxiliary engine"; a vessel whose mission is to supply or support combatant forces.
Balances cargo	A mixture of heavy and light cargo, which approximately fills the cargo space and weighs the ship down to its legal maximum draft.

Bale cubic	The space available for cargo, measured in cubic feet, to the inside of the cargo battens on the frames of the vessel and to the underside of the beams.
Ballast	Heavy material, other than cargo, carried in the hold of a vessel to provide stability.
Bareboat charter	The charter of a bare vessel from the owner, without crew, fuel, stores, etc.; all such items being furnished by the charterer at the latter's expense.
Black gang	The engine-room crew of a steamship or motorship, so-called (no reference to skin color) because of their variously sooty and oily environment, which, especially in the days of coal-fired boilers, blackened the clothing and exposed skin of wipers, oilers, firemen-water-tenders, and the engineer on watch.
Boatswain	Shortened to "bo'sun."
Bogey	Unidentified aircraft.
Bow	The foremost point of a boat or ship; anything in the sea between dead ahead and abeam is said to be off its (port or starboard) bow.
Caliber	The diameter of a gun barrel; a gun's length is also often expressed in calibers; e.g., a 4-inch/33-caliber gun would be 4 x 33 inches (132 inches or 11 feet) long.
Chief mate	A term for first mate.
Chief	The merchant crew's term for the chief engineer.
Coaster	Or coastal type vessel. A vessel designed to operate primarily on coastal or inter-island voyages, distinguished from a trans-ocean vessel by its smaller size, lighter construction, and less stringent safety requirements.
Combat loader	Or "battle loader." A vessel specially equipped for combat loading. The Navy provided two types: APA (transport, attack) and AKA (cargo ship, attack). (LSTs were also considered combat loaders.)
Combat loading	Loading a ship with an assortment of equipment and supplies required by troops entering combat, and stowing the various items in such a manner that they can be unloaded quickly and in the order needed.
Combatant ship	A ship whose primary mission is combat.

Commercial basis	The use of a vessel at normal commercial rates for carrying passengers and cargo, but in World War II, usually not on its regular schedule nor on its regular route.
Condition I	All stations fully-manned and on alert.
Condition II	A state of readiness which required only half the crew to be on watch.
Conn	Station, usually on the bridge, from which a ship is controlled; the act of so controlling.
Conversion	Major alteration of a vessel to fit it for a specific purpose other than that for which it was originally constructed.
Coxswain	Enlisted person in charge of a boat.
Deadweight tonnage	The total weight of cargo, fuel, water, stores, crew, and passengers that a ship can carry.
Deck engineer	On a freighter, the person responsible for operating and maintaining winches and associated deck machinery used for handling cargo.
Displacement tonnage	The total weight of a ship when afloat, equal to the weight of the water displaced, generally expressed in long tons.
Division	The main subdivision of a ship's crew; an organization composed of two or more ships of the same type.
Dock	The space alongside a pier.
Doctrine	Something taught, as the principles or creed of a military organization, religion, or political party.
Draft	(of a ship). The distance between a ship's keel or bottom and the waterline; e.g., her draft is eight feet, or she draws eight feet.
Dry dock	A dock, either floating or built into the shore, from which water may be removed for the purpose of inspecting or working on a ship's bottom; to be put in dry dock.
Dumb barge	An unpowered barge.
Explosives cargo	Live ammunition and bulk explosives.
Full and down	Term indicating that a vessel has all cargo space filled and that the cargo is sufficiently heavy to take the ship down to the legal maximum draft.

Fleet	An organization of ships, aircraft, marine forces, and shore-based fleet activities, all under one commander, for conducting major operations.
Forecastle	Shortened to "fo'c'sle." The bow section of the ship where, in earlier times, the crew lived. Today, as generally they did during World War II, the crew lives amidships or aft in cabins allotted for one or more men.
Freighter	A ship designed to carry all types of general cargo, or "dry cargo."
Full and down	Term indicating that a vessel has all cargo space filled and that the cargo is sufficiently heavy to take the ship down to the legal maximum draft.
General cargo	Broadly used, the term includes all except bulk cargoes, but in Army usage it may exclude explosives.
General Quarters	"GQ." The condition of full readiness for battle.
Gross tonnage	The total cubic measurement of the permanently enclosed internal capacity of a vessel, in units of 100 cubic feet to a ton.
Gunwale	Pronounced "gunn'l". The upper edge of the side of a ship, used, in earlier times, to support muskets and wallpieces, with openings cut into it for cannons.
Head	Sailors' term for the toilet.
Hook	Term for anchor.
Knot ship	A World War II diesel-powered coastal cargo ship of the Maritime Commission C1 category, generally named for a knot or splice, having superstructure and engine spaces aft.
Knot	A nautical mile, or 1.15 statute miles. Also a measure of speed; a speed of 10 knots is 10 nautical miles per hour.
Ladder	Sea term for stairs.
Laker	Broadly, any vessel built on the Great Lakes; more specifically, a mass-produced U.S. Shipping Board well-deck freighter of about 250-foot length, originally carrying the name of a lake.
"Lame duck"	Term for disabled vessel that had to fall out of a convoy and thus became easy prey for submarines.
Landing craft	A vessel designed for landing troops and combat equipment directly on a beach.

Landing ship	A large seagoing ship designed for landing personnel, heavy equipment, or both, directly on a beach.
Liberty ship	The EC2 freighter that was credited with changing the course of the war and making the eventual Allied victory possible. All together 2,710 Liberties were built between 1941 and 1944. More than 200 were sunk or only partly salvageable.
Loan basis	A term applicable for a few vessels only, which were owned by the Maritime Commission (or the War Shipping Administration), and which were released to the Army or Navy Department for service operation without charter hire, and to be returned on a mutually agreeable date.
Log	A ship's speedometer; book, or ledger in which data or events that occurred during a watch are recorded; to make a certain speed, as in "the ship logged 20 knots"
Logistics	The branch of military science having to do with procuring, maintaining, and transporting materiel, personnel and facilities.
Long ton	Weight ton of 2,240 pounds; customarily used in connection with ocean freight, whereas the railroads customarily use the short ton of 2,000 pounds.
Master	Term for the captain; a holdover from the days when the merchant marine captain was literally, and legally, the "master" of the ship and crew. His word was law.
Measurement ton	40 cubic feet; sometimes called ship ton, since it is used chiefly in connection with ocean transportation.
Messman	A member of the steward's department who served meals to officers and crew.
Pier	Structure extending from land into water to provide a mooring for vessels.
Pennant	Properly "pendant," though universally pronounced "pennant." A long, narrow pendant or flag flown at the masthead of a warship commanded by a commissioned officer. It was flown day and night as long as a ship was in commission.
Plan of the day	Schedule of a day's routine and events ordered by the executive officer and published daily aboard ship or at a shore activity.

Pollywog	A person who has never crossed the equator.
Ponton	The Army's term and spelling for a float that supports bridges or serves as a causeway or barge. "Pontoon" is the Navy's spelling.
Port	To the left of the centerline, when facing forward.
Reconversion	The opposite of conversion; namely, changing a converted vessel back to its former condition.
Sea anchor	A drag resembling a tapered, bottomless, canvas bucket attached by line to a lifeboat or raft to retard its drifting and keep its bow to the wind.
Shaft alley	A tunnel between engine room and the very stern of a propeller-driven ship; it houses the drive shaft by which the engine turns the propeller.
Short ton	Weight ton of 2,000 pounds, customarily used by the domestic carriers.
Space charter	The chartering of all or a portion of the cargo or passenger space on a vessel at an agreed rate for a specific period, route or voyage.
Sparks	Universal seafaring term for the radio operator.
Squadron	Two or more divisions of ships or aircraft.
Standard type vessels	Vessels constructed in considerable quantity from adopted "standard" plans, under the jurisdiction of the Maritime Commission, in accordance with a long-range, rapid-delivery construction program to meet the shipping needs of World War II.
Starboard	To the right of the centerline, when facing forward.
Steam schooner	A small freighter developed on the West Coast early in the twentieth century of either steel or wood construction, generally powered by steam, often with the house and machinery aft.
Stem	Extreme forward line of bow.
Stern	The aftermost part of a vessel.
Strategy	a) The science of planning and directing large-scale military operations (as distinguished from Tactics), of maneuvering forces into the most advantageous position prior to actual engagement with the enemy; b) a plan or action based on this.

Tactics	a) The science of arranging and maneuvering military and naval forces in action or before the enemy (as distinguished from Strategy) with reference to short-range objectives; b) actions in accord with this science.
Tanker	A tank ship for transporting petroleum products and other liquids in bulk.
Tender	A smaller vessel attending a warship, carrying provisions and serving as a sort of nautical errand boy.
Theater of operations	A military command including the area of actual fighting (combat zone) and the adjacent area utilized for supporting administrative and supply activities.
Time charter	A charter in which the owner furnishes the crew and meets all other ship operating expenses, the charterer paying an agreed rate for an agreed period of time for all consolidated services furnished with the vessel.
Victory ship	The VC2 freighter first launched in 1944 as a faster (16+ knots) replacement of the Liberty ship (11 knots). A total of 531 Victories were built: 414 cargo ships and 117 transports.
Voyage charter	A special case of time charter in which the charterer pays the owner for use of the entire vessel to and from specified ports on specified or approximate dates.
Watch	One of the periods, usually four hours, into which a day is divided; a particular duty, as in "life buoy watch."
Weigh anchor	To hoist the anchor clear of the bottom.
West Coaster	A 410-foot ship of U.S. Shipping Board design built at West Coast yards.
Wharf	Structure similar to a quay (pro. "key") but constructed like a pier.
Windward	In the direction of the wind.
Yardcraft	Term for harbor vessels.
Zone of interior	The area which furnishes manpower and materiel to the forces in theaters of operations. The United States and Canada constituted the zone of interior for the U.S. Army in World War II.

Bibliography

I. Works Cited

Books

Browning Jr., Robert M. *U.S. Merchant Vessel War Casualties of World War II.* Annapolis, MD: Naval Institute Press, 1996.

Bunker, John Gorley. *Liberty Ships: The Ugly Ducklings of World War II.* Annapolis, MD: Naval Institute Press, 1972.

Bureau of Supplies and Accounts, Navy Department. "History of the Transportation Division." Reports. Washington, D.C.: 1 June 1944.

Bureau of Yards and Docks, Department of the Navy. *Building the Navy's Bases in World War II: History of the Bureau of Yards and Docks and the Civil Engineer Corps, 1940-1946.* 2 vols. Washington, D.C.: U.S. Government Printing Office, 1947.

Carter, Rear Admiral Worrall Reed, USN (Ret). *Beans, Bullets, and Black Oil: The Story of Fleet Logistics Afloat in the Pacific During World War II.* Washington, D.C.: U. S. Government Printing Office, 1953.

Dyer, Vice Admiral George Carroll, USN (Ret). *The Amphibians Came to Conquer: The Story of Admiral Richmond Kelly Turner.* 2 vols. Washington, D.C.: U.S. Government Printing Office, 1971.

Felknor, Bruce L., ed. *The U.S. Merchant Marine at War, 1775–1945.* Annapolis: Naval Institute Press, 1998.

Grover, David H. *U.S. Army Ships and Watercraft of World War II.* Annapolis: Naval Institute Press, 1987.

Huie, Lieutenant (jg) William Bradford, CEC, USNR. *Can Do!—The Story of the Seabees.* New York: E. P. Dutton & Company. Inc., 1944.

Land, Vice Admiral Emory Scott, USN. *Winning the War with Ships: Land, Sea and Air, Mostly Land.* New York: Robert M. McBride Co., 1958.45

Lane, Frederic C. *Ships for Victory: A History of Shipbuilding under the U.S. Maritime Commission in World War II.* Baltimore: The Johns Hopkins Press, 1951. Reprint, with a new preface by Arthur Donovan, Johns Hopkins Paperbacks edition, 2001.

McGee, William L. *Amphibious Operations in the South Pacific in World War II.* Santa Barbara, CA: BMC Publications. Vol. 1, *The Amphibians Are Coming!: Emergence of the 'Gator Navy and its Revolutionary Landing Craft,* 2000; Vol. 2, *The Solomons Campaigns, 1942-1943: From Guadalcanal to Bougainville, Pacific War Turning Point,* 2002.

———. *Bluejacket Odyssey, 1942-1946: Guadalcanal to Bikini, Naval Armed Guard in the Pacific.* Santa Barbara, CA: BMC Publications, 2000.

Moore, Captain Arthur R. *A Careless Word...A Needless Sinking: A History of the Staggering Losses Suffered by the U.S. Merchant Marine, both in Ships and Personnel, during World War II.* Kings Point, NY: American Merchant Marine Museum at the U.S. Merchant Marine Academy, 1983.

Morison, Samuel Eliot. *History of United States Naval Operations in World War II.* Boston: Little, Brown and Company. Vol 5, *The Struggle for Guadalcanal, August 1942-February 1943,* 1948; vol. 6, *Breaking the Bismarcks Barrier, 22 July 1942-1 May 1944,* 1950; vol. 15, *Supplement and General Index,* 1962.

Wardlow, Chester. *United States Army in World War II series. The Technical Services, The Transportation Corps: Responsibilities, Organization, and Operations.* Washington, D.C.: U.S. Government Printing Office, 1951.

Periodicals, Reports, Pamphlets and Other Publications

Browning Jr., Robert M. *The Coast Guard and the Pacific War.* Pamphlet. Washington, D.C.: Office of the Coast Guard Historian, 1995.

DeVries, Captain Larry G., CEC, USNR, (Ret). "Builders at the Front: U.S. Naval Construction Battalion Seabees at Guadalcanal in World War II." Unpublished mss., 1996.

———. "Seabees on Guadalcanal." *WWII Naval Journal* (July/August 1994).

Frank, Winn B. "Farewell to the Troopship." *Naval History* (January/February 1997).

Frazer, Lieutenant Colonel James G., USMC. "Building Under Fire: Marine Corps Engineers." *Engineering News-Record* (February 1944).

Gulbranson, Claude S. *History of the First Special U.S. Naval Construction Battalion, 1942-1946.* Privately published, 1994.

Johnson, Robert Erwin. *Coast Guard-Manned Naval Vessels in World War II.* Pamphlet. Washington, D.C.: Office of the Coast Guard Historian, 1993.

Jordan, Mark H., CEC, USN. *Saga of the Sixth.* Privately published: n.d.

Land, Vice Admiral Emory Scott, USN. "The United States Merchant Marine at War: Report of the War Shipping Administrator to the President." Washington, D.C.: U.S. Government Printing Office (15 January 1946). Courtesy: Office of External Affairs, Maritime Administration, U.S. Department of Transportation, Washington, D.C.

Scheina, Robert L. *The Coast Guard at War.* Pamphlet. Washington, D.C.: Office of the Coast Guard Historian, January 1, 1987.

ServRonSoPac, World War II Diaries and Action Reports, 1942–43.

USMC, "Engineering on Guadalcanal." Reprinted in *Headquarters Bulletin* (January 1944) by permission of *Construction* Magazine. Courtesy: Marine Corps Historical Center, Washington, D.C. Navy Yard.

Interviews conducted in person or by telephone
1993–1997, by William L. McGee

Seabee, Guadalcanal Beachmaster
John D. Case

USS *Aludra* (AK-72) survivors
Marvin Acree
Primo Saraiba
Eugene M. Hopper
Clinton Slater
Roy Lucy
Merle Luther
Ross Osborn
William Earl Hartman

USS *Celeno* (AK-76)
Anthony Gray

USS *Deimos* (AK-78) survivors
Richard T. Rogers
Walter P. Ballow
Edval Helle Sr.
Bernard Barker
Erwin Holan
Mike Hosier
Kenneth F. Keller

Charles Maiers
J. B. Morrison
Pat Paones
Stan Voorheis
Bob Parker
Robert E. Vorhies
Donald R. Waterhouse
Robert B. Phillips
Lester "Ray" Weathers
Jay S. Rider Jr.
David Haugh

USS LST-340
Don Sterling
Anthony Tesori

USS LST-353
Cal McGowan

USS *Skylark* (AM-63)
Leonard D. Honeycutt

SS *Nathaniel Currier*
Duane Curtis

II. Additional Reference Works

Allston, Rear Admiral Frank J., SC, USNR (Ret). *Ready for Sea: The Bicentennial History of the U.S. Navy Supply Corps.* Annapolis: Naval Institute Press, 1995.

Baker, G. S., O.B.E., D.Sc., *The Merchant Ship: Design Past and Present.* London: Sigma Books Limited, 1948.

Ballantine, Duncan S. *U.S. Naval Logistics in the Second World War.* Princeton, NJ: Princeton University Press, 1947.

Barbey, Daniel E. *MacArthur's Amphibious Navy: Seventh Amphibious Force Operations, 1943-1945.* Annapolis: Naval Institute Press, 1969.

Barry, Robert. "What of the Auxiliaries." *U.S. Naval Institute Proceedings* 62, no. 7 (July 1936).

Berry, Lieutenant Bob. *Gunners Get Glory: Lt. Bob Berry's Story of the Navy's Armed Guard.* New York: The Bobbs-Merrill Co., 1943.

Bowman, Waldo G., Harold W. Richardson, and Nathan A. Bowers. *Bulldozers Come First: The Story of U.S. War Construction in Foreign Lands.* New York: McGraw-Hill Book Company, Inc, 1944. (Firsthand accounts by the war correspondent editors of *Engineering News Record*, a civil engineering journal.)

Boyd, Carl and Akihiko Yoshida. *The Japanese Submarine Force and World War II.* Annapolish: Naval Institute Press, 1995.

Bunker, John. *Heroes in Dungarees: The Story of the American Merchant Marine in World War II.* Annapolis: Naval Institute Press, 1995.

Bykofsky, Joseph and Harold Larson. *United States Army in World War II. The Technical Services, The Transportation Corps: Operations Overseas.* Washington, D.C.: U.S. Government Printing Office, 1957.

Cant, Gilbert. *The Great Pacific Victory: From the Solomons to Tokyo.* Omaha, NE: The John Day Company, 1946.

Carpenter, D. and N. Polmar. *Submarines of the Imperial Japanese Navy.* Annapolis: Naval Institute Press, 1986.

Charles, Roland W. *Troopships of World War II.* Washington, D.C.: Army Transportation Association, 1947.

Coll, Blanche D., Jean E. Keith, and Herbert H. Rosenthal. *The Corps of Engineers: Troops and Equipment.* Washington, D.C.: Office of the Chief of Military History, 1958.

Cressman, Robert J. *The Official Chronology of the U.S. Navy in World War II.* Annapolis: Naval Institute Press, 2000.

Dillon, E. S., L. C. Hoffman, and D. P. Roseman. "Forty Years of Ship Designs under the Merchant Marine Act, 1936–1976." Pamphlet. *Transactions of the Society of Naval Architects and Marine Engineers* (1976).

Dinger, H. C. "Fueling at Sea." *U.S. Naval Institute Proceedings* 45, no. 9 (September 1919).

Disher, Robert C. "Future Concepts of Mobile Logistic Support." *U.S. Naval Institute Proceedings* 85, no. 6 (June 1959).

Dupra, Lyle E. *We Delivered! The U.S. Navy Armed Guard in World War II.* Manhattan, KS: Sunflower University Press, 1997.

Dyer, George C. *Naval Logistics.* Annapolis: Naval Institute Press, 1960.

Ellis, Captain E. H., USMC. *"Naval Bases: Their Location, Resources and Security," "The Denial of Bases," "The Security of Advanced Bases and Advanced Base Operations," "The Advanced Base Force."* Various papers written in 1921.

Finnie, Richard, ed. *Marinship: The History of a Wartime Shipyard.* San Francisco: Marinship Corp., 1947.

Fischer, Gerald T. *A Statistical Summary of Shipbuilding under the U.S. Maritime Commission During World War II. Historical Reports of the War Administration.* Washington, D.C.: U.S. Maritime Commission, 1949.

Friedman, Norman. "The Fleet Train" in *The Eclipse of the Big Gun: The Warship, 1906–1945.* Robert Gardiner, ed. London: Conway Maritime Press, 1992.

Gailey, Harry A. *The War in the Pacific: From Pearl Harbor to Tokyo Bay.* Novato, CA: Presidio Press. 1995.

Galati, Bob. *Gunner's Mate: On-Ship and On-Shore Memoirs of World War II and the Naval Armed Guard.* Irving, TX: Innovatia Press, 1993.

Gibson, Charles Dana, with E. Kay Gibson. *Over Seas: U.S. Army Maritime Operations, 1898 through the Fall of the Philippines.* Camden, ME: Ensign Press, 2002.

Gleichauf, Justin F. *Unsung Sailors: The Naval Armed Guard in World War II.* Annapolis: Naval Institute Press, 1990.

Halsey, Fleet Admiral William F. and Lieutenant Commander J. Bryan III. *Admiral Halsey's Story.* New York: McGraw-Hill Book Company, Inc., 1947.

Harms, Norman E. *Hard Lessons*, Vol. 1, *U.S. Naval Campaigns Pacific Theater, February 1942-1943.* Fullerton, CA: Scale Specialties, 1987.

Hoehling, A. A. *The Fighting Liberty Ships: A Memoir.* Annapolis, MD: Naval Institute Press, 1996.

Hoof, Wayne. "Design of FAST Combat Support Ship AOE," *Bureau of Ships Journal* 10, no. 8 (August 1961).

Isely, Jeter A. and Philip A. Crowl. *The U.S. Marines and Amphibious War: Its Theory and Its Practice in the Pacific.* Princeton, NJ: Princeton University Press, 1957.

Kilmarx, Robert A., ed. *America's Maritime Legacy: A History of the U.S. Merchant Marine and Shipbuilding Industry Since Colonial Times..* Boulder, CO: Westview Press, 1979.

Klawonn, Marion J. *Cradle of the Corps: A History of the New York District U.S. Army Corps of Engineers, 1775–1975.* New York: U.S. Army Corps of Engineers, New York District, 1977.

Kludas, Arnold. *Great Passenger Ships of the World, Volume 4: 1936-1950.* Wellingborough, England: Patrick Stephens, 1977.

Land, Emory S. "How My Career Was Controlled by the Roosevelts." *Navy* 3, no. 10 (October 1960).

———. "Progress of the Shipbuilding Program." *Marine Engineering and Shipping Review* (October 1941).

Lane, Lieutenant Colonel Kerry, U.S. Marine Corps (Ret.). *Marine Pioneers: The Unsung Heroes of World War II.* Atglen, PA: Schiffer Military/ Aviation History, 1997.

Leighton, Richard M. and Robert W. Coakley. *Global Logistics and Strategy, 1943–1945: U.S. Army in World War II, The War Department.*

Washington, D.C.: Office of the Chief of Military History, U.S. Army, 1968.

Lisle, Orchard. "Tankers as Naval Auxiliaries." *U.S. Naval Institute Proceedings* 64, no. 9 (September 1938).

Lorelli, John A. *To Foreign Shores: U. S. Amphibious Operations in World War II.* Annapolis: Naval Institute Press, 1995.

Lundstrom, John B. *The First Team and the Guadalcanal Campaign: Naval Fighter Combat from August to November 1942.* Annapolis: Naval Institute Press, 1994.

Manning, Rear Admiral J. J., CEC, USN. "The Saga of the Seabees." *Think* (May 1947)

Marines in World War II Commemorative Series. Fourteen booklets by various military authors. Washington, D.C.: Marine Corps Historical Center, 1992–1996.

Masterson, James R. *U.S. Army Transportation in the Southwest Pacific Area: 1941–1947.* Washington, D.C.: U.S. Government Printing Office, 1949.

McCleary, Lieutenant (jg) Eugene E. *History of U.S. Advanced Base, Guadalcanal, 1942–1945.* 2 vols. Shore Establishment, 1945. Naval Historical Archives. History of Advanced Naval Base, Tulagi, British Solomons Islands.

McMillan, George. *The Old Breed: A History of the First Marine Division in World War II.* Washington, D.C.: Infantry Journal Press, 1949.

Miller Jr., John P. *The War in the Pacific, Guadalcanal: The First Offensive. U.S. Army in World War II: The Army Ground Forces.* Washington, D.C.: Office of the Chief of Military History, Department of the Army, 1949.

———. *The War in the Pacific. Cartwheel: The Reduction of Rabaul. U.S. Army in World War II.* Washington, D.C.: Office of the Chief of Military History, Department of the Army, 1959.

Miller Jr., Thomas G. *The Cactus Air Force.* New York: Harper & Row, 1969.

Miller, Jake. *Round Trip, Looneyville/Tokyo: Via the USS George F. Elliott Lines.* White Sulphur Springs, WV: The Fightin' Foxes, Inc., 1998.5

Millet, Jeffrey R. *U.S. Navy Seabees: The First 50 Years, 1942–1992.* Dallas, TX: Taylor Publishing Company, 1993.

Millett, John D. *The Organization and Role of the Army Service Forces.* Washington, D.C.: Office of the Chief of Military History, 1954.

Moreell, Admiral Ben, CEC, USN (Ret). "The Seabees in World War II." *U.S. Naval Institute Proceedings,* LXXXVIII (March 1962).

Potter, E. B. *Bull Halsey.* Annapolis: Naval Institute Press, 1985.

———. *Nimitz.* Annapolis: Naval Institute Press, 1976.

Sawyer, L. A. and W. H. Mitchell. *The Liberty Ships: The History of the "Emergency" type Cargo ships constructed in the United States during the Second World War.* London: Lloyds of London Press Ltd., 1970.

———. *Victory Ships and Tankers: The History of the "Victory" type Cargo ships and of the Tankers built in the United States of America during World War II.* Newton Abbott, England: David & Charles, 1974. Cambridge, MD: Cornell Maritime Press, 1974.

Scheina, Robert L. *U.S. Coast Guard Cutters and Craft of World War II.* Annapolis: Naval Institute Press, 1982.

"Seabees: Where They Worked and Fought in World War II." *Seabee News Service* (October 10, 1945).

Shaw Jr., Henry I. and Major Douglas T. Kane, USMC. *History of U.S. Marine Corps Operations in World War II.* Vol. 2, *Isolation of Rabaul.* Historical Branch, G-3 Division, Headquarters, U.S. Marine Corps, 1963.

Skordiles, Kimon. *The Seabees in War and Peace.* 2 vols. CA: Argus Communications, 1973.

Stauffer, Alvin P. *United States Army in World War II series. The Technical Services, The Quartermaster Corps: Operations in the War Against Japan.* Washington, D.C.: U.S. Government Printing Office, 1956.

Stewart, E. L. "New Developments in Tanker Design." *Marine Engineering and Shipping Review* (December 1944).

van der Vat, Dan. *The Pacific Campaign: The U.S.-Japanese Naval War, 1941–1945.* New York: Simon & Schuster, 1991.

Vandegrift, General A. A., USMC (Ret). *Once a Marine: The Memoirs of General A. A. Vandegrift, Commandant of the U.S. Marines in World War II.* NY: W. W. Norton, 1964.

Whitehurst Jr., Clinton H. *The U.S. Shipbuilding Industry: Past, Present, and Future.* Annapolis: Naval Institute Press, 1986.

Wildenberg, Thomas. *Gray Steel and Black Oil: Fast Tankers and Replenishment at Sea in the U.S. Navy, 1912–1992.* Annapolis: Naval Institute Press, 1996.

Willoughby, Lieutenant Malcolm F., USCGR (T). *The U.S. Coast Guard in World War II.* Annapolis: United States Naval Institute, 1957.

BMC Catalog and Order Form

BMC PUBLICATIONS   *Estab. 1971*

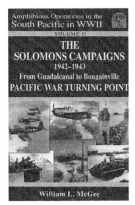
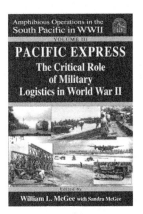

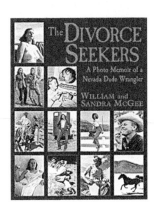

TITLES IN PRINT

For a "Look Inside" visit www.BMCpublications.com

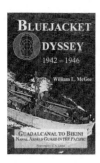

Bluejacket Odyssey, 1942–1946
Guadalcanal to Bikini—Naval Armed Guard in the Pacific
By William L. McGee

"Little has been written about service in the Armed Guard in which nearly 145,000 men served. McGee remedies this with a book that has value for historians."

—Naval History Magazine

In 1942, Montana cowboy Bill McGee joined the U.S. Navy on his seventeenth birthday. He was assigned to the Naval Armed Guard, the branch of the Navy that protected merchant ships and their valuable cargo and crew from enemy attacks. Within weeks, McGee was in the middle of two major enemy attacks in the South Pacific. His "kid's cruise" ended in 1946 on the heavy cruiser, *Fall River,* and the atomic bomb tests at Bikini. McGee draws on his shipboard journal, extensive research, and interviews with former shipmates and other survivors to produce an engrossing book that has the inimitable mark of one who has "been there, done that."

546 pp., 250 b&w photos, plus appendices, bibliography, index, 6" x 9", ISBN 13: 978-0-9701678-0-4, Softcover: $29.95. Foreword by C. A. Lloyd, Chairman, USN Armed Guard Veterans of WWII.

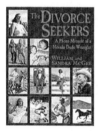

The Divorce Seekers
A Photo Memoir of a Nevada Dude Wrangler
By William L. McGee and Sandra McGee

"Former dude ranch wrangler Bill McGee may have written the ultimate Western kiss-and-tell…a firsthand account of the epic era of the Reno six-week divorce."

—Cowboys & Indians Magazine

"Best book yet about Nevada's famous dude-divorce ranch business."

—Eric Moody, Nevada Historical Society

In 1947, Bill McGee had the coveted job of head dude wrangler on an exclusive Nevada divorce ranch twenty miles south of Reno that catered to wealthy divorce seekers who came for a six week divorce. True stories mixed with history provide delightful reading about bygone times and glamorous people. A brief but glimmering epoch of the American West.

444 pp., 502 b&w photos, plus maps, appendices, notes, bibliography, index, 8½" x 11", ISBN 13: 978-0-9701678-1-1, Hardcover: $39.95. Foreword by William W. Bliss.

**View the authors in interview clips from TV and 20th Century Fox.
Visit www.BMCpublications.com**

Amphibious Operations in the South Pacific in World War II series

The Amphibians Are Coming!
Emergence of the 'Gator Navy and its Revolutionary Landing Craft, Vol. I
By William L. McGee

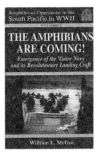

"McGee combines exhaustive research with the words of the men who took the theory of the amphibious doctrine and the new machines to sea. His dedicated work will surely help keep the day-to-day naval record of the 'Greatest Generation' from being lost."
—*John Lorelli, Author of "To Foreign Shores, U.S. Amphibious Operations in World War II"*

A Biographical History of the Revolutionary WWII Landing Craft and the Unsung Heroes Who Manned Them.

308 pp., 110 b&w photos, 13 maps, plus charts, appendices, notes, bibliography, index, 6" x 9", ISBN 13: 978-0-9701678-6-6, Softcover: $29.95

The Solomons Campaigns, 1942–1943
From Guadalcanal to Bougainville, Pacific War Turning Point, Vol. II
By William L. McGee

"Enough gripping drama, heroism, and heartbreak in McGee's almost encyclopedic work to supply Hollywood with material for a century."
—*Marine Corps League*

All the Solomons Campaigns—from Guadalcanal to Bougainville—are covered and tell the story of America's first offensive after Pearl Harbor.

688 pp., 310 b&w photos, 44 maps, plus charts, notes, appendices, bibliography, index, 6" x 9", ISBN 13: 978-0-9701678-7-3, Softcover: $39.95

Pacific Express
The Critical Role of Military Logistics in World War II, Vol. III
Edited by William L. McGee with Sandra McGee

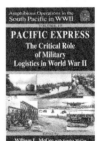

Victory is won or lost in battle, but all military history shows that adequate logistics support is essential to the winning of the battle. In WWII, for every one individual who served in combat, ten served in a support role.

Under one cover, an edited collection of the best works by other historians on the importance of military logistics in WWII. Profiles the many major components that made up the "Pacific express."

560 pp., 104 b&w photos, 7 maps, 21 figures, tables & charts, plus appendix, notes, bibliography, index, 6" x 9", ISBN 13: 978-0-9701678-8-0, Softcover: $39.95

▮BMC▮ PUBLICATIONS

ORDER FORM

For a "Look Inside" visit www.BMCpublications.com

BMC Publications titles are available from Amazon.com and bookstores. To order direct from the publisher, complete this order form and mail with your check payable to BMC Publications:

BMC Publications
PO Box 1012
Tiburon, CA 94920

ORDERED BY

Name _____

Address _____

City _____ State _____ Zip _____

Daytime Phone _____ Email: _____

I would like the author to sign my book(s). _____ yes _____ no

If yes, please inscribe my book(s) to _____

Qty	Title	Price	Total
	The Amphibians Are Coming!, Vol. I Softcover, 6"x9", 308 pp, 110 B&W Illus. plus Maps, Charts, Appendices, Notes, Bibliography, Index.	$29.95	
	The Solomons Campaigns, 1942–1943, Vol. II Softcover, 6"x9", 688 pp, 310 B&W Illus. plus Maps, Charts, Appendices, Notes, Bibliography, Index.	$39.95	
	Pacific Express, Vol. III Softcover, 6"x9", 560 pp, 104 B&W Illus. plus Maps, Figures, Charts, Appendix, Notes, Bibliography, Index.	$39.95	
	Bluejacket Odyssey, 1942–1946 Softcover, 6"x9", 546 pp, 250 B&W Illus plus Appendices, Bibliography, Index.	$29.95	
	The Divorce Seekers Hardcover, 8½"x11", 444 pp., 502 B&W Illus. plus Maps, Appendices, Notes, Bibliography, Index.	$39.95	
	Subtotal		
	Save 30% on orders for any two or more books		
	Subtotal		
	Postage & Handling — $5.00 + $3.00 for each addt'l book		
	Subtotal		
	CA Residents add 9.00% sales tax		
	TOTAL		

All prices are in U.S. dollars. U.S. orders shipped via U.S. Media Mail. Allow 14 days for delivery. For faster delivery or international orders, call 415-435-1883 or email bmcpublications@aol.com.

THANK YOU FOR YOUR ORDER

Index

Notes:

1. Names of ships and lettered-numbered vessels like LSTs, LTs, PCs and YPs are all in *italics*.

2. Page references in **boldface** indicate information contained in photographs. Page references in *italic* indicate information contained in tables or figures.

Printed in Great Britain
by Amazon

78802673R00322